AF594116

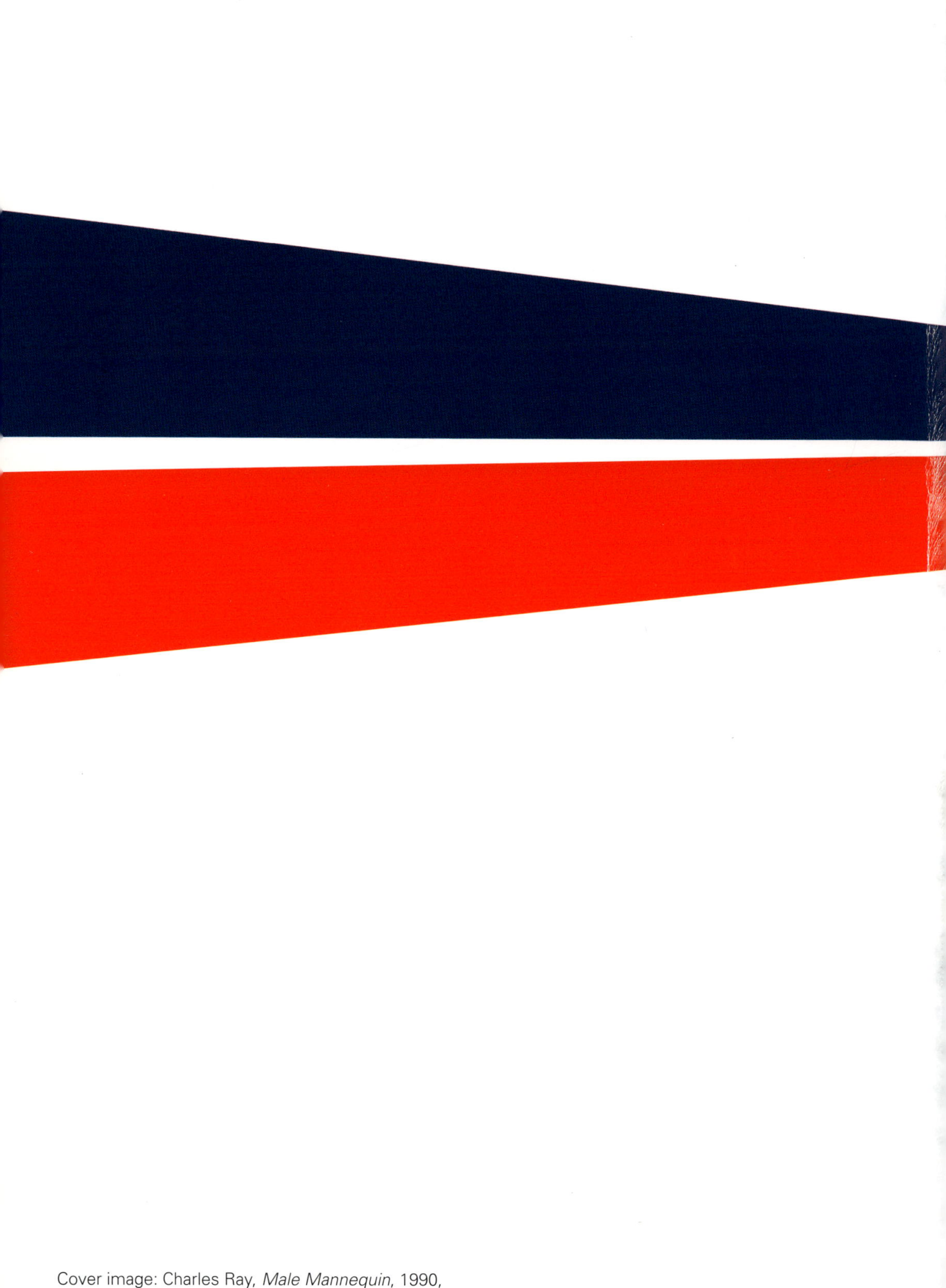

Cover image: Charles Ray, *Male Mannequin*, 1990,
Mannequin and painted fiberglass, Ed. of 3, 73 3/4 x 27 1/4 x 21 1/4 in. (186 x 69.2 x 54 cm)

RED EYE

L.A. ARTISTS from the RUBELL FAMILY COLLECTION

December 6, 2006 - May 31, 2007

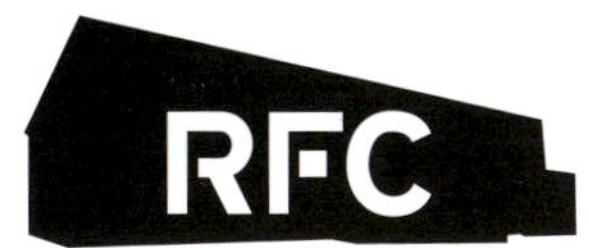

First published in 2007 by the
Rubell Family Collection
95 NW 29th Street
Wynwood Art District
Miami, Florida 33127
United States of America
Telephone: 305 573 6090
Facsimile: 305 573 6023
Bookstore: 305 573 6033
info@rubellfamilycollection.com
www.rubellfamilycollection.com

Published in conjunction with the exhibition
RED EYE: L.A. Artists from the
Rubell Family Collection
organized by the Rubell Family Collection

Presented at:

Rubell Family Collection
(95 NW 29th Street, Miami, FL 33127)
December 6, 2006 - May 31, 2007

Editor: Mark Coetzee
Essays: Michael Darling and Michael Holte
Director: Mark Coetzee
Registrar: Juan Valadez
Book Design: Chi Lam
Archivist and Assistant Registrar: Carolina Wonder
Curatorial Assistant: Mark Clintberg
Copy-Editing: Elizabeth Martinez
Photography: Chi Lam and Simon Hare
Additional Photography: Markus Haugg
Biographical Research: Meredith Carruthers, Mark Clintberg, Rebecca Duclos, Larissa Holman, Tatiana Mellema, David Ross and Jacqueline Sischy
Preparators: Sonia Alvarez, Juan Gonzalez, Ricky Jiminez, Richard Kern, Diego Machado, Paul Pisoni, Susanne Slauenwhite, Matthew Snitzer and Mark Stark
Promotion and Sales: Stephanie Garcia
Museum Educator: Linda Mangual
Accounting: Liliana Zarif
Promotion and Sales Assistants: Kiwi Farah and Cecilia Fernandez
Office Assistant: Katherine Garcia
Conservation Interns: Anne Blazejack and John Witty
Visitor Services Interns: Sheila Cordova, Yadian Fonseca and Jacob Guerin
Archive Intern: Katrina Miller

Printing and Binding: Imprenta Mariscal, Quito, Ecuador

Distribution: D.A.P. / Distributed Art Publishers, Inc.
155 6th Avenue, 2nd Floor
New York, New York 10013
United States of America
Customer Service Telephone: 800 388 2665
Editorial amd Marketing Telephone: 212 627 1999
Facsimile: 212 627 9484
Orders: dap@dapinc.com
www.artbook.com

First Edition: December 2007
ISBN: 978-0-9789888-7-6
Library of Congress Control Number: 2007908593

The type for this book was set in
Univers, Conduit and Charcoal CY

This book was printed on
Torraspapel CreatorMatt (150gsm)
with white Bristol fine cardboard endsheets (160gsm)
sewn and case bound in 2.5 mm board
covered with Torraspapel CreatorGloss (150gsm)
with a matte film lamination

Printed in Ecuador

Doug Aitken
John Baldessari
Frank Benson
Amy Bessone
Mark Bradford
Chris Burden
Brian Calvin
Aaron Curry
Brian Fahlstrom
Mark Grotjahn
Karl Haendel
Richard Hawkins
Evan Holloway
Violet Hopkins
Thomas Houseago
Mike Kelley
Barbara Kruger
Nathan Mabry
Paul McCarthy
Jason Meadows
Matthew Monahan
Kristen Morgin
Catherine Opie
Kaz Oshiro
Laura Owens
Raymond Pettibon
Charles Ray
Jason Rhoades
Ry Rocklen
Sterling Ruby
Lara Schnitger
Jim Shaw
Yutaka Sone
Catherine Sullivan
Ricky Swallow
Henry Taylor

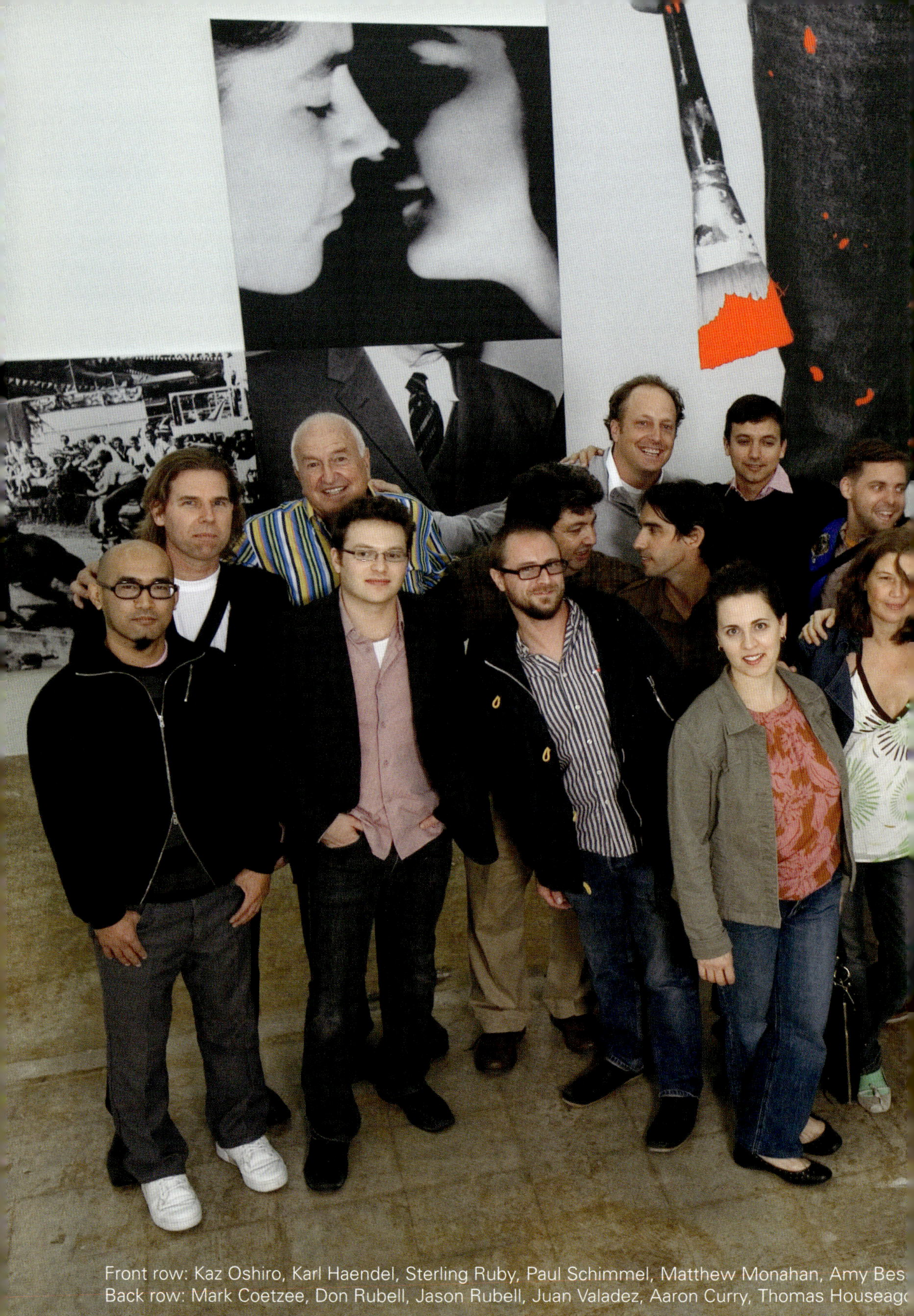

Front row: Kaz Oshiro, Karl Haendel, Sterling Ruby, Paul Schimmel, Matthew Monahan, Amy Bes
Back row: Mark Coetzee, Don Rubell, Jason Rubell, Juan Valadez, Aaron Curry, Thomas Houseago

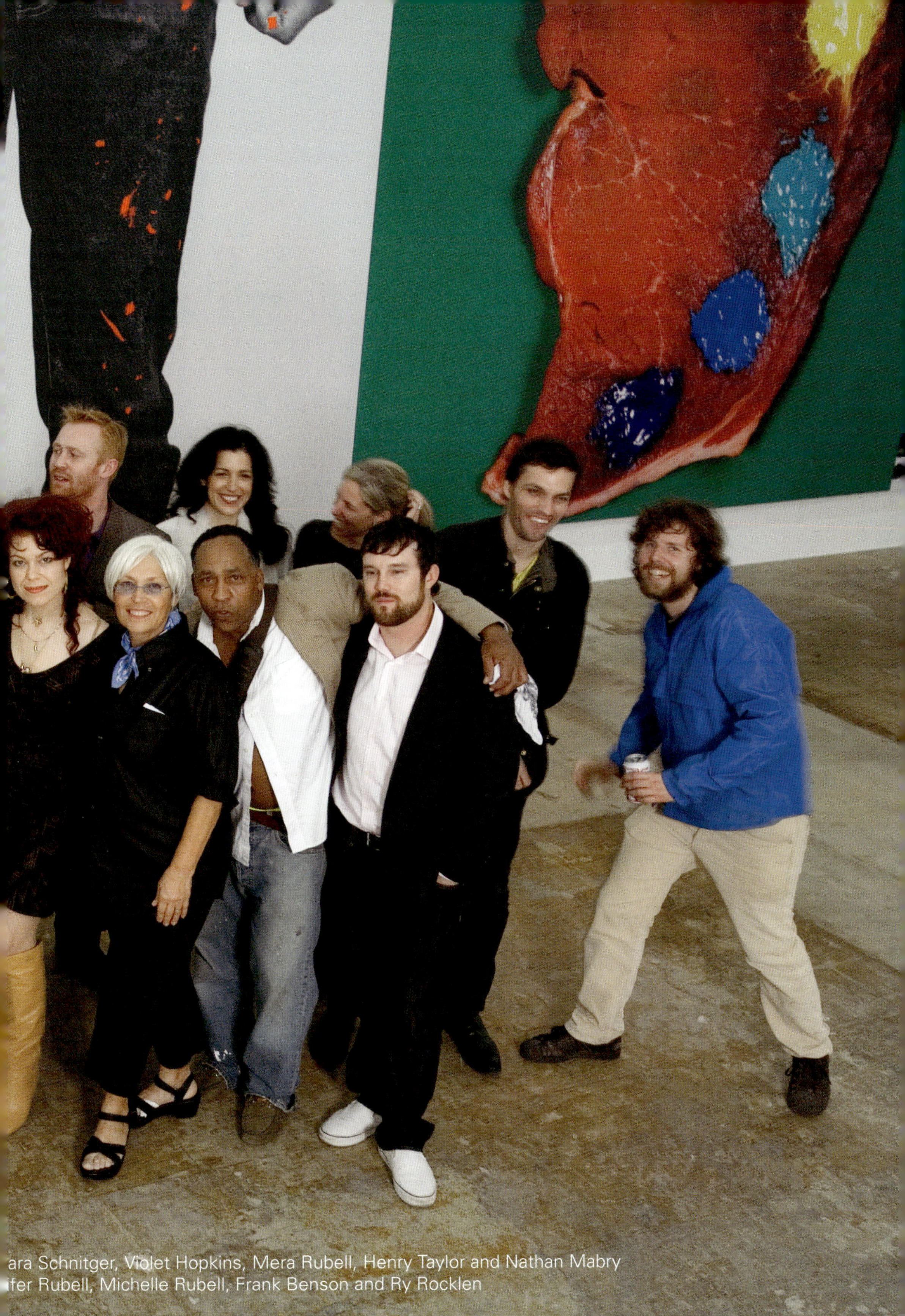

ara Schnitger, Violet Hopkins, Mera Rubell, Henry Taylor and Nathan Mabry
ifer Rubell, Michelle Rubell, Frank Benson and Ry Rocklen

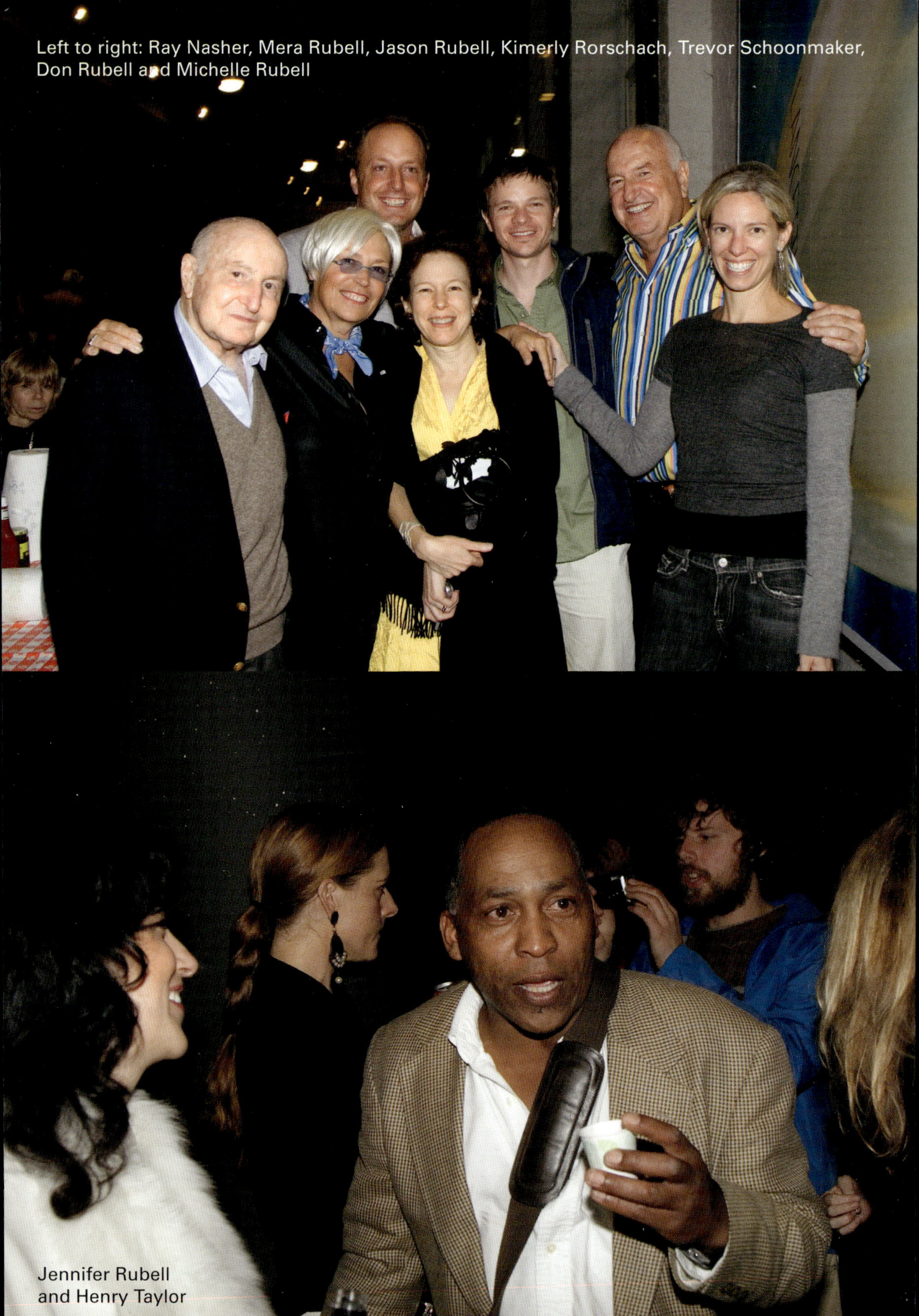
Left to right: Ray Nasher, Mera Rubell, Jason Rubell, Kimerly Rorschach, Trevor Schoonmaker, Don Rubell and Michelle Rubell

Jennifer Rubell and Henry Taylor

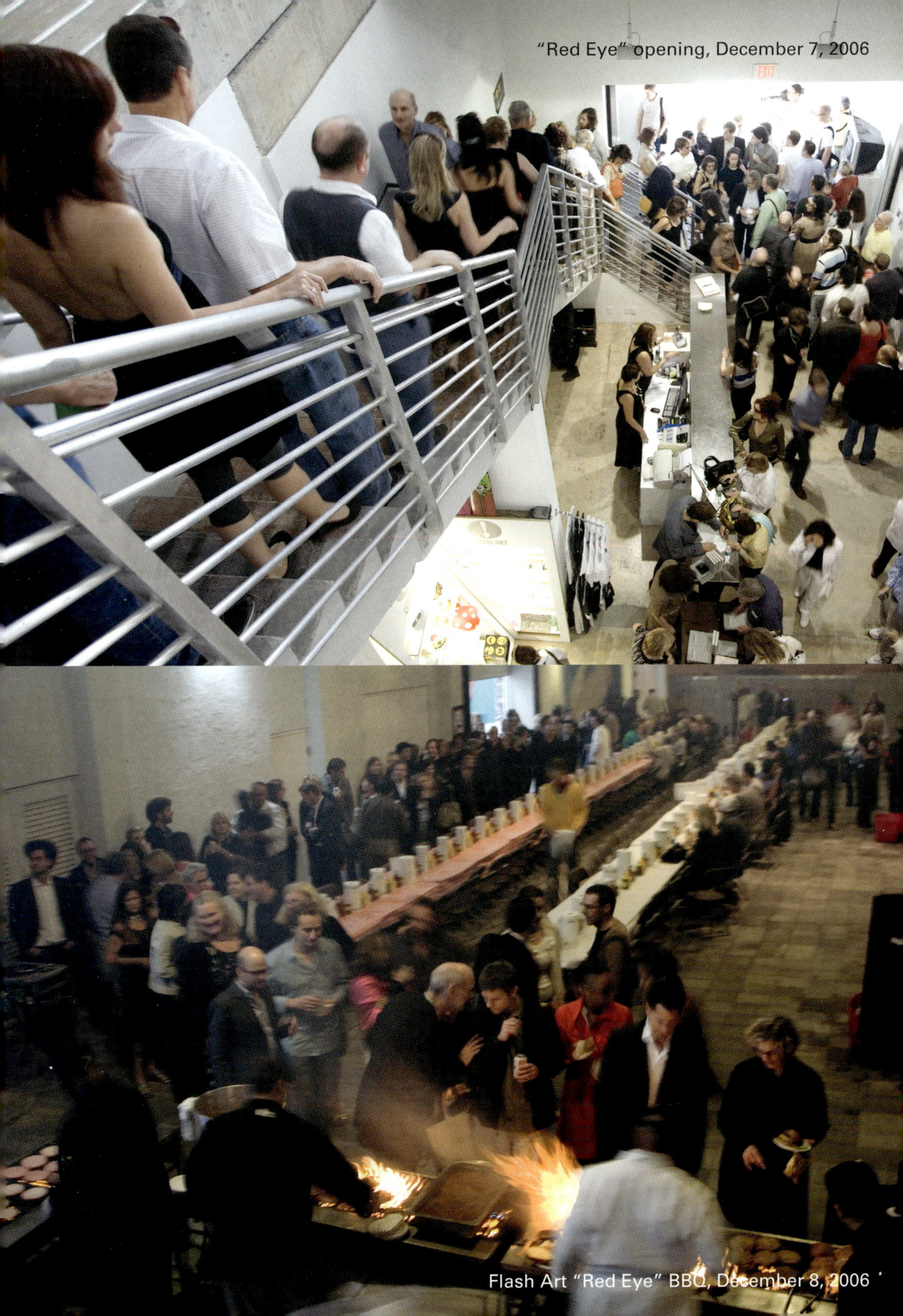

"Red Eye" opening, December 7, 2006

Flash Art "Red Eye" BBQ, December 8, 2006

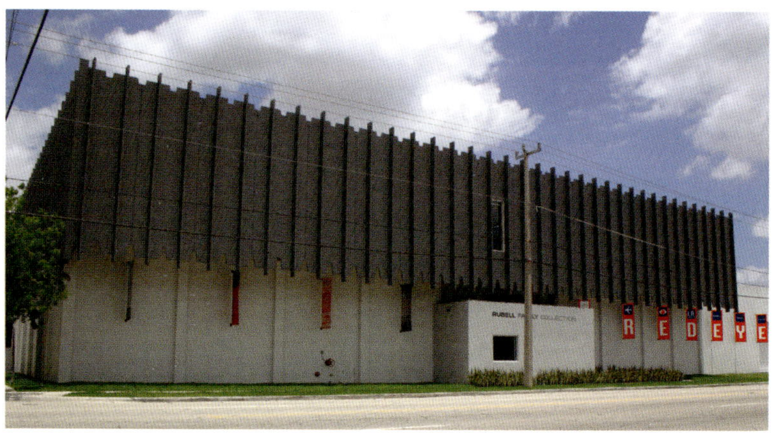
R E D E Y E

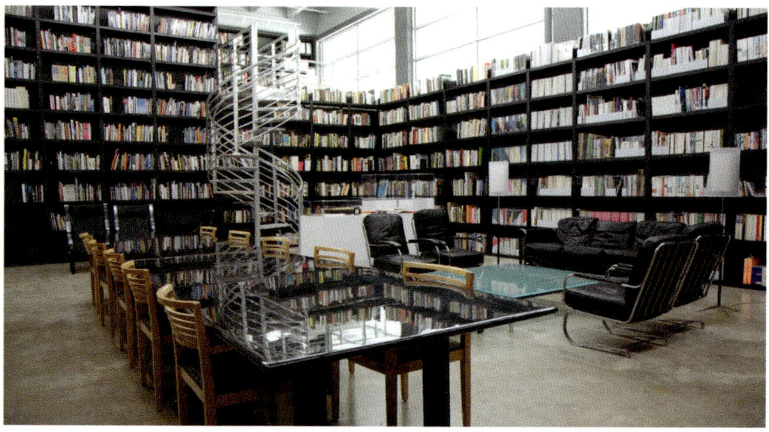

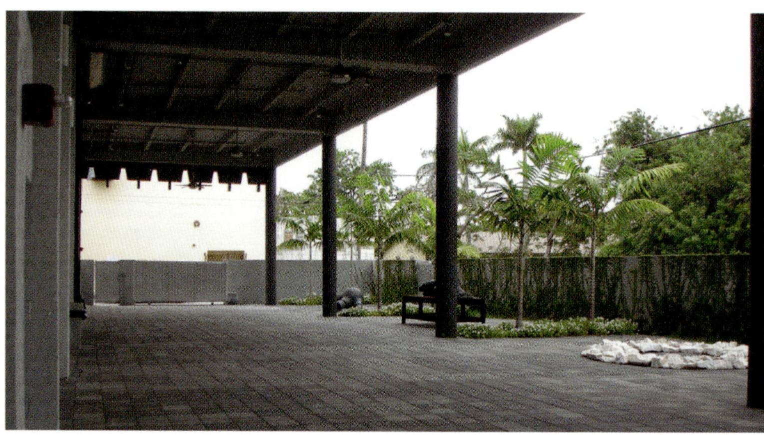

Founded in 1994, the Contemporary Arts Foundation (CAF) is a 501(c)(3) non-profit foundation located in the Wynwood Art District, in downtown Miami, Florida. CAF has been a public-access facility since 1996, and the locus for housing, preserving, archiving and presenting works from the collection of the Rubell family, one of the world's leading collections of contemporary art. In addition, the CAF presides over an in-house research library containing over 30,000 volumes, including many rare texts and periodicals. The library is open to the public.

CAF believes that great works of art are an intrinsically transcendent, elevating, liberating and empowering force, and that the artifacts of our time are the legacy of society as a whole. Based on this premise, the Foundation seeks to prompt social intercourse and debate, an essential freedom of a democratic society, by sharing with the world the physical, sensual and intellectual properties of cutting-edge art.

CAF advances public interaction at the Rubell Family Collection (RFC) by presenting works from the collection of the Rubell family in rotating, curated exhibitions with accompanying documentation, throughout its 27 galleries, new media room and Sculpture Garden, as well as through a variety of educational and community outreach programs. CAF commissions new works of art and produces traveling exhibitions, which are presented throughout the world. In addition, CAF operates as a lending resource for curators and museums.

The title for this exhibition came from the process that brought it into existence: the many bleary-eyed cross-continental trips we took over the last two years—armed with our hunches, our eyes and our GPS— as we attempted to understand the Los Angeles art scene. "Red Eye" expressed our feelings of displacement and anxiety as we shifted from one paradigm to another. Every time we left Los Angeles late at night and arrived in Miami in the early morning hours, we lost our sense of today, our sense of now. For what happened today in L.A. actually occurred yesterday in Miami.

That displacement of time, place and body is analogous to our process of collecting in general. We begin with a feeling, a sort of hunch about a place, about artistic or creative energy coming from that place. The hunch leads to a journey that opens exciting and extraordinary doors to artists, dealers, curators, museums, writers, collectors, and to the unknown. With each of these magical encounters, we begin to form a cohesive set of ideas about a place; these ideas become the seeds of a collection exhibit. After condensing these many experiences into a few brief days, we are ready to head back home to Miami. As is the case when leaving Los Angeles, we take the "Red Eye."

Our Los Angeles journey began in 1992 at the Los Angeles Museum of Contemporary Art, with Paul Schimmel's seminal exhibition "Helter Skelter." This show introduced us to the unexpectedly diverse and geographically scattered, art community in L.A. Influenced and inspired by this exhibition, we began to collect many of the important artists from the L.A. art scene of the late 1980s and early 1990s;

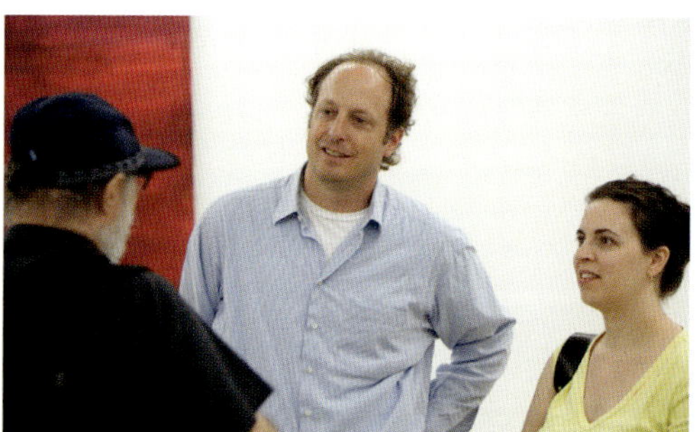

Paul McCarthy, Jason Rubell and Amy Bessone

their work immediately stood out as some of the most significant in our collection. In the last few years, we began to feel that an examination of more recent trends in L.A. would form a fascinating exhibition that showcased the juxtapositions and interrelationships between the new L.A. and the old. Thus, in 2004 we decided to revisit both the place that so influenced our development as collectors, and the artworks that had formed the backbone of the entire collection over the last twenty years.

Combining this specific focus of collecting with our mission to exclusively exhibit work we own, creates interesting dynamics and challenges. Time, money, place and fate are distractions to this process. We cannot expect to distill an entire art scene (nor would we ever try), but the inclusion and exclusion of artists and ideas within the paradigm of collecting creates a unique set of questions: Can we afford this work? Are there even works available by a specific artist? Are we missing something? Or, most importantly, are we looking hard enough? These are some of the questions that continually present themselves as we struggle to grow intelligently as collectors. But these vexing questions are what make this process of searching, learning and collecting so personally vital and compelling.

"Red Eye" epitomizes the very heart of our collecting. We push and pull, push and pull, push and pull again, and then we get on an airplane, head back home, wake up in a new place on a new day—bleary-eyed and trying to make sense of it all.

Jason Rubell
December 2006

Doug Aitken
John Baldessari
Frank Benson
Amy Bessone
Mark Bradford
Chris Burden
Brian Calvin
Aaron Curry
Brian Fahlstrom
Mark Grotjahn
Karl Haendel
Richard Hawkins
Evan Holloway
Violet Hopkins
Thomas Houseago
Mike Kelley
Barbara Kruger
Nathan Mabry
Paul McCarthy
Jason Meadows
Matthew Monahan
Kristen Morgin
Catherine Opie
Kaz Oshiro
Laura Owens
Raymond Pettibon
Charles Ray
Jason Rhoades
Ry Rocklen
Sterling Ruby
Lara Schnitger
Jim Shaw
Yutaka Sone
Catherine Sullivan
Ricky Swallow
Henry Taylor

For the first time in its history, the Rubell Family Collection (RFC) has dedicated its entire 45,000-square-foot exhibition space to a single exhibition. "Red Eye: L.A. Artists from the Rubell Family Collection" presents a cross section of the artwork produced in Los Angeles over the past 20 years by 36 L.A.-based artists—some iconic, some mid-career, some relatively new. When exhibited collectively the artworks created by this multi-generational group represent a substantial history, both of L.A.'s art scene and of RFC itself. As part of the RFC mission all works exhibited are drawn exclusively from the collection of the Rubell family.

The compelling nature of the work, the great number and diversity of the pieces, and the significant scale of many of the objects demanded that we dedicate the whole building to this exhibition to adequately represent the breadth and depth of the pieces we have here. The exhibition encompasses all media, from painting to sculpture and video installation. Many of the artists featured in "Red Eye" have made work specifically for the exhibition, taking into account what already exists in the collection to create an organic and continuous dialogue. These pieces will in turn become part of the history of the collection at RFC.

"Red Eye" continues an RFC tradition of presenting at least one geographically centered exhibition each year. In the past we presented "Northern Light" and "Life After Death," which focused on Leipzig painters, "At This Time" featured 10 Miami artists, and "Poles Apart" investigated Poland. This December we are opening "Euro-Centric, Part 1," the first in a series of exhibitions that will question issues surrounding European identity, aesthetics, and culture.

The title "Red Eye" was born from conversations and debates on the overnight flights from the West to the East Coast that are fondly referred to as the Red Eye by bleary-eyed travelers. In this case those travelers were Mera, Don and Jason Rubell. "Traveling back and forth to L.A. we were like voyeurs looking into that scene," explains Mera Rubell. "For us, L.A. is never a complete experience, but at best an imperfect exploration—a vision found from the outside. For the last 18 months, like modern explorers armed with a Global Positioning System, we combed the breadth of the infamous L.A. sprawl, visiting studios, galleries and museums."

In 1992 the Rubells visited Paul Schimmel's seminal show, "Helter Skelter," at The Museum of Contemporary Art in Los Angeles. This exhibition proved pivotal to the family's engagement with art and L.A.: since that show the Rubell family has actively collected Los Angeles-based artists. "Red Eye" brings these seemingly disparate groups of artists together; that they talked, taught and trained together makes them invariably connected—if not artistically, then psychologically. The older generation of artists represented here, a major force in their own day, exerted certain influence over the next generation, who in turn became the teachers of the next. "We are very excited about the possibility of connecting the older influential artists from the late 80s and early 90s with those starting to work today," says Jason Rubell. The heart of the Rubell collection is centered on this generation of L.A. artists from the 80s and 90s. Mera Rubell adds, "we wanted to revisit the core of this collection, study its influence and cross reference it to the newer generations and in so doing analyze new developments. What we discovered was an extremely self-reflective art scene, both celebrating and rejecting, yet largely influenced by the generation of artists that came before."

Such artists as Charles Ray and Paul McCarthy, both widely collected by the Rubell family, largely determined much of the debate and dialogue around art-making in L.A. at the time. This in turn influenced contemporary art practices over the many years that followed, and affected the way the Rubell family collects even today. "As many of the artists went on to teach, we were curious to explore the effect they might have had on the next generation," explains Don Rubell. "We discovered L.A. is not in fact stuck inside itself and its history; it is an open-ended, dynamic and evolving environment."

L.A. has enough of a history to have established great teaching institutions, museums and collections, supported by a sophisticated gallery system that facilitates critical dialogue and a sympathetic approach to art. It is, however, still new enough to encourage freedom and to expect individuality among its artists, curators and writers.

The Rubell Family Collection (RFC) is one of the leading collections of contemporary art in the world. Started in 1964, soon after Don and Mera Rubell were married, the collecting group expanded some years later when their children Jason and Jennifer, then quite young, joined their parents in buying and collecting art. Recently Jason's wife Michelle joined the collecting team alongside her husband. The family's extensive collection of works dates from the 1960s to the present.

The collection is housed and exhibited in a converted former Drug Enforcement Agency (D.E.A.) confiscated-goods warehouse. Open to the public since 1996, the collection features rotating exhibitions of work by such prominent artists as Maurizio Cattelan, Marlene Dumas, Keith Haring, Damien Hirst, Anselm Kiefer, Jeff Koons, Paul McCarthy, Takashi Murakami, Neo Rauch, Charles Ray, Gregor Schneider, Cindy Sherman and Luc Tuymans. The institution features 27 galleries, a research library with over 30,000 volumes, a film and lecture theatre, a new media room, a bookstore, a gift shop and a sculpture garden.

Over the last number of years, the Rubell Family Collection has presented large solo exhibitions of such historical and influential figures as Keith Haring, Richard Prince and John Stezaker. We have also presented solo exhibitions of a new generation of artists, such as Franz Ackermann, Francis Alÿs, Hernan Bas, Eberhard Havekost, Jim Lambie, Andrea Lehmann and Andro Wekua.

RFC operates as a public institution with a strong policy of loaning works to other institutions to support their exhibition activities. Some recent loans have gone to the following institutions: The Hayward Gallery, London; Kunstmuseum Wolfsburg; Modern Art Museum of Fort Worth; The Museum of Contemporary Art in Los Angeles; The Museum of Modern Art in New York; Schaulager in Basel; Tate Modern; and Whitney Museum of American Art.

In addition, as part of its exhibition services, the RFC regularly produces exhibitions that travel from the Contemporary Arts Foundation (CAF) in Miami to museums, university galleries and other educational institutions around the world, thereby presenting the work to a larger audience. Recent traveling exhibitions include "Memorials of Identity: New Media from the Rubell Family Collection," which was presented at The Art Gallery of Florida Gulf Coast University, Corcoran Gallery of Art / College of Art + Design, Haifa Museum of Art, Museo de Arte de Puerto Rico, Nasher Museum of Art at Duke University, and Tampa Museum of Art; and "Life After Death: New Leipzig Paintings from the Rubell Family Collection," which was also presented at American University Museum, Frye Art Museum, Kemper Museum of Contemporary Art, MASS MoCA, Richard E. Peeler Art Center, Salt Lake Art Center, and SITE Santa Fe.

"Eberhard Havekost 1996-2006: Paintings from the Rubell Family Collection" was presented at American University Museum, The Art Gallery of Florida Gulf Coast University, and Tampa Museum of Art.

The Rubell family is passionately committed to the art and artists to which they respond. As art patrons first and foremost, and as the heart and soul of an innovative collecting institution, the Rubells focus their efforts on acquiring a large body of work from a particular artist, and conserving that body of work for future generations. During focused exhibitions, each of the artists in the collection have many of their works on display simultaneously, offering visitors a complete overview of an artist's oeuvre.

The Rubell family went to great lengths to acquire exceptional examples of work produced in Los Angeles. As always, the Rubells' enthusiasm and support for this exhibition and publication were unfailing. I am forever grateful to the Rubells for their guidance and constancy, and for always encouraging me to find personal enrichment in my work here. With collaborators and supporters such as these, all of us at RFC can't help but take pride in our work and our mission. Of course, being surrounded by brilliant and provocative art adds to our delight. I trust you too will share in this delight.

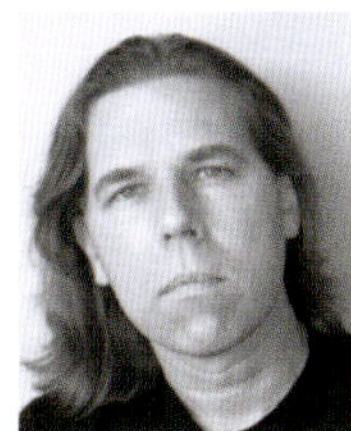

Mark Coetzee
Director
Rubell Family Collection
Miami, FL

"Red Eye" Indeed

Michael Darling

L.A. artists work hard. The precedents have been set and there is no getting around them. The older generation paid its dues, labored in obscurity and at the edge of financial viability through two boom periods (only one of which really benefited them) and at least one bust, making dogged determination and devoted labor the only way to earn respect in this surprisingly rigorous town. There is a bit of Darwinism to L.A. art, as the notoriously tough art schools grind students down through critique, making them defend their work to ridiculous extremes, and as a result, the ones who continue and thrive are the ones that make art because they can't get it out of their systems. Those cursed survivors also possess a bold belief that history can be made, and luckily there are ample examples working and living and teaching around them to show that this is the case. L.A. artists also realize that they are now center stage, as this exhibition attests, and while the world is watching they are taking advantage by producing ever tougher, smarter, and more ambitious work.

Much has been made of the fact that the L.A. art ecology owes its peculiar depth and breadth to the fact that the best artists stay in the city and teach, helping to nurture subsequent generations—and this is certainly true. Those same influential teachers, however, are like Depression-era businessmen who have seen the bad times and know they are right around the corner again, so teaching has been a form of survival when sales were slow (to non-existent) and a bonus when their dealers found that elusive buzz that moves art out the door. Another common denominator of much of the best art that has been made in L.A. during the past 20 years, is its ambition and complexity. Some of this can be attributed to the wide open spaces that sprawl allows, coupled with once-affordable studio buildings, but the benign neglect that many artists enjoyed in the early part of this period also allowed more gestation time for complex languages to develop that are now sustaining these artists well into maturity. John Baldessari, Mike Kelley, Paul McCarthy, Chris Burden, Charles Ray and Jim Shaw are six such exemplars within this exhibition—artists who embody all of the aforementioned traits and conditions, and who have set the bar very high for the artists who followed. As the increasingly rich and varied outputs of these artists unspool in front of us, gathering momentum and meaning along the way, the international artistic landscape has been inscribed with their achievements, and their students and studio assistants have witnessed these examples and set similar standards for their own practices.

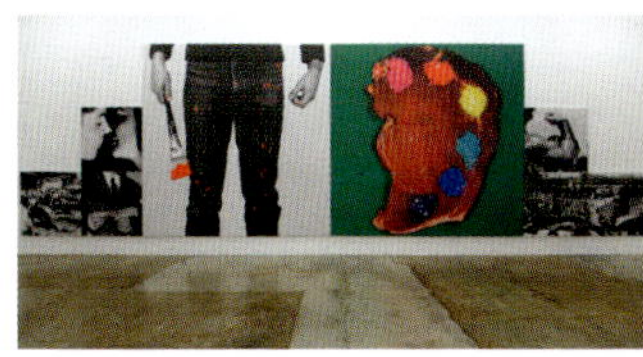

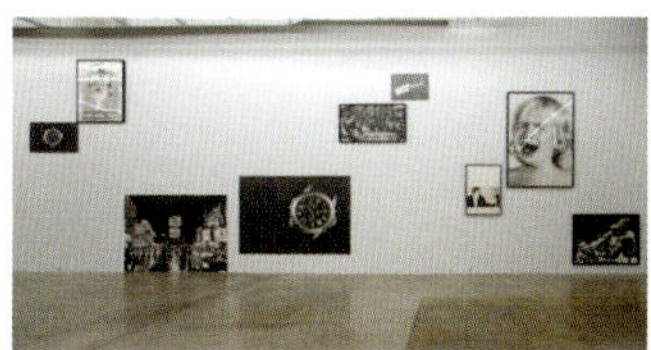

How heartening to see, for example, a giant wall in the Rubell space filled with John Baldessari's work from the past 20 years tracing his revolutionary manipulation of photographic imagery, and next to it an equally large wall, equally dominated by the recently emerged Karl Haendel. Like Baldessari famously did with photographs, Haendel doesn't allow drawing to be limited to circumscribed rectangles, but deploys multiple sheets with diverse imagery and a range of techniques to form installational, often architectural, dissertations on politics, perception and polyphony that transcend all expectations for graphite on paper. Doug Aitken's multichannel video installations such as *Diamond Sea* (1997), perform a similar detonation of single-image authority, using moving imagery where Baldessari employed stills, and activating space with an exacting degree of control, elegance and cinematic élan.

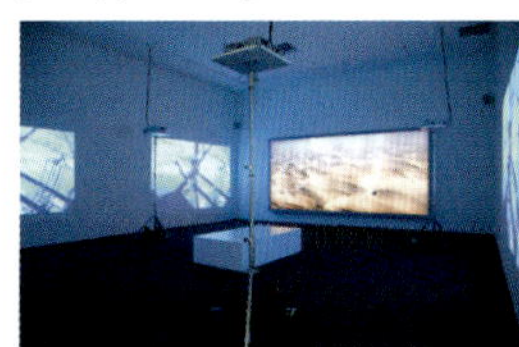

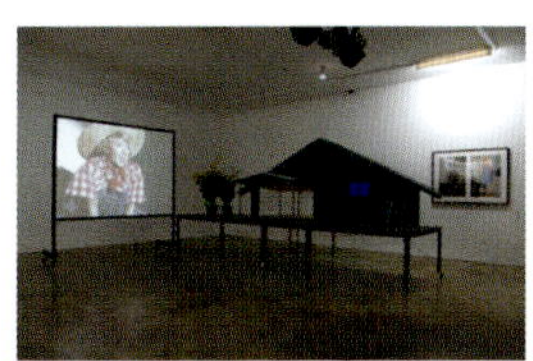

Mike Kelley is well represented within the "Red Eye" exhibition, and he has become indispensable to the health and success of the L.A. scene through teaching, as well as through the post-graduate program that working in his studio has become for legions of artists. His multidisciplinary approach, as sketched by the works in this show and the sheer ambition of his projects, has been a beacon for artists near and far. Where else can one imagine an artist like Catherine Sullivan (a Kelley studio graduate) emerging onto the scene, not slowly with meek single monitor videos, but right out of the gate with multichannel installations that are packed with formal, technical and dramatic complexity and which demand institutional display? (One-night, DIY garage shows need not apply.) Or Sterling Ruby, who has catapulted onto the stage with not one identifiable riff, but a barrage of complex references and forms channeled through every imaginable medium—from painting to sculpture, photography, collage, video and ceramics? An approach

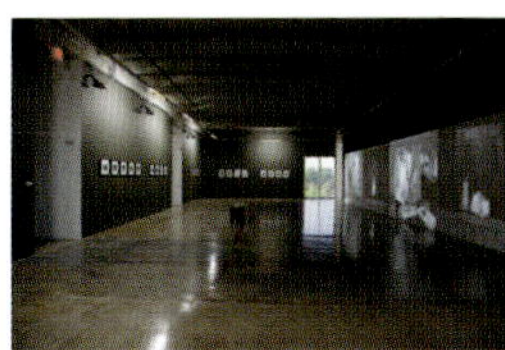

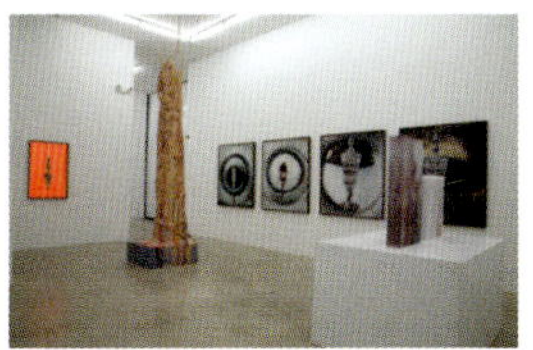

such as Ruby's, where the audience is flooded with material at such an early stage, portends a long career that could be easily sustained by just following up on all the discussions he's already started. So too with Aaron Curry,

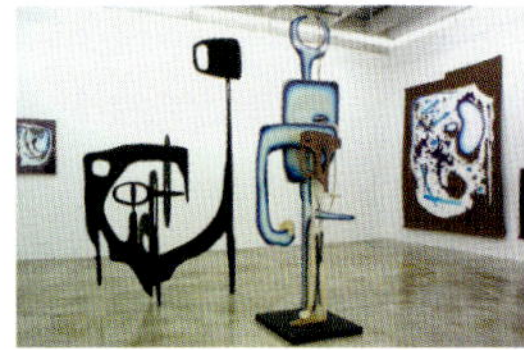

whose sculpture / painting / collage hybrids ramble in a dizzying lexicon pulled from 20th-century classics, but also talk the trash of disposable contemporary culture. First outings such as those by Sullivan, Ruby or Curry in the past couple of years just seem more auspicious and smart and risky than what used to be expected of young artists, and I think the hothouse of the L.A. community has a lot to do with that.

Paul McCarthy's protean output of the past 10 to 15 years has not only moved him into elite status when speaking about artists with global influence and admiration, but it has also established a pattern by which a seemingly maniacal pursuit of a theme (or series of interrelated themes) begets extraordinarily rich bodies of work. Thus performances produce videos and photographs, but not until the props are built that become sculptures; the drawings and collages that map out the characters also enter the realm of art along with the costumes and relics that are part of the undertaking. None of this would be of interest if it weren't for the searing commentaries that the artist builds into his spoofs of painters and pirates and Pinocchios. And as a sculpture like *Tripod* (2006)

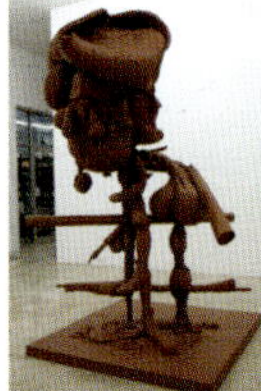

can attest, what may seem abject and slapdash at first glance is in reality a highly conceived and masterful manipulation of form. The late Jason Rhoades was a benefactor of McCarthy's pioneering use of performance as a vehicle for a wide range of artistic residue; he developed his own signature method of single-mindedly pursuing a theme that through sheer volume and often hilarious extrapolation

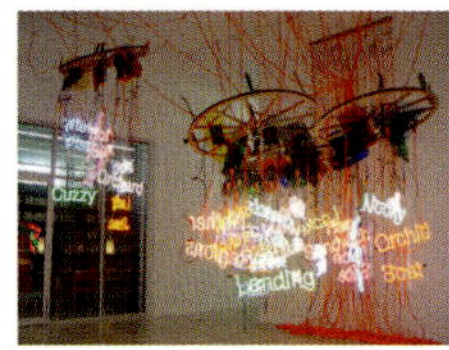

yielded complex installations. Rhoades' pieces within "Red Eye" achieve a certain formal elegance through such excess, balancing an amazing amount of research and artistic intent with materials that have been marshaled primarily through the purchasing power of shopping.

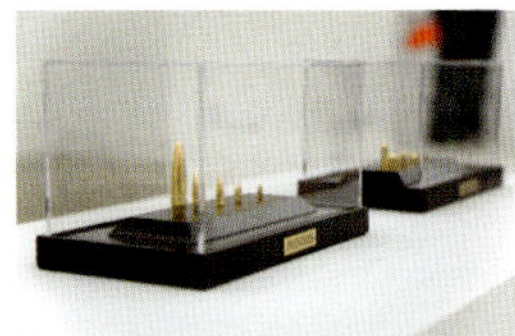

Chris Burden also famously came out of performance art, and it could even be said that he embodies the extremes of performance art more than any other artist, with such pieces as *Shoot* (1971) or *Five Day Locker Piece* (1971). While relics from his performances keep the aura of those actions alive, as with *Gold Bullets* (2003) in the Rubell Family

Collection, he has also developed a wide-ranging body of sculpture and even mentored young artists in his Topanga Canyon studio the way his UCLA faculty peers did. Although the performance of making or assembling his pieces is surely a subtext, mind-boggling labor and accumulation has been a hallmark of Burden's non-performance practice, from such works as *All the Submarines of the United States of America* (1987), to his Erector Set-like architectural exercises in *21 Foot Truss Bridge* (2003). And while Lara Schnitger didn't study with Burden, there is something to her "Tatlin-meets-Butterick" tower of cow print and lace that recalls the older artist, substituting feminine-coded patchwork for juvenile male building fantasies.

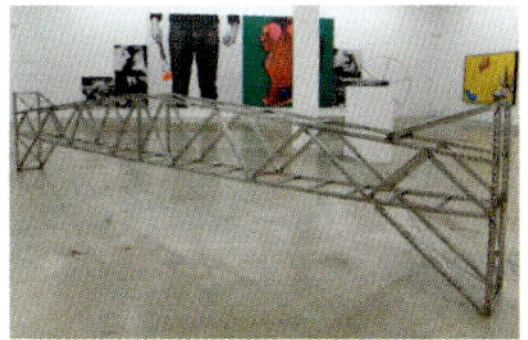

Charles Ray, a longtime colleague of Burden's and McCarthy's at UCLA, has likewise sustained an amazing array of younger artists, both in his courses and in his own studio as assistants. Ray's particular focus on sculpture, both Modernist formalism and an ever-widening historical context that has recently included Assyrian reliefs, has fostered a culture of serious thinking about sculpture that is unprecedented in Los Angeles. His own work (*Oh! Charley, Charley, Charley...* , (1992) for example) lampoons the kind of insular hermeticism of the romantic artist coaxing form from a block of marble with only his divine gifts, by making an obscenely narcissistic and perhaps schizophrenic self-portrait. Evan Holloway's freedom from stylistic singularity can be traced to Ray's example without toiling in the older artist's shadow, and the very different work of Jason Meadows can be seen as an offshoot of one aspect of Ray's practice, before it developed into a wholly original language of tectonic composition. It is hard not to think of Ray when one looks at Frank Benson's *Human Statue* (2005) installed in the same building as Ray's *Male Mannequin* (1990), but whereas Ray's piece unleashes the shock of the real within the acceptably fake convention of the department store model, Benson goes to a more confusing extreme, making a figure so believable yet unconventional that it is impossible to get one's mind to work in accordance with one's eyes.

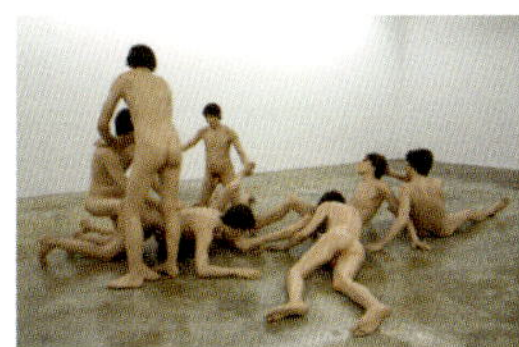

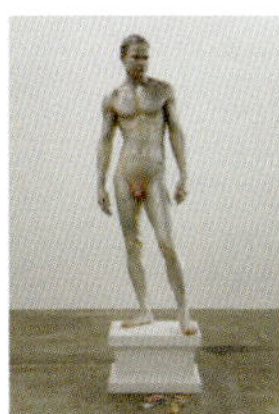

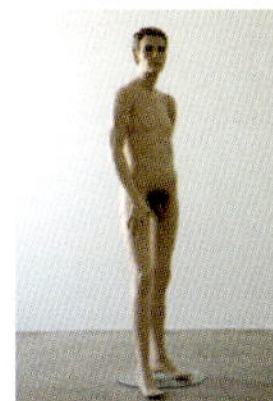

Nathan Mabry takes up yet another strand of Ray's legacy and is represented by no less than 12 pieces within the "Red Eye" exhibition, a testament to his lightning-quick establishment within the artworld. In his case, the modernist in-jokes of Ray's early work with cubes or planks is made more blatantly referential, but arguably weirder too, jamming together juxtapositions across time and space that are not only funny, but surprisingly harmonious. Like Ray and most of his protégés, Mabry does not shy away from complicated fabrication or the chores of finishing his

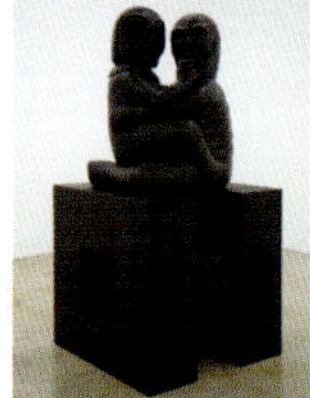

pieces to a high level of craft, and this attention to detail is an important balance for the goofiness of his subjects. *A Very Touching Moment (Cunning Linguist)* (2005) for instance, relies on wordplay and an irreverent adaptation of minimal sculpture to bring long-forgotten (at least within contemporary art) traditions of pre-Columbian art back into the dialogue.

Jim Shaw has been an artist's artist for a long time now, making such landmark bodies of work as his *Thrift Store Paintings* project and *Dream Drawings*

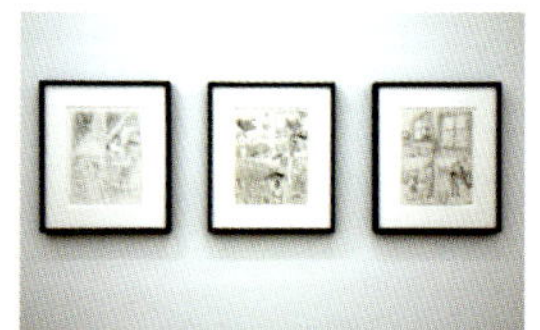

that are cherished by his peers, but just recently earned the institutional and commercial success such dedication deserves. His resuscitations of lowbrow popular culture make a fascinating portrait of the trickle-down assimilation of avant-garde ideas into the mainstream, and have been idiosyncratic beacons for many artists. Amy Bessone is interesting to consider within the context of Shaw's work, for her

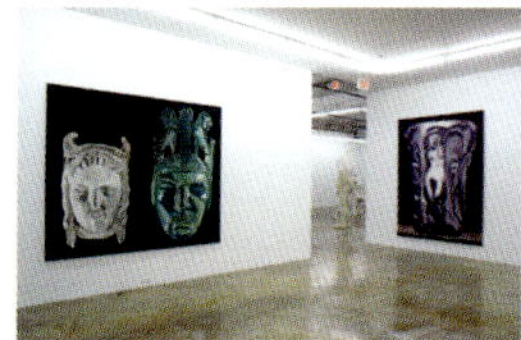

recent paintings take secondhand store tchotchkes and elevate them to heroic proportions, closing a circle of appropriation that may lead from Greek sculpture to Roman copy to tourist trade miniature, aggrandizing these bastardized, orphaned objects into strange monuments of modernity. Bessone's work hits a tone that is familiar to the ears of the irony peddlers of L.A., but much of her training was done in Europe and her sources and inspirations perhaps owe more to the louche robberies of Picabia or the airless metaphysics of De Chirico, than to the tongue-in-cheek discoveries of the Rose Bowl swap meet. Similarly, Matthew Monahan

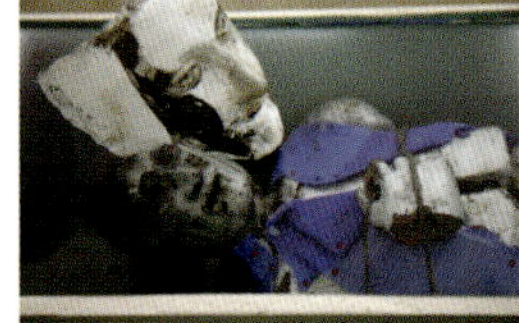

and Thomas Houseago, who also moved to L.A. after schooling in Holland, have found support and camaraderie in a city that appreciates their relentless work ethic and their fearless disregard for what cool contemporary art is supposed to look like. All too often, Monahan's art makes one wince when it gets dangerously close to the sort of romantic figuration that plies its trade with angels and saints, but his equal taste for the goulish and crude keeps his virtuoso work teetering thrillingly on a knife's edge. I can only imagine after seeing Houseago's installation at the Rubell

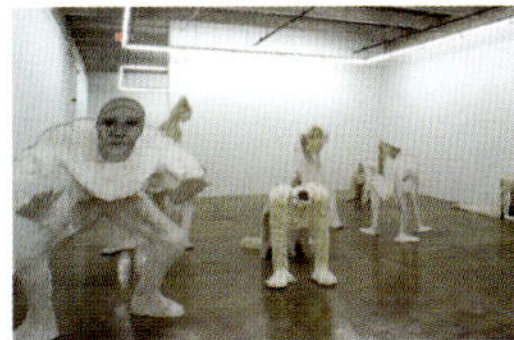

Family Collection that they were as blown away as I was upon first entering his studio and being stared down by an army of monumental white plaster figures that seem to be test dummies for formal experimentation. The sheer volume of his output, coupled with his fervent curiosity and an aesthetic that has few if any counterparts in current artmaking, certainly makes an impression and makes one yearn to see more.

This is the car-crash fascination at the heart of so much of the art coming out of Los Angeles these days. These artists pack so much thought and vision into their work, pumped up by confident ambition that signals a desire and ability to mark out a place of their own in the history of art, that it is virtually impossible to look away. Perhaps "Red Eye" does not just refer to a grueling air travel route, but to the condition that derives from trying to digest the incredible array of artmaking in L.A. today.

October 2007
Michael Darling
Jon and Mary Shirley Curator of Modern and Contemporary Art
Seattle Art Museum
Seattle, WA

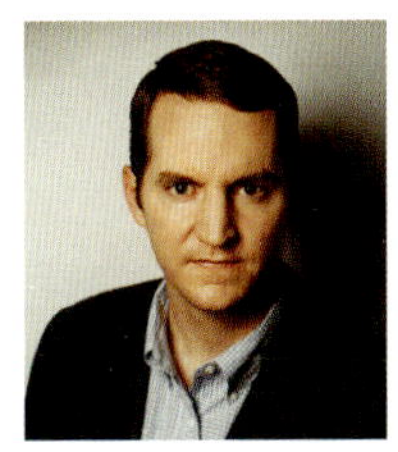

Michael Darling is the Jon and Mary Shirley Curator of Modern and Contemporary Art at the Seattle Art Museum (SAM), where he is currently working on an exhibition titled "Target Practice: Critiques of Painting 1949-1976," planned for 2009. Darling previously was Associate Curator at The Museum of Contemporary Art in Los Angeles, where he helped organize and author accompanying catalogues, including *Painting in Tongues* (Los Angeles: The Museum of Contemporary Art, 2006) and *Roy McMakin: A Door Meant as Adornment* (Los Angeles: The Museum of Contemporary Art, 2003). He has written for numerous publications including *L.A. Weekly, Flash Art* and *New Art Examiner,* and was a co-author of the book *Sam Durant* (Los Angeles: The Museum of Contemporary Art, 2002). Darling has a Ph.D. in Art History from the University of California at Santa Barbara.

ON LOCATION

Michael Ned Holte

I.

Driving through a rain-slicked Miami for the first time in my life and crossing the MacArthur Causeway to Miami Beach, with the nighttime skyline of downtown Miami in the background and a steady stream of palm trees whizzing by in the foreground, I can't help but think I've seen it before—that I've known this exotic locale implicitly since watching "Miami Vice" (or, I hate to admit, "Golden Girls") during my awkward teen years in a decidedly unexotic Middle American living room. Nothing conjures déjà vu as efficiently as the entertainment industry.

This sun-drenched, beach-edged, palm-dotted city has, of course, served as a popular destination for the film and television industry that seems to define the imaginary if not the reality of Los Angeles—my own sun-drenched, beach-edged, palm-dotted metropolis for the past 12 years. Miami is remarkably different from Los Angeles, not only in climate (tropical and relentlessly humid in Miami, dry and mild in Los Angeles) but also in culture. The camera's lens however, usually fails to register the differences. Facing the ocean, the camera (or an audience from the Midwest or Middle East) might not realize that there really is a difference between the beach of Santa Monica and the whiter, brighter sands of South Beach. Like Los Angeles, cinematic Miami even has its own shadow named Hollywood.

Somehow it should not come as a surprise that the Rubell Family Collection of contemporary international art is exhibited to the public in a former Drug Enforcement Agency warehouse—a 45,000 square-foot, raw concrete facility intended to house confiscated ... well, ... "Miami vice." Now, of course, the only vice on display is the loot acquired from art galleries and studios around the world. To sharpen the point, Don Rubell has referred to his family's proclivity for collecting contemporary art, which began in the late 1960s, as an "addiction" where something exciting and new is always a quick plane trip away.

The exhibition "Red Eye: L.A. Artists from the Rubell Family Collection" takes its title from this impulse. Don and Mera Rubell, and their son Jason, would frequently fly back to Miami from Los Angeles on the red-eye flight (arriving bleary-eyed the next morning) all to stay atop the ever-burgeoning L.A. contemporary art scene. In the past decade a series of notable gallery enclaves have emerged in the city, all of which remain viable and heavily trafficked: first, the Bergamot Station complex in industrial Santa Monica; followed by the 6150 Wilshire building on the city's Miracle Mile; followed by the then-young upstart galleries of Chinatown; followed more recently by the seemingly improbable explosion of commercial activity on the otherwise anonymous eastern edge of Culver City (pitched as "the next Chelsea" by The New York Times); and just in the past year, Hollywood proper is considered a new pocket of important contemporary art activity—again. And this is not even accounting for the geography of L.A.'s much-ballyhooed graduate art programs (to many, they are the heart of, and surely the primary audience for, the energetic Southern California art world), with MFA studios and exhibitions stretching from Westwood to Pasadena, from Valencia to the southern edge of downtown, from San Diego to Riverside, reminding the intrepid (or thorough) art connoisseur just how expansive and endless Los Angeles really is.

II.

The second occurrence of déjà vu washes over me inside the Rubells' warehouse. Much of the "Red Eye" exhibition was already familiar to me from my regular rounds of gallery, museum and studio visits in Los Angeles, though the specific combination and sheer quantity of work on display in Miami, as well as the change of venue, surely encouraged me to see the work anew. On location and divorced from their familiar context, the objects gathered by the Rubell family and configured in the generous gallery spaces conjured new understandings of old favorites, and suggested new circuits of significance between individual works and artists.

My introduction pointed to the entertainment industry because Hollywood seems to cast its shadow over all other forms of cultural production in Los Angeles, and of course the proper name "Hollywood"—as much an imago as an actual place—literally looms over the city. It will generally be the first thing anybody knows about Los Angeles; the flicker of abstract images that pops into the mind's eye.

This isn't to suggest that Hollywood (which may connote many things, from "cinema," to "glamour," to "Sunset Boulevard," to "Lindsay Lohan," to "broken dreams," and so on) is already inscribed on the artwork made in Southern California. That would be nonsense because obviously no single category or perspective could possibly contain the pluralistic range of practices in the region. Yet, when it's not inscribed in the work, Hollywood surely acts as a foil for the Los Angeles artist working individually in the studio—a scale of production (or ambition) worthy of consideration if not admiration. In recent years, Paul McCarthy and Mike Kelley—both crucial figures in defining the Los Angeles art world and featured prominently in "Red Eye"—have started approaching that scale of operation without sacrificing the strength or clarity of their early low-budget performance and installation work.

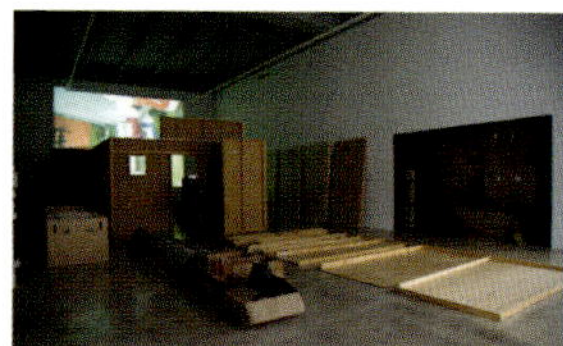

McCarthy's video installation *Painter Reformed* (1995-2006) is the first major work confronted in the "Red Eye" show, and it definitively sets the tone for the entire exhibition. Originally executed in 1995, the installation is centered on a video in which McCarthy sardonically adopts a cartoonish, De Kooning-esque persona, compulsively bumbling about his wood-paneled studio, treating enormous tubes of paint as excremental and / or sexual objects, while producing some fatuous Ab-Ex-style paintings. Typical of McCarthy's significant work in the 1990s, the video and stage set recall a low-budget sitcom production gone haywire. During several interludes, a married collecting couple meets with the artist and attempt to purchase a work despite the artist's juvenile, destructive behavior. In 2000, the original *Painter* installation, which included a single-channel video, the stage set, the paintings, and a number of the props, was severely damaged while in transit from the Rubell Family Collection in Miami to the Biennale of Sydney. After much negotiation (and a financial settlement akin to purchasing a major new work) McCarthy finally rewarded the Rubells with a "reformed" installation that included insurance photographs of the damaged work, crates with the ruined props, and most critically, a series of large panels leaned against the wall documenting the correspondence between the annoyed artist, the Rubells, and the insurance company. In a passive-aggressive gesture, McCarthy also projected the video upside-down. *Painter Reformed* provides a risky opening gambit for "Red Eye": it puts the collectors in a precarious position by exposing the damage resulting from the art shipper's disastrous handling of the original installation, but it also intimately reveals the extent to which the Rubells become involved in the lives of the artists they collect. More importantly, the artwork matches McCarthy's caustic satire—the ugly mechanisms behind the scenes of the artwork are exposed.

Similarly ambitious time-based installations by Catherine Sullivan, Doug Aitken, and Mike Kelley, all taking the film director as an implicit model, anchor

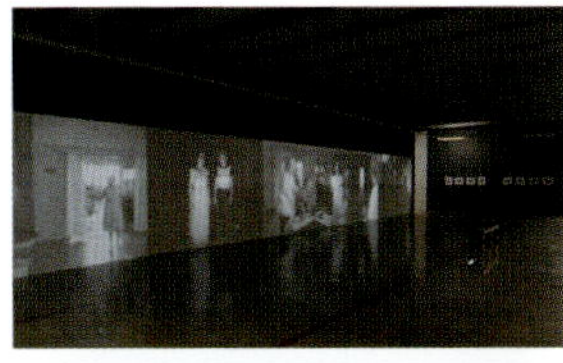

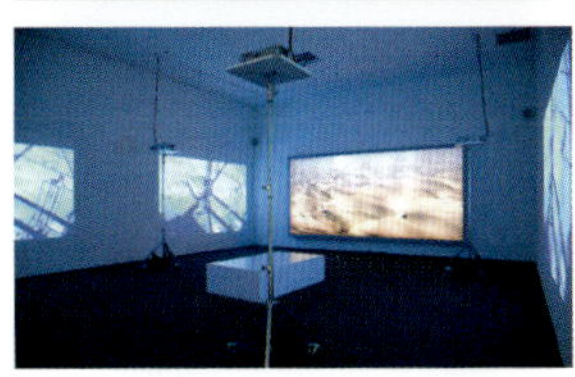

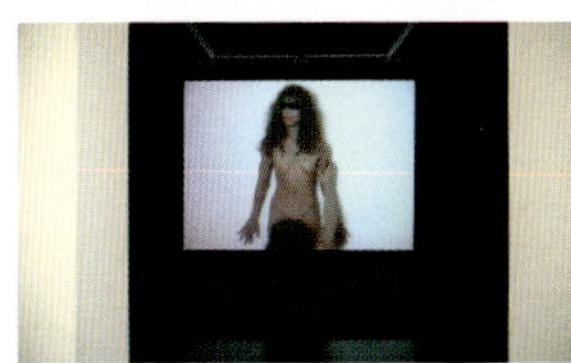

"Red Eye." Sullivan's *Big Hunt* (2002) restages and reinterprets scenes from films including "The Miracle Worker," "Marat / Sade," "Tim," and "Whatever Happened to Baby Jane?" as a linear, simultaneous black-and-white, five-channel video projection. Aiken's *Diamond Sea* (1997) surrounds the viewer with a vaguely apocalyptic multichannel document of the vast, inhuman desert in southwestern Africa, sealed off to the public since 1908. The result is like a multimedia National Geographic episode crossed with music video poetics. Likewise, Mike Kelley and Paul McCarthy's disturbing collaborative video, *Fresh Acconci* (1995) which also includes a series of 15 photographs, suggests a hybridization of genres—something between soap opera and porno. Tellingly, both narrative genres are often considered inferior to mainstream Hollywood film, but are in actuality just as crucial to the Hollywood ecology and economy. The respective industries quickly turn out new products following established codes and conventions, as familiar to their audiences as they are to their production crews.

III.

The provincial reality of Hollywood's presence (stars, sure, but also the unexpected street closures, the caravans of production trailers hogging valuable parking space, cops casually overlooking make-believe disasters on La Brea or Exposition, scruffy screenwriters in residence at the local Starbucks, etc.,) might well be as influential as the fantasy product exported to a global audience. That Los Angeles is the image-making (or "Imagineering" in the trademarked parlance of Disney) center of the world, and that the Rubell Collection includes numerous examples of images literally constructed (*made* as much as *taken*) in vastly different ways by such pioneers as Barbara Kruger, John Baldessari, Raymond Pettibon, Richard Hawkins, and Mike Kelley, as well as younger artists including Aaron Curry, Karl Haendel, and Sterling Ruby, suggests Hollywood is a model for aesthetic production, even if that model is less one of glamour than one of creative borrowing, recycling (call the script doctor!) and highbrow dumpster-diving.

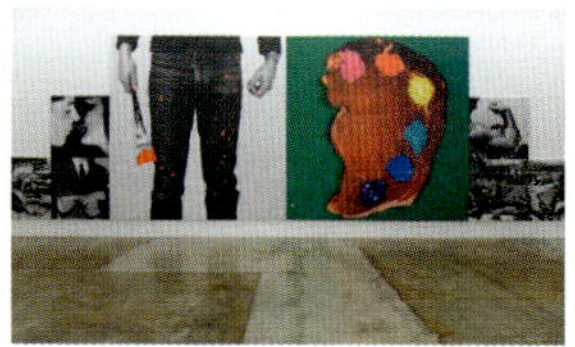

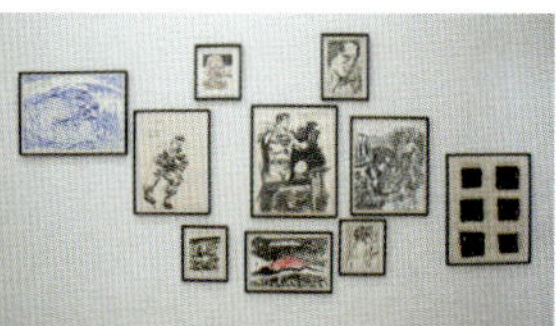

Baldessari, for example, has long relied upon his vast files of production stills, purchased cheaply on Hollywood Boulevard, to create his multipanel images. Pettibon's iconic, text-littered ink and watercolor drawings dig deep into the detritus of high and low culture, as do Shaw's

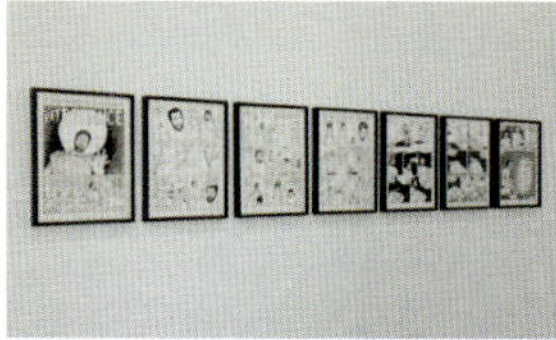

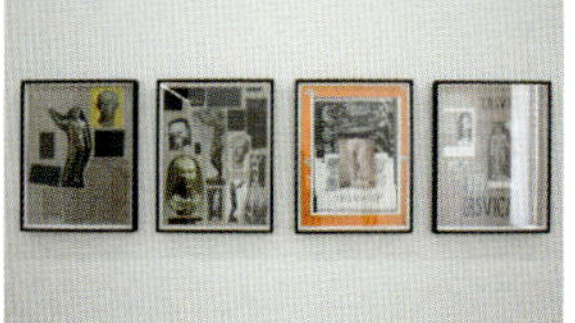

consistently unsettling comic book style drawings based on his dreams. With typical economy, Hawkins' collages and pages cut out of fashion magazines and marked with ejaculate-like daubs of oil paint reveal profound longing and subconscious desire inscribed in a Hollywood newsstand, while Mark Bradford's large collage on canvas, provocatively titled *Whore in the*

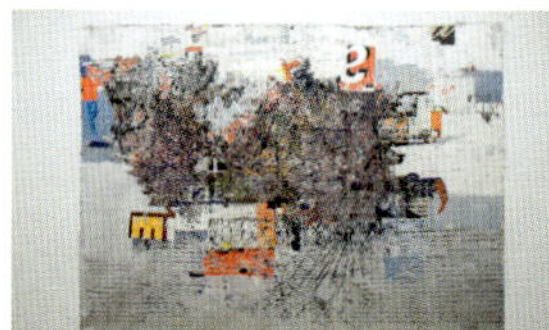

Church House (2006) recalls the density of abstract expressionist painting, but is constructed from ragged fragments of words and bits of color culled from posters and signage in the urban environment, layered toward a purposefully ruinous whole.

Perhaps the model most appropriate to the Los Angeles artist is the *bricoleur* who constructs mythology from scraps already in the world and ready-at-hand, like a production designer on a tight budget. (In "The Savage Mind," anthropologist Claude Levi-Strauss opposed the *bricoleur* in favor of the engineer who instead invents the world around himself from whole cloth.) One can easily look to pioneering garbage collectors-*cum*-sculptors George Herms and Ed Kienholz as an influence on this tendency, not to mention the wildfire-spread of the ready-made in L.A. following Marcel Duchamp's retrospective (his first) at the Pasadena Art Museum in 1963.

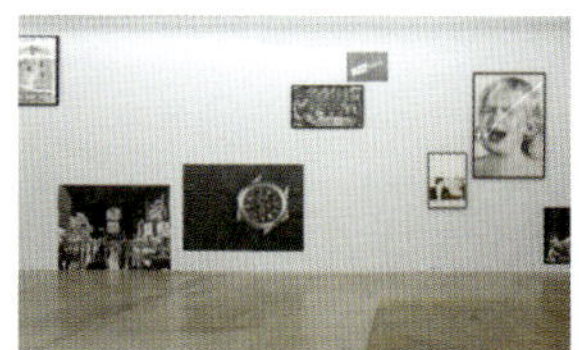

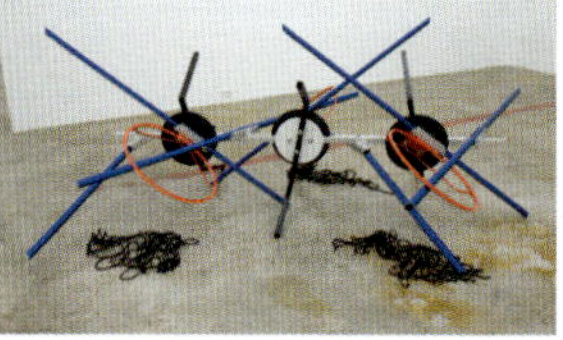

A number of objects in "Red Eye" oscillate between ready-made and fabrication. The images in Karl Haendel's labor-intensive grisaille drawings, typically installed in associative clusters, are taken directly from pop culture sources. Jason Meadows' *Web of Spiderman* (2001) conjures the superhero with a low slung, spider-like assemblage of blue anodized aluminum pipe, red

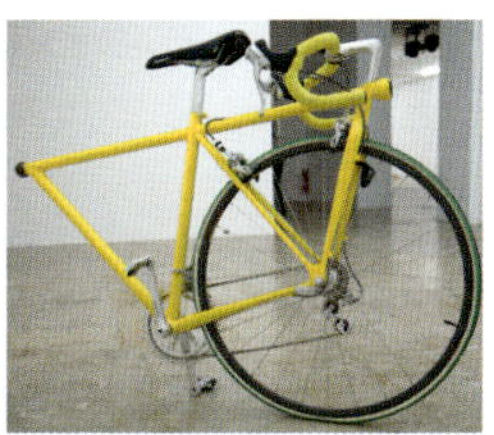

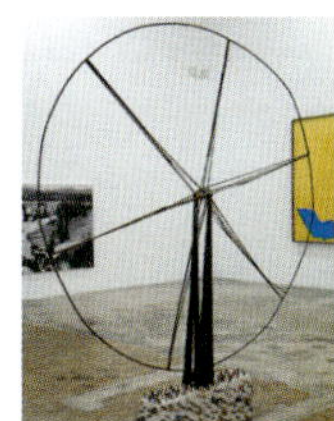

basketball hoops and nylon nets. Likewise, Yutaka Sone's *Alpine Attack* (1999), reconfigures parts of a yellow bicycle to create a strangely stationary object that suggests allegiance with Duchamp's *Bicycle Wheel* of 1913. Evan Holloway has literally

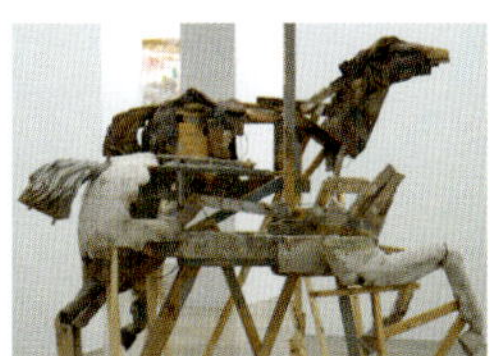

proposed recycling as a sculptural tactic. His *Second Law* (2006) invokes the principle of entropy and features a large metal wheel supported by a concrete base covered with depleted batteries; it too recalls Duchamp's influential ready-made. Likewise, Kristen Morgin's *Carousel Horses* (2006) which incorporates unfired clay, wire, and paint over wooden armatures, exists ambiguously between construction and ruin.

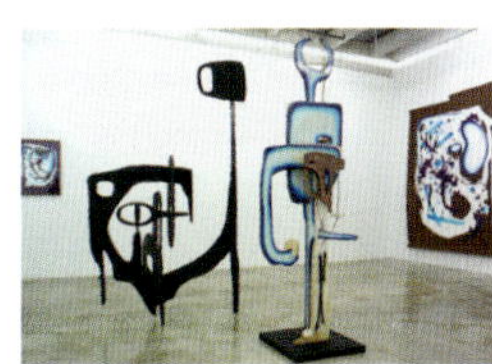

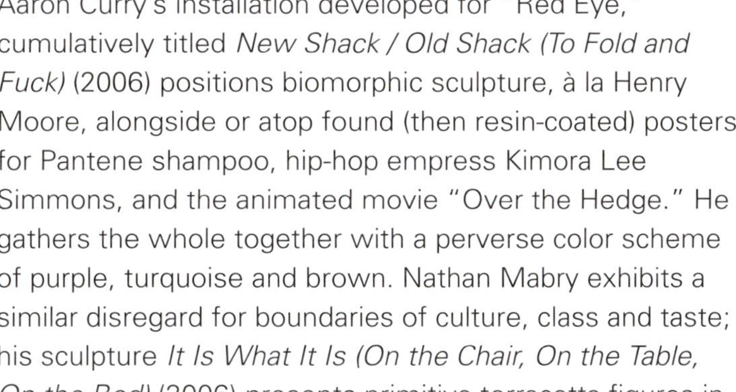

Aaron Curry's installation developed for "Red Eye," cumulatively titled *New Shack / Old Shack (To Fold and Fuck)* (2006) positions biomorphic sculpture, à la Henry Moore, alongside or atop found (then resin-coated) posters for Pantene shampoo, hip-hop empress Kimora Lee Simmons, and the animated movie "Over the Hedge." He

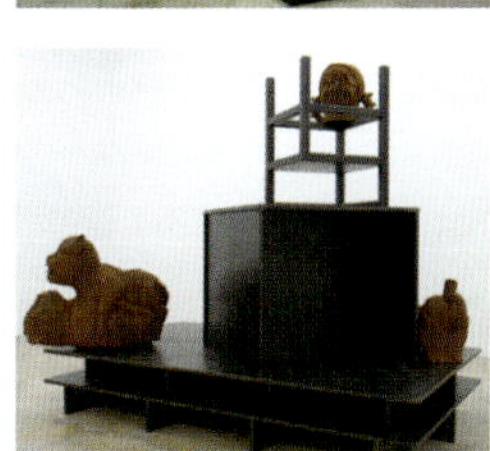

gathers the whole together with a perverse color scheme of purple, turquoise and brown. Nathan Mabry exhibits a similar disregard for boundaries of culture, class and taste; his sculpture *It Is What It Is (On the Chair, On the Table, On the Bed)* (2006) presents primitive terracotta figures in sexual positions, atop a steel platform based on several pieces of Donald Judd's stark, minimalist furniture.

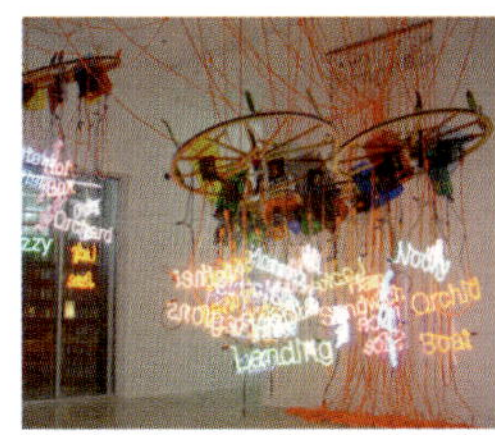

Perhaps the most extreme *bricoleur* in "Red Eye" is Jason Rhoades, who died unexpectedly in 2006. In his two raucous sculptures *Untitled Chandelier* (2004) euphemisms for female genitalia—"Knot's Landing," "Ham Sandwich," and "Ninja Boot," among countless others—take the form of neon sculptures that dangle from wagon wheels

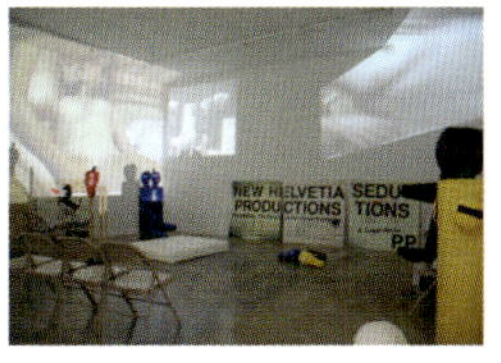

adorned with plastic phallic-looking produce, such as yams, eggplants, and corn cobs. Rhoades' performative installation *Propposition* (1999) made in collaboration with his former teacher McCarthy, employs self-defense equipment and upturned folding chairs along with a video of the artists making a delirious boardroom presentation conflating, according to Rhodes, "the art of production and the production of art."

IV.

Los Angeles' international reputation as a significant hub for sculpture—a medium well-represented in "Red Eye"—reminds me that an avalanche of remarkable, frequently weird objects are produced in prop houses and creature

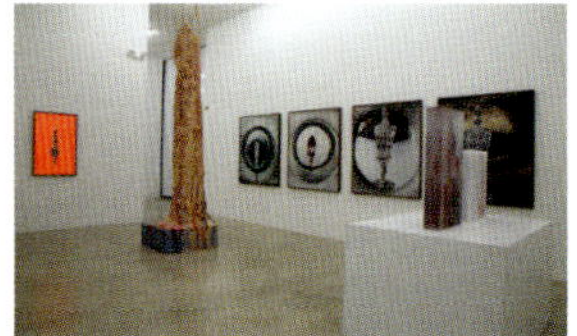

shops on a daily basis. Such "production value" has also been a trademark of Los Angeles sculpture since the "finish fetish" of 1960s sculptors John McCracken and Craig Kauffman, and remains fundamental to the work of many contemporary sculptors in Southern

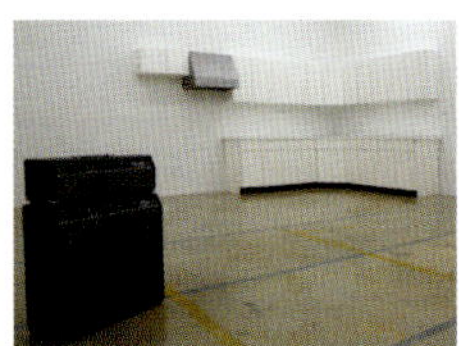

California. Sterling Ruby's luminous rectangular urethane slabs, situated on vandalized Formica pedestals, seem to acknowledge McCracken's influence, but are inflected by feathery skeins of colored liquid that inevitably recall creepy bodily fluids. Kaz Oshiro's Fender amplifier and

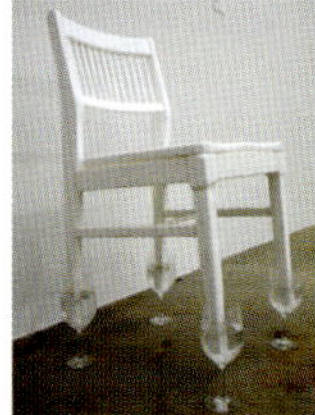

kitchen cabinetry are hollow yet hyper-real simulacra of the real things, constructed from paint and Bondo on mundane canvas stretchers. In Ry Rocklen's evocatively titled *10,000 Year Wait* (2006) a chair, painstakingly carved from Styrofoam, floats in four wine glasses—creating an effective illusion of gravity defied with humble materials.

Charles Ray continues to be the most influential figure in contemporary Los Angeles sculpture. (Holloway, Mabry, Meadows, Rocklen, and Frank Benson—all in "Red Eye"—are among his former students.) Ray's labor-intensive work is inflected by his interest in minimalist theatricality and the psychological presence of objects, which often extend to the figure. Here, he is represented by two disturbing self-portraits: *Male Mannequin* (1990) a ready-made figure

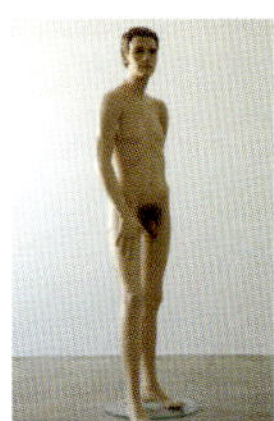

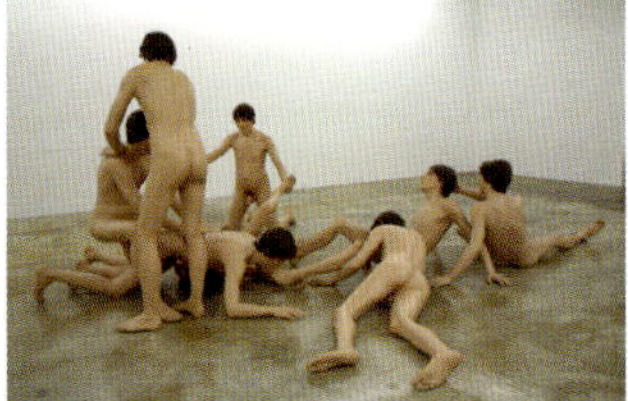

that features a painted cast of Ray's genitals along with a startling patch of brown pubic hair; and *Oh! Charley, Charley, Charley...* (1992) a freaky, onanistic orgy of eight "Charles Rays" in a variety of contiguous positions.

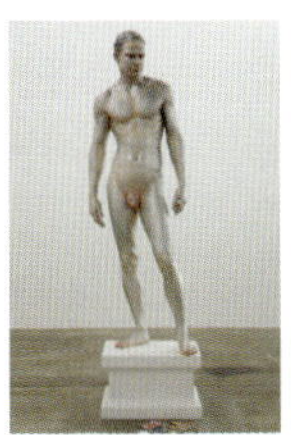
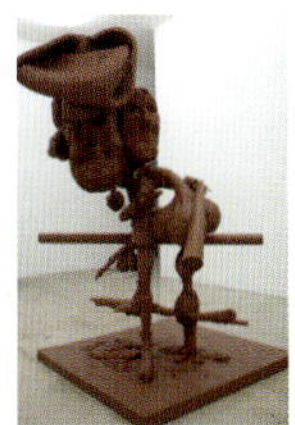
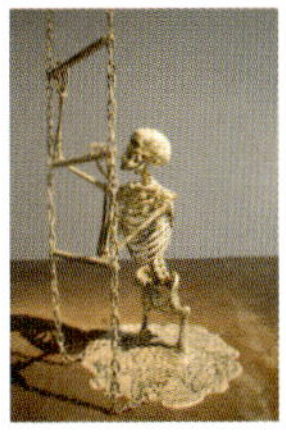

A similar interest in laborious fabrication in the service of making, unmaking, and remaking the human figure is also seen in Benson's eerily lifelike, but just-smaller-than life-size *Human Statue* (2005); McCarthy's *Tripod* (2006) a grotesque, aggregated pirate in shit-brown resin; Ricky Swallow's *The First One Now* (2000) in which a pigmented resin skeleton emerges from (or sinks into?) a

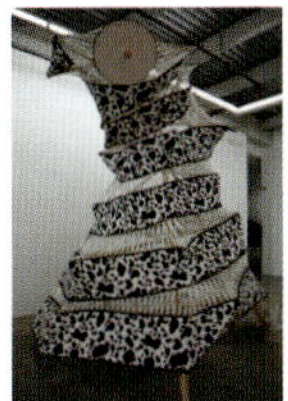

puddle of the same material while desperately hanging from a chain link ladder; and Lara Schnitger's *The Mothership* (2006) in which a large, abstract tensegrity structure of wood, cotton lace, and garish black-and-white spotted fabric unexpectedly emerges as a figure. The addition of a circular pink breast acts much like the exclamation point of Ray's genitals.

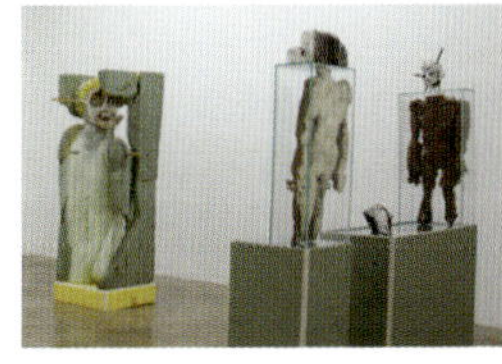

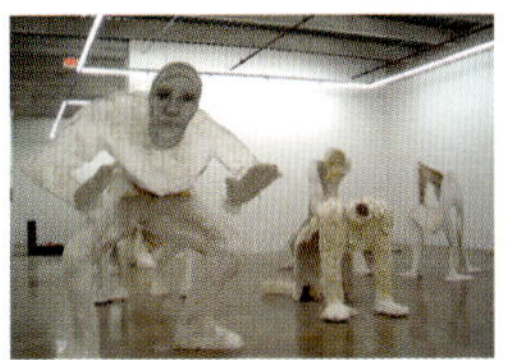

Matthew Monahan's sculptures have a funereal vibe, and merge the human figure with the museological display using ancient and contemporary materials: beeswax, canvas, green drywall with industrial stamps, glass, foam, and crumpled drawings which become sculptural. Like Monahan's hybrids, the nearly monochromatic white figures of Thomas Houseago's aggressive installation each occupy some space between drawing and objecthood, and seem to defy time and place. Roughly hewn or cobbled from plaster, rebar, clay, Tuf-Cal, graphite and hemp, Houseago's plaintive figures unexpectedly remind me of the murder victims literally made into plaster sculptures by beatnik artist Walter Paisley (played to the hilt by Dick Miller) in Roger Corman's 1959 film "A Bucket of Blood"—and I mean this as a sincere compliment. Working well outside of Hollywood, with a paper-thin artist's budget, Corman thriftily re-used the sets from his "Little Shop of Horrors" to augment the Venice Beach location of "A Bucket of Blood," which remains, for me at least, the best and most honest movie about art in Los Angeles.

V.

I arrive near the end of this essay with the sneaking suspicion that I have been slightly overbearing with my premise, by casting a claustrophobic shadow of Hollywood over a diverse group of artists who mostly operate independent of this imposition. And frankly, even as I travel across Los Angeles, moving from gallery to gallery or studio to studio, Hollywood as a concept is lurking mostly in the background, along with our infamous smog. It's only when I'm in Miami to see what Los Angeles art looks like, that I am able to see this thematic connective tissue.

Again, personal memories come flooding back: It's 1995, and I arrive in Los Angeles as a naive kid from the Midwest, in L.A. to pursue a career in the film industry. (Welcome to the jungle, baby.) My idea, that film was a creative or even self-critical discipline (an idea nourished by watching "Week-End" and "The Cabinet of Dr. Caligari" and "October" and "Pink Flamingos" as an undergrad), was revealed to be a grotesque fantasy. As a serf in Tinseltown, it didn't take me long to feel out-of-place, outnumbered, and dicked over. Thankfully, I was rescued by the realization that an amazing accumulation of art objects was lurking in the shadows, and was actually being produced here, and not in New York as I would have expected. I was excited to be in the midst of Mike Kelley, Raymond Pettibon, Paul McCarthy, Charles Ray—artists whose work I already knew and loved—and a witness to the impressive solo debuts of artists including Jason Meadows, Evan Holloway, Kaz Oshiro, and Aaron Curry, along with everything (and everyone) else that's emerged in the past 12 years. When I walked into the "Red Eye" show, I recognized that excitement again, preserved and on display, shared by the Rubells. Sometimes, you have to go on location to know how happy you are at home.

October 2007
Michael Ned Holte
Writer and Independent Curator
Los Angeles, CA

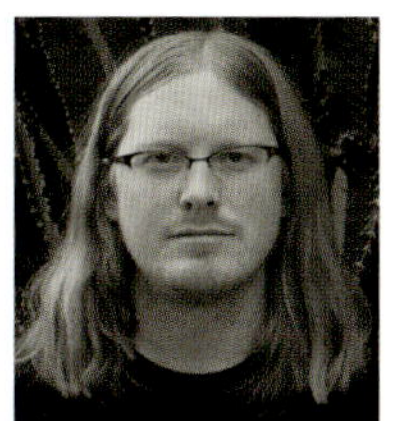

Michael Ned Holte is a Los Angeles-based writer and independent curator. He is a regular contributor for *Artforum*, and writes for other periodicals including *Afterall*, *Art Review*, *frieze*, and *Interview*. His most recent book publications include *Mindy Shapero: Heavy Lighght* (Athens: Breeder Gallery, 2007), and the *2006 California Biennial* (Newport Beach: Orange County Museum of Art, 2006). He has organized exhibitions for the USC Roski School of Fine Arts, Los Angeles, and the Anna Helwing Gallery, Los Angeles, and currently teaches at the University of Southern California. Holte has an M.A. in Theory and Criticism from Art Center College of Design in Pasadena, California.

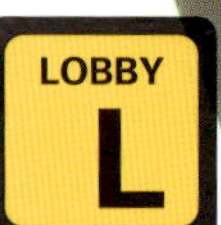

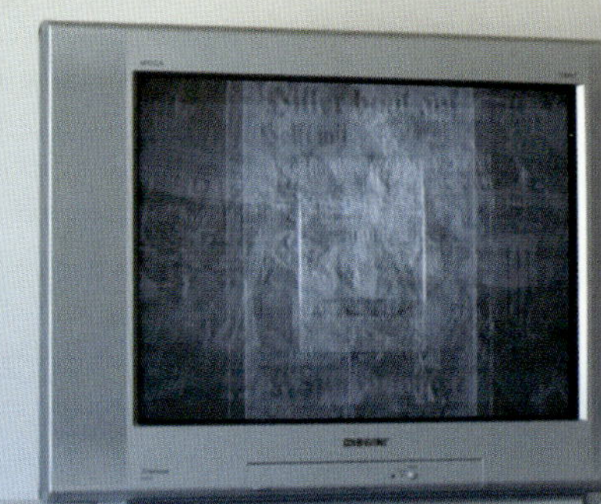

Paul McCarthy
Documents-Flicker Video, 2005
DVD, Ed. 5/10 + 2 AP
Loop

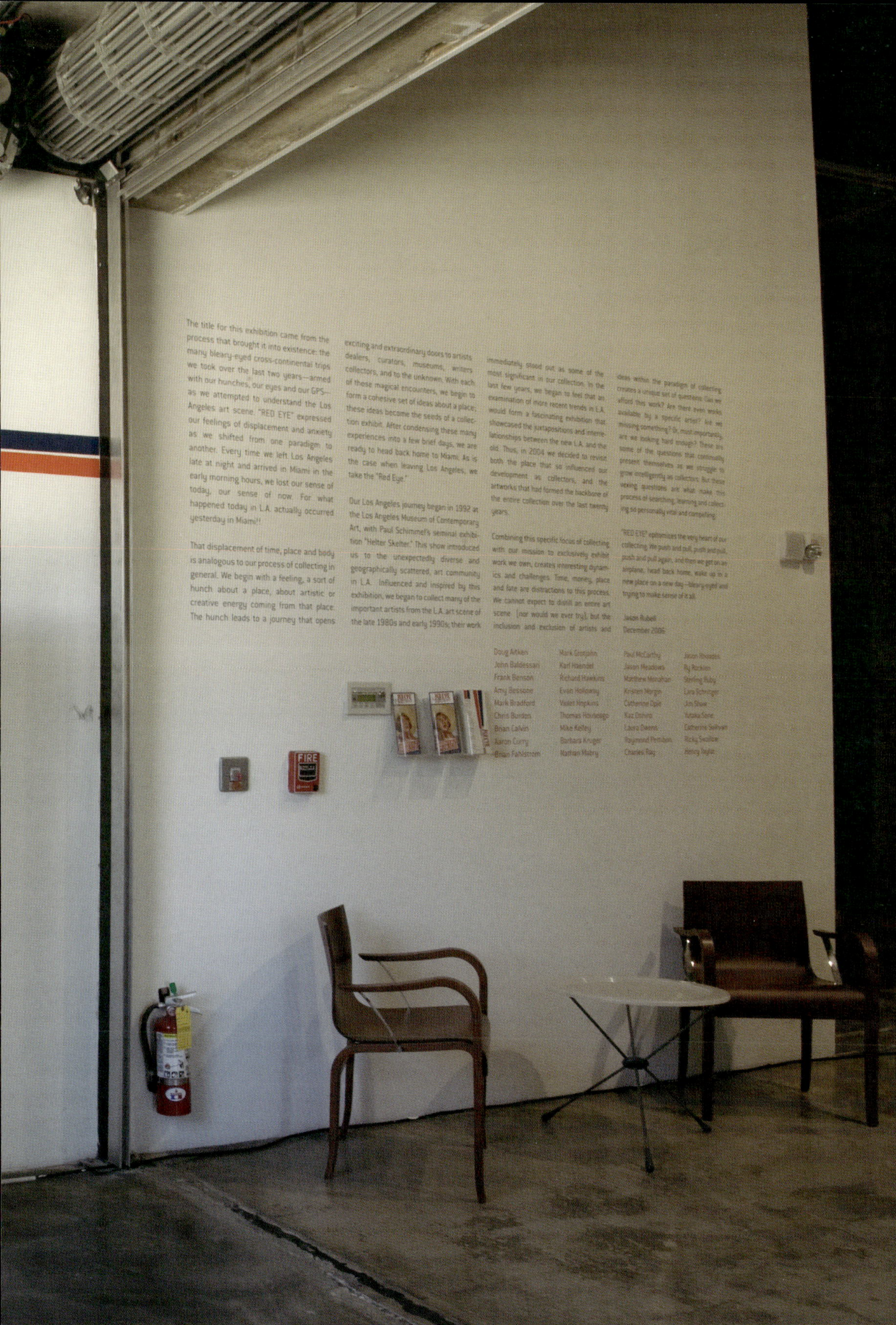
The title for this exhibition came from the process that brought it into existence: the many bleary-eyed cross-continental trips we took over the last two years—armed with our hunches, our eyes and our GPS—as we attempted to understand the Los Angeles art scene. "RED EYE" expressed our feelings of displacement and anxiety as we shifted from one paradigm to another. Every time we left Los Angeles late at night and arrived in Miami in the early morning hours, we lost our sense of today, our sense of now. For what happened today in L.A. actually occurred yesterday in Miami!!
That displacement of time, place and body is analogous to our process of collecting in general. We begin with a feeling, a sort of hunch about a place, about artistic or creative energy coming from that place. The hunch leads to a journey that opens exciting and extraordinary doors to artists, dealers, curators, museums, writers, collectors, and to the unknown. With each of these magical encounters, we begin to form a cohesive set of ideas about a place; these ideas become the seeds of a collection exhibit. After condensing these many experiences into a few brief days, we are ready to head back home to Miami. As is the case when leaving Los Angeles, we take the "Red Eye."
Our Los Angeles journey began in 1992 at the Los Angeles Museum of Contemporary Art, with Paul Schimmel's seminal exhibition "Helter Skelter." This show introduced us to the unexpectedly diverse and geographically scattered art community in L.A. Influenced and inspired by this exhibition, we began to collect many of the important artists from the L.A. art scene of the late 1980s and early 1990s; their work immediately stood out as some of the most significant in our collection. In the last few years, we began to feel that an examination of more recent trends in L.A. would form a fascinating exhibition that showcased the juxtapositions and interrelationships between the new L.A. and the old. Thus, in 2004 we decided to revisit both the place that so influenced our development as collectors, and the artworks that had formed the backbone of the entire collection over the last twenty years.
Combining this specific focus of collecting with our mission to exclusively exhibit work we own, creates interesting dynamics and challenges. Time, money, place and fate are distractions to this process. We cannot expect to distill an entire art scene (nor would we ever try), but the inclusion and exclusion of artists and
Jason Rubell
December 2006
FIRE

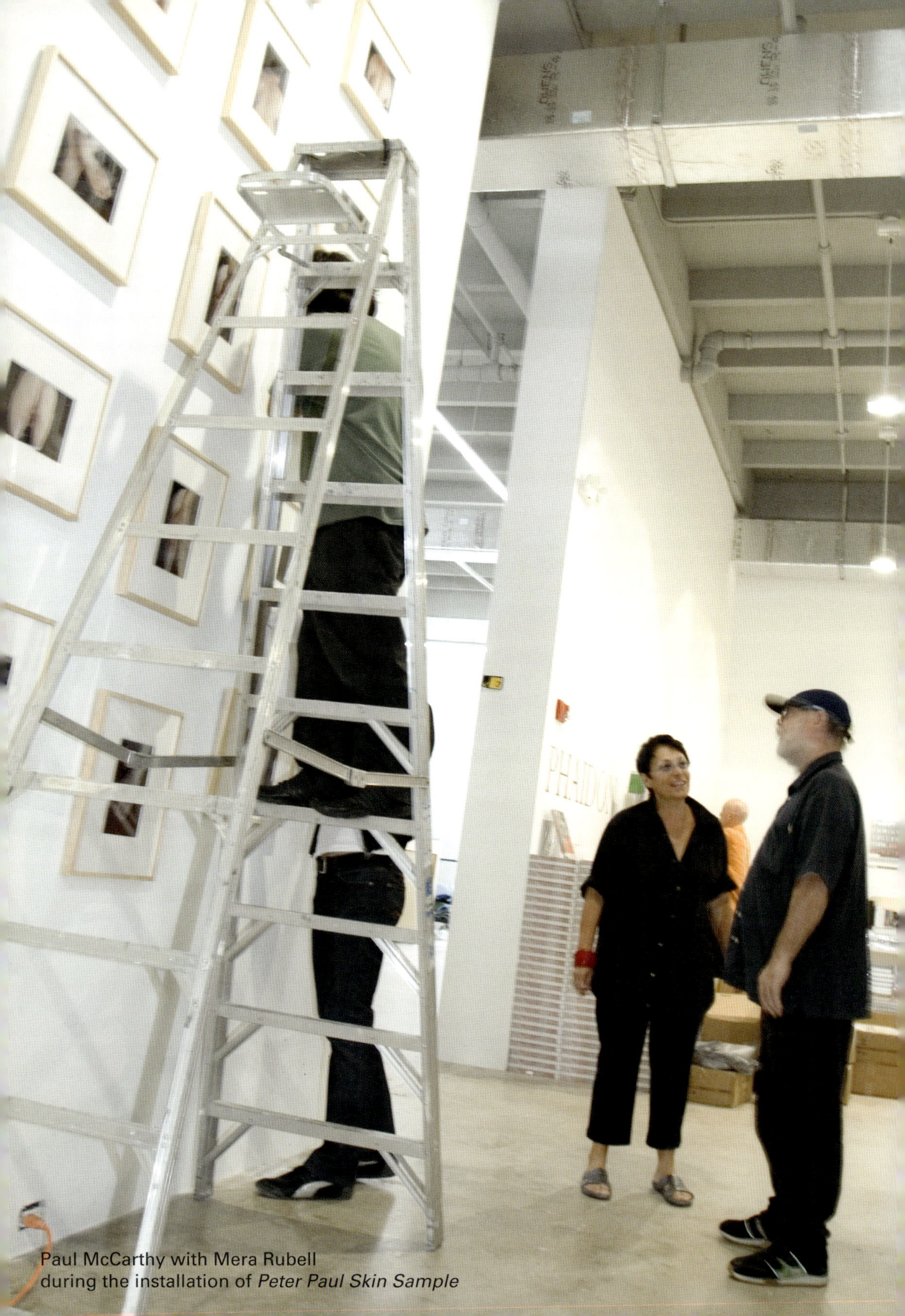

Paul McCarthy with Mera Rubell
during the installation of *Peter Paul Skin Sample*

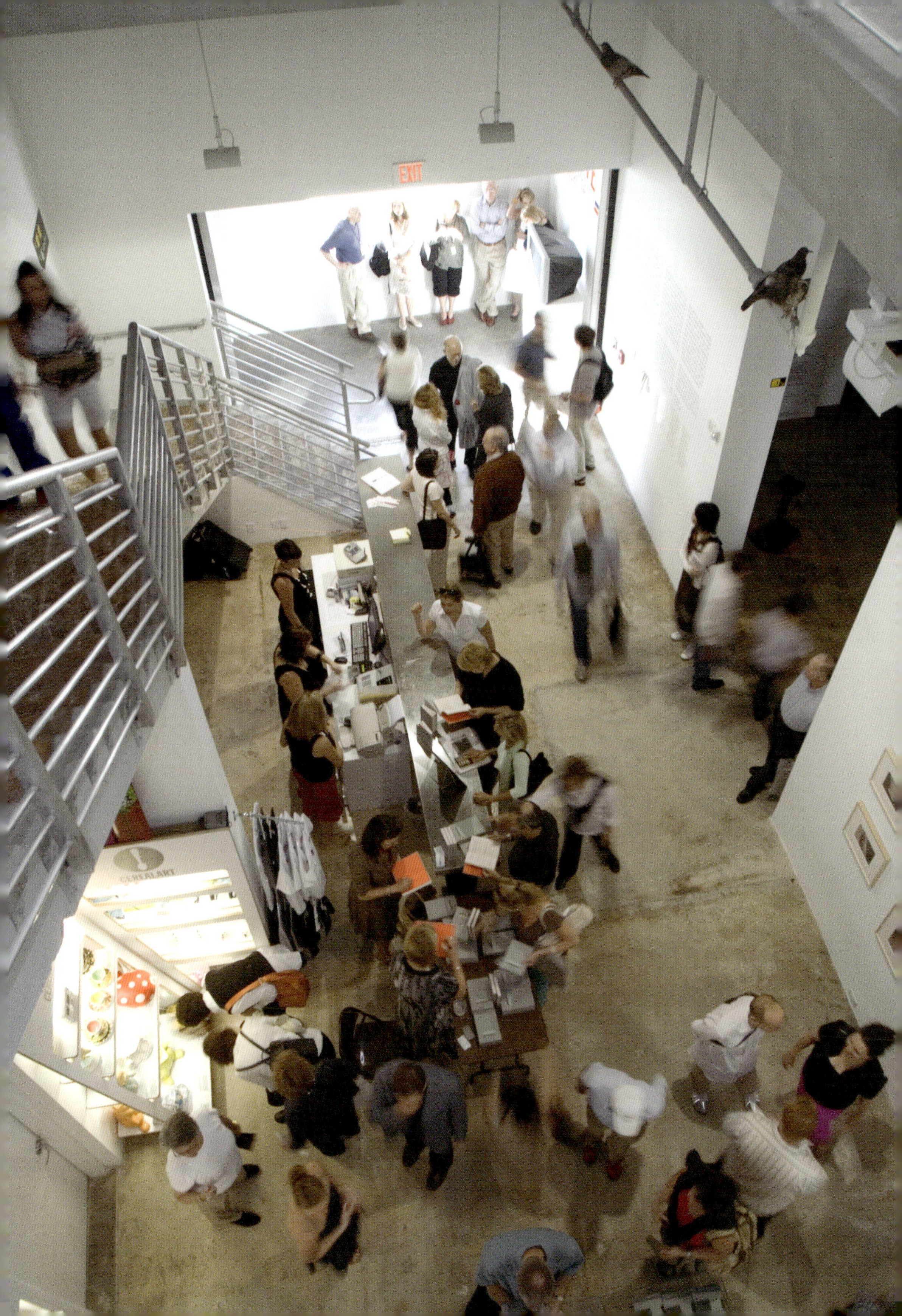
EXIT

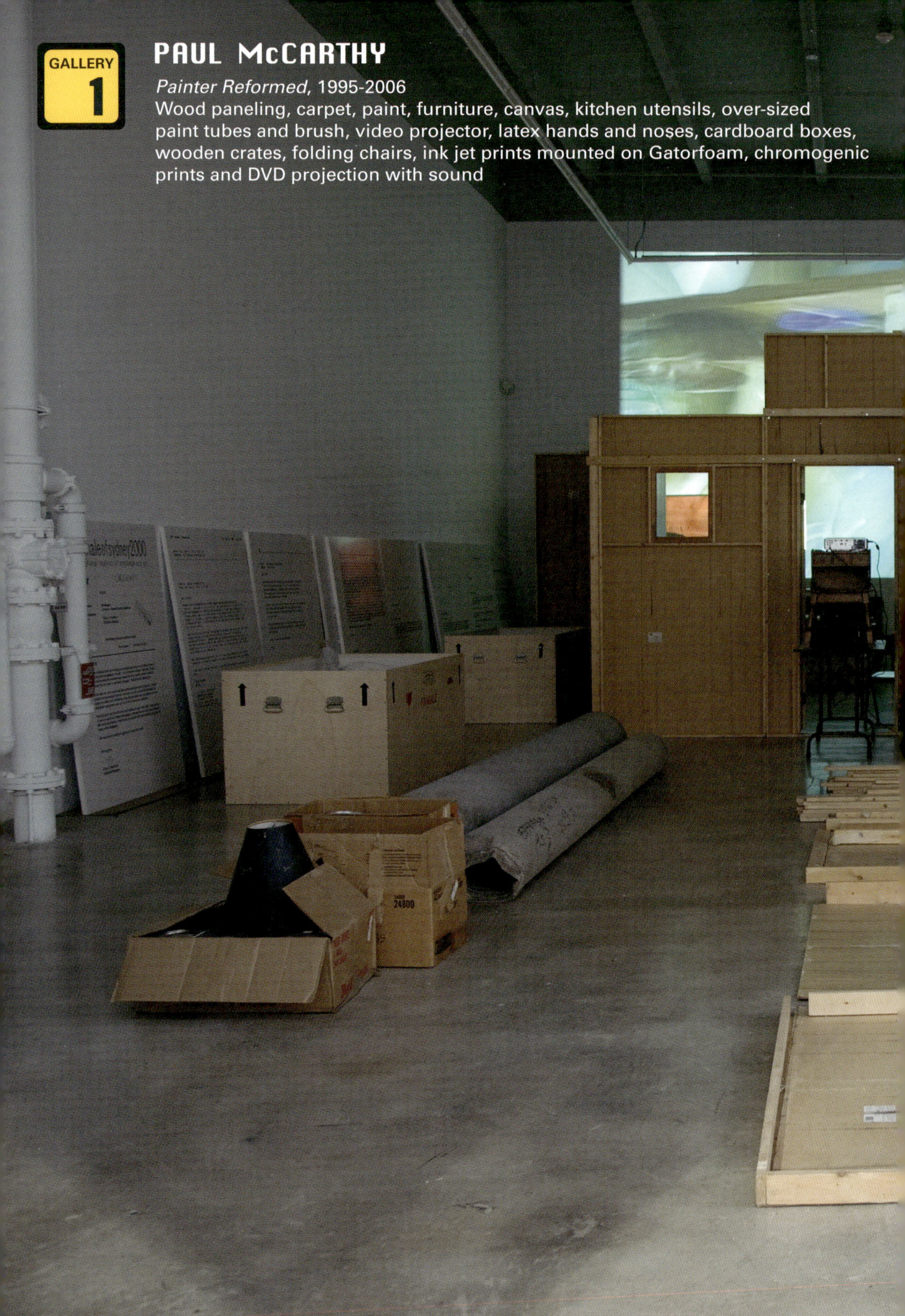

GALLERY 1

PAUL McCARTHY

Painter Reformed, 1995-2006
Wood paneling, carpet, paint, furniture, canvas, kitchen utensils, over-sized paint tubes and brush, video projector, latex hands and noses, cardboard boxes, wooden crates, folding chairs, ink jet prints mounted on Gatorfoam, chromogenic prints and DVD projection with sound

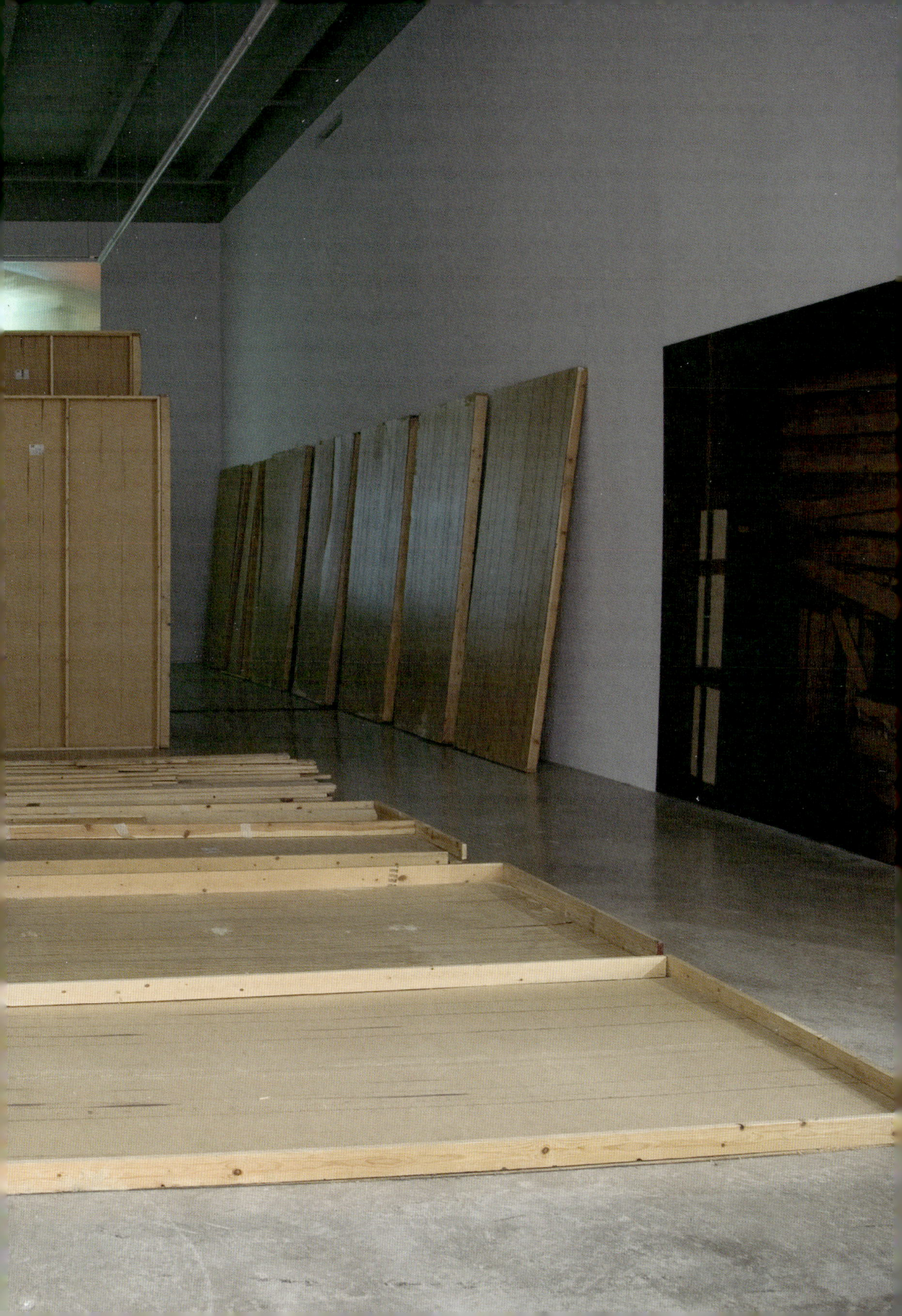

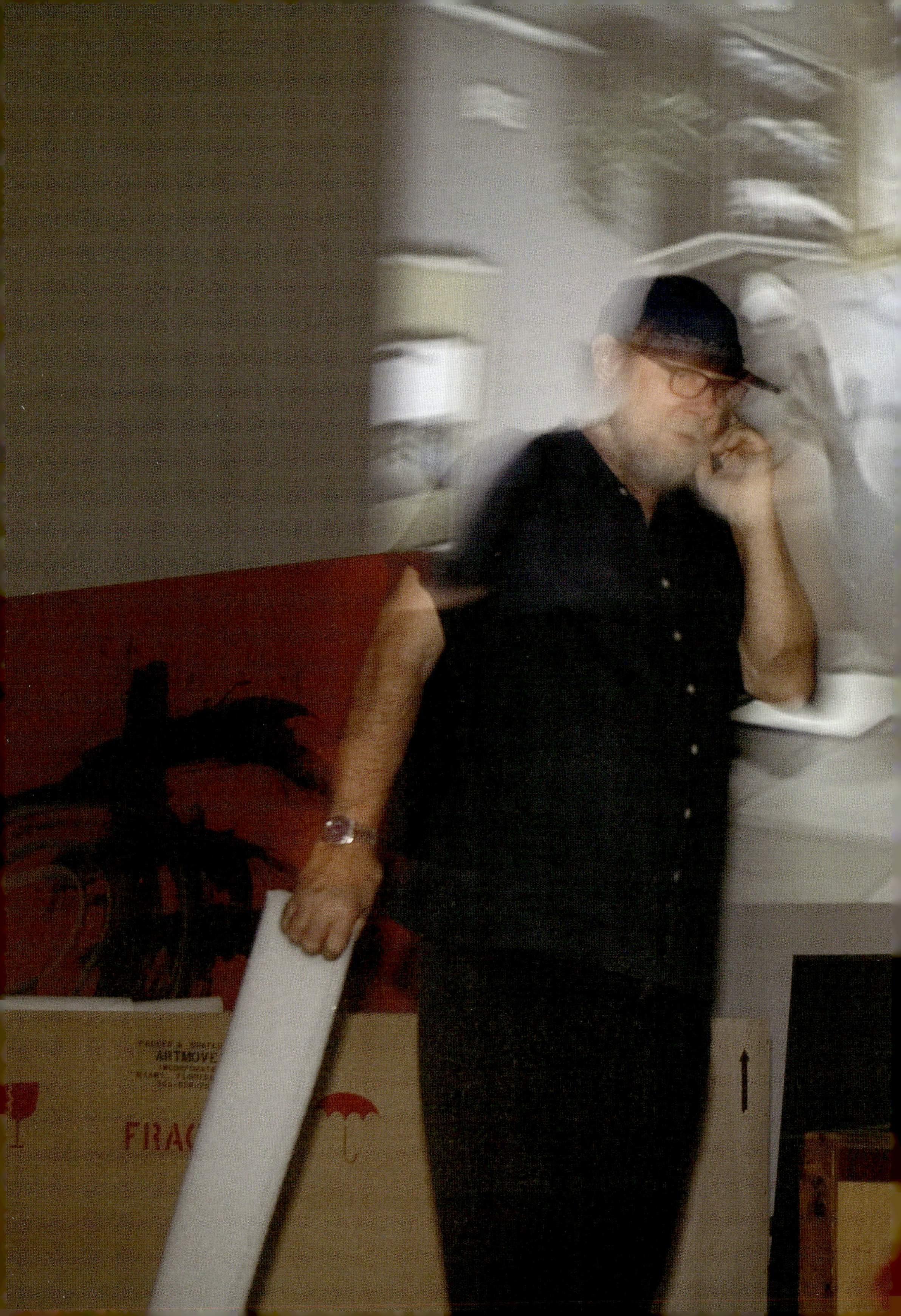

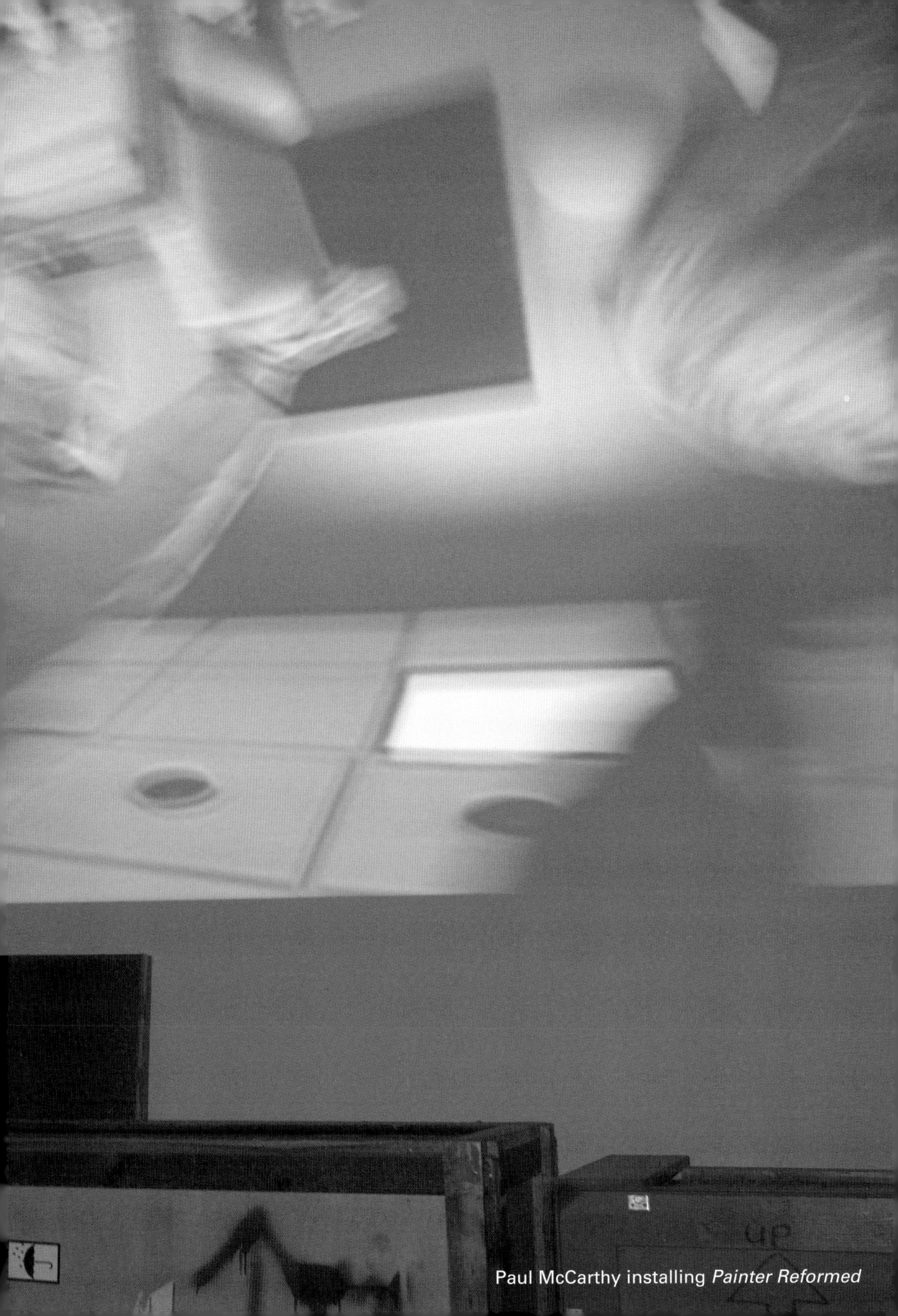

Paul McCarthy installing *Painter Reformed*

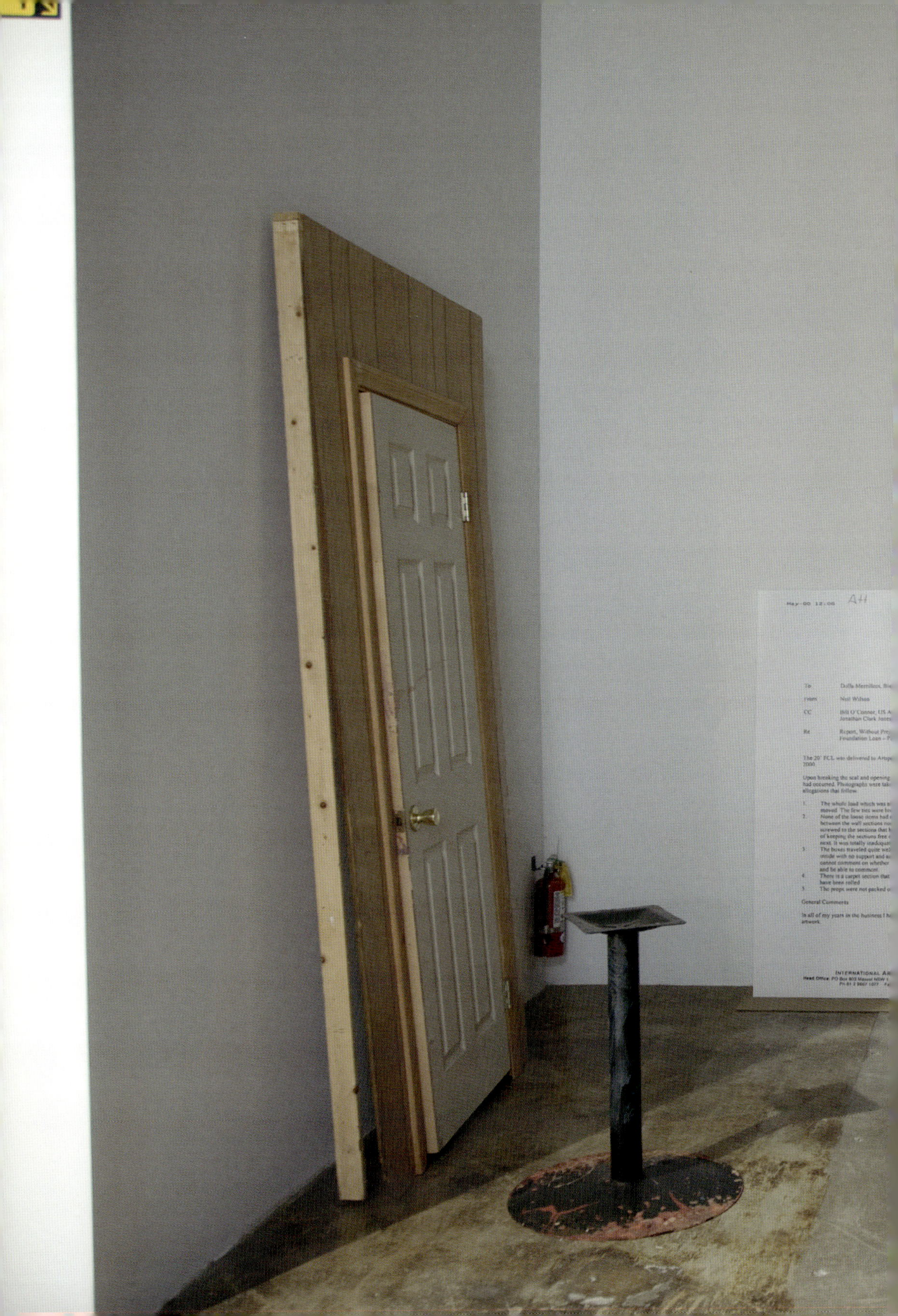

May-00 12:00
AH
To
From
Neil Wilson
CC
Re
General Comments
INTERNATIONAL

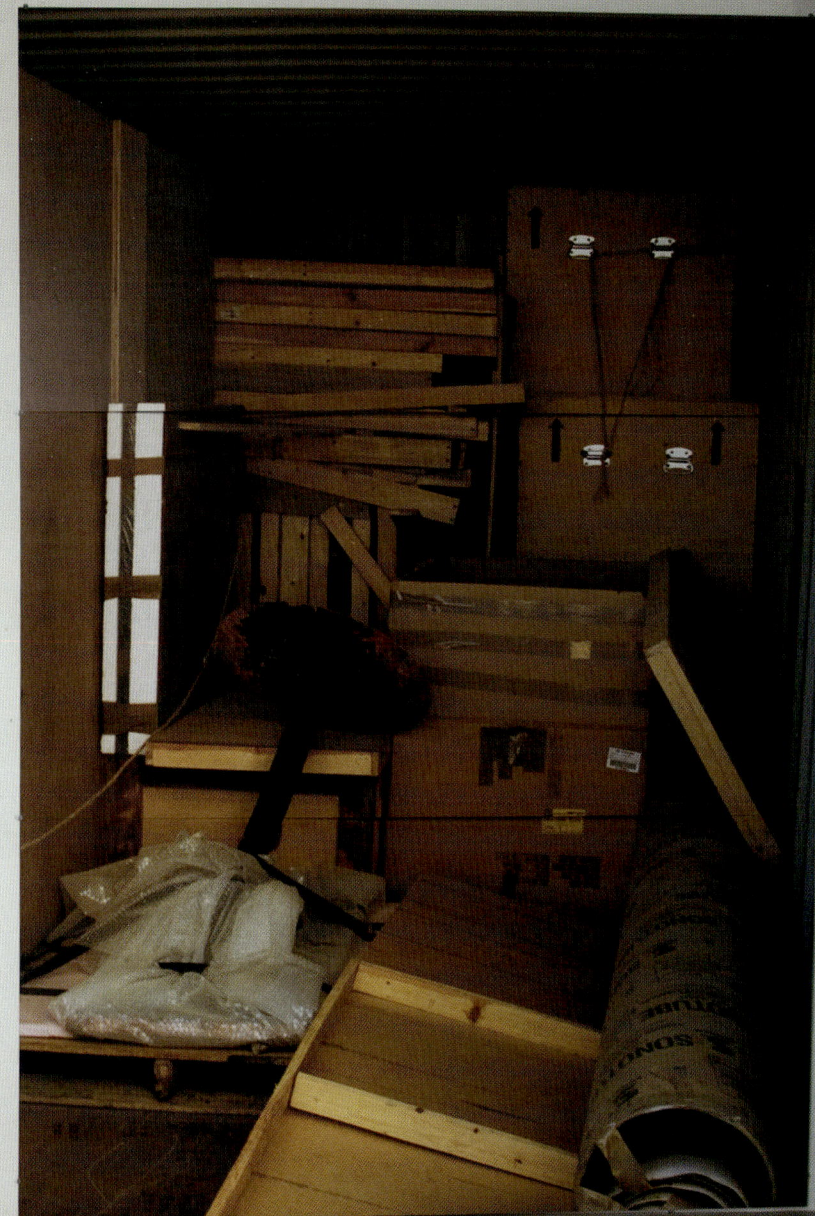

Painter Reformed (detail), 1995-2006

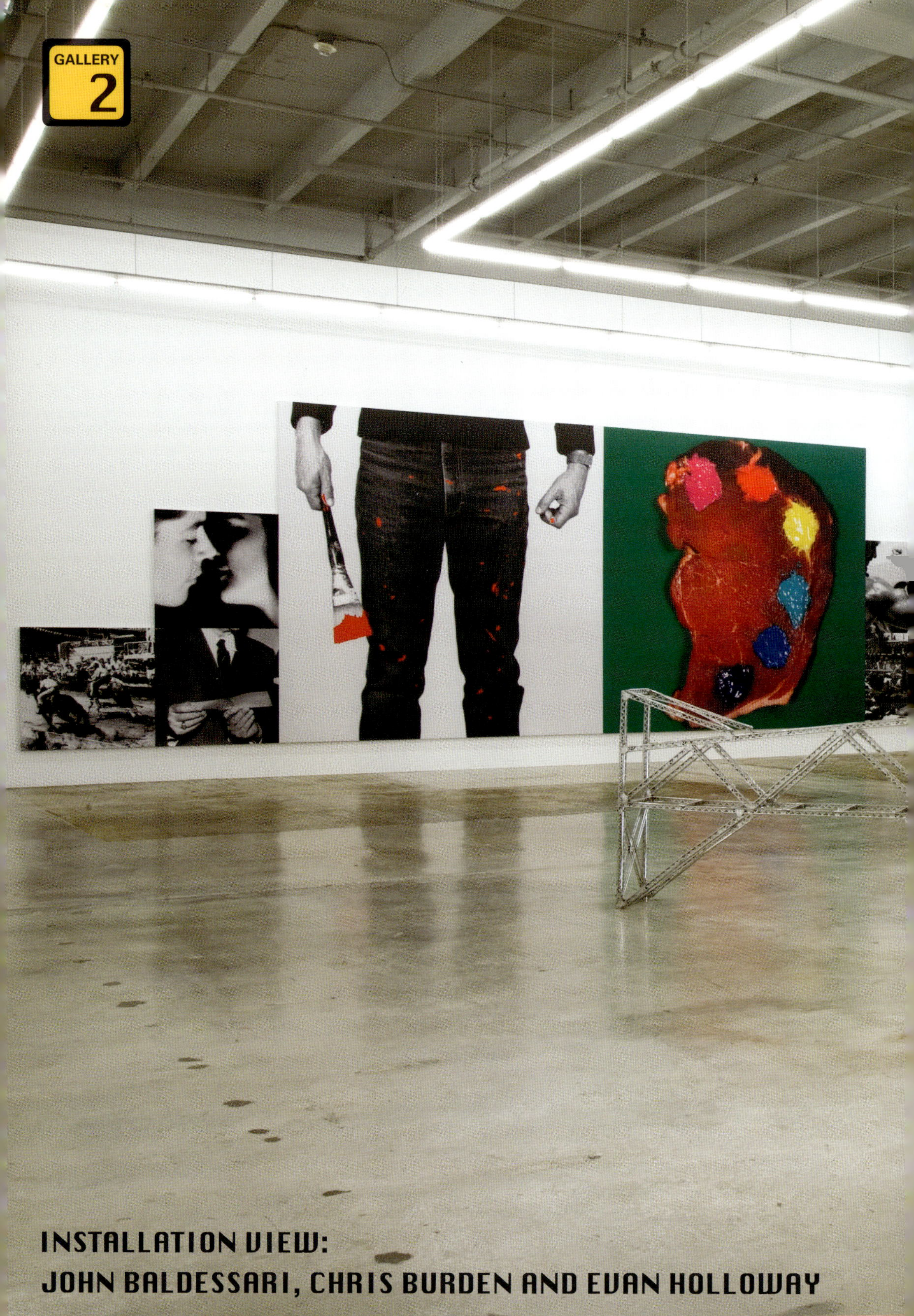

INSTALLATION VIEW:
JOHN BALDESSARI, CHRIS BURDEN AND EVAN HOLLOWAY

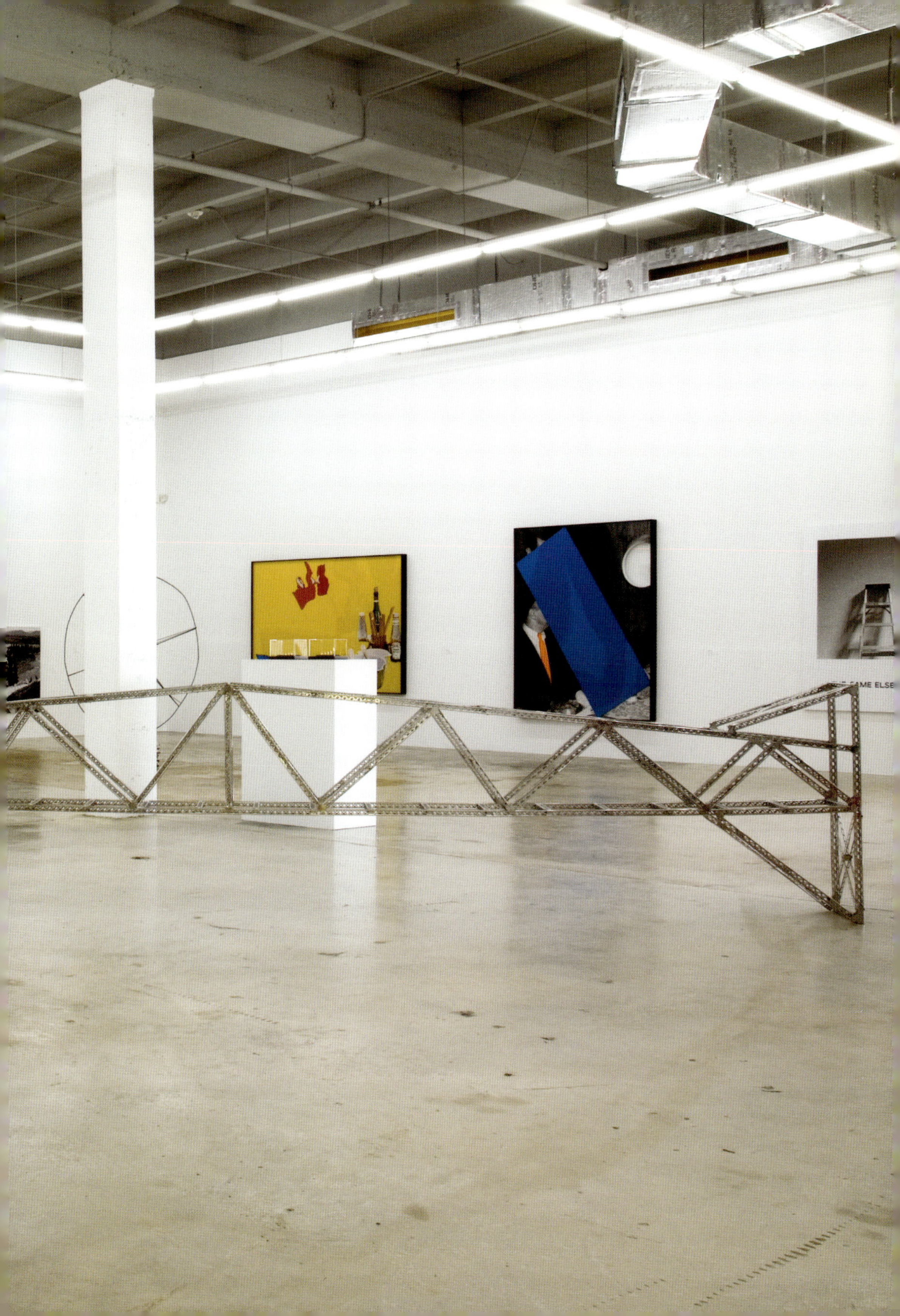

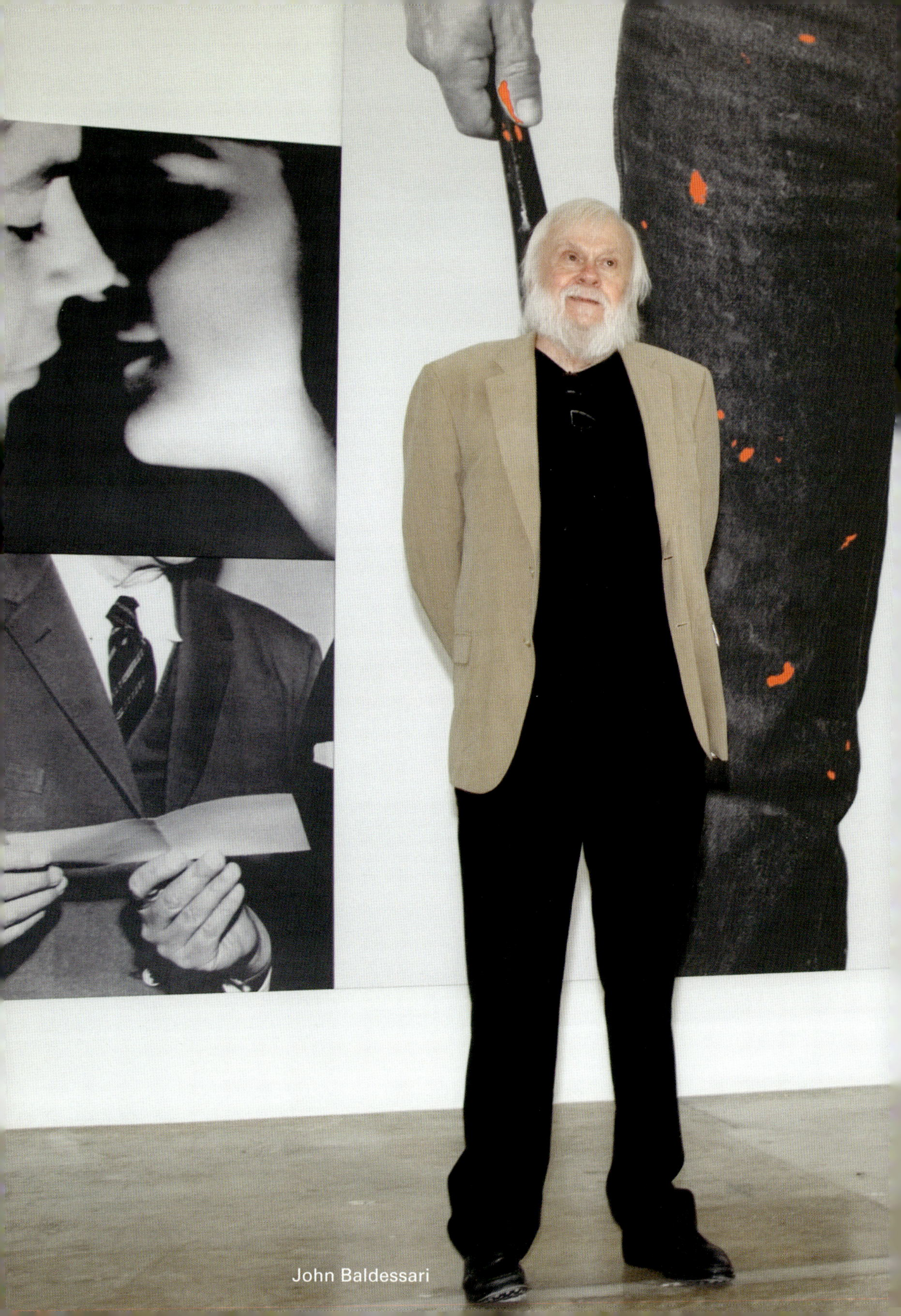

John Baldessari

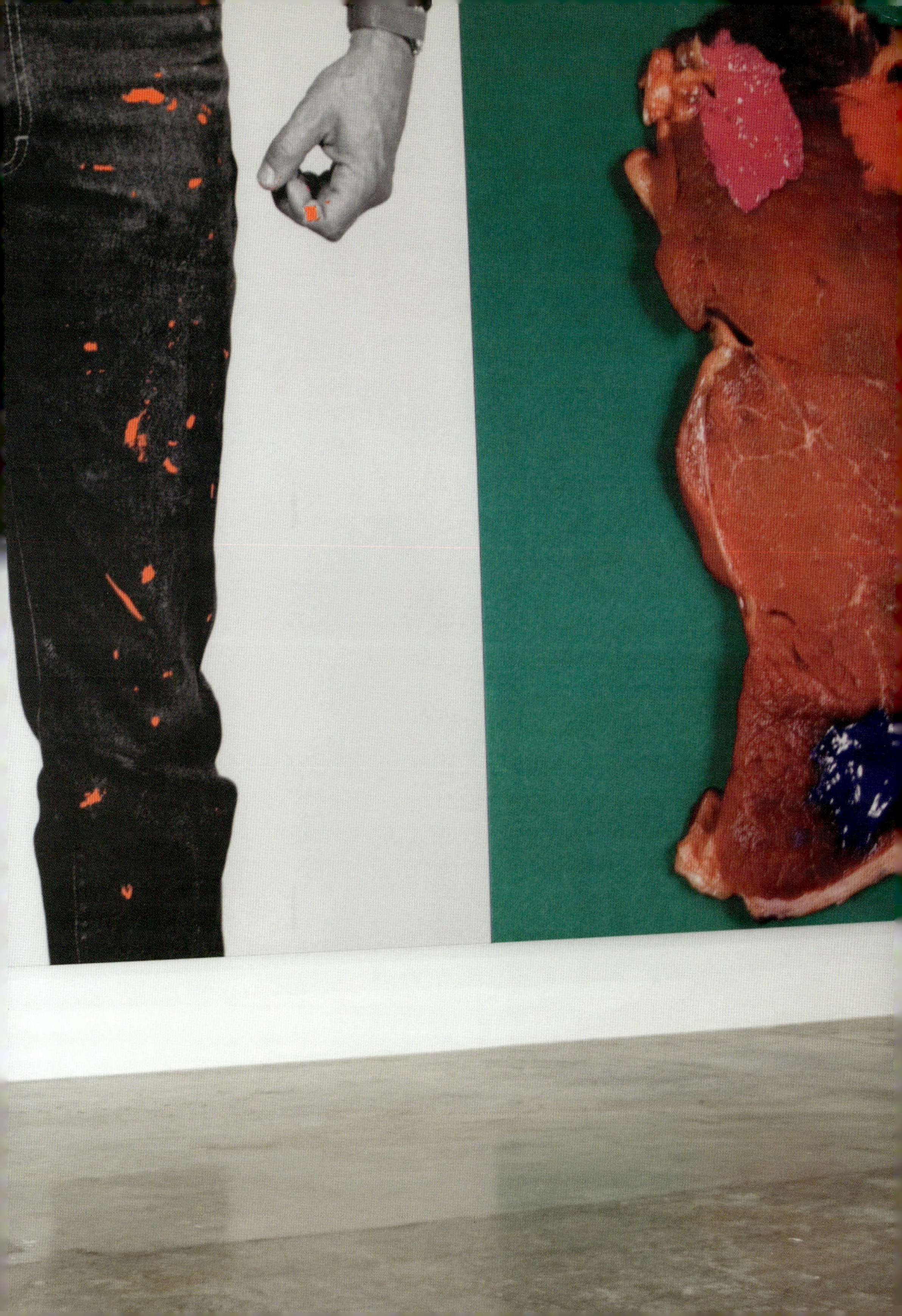

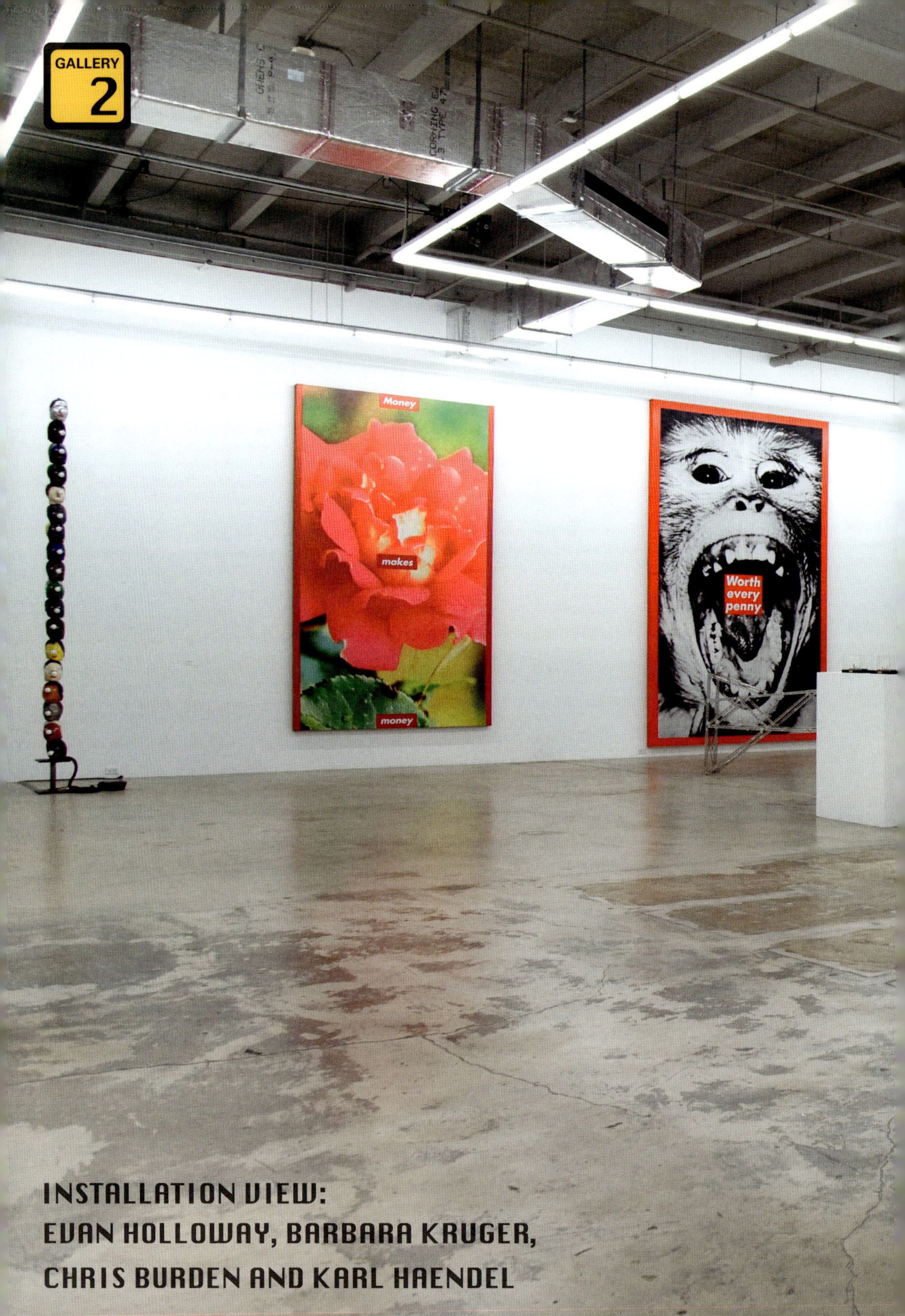

INSTALLATION VIEW:
EVAN HOLLOWAY, BARBARA KRUGER,
CHRIS BURDEN AND KARL HAENDEL

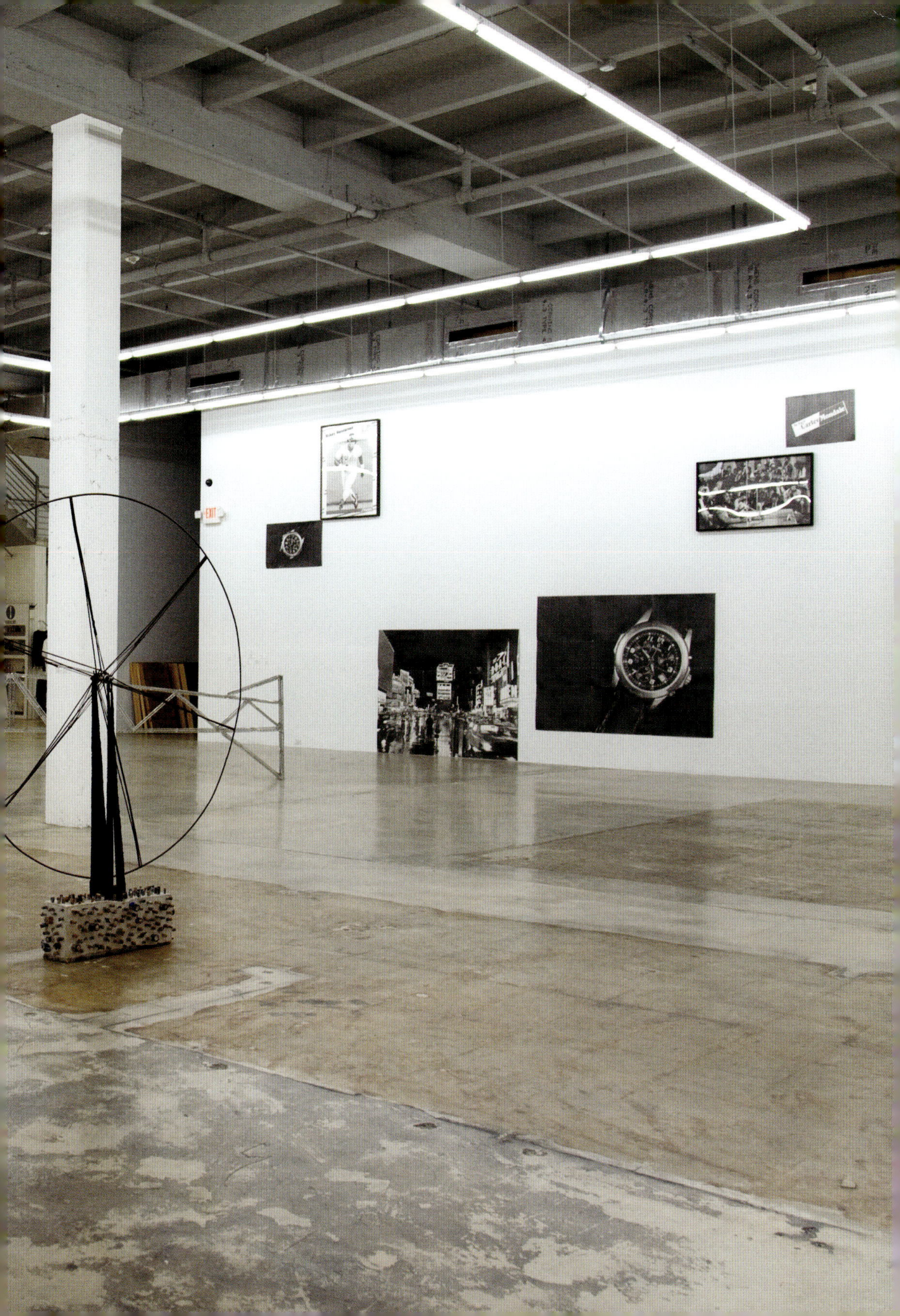

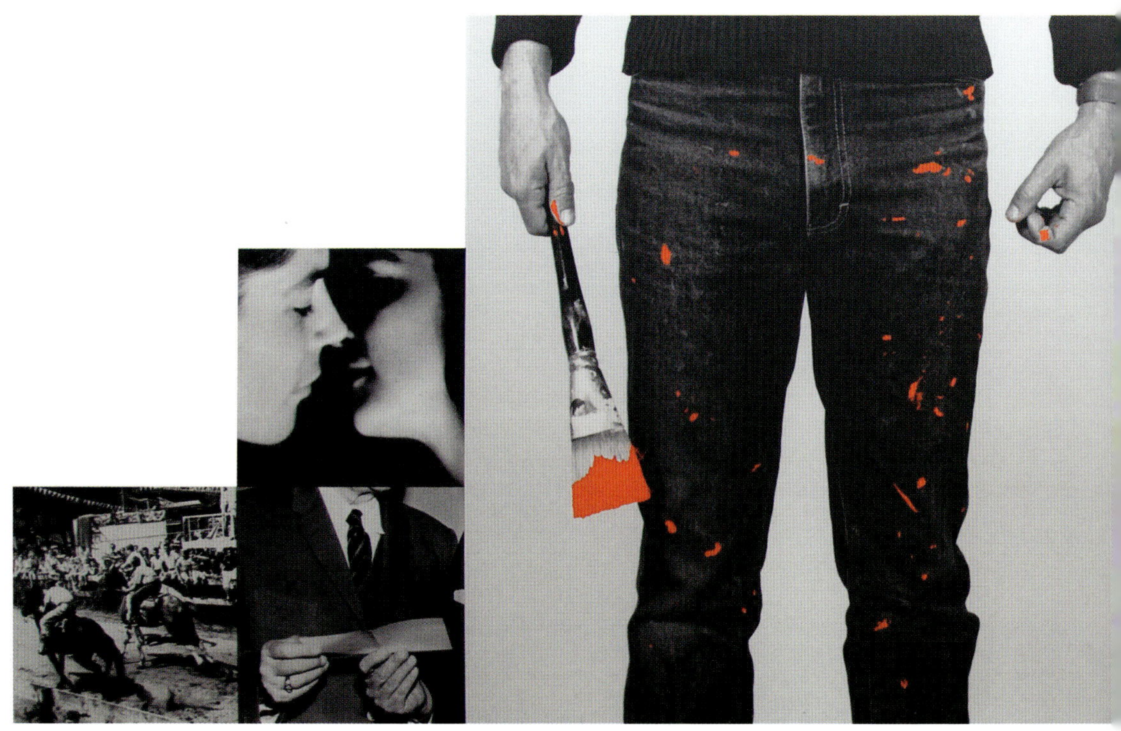

John Baldessari
Stake: Art is Food for Thought and Food Costs Money, 1985
Black-and-white photographs, color photograph and acrylic paint
144 x 480 in. (365.8 x 1219.2 cm)

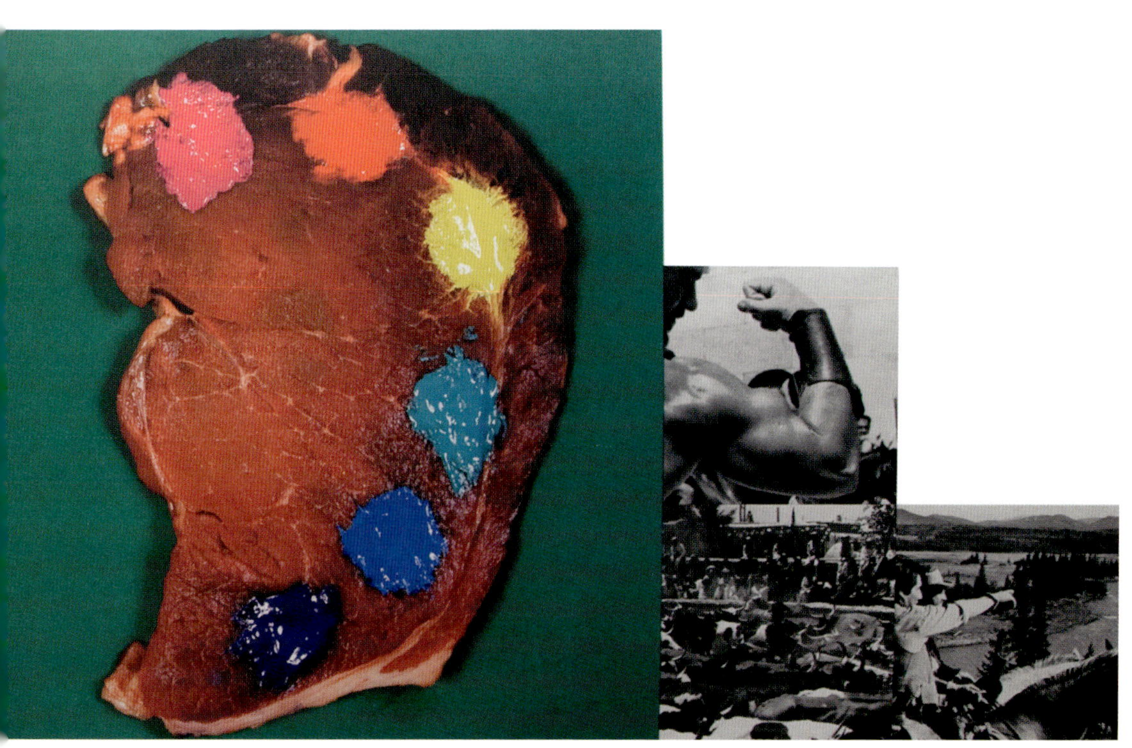

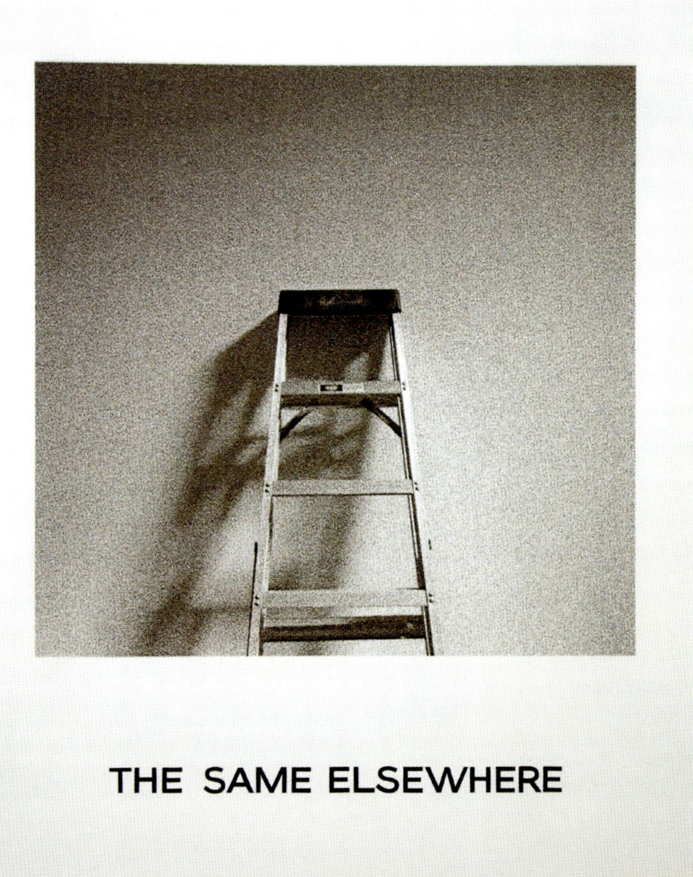

John Baldessari
Goya Series: The Same Elsewhere, 1997
Ink jet print and hand lettering on canvas
75 x 60 in. (190.5 x 152.4 cm)

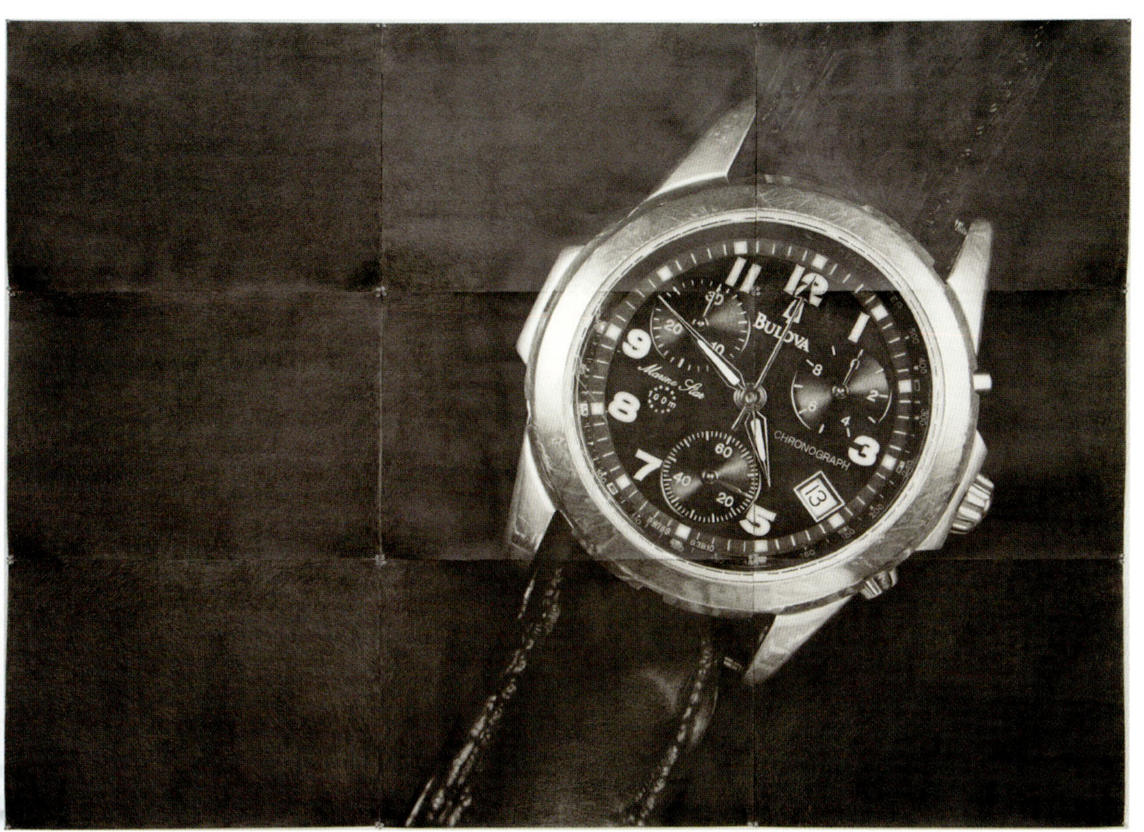

Karl Haendel
Watch #2, 2006
Charcoal on nine sheets of paper
66 x 90 3/4 in. (167.6 x 230.5 cm)

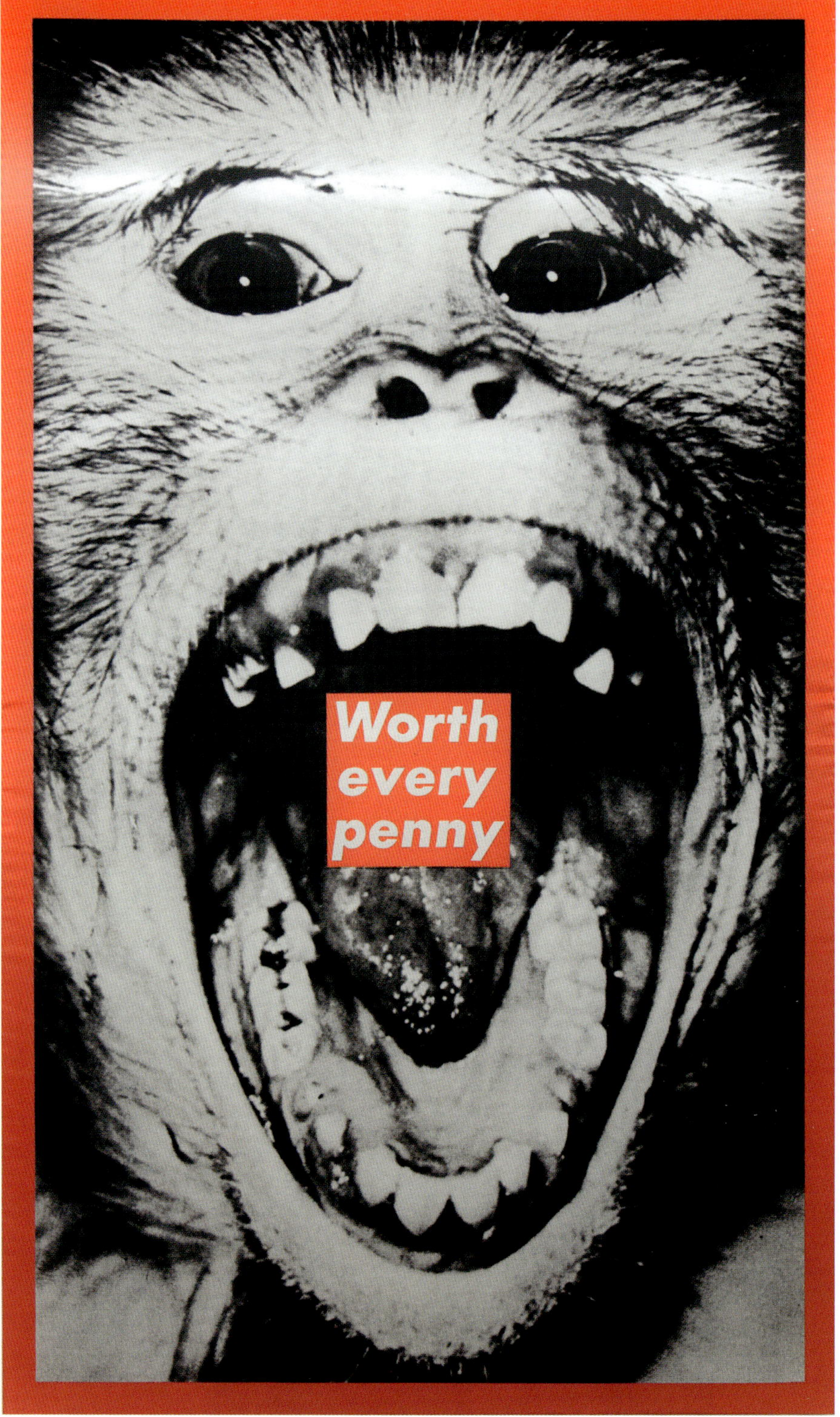

Barbara Kruger
Untitled (Worth Every Penny), 1987
Silkscreen on vinyl
182 x 110 in. (462.3 x 279.4 cm)

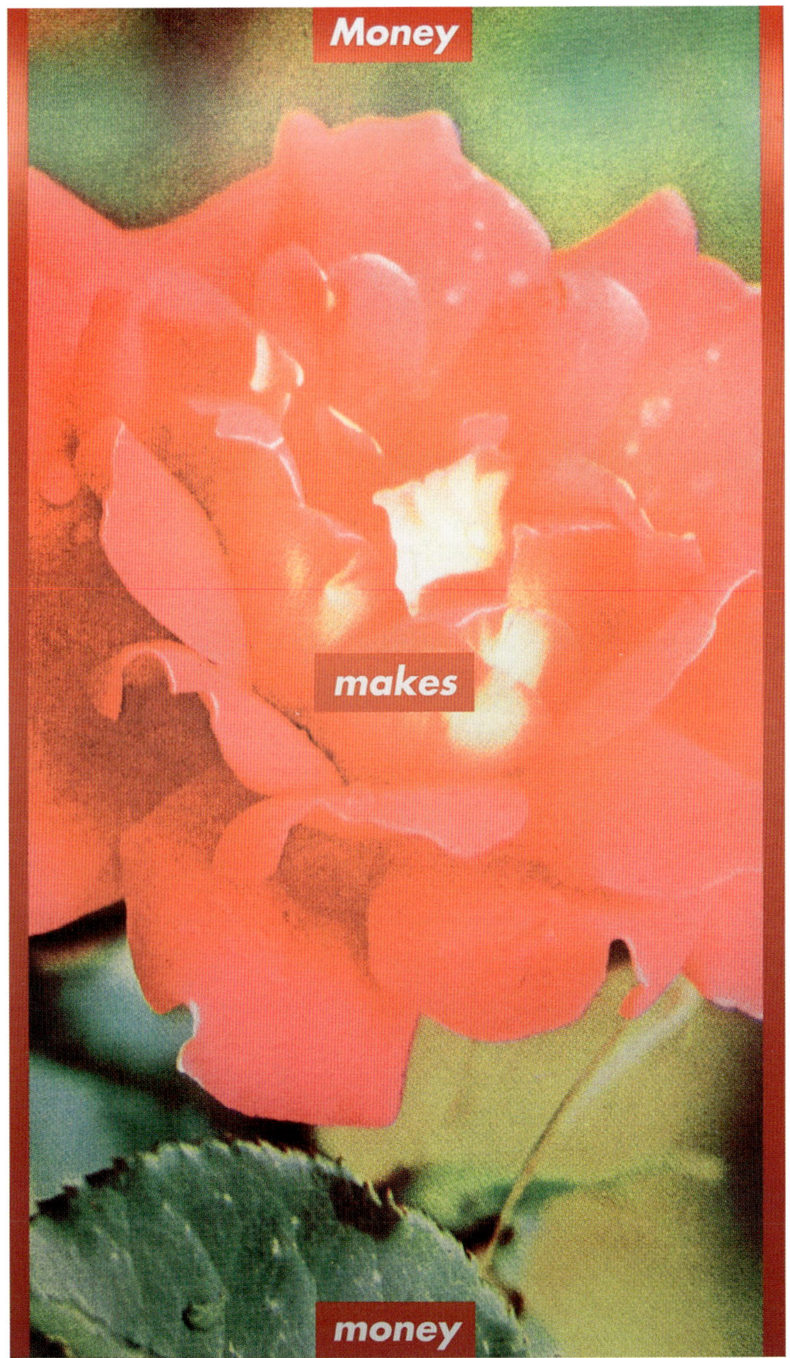

Barbara Kruger
Untitled (Money Makes Money), 2001
Silkscreen on vinyl
164 3/8 x 102 6/8 in. (417 x 260 cm)

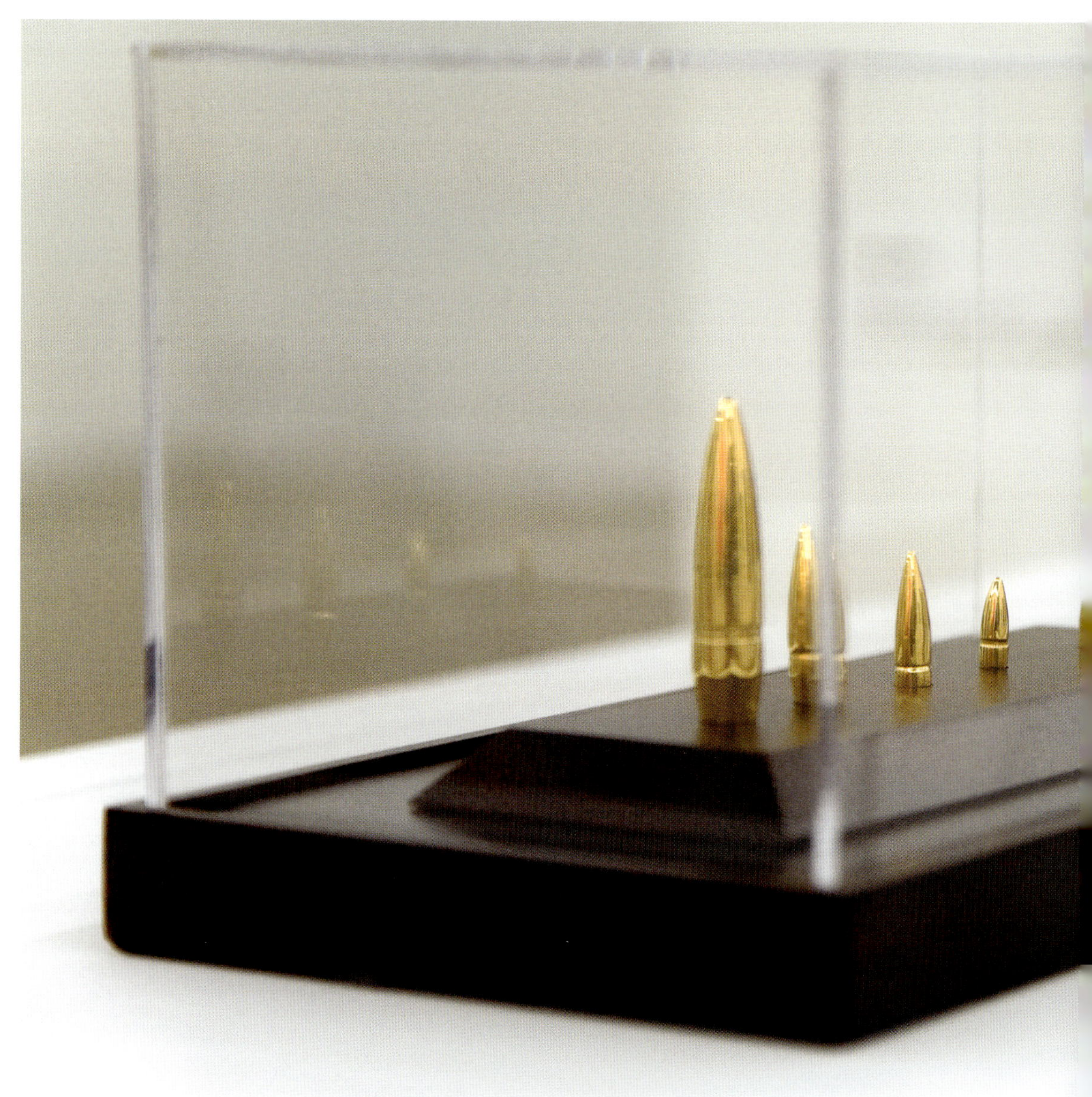

Chris Burden
Gold Bullets, 2003
Ten twenty-two karat gold bullets and two wood and Plexiglas vitrines, Ed. 8/10
Bullets: variable dimensions
Each vitrine: 10 1/4 x 5 3/4 x 6 1/4 in. (26 x 14.6 x 15.9 cm)

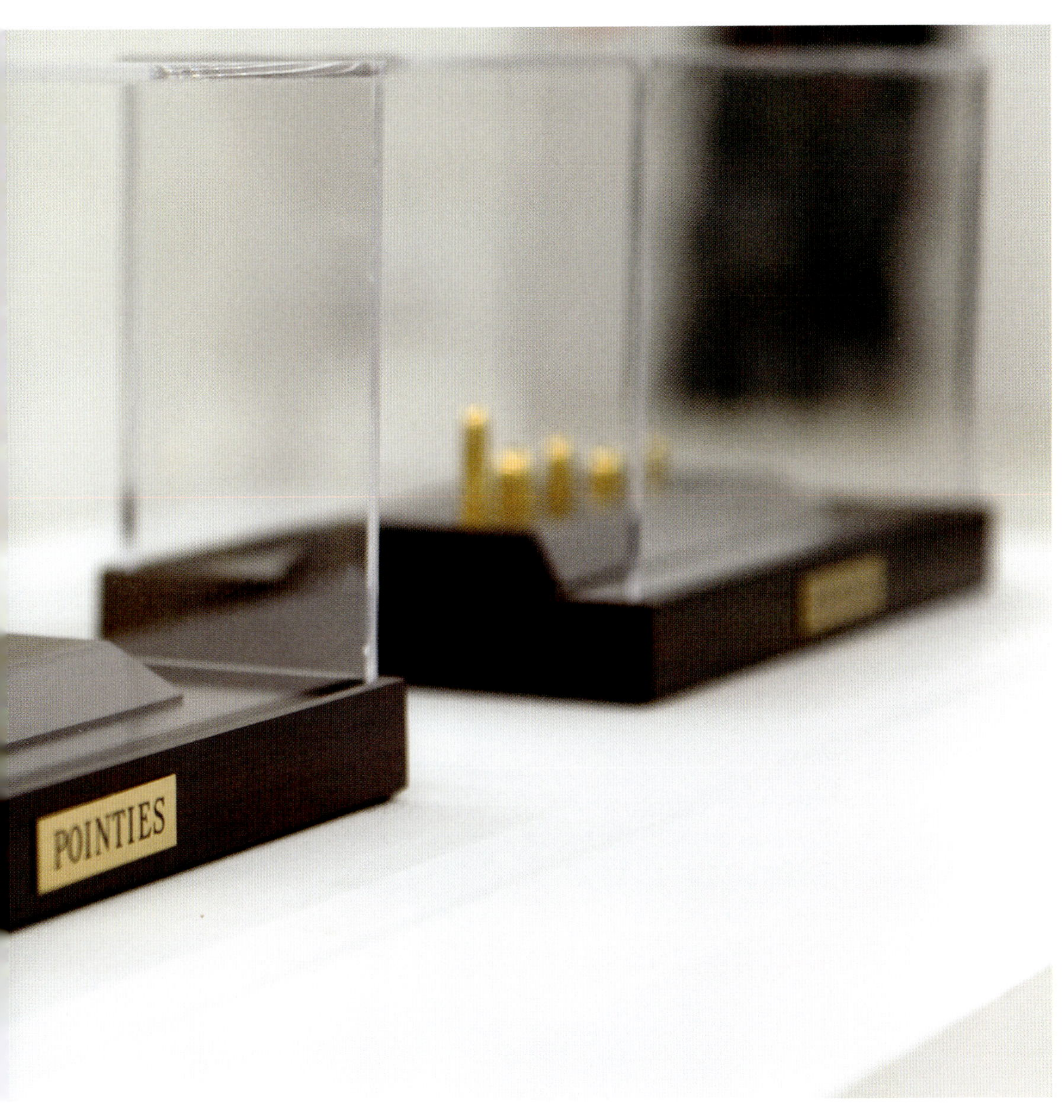
POINTIES

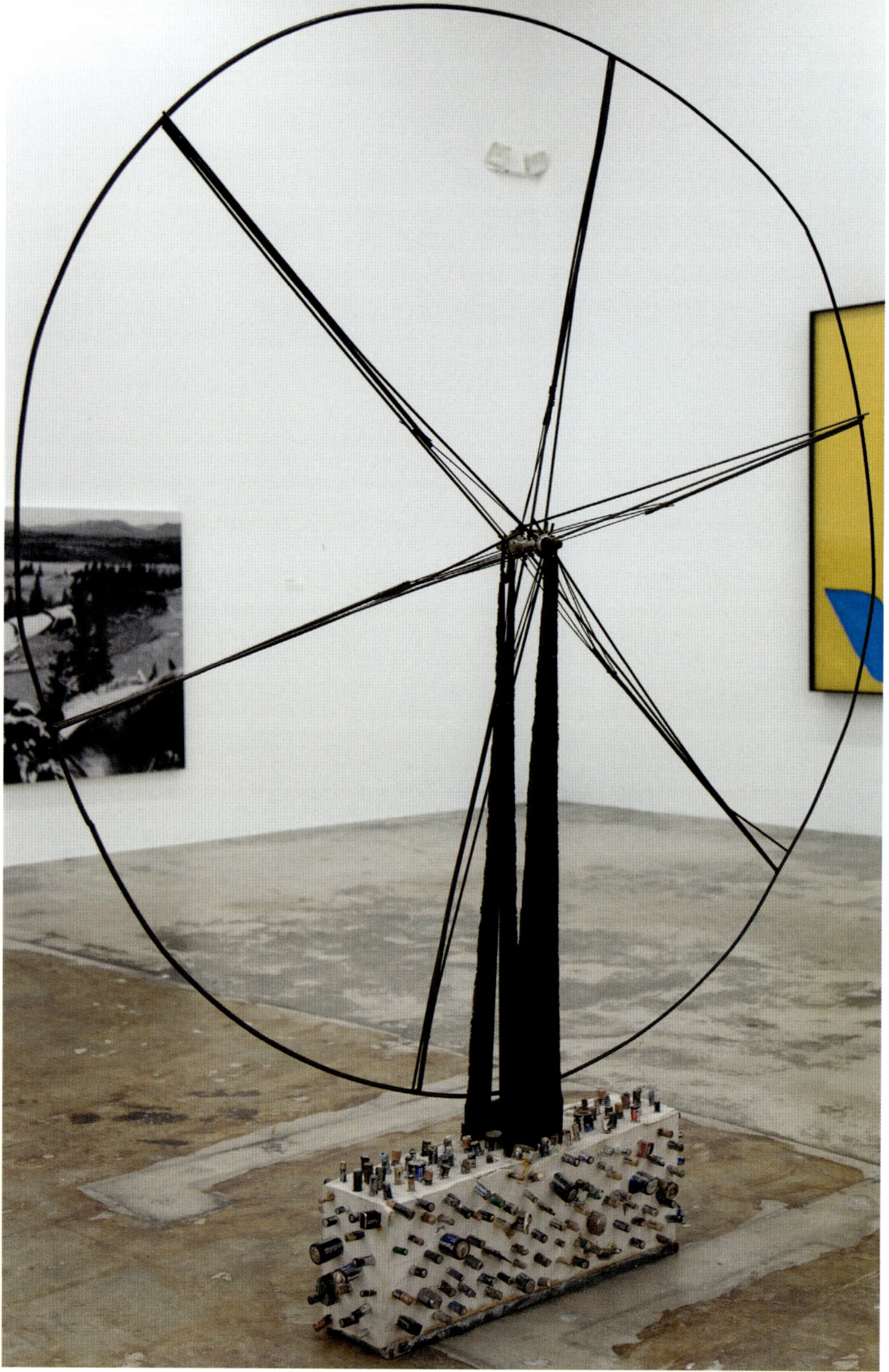

Evan Holloway
Second Law, 2006
Steel, plaster, batteries and bicycle parts
86 x 86 x 11 in. (218.4 x 218.4 x 27.9 cm)

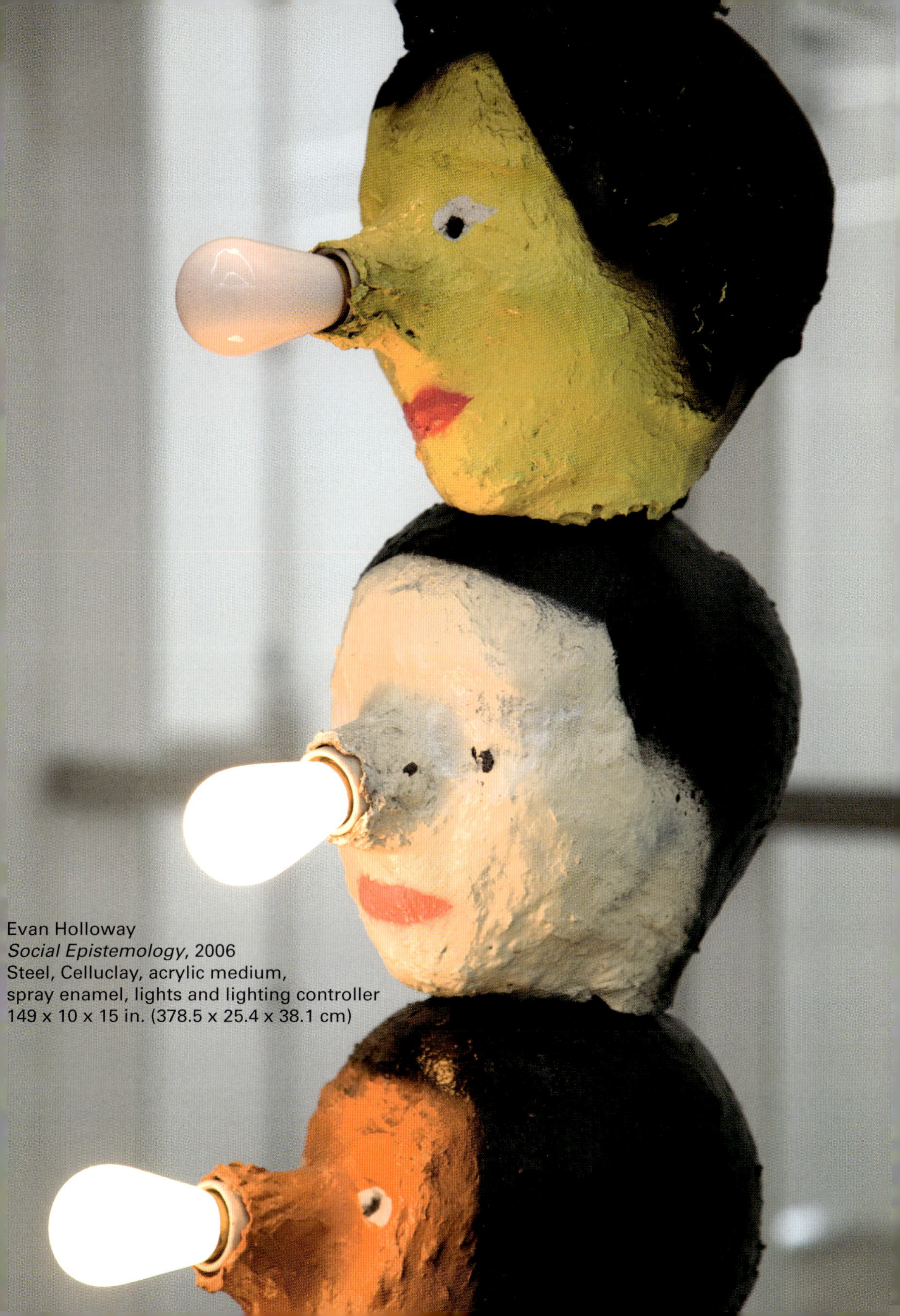

Evan Holloway
Social Epistemology, 2006
Steel, Celluclay, acrylic medium, spray enamel, lights and lighting controller
149 x 10 x 15 in. (378.5 x 25.4 x 38.1 cm)

GALLERY 3

INSTALLATION VIEW: PAUL McCARTHY

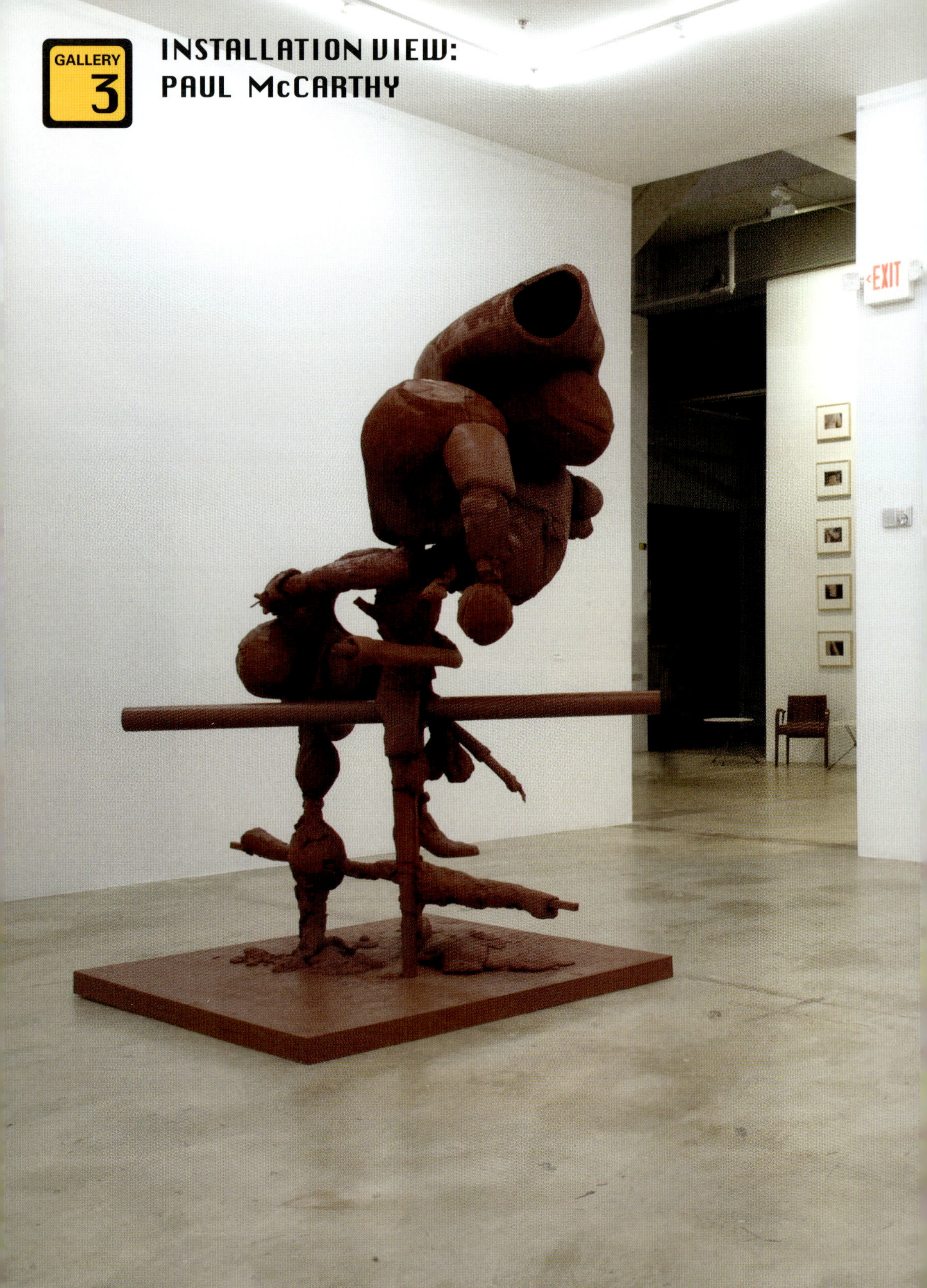

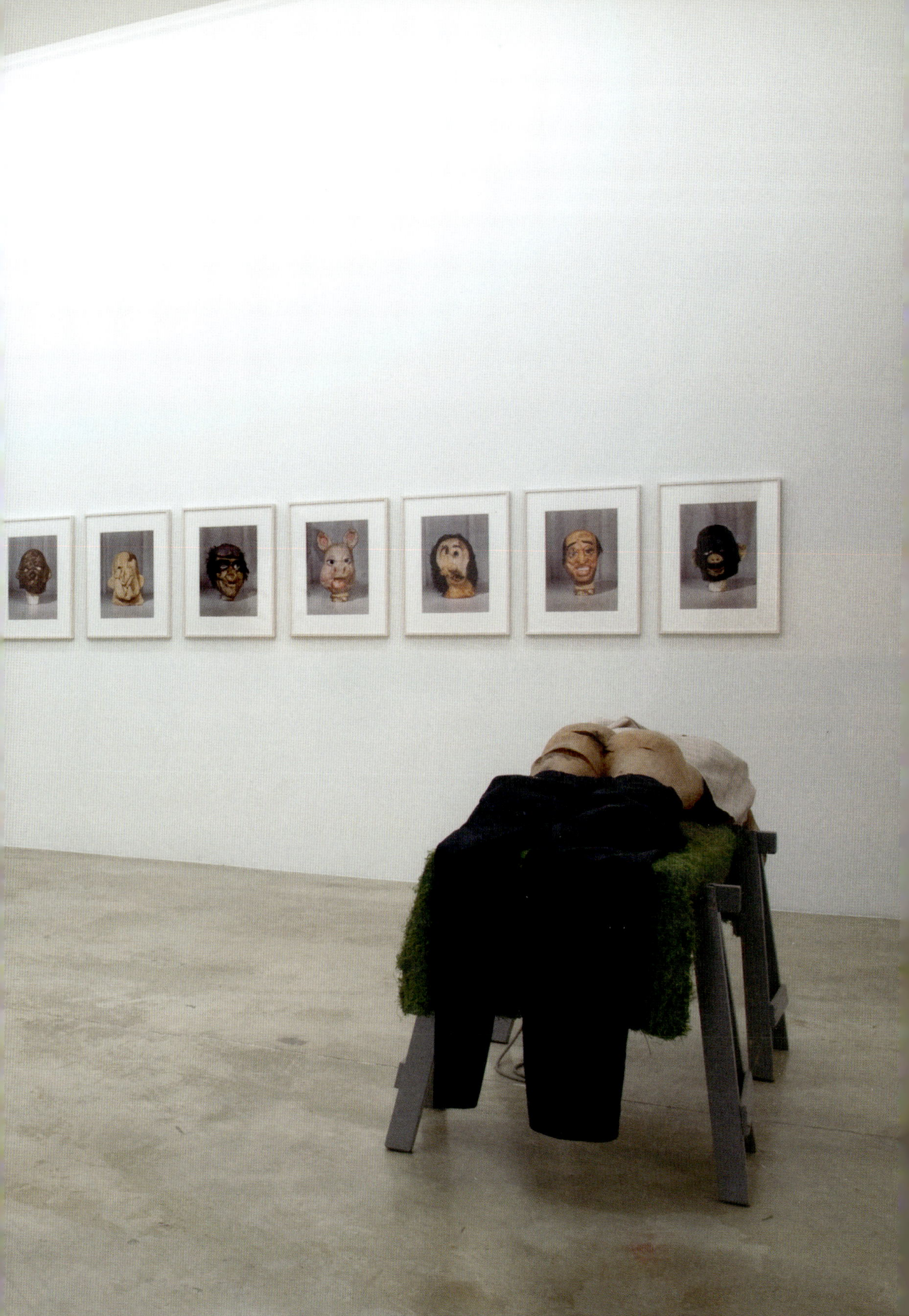

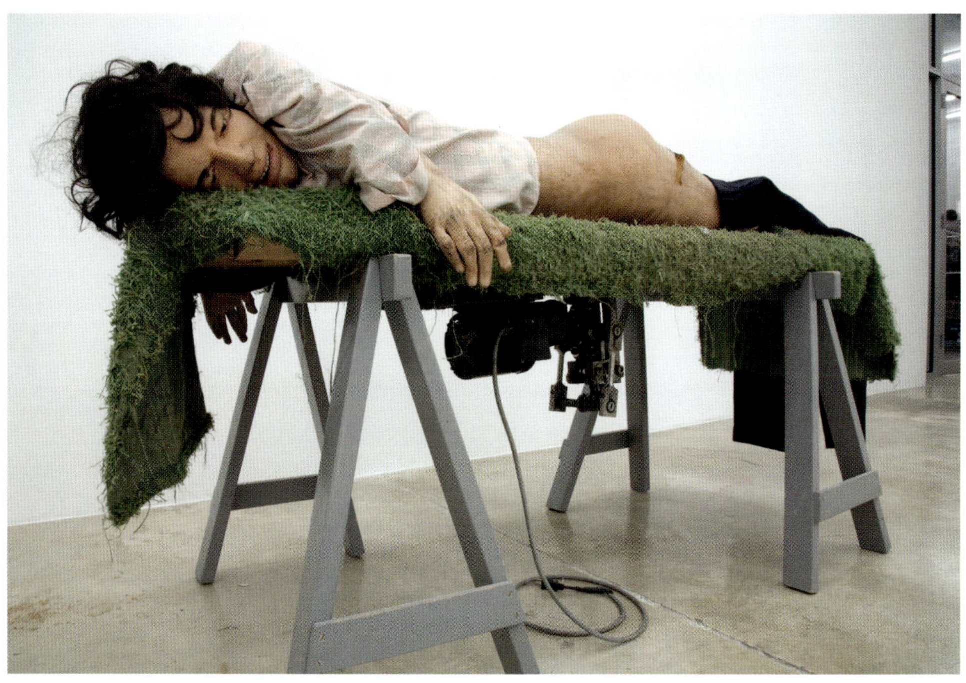

Paul McCarthy
MoCA Man, 1992
Latex rubber, urethane foam, clothing, wig, wood, motor, artificial turf and saw horses
36 x 72 x 36 in. (92.4 x 182.9 x 91.4 cm)

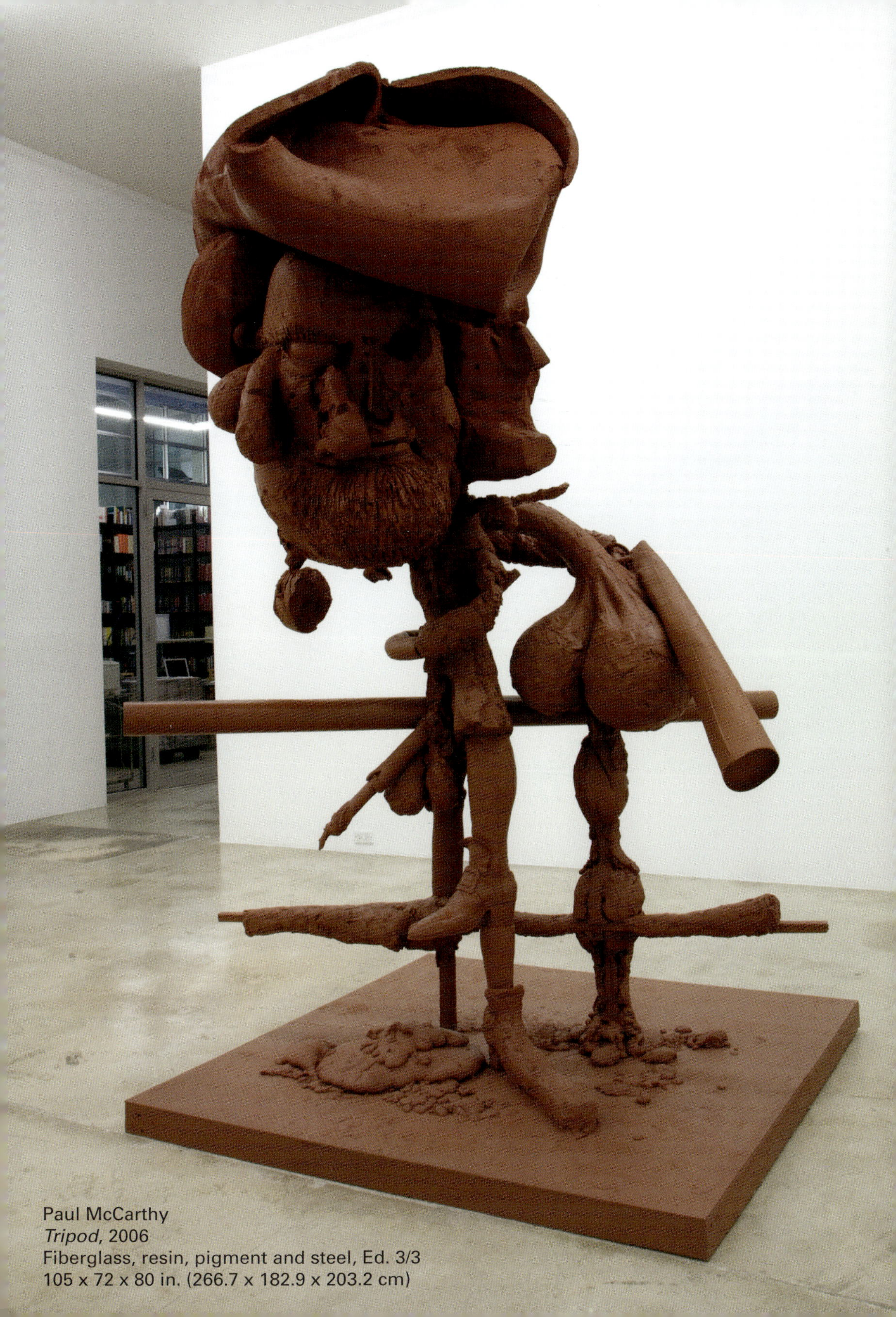

Paul McCarthy
Tripod, 2006
Fiberglass, resin, pigment and steel, Ed. 3/3
105 x 72 x 80 in. (266.7 x 182.9 x 203.2 cm)

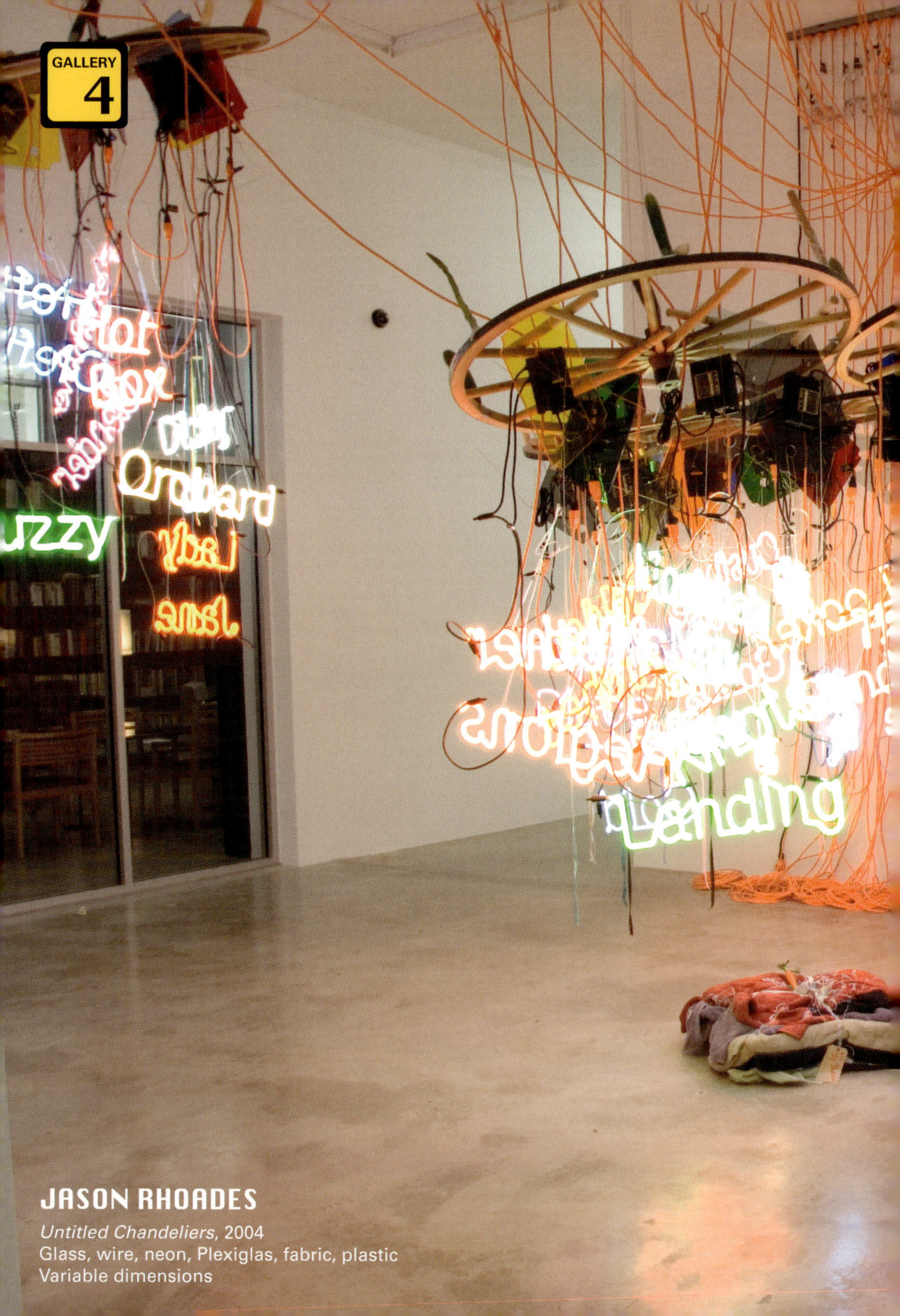

JASON RHOADES

Untitled Chandeliers, 2004
Glass, wire, neon, Plexiglas, fabric, plastic
Variable dimensions

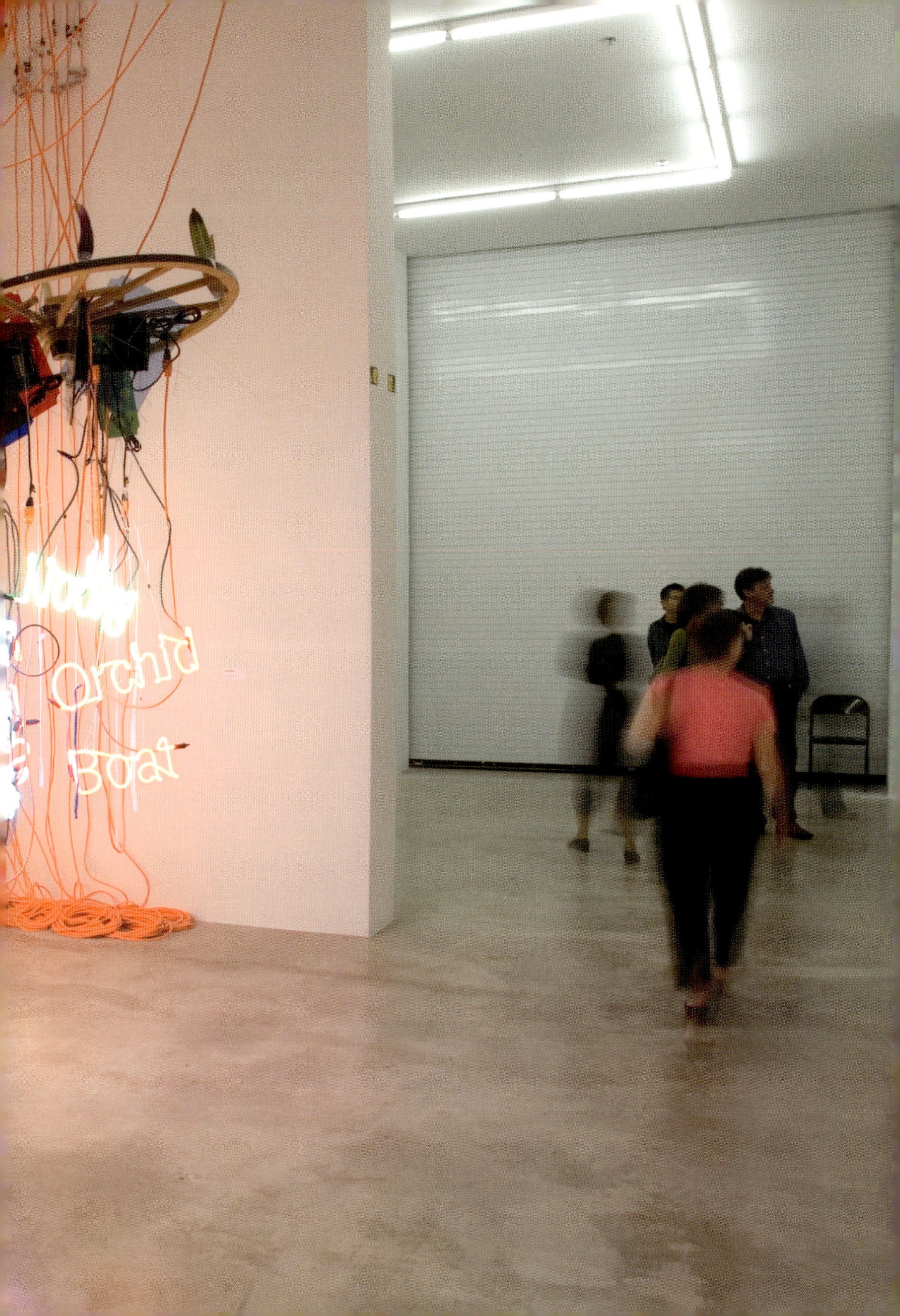
Orchid
Boat

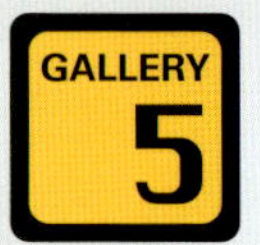

INSTALLATION VIEW: RAYMOND PETTIBON AND PAUL McCARTHY

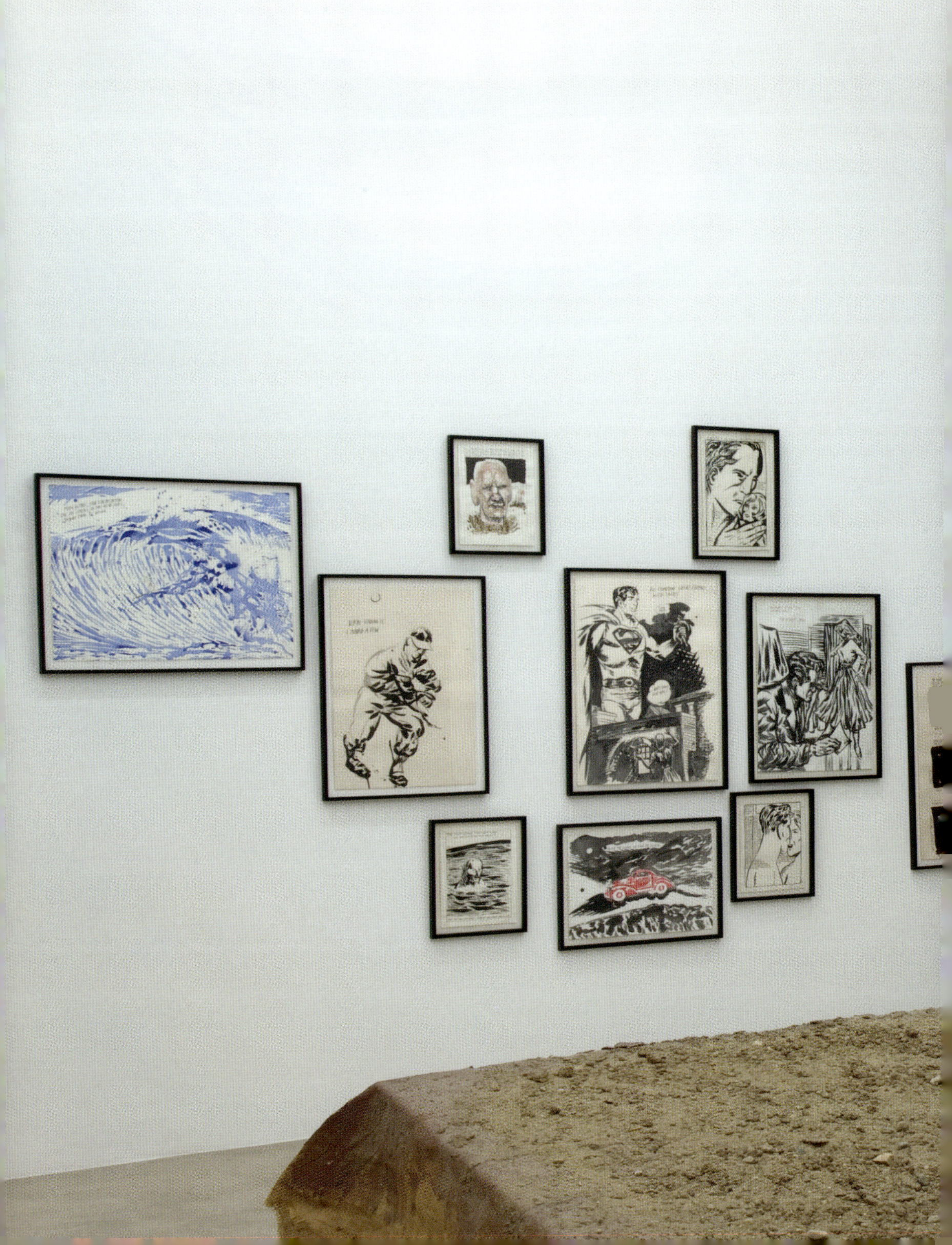

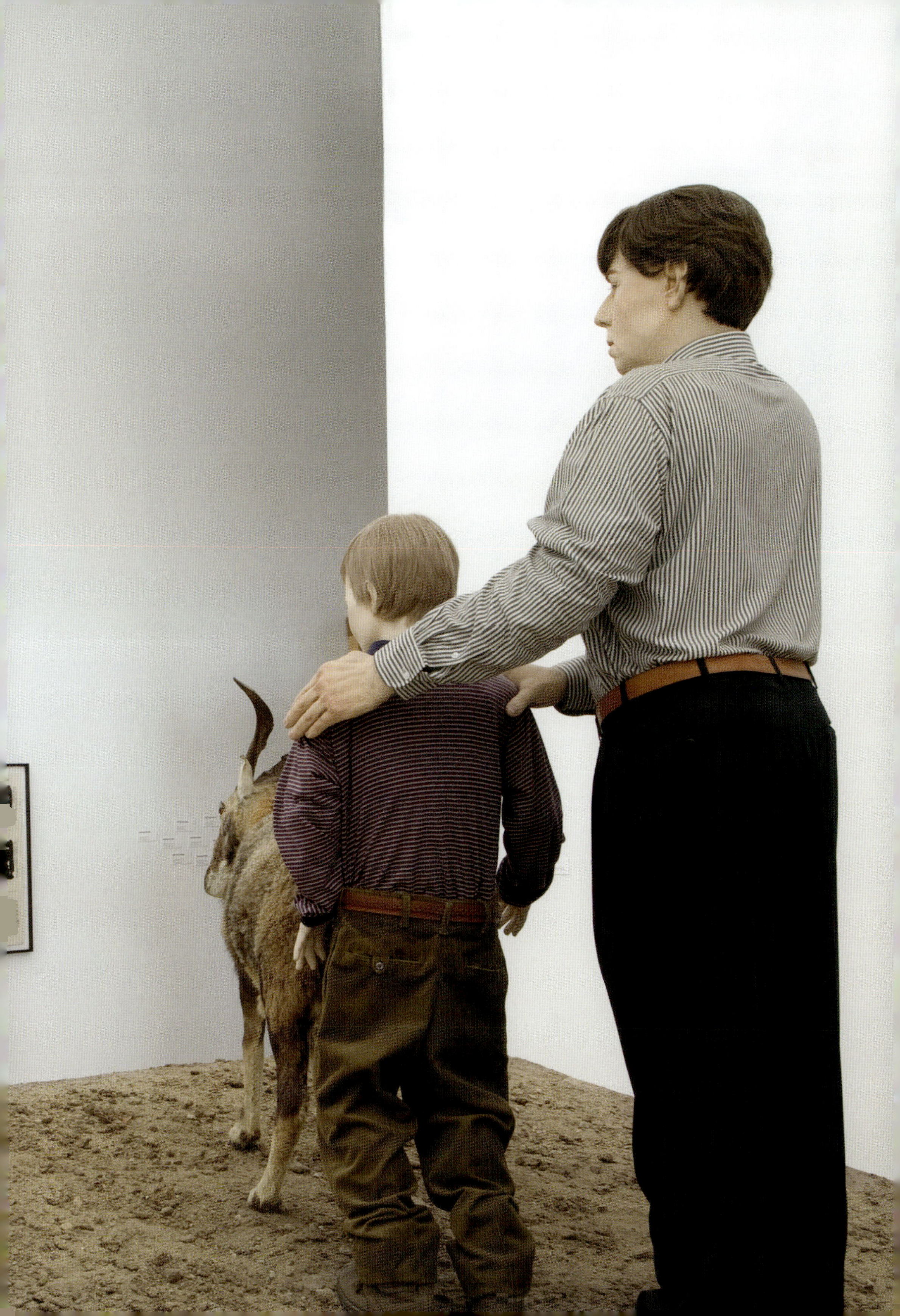

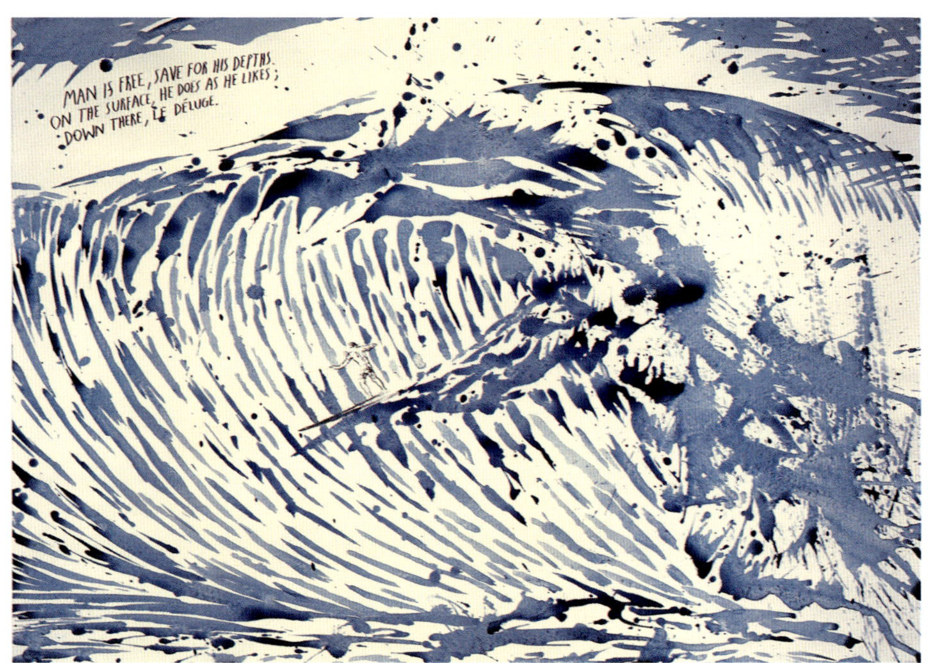

Raymond Pettibon
No Title (Man is free), 1999
Pen and ink on paper
22 1/4 x 30 in. (56.5 x 27.9 cm)

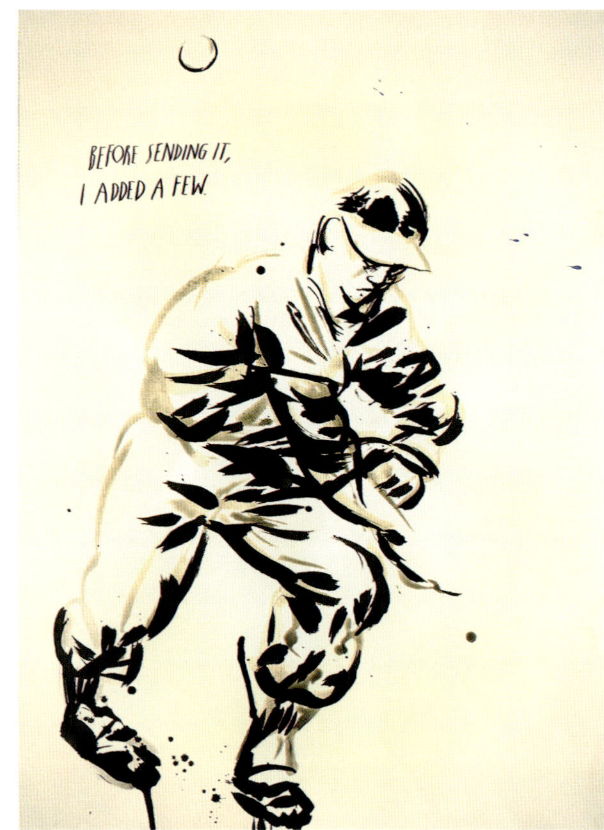

Raymond Pettibon
No Title (Before sending it), 1999
Pen and ink on paper
27 3/4 x 19 3/4 (70.5 x 50.2 cm)

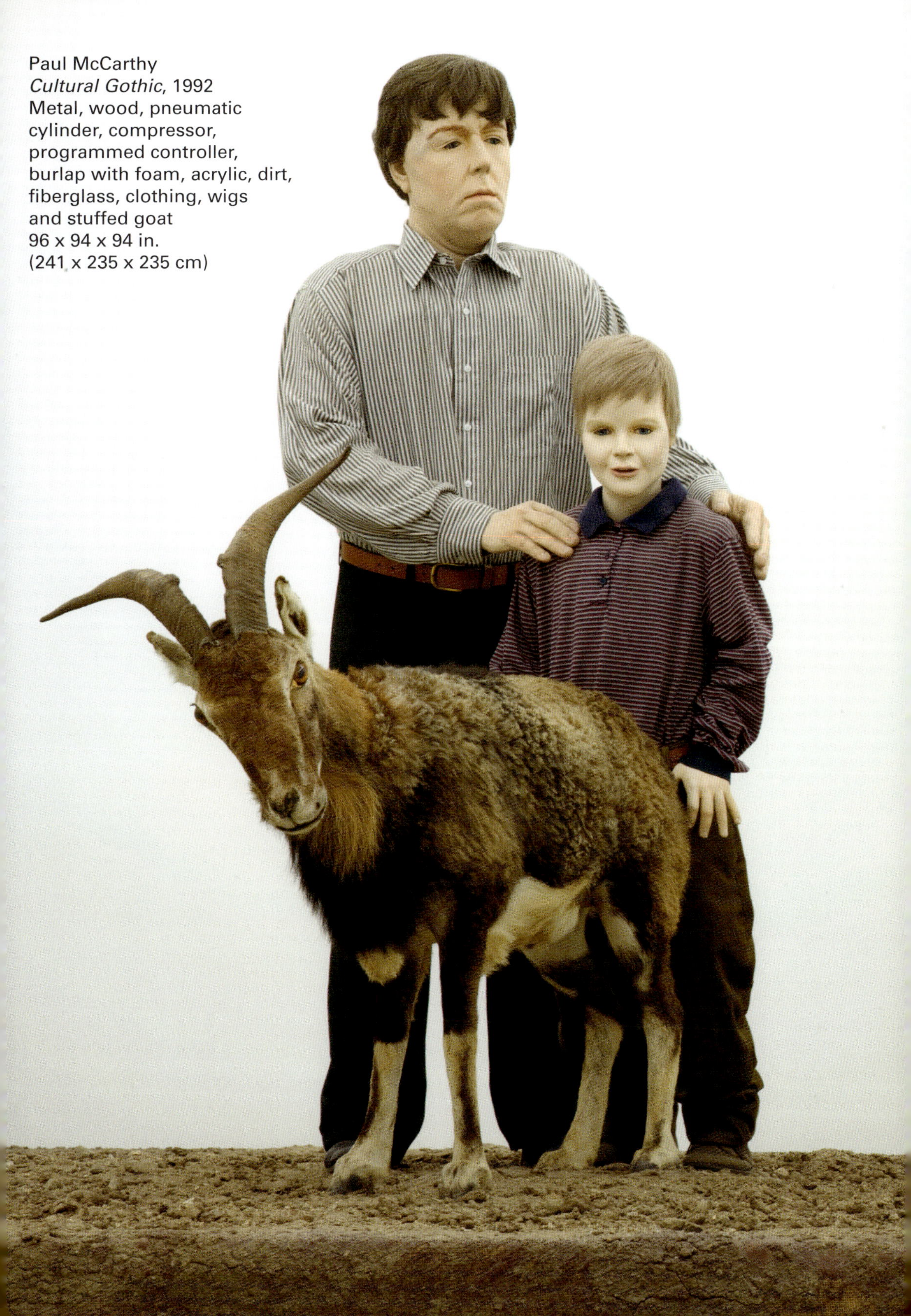

Paul McCarthy
Cultural Gothic, 1992
Metal, wood, pneumatic
cylinder, compressor,
programmed controller,
burlap with foam, acrylic, dirt,
fiberglass, clothing, wigs
and stuffed goat
96 x 94 x 94 in.
(241 x 235 x 235 cm)

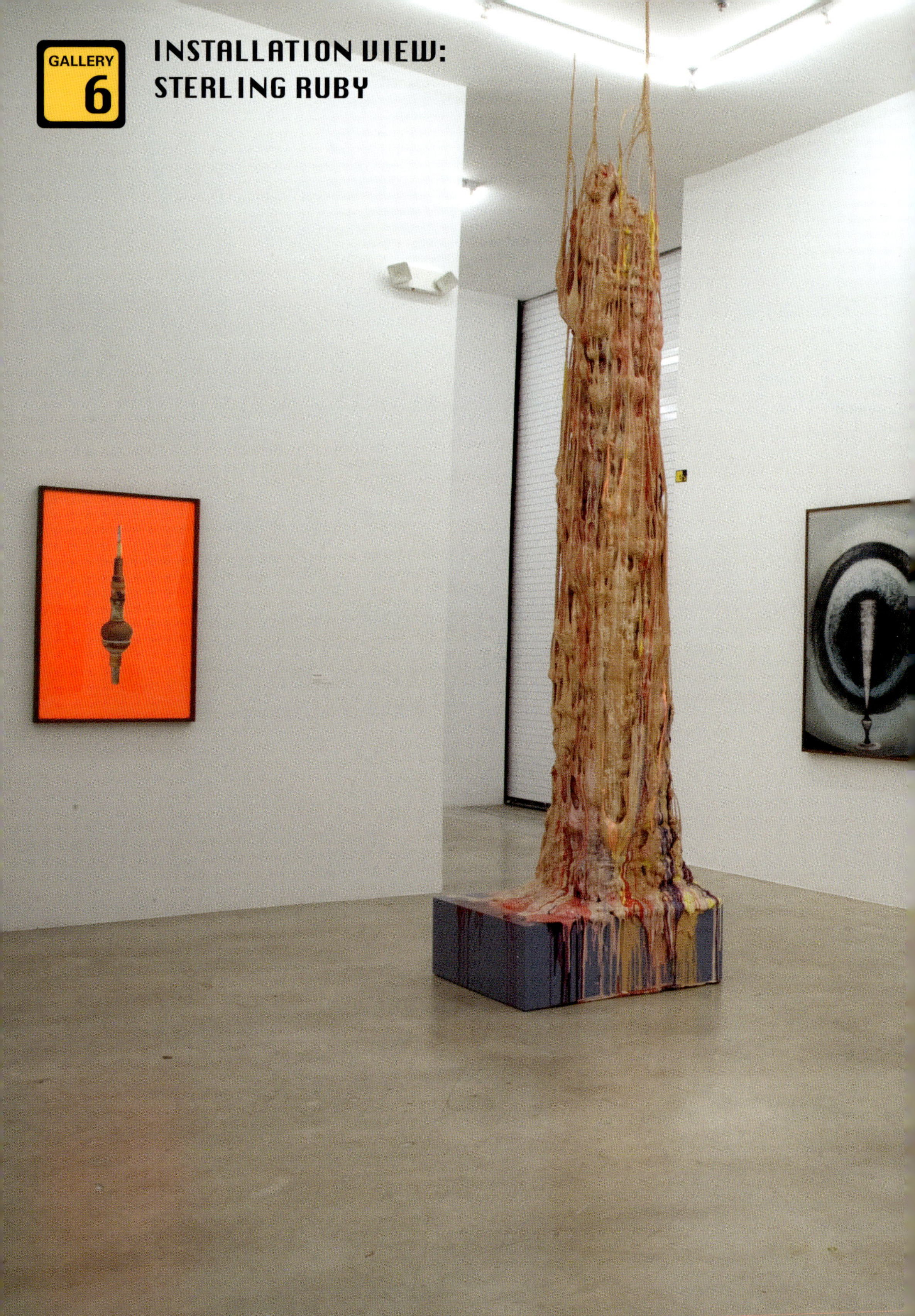
GALLERY
6
INSTALLATION VIEW:
STERLING RUBY

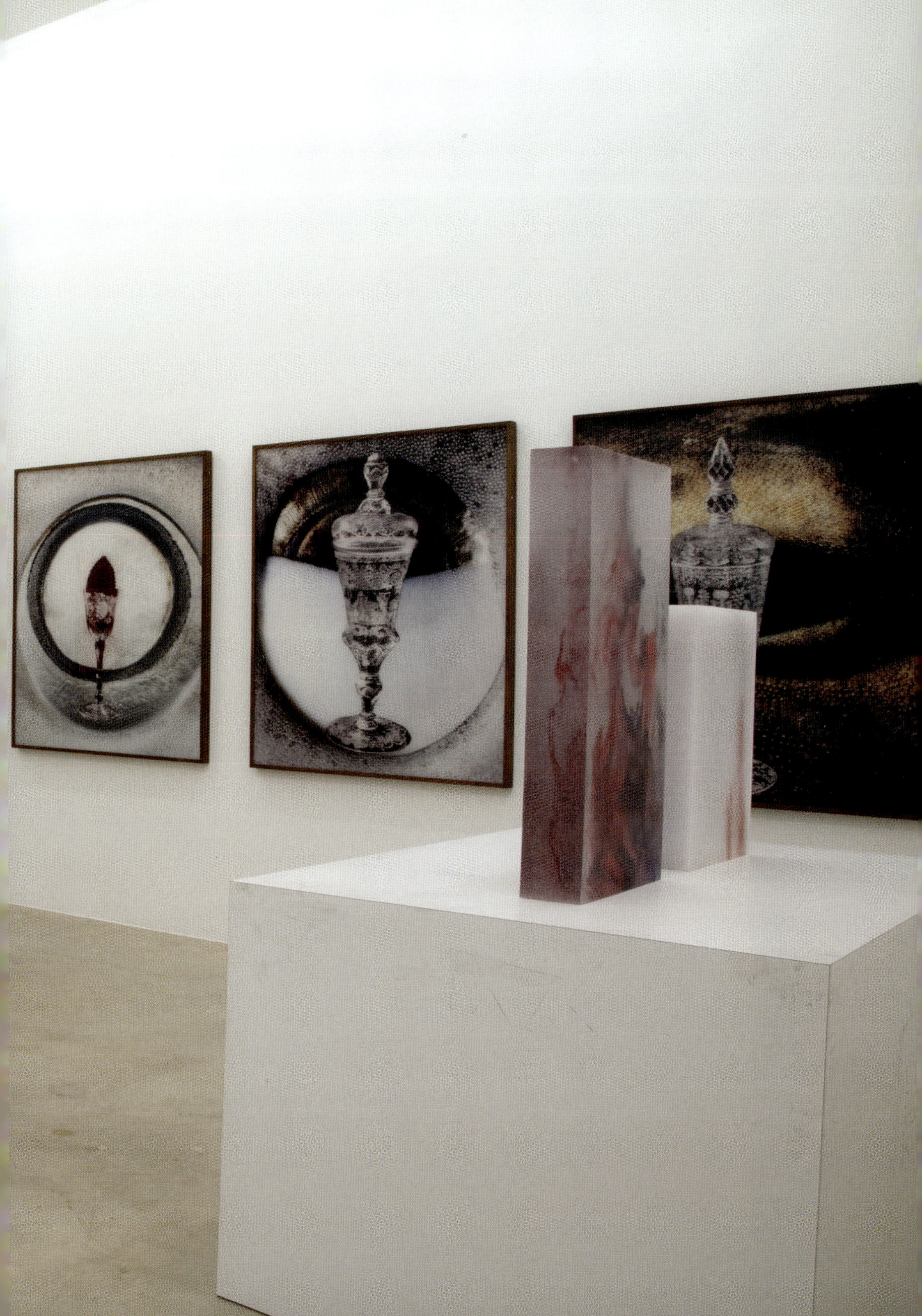

Sterling Ruby
Absolute Contempt for Total Serenity (Double), 2006
Urethane, Formica and wood
72 7/8 x 60 x 45 in. (184 x 152.4 x 114.3 cm)

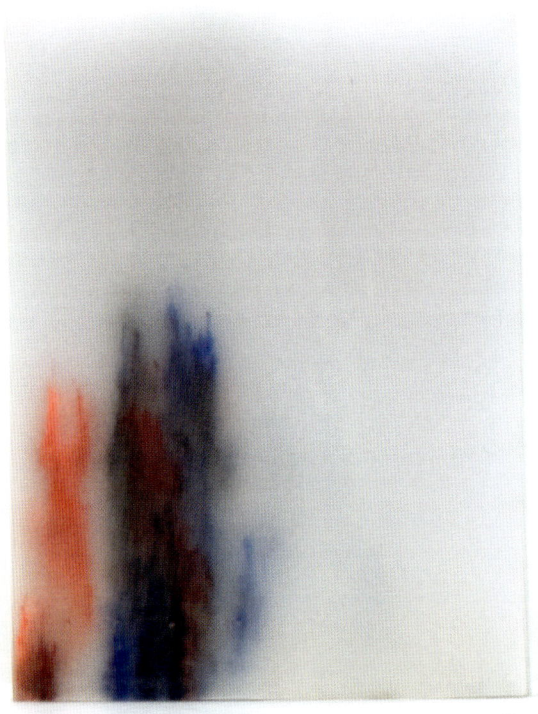

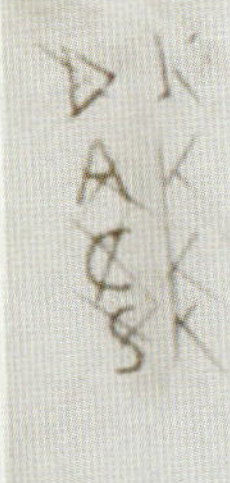

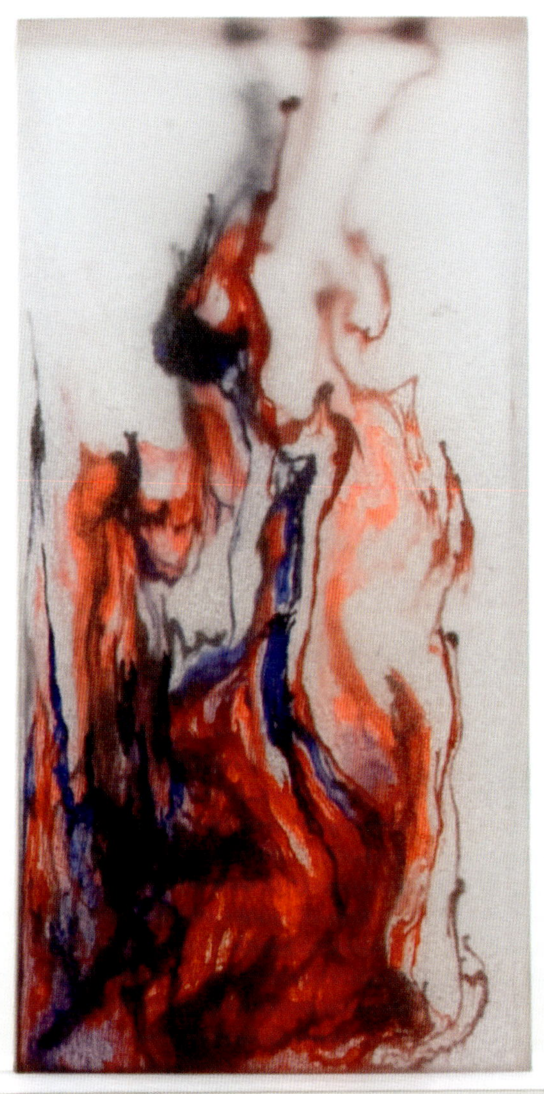

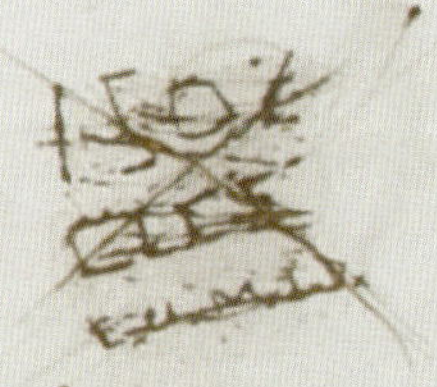

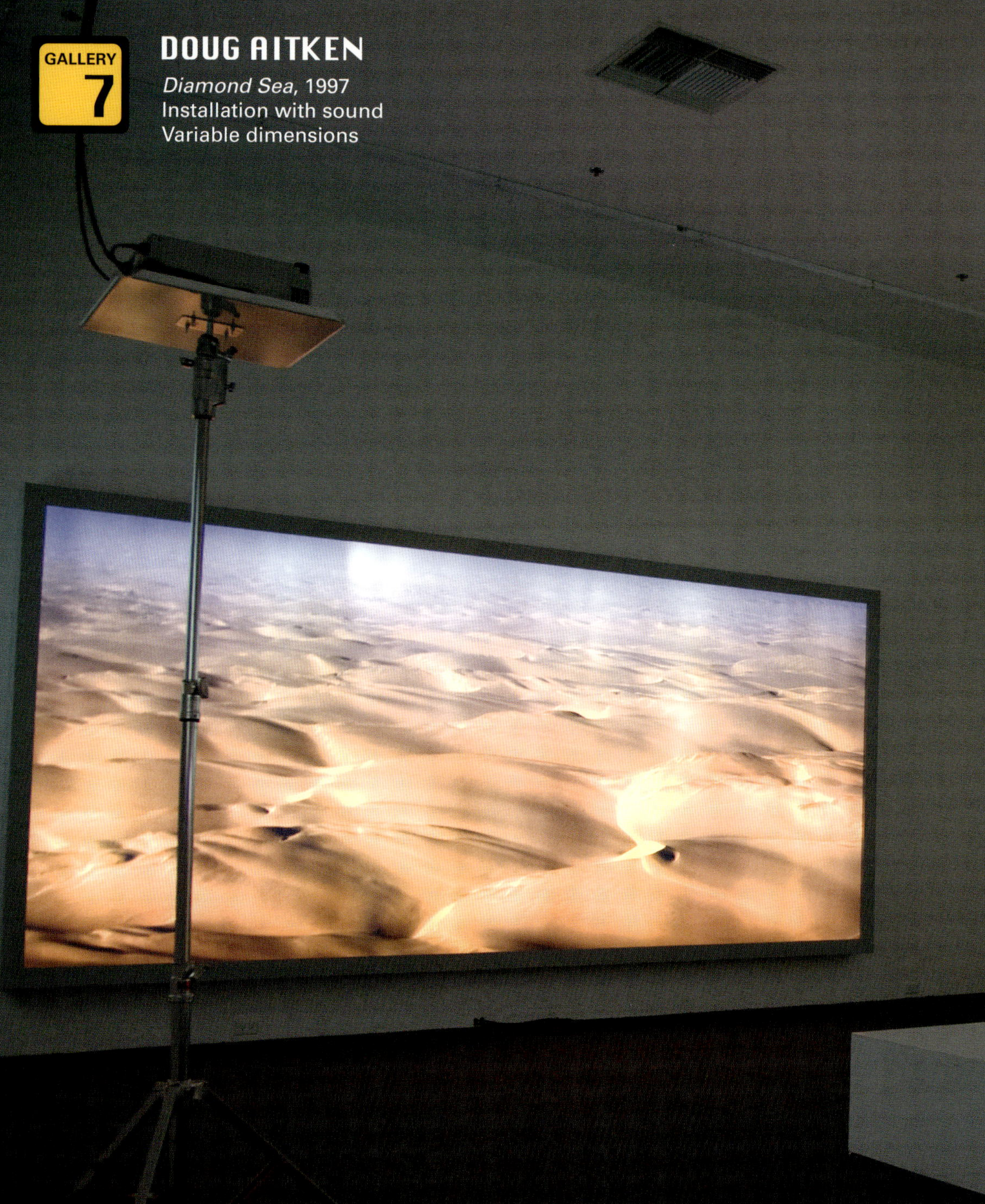

DOUG AITKEN

Diamond Sea, 1997
Installation with sound
Variable dimensions

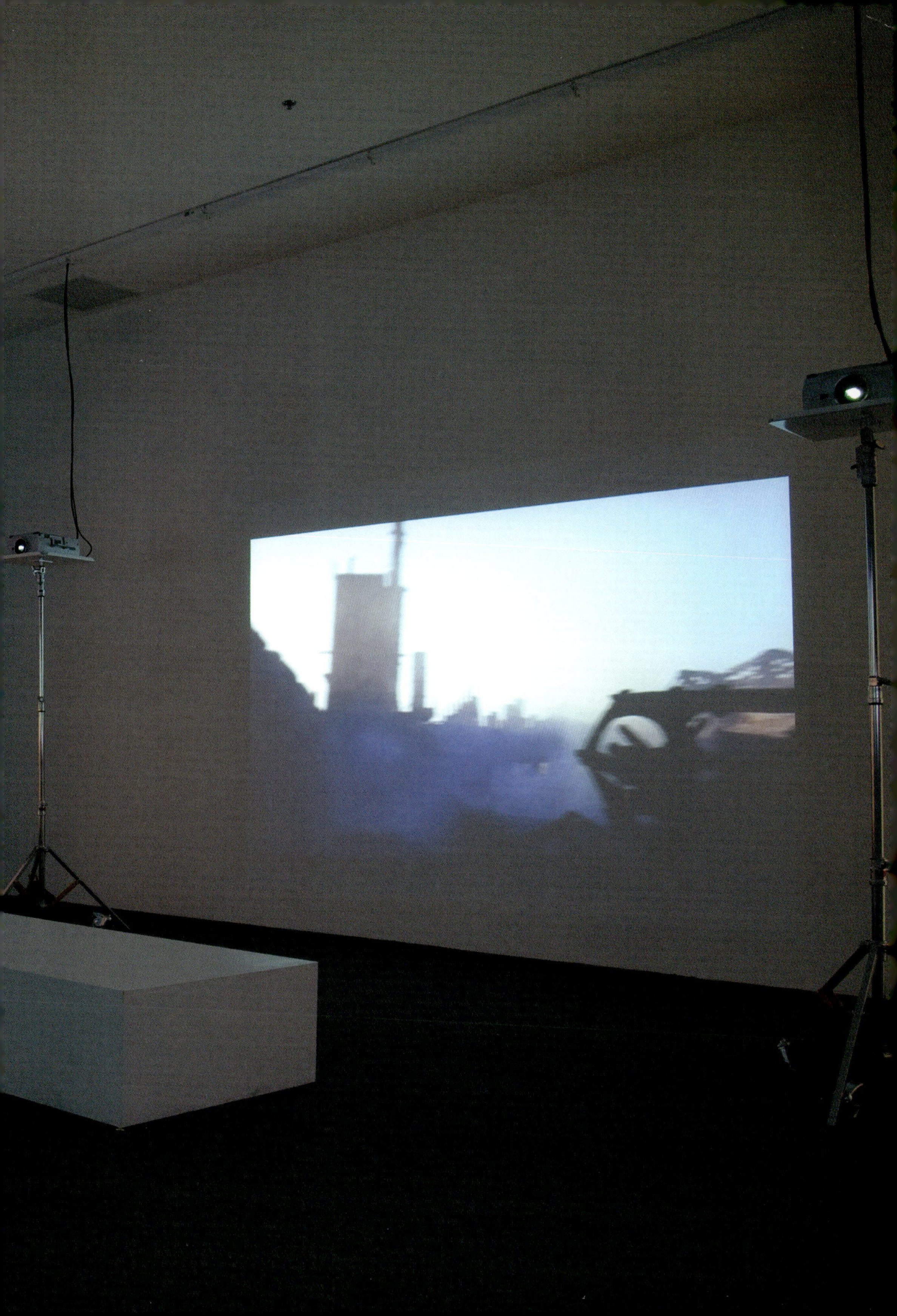

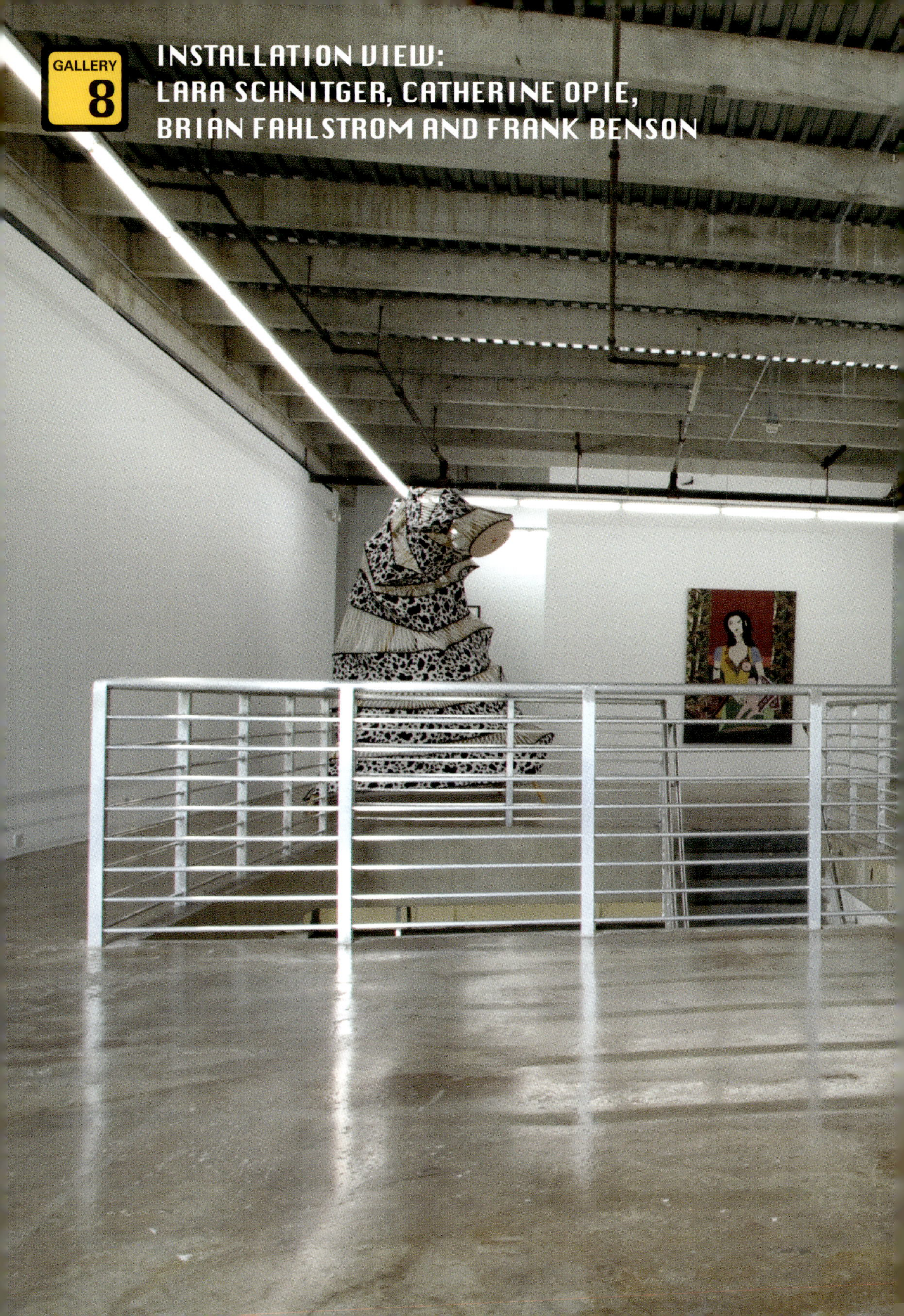

INSTALLATION VIEW:
LARA SCHNITGER, CATHERINE OPIE,
BRIAN FAHLSTROM AND FRANK BENSON

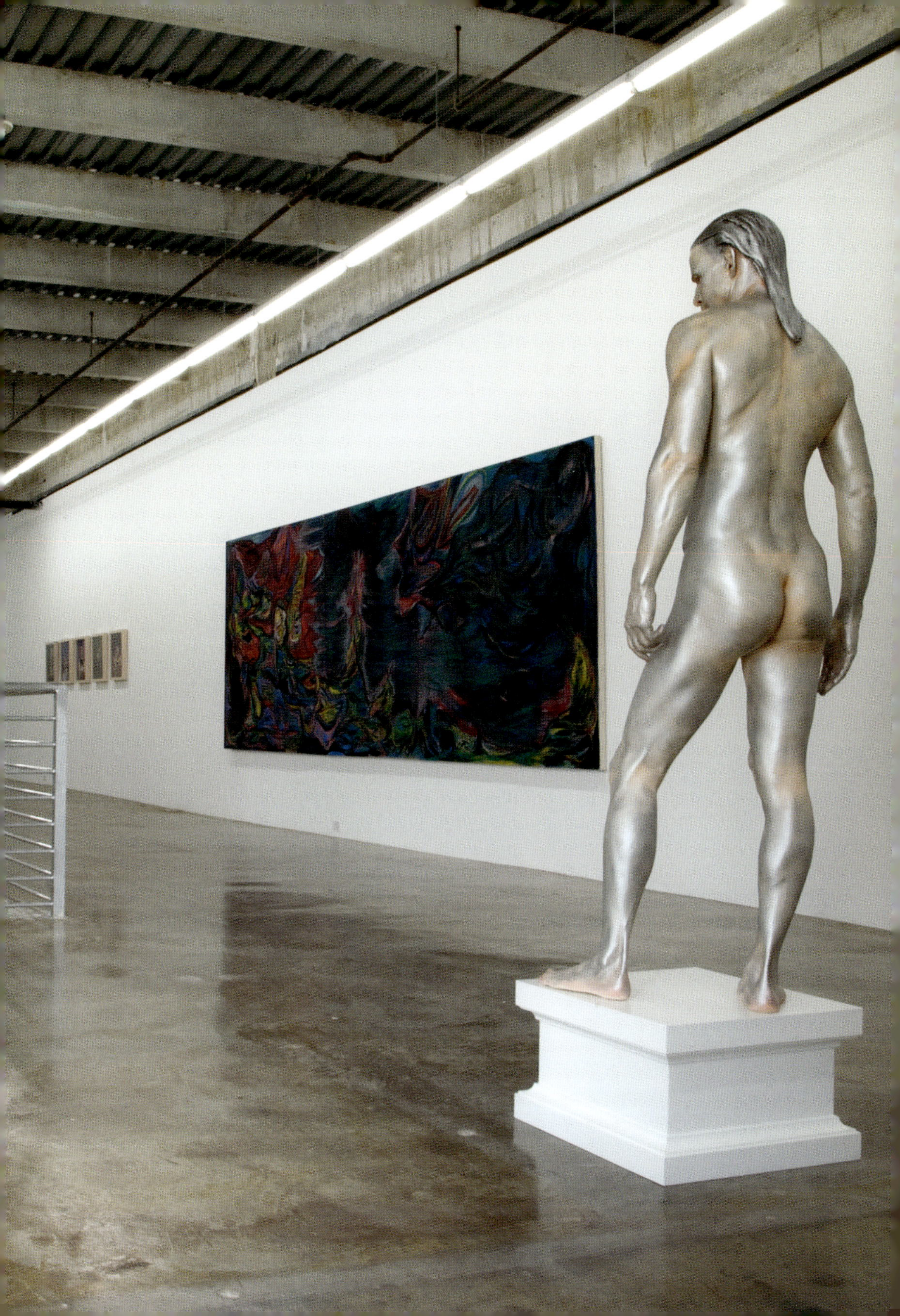

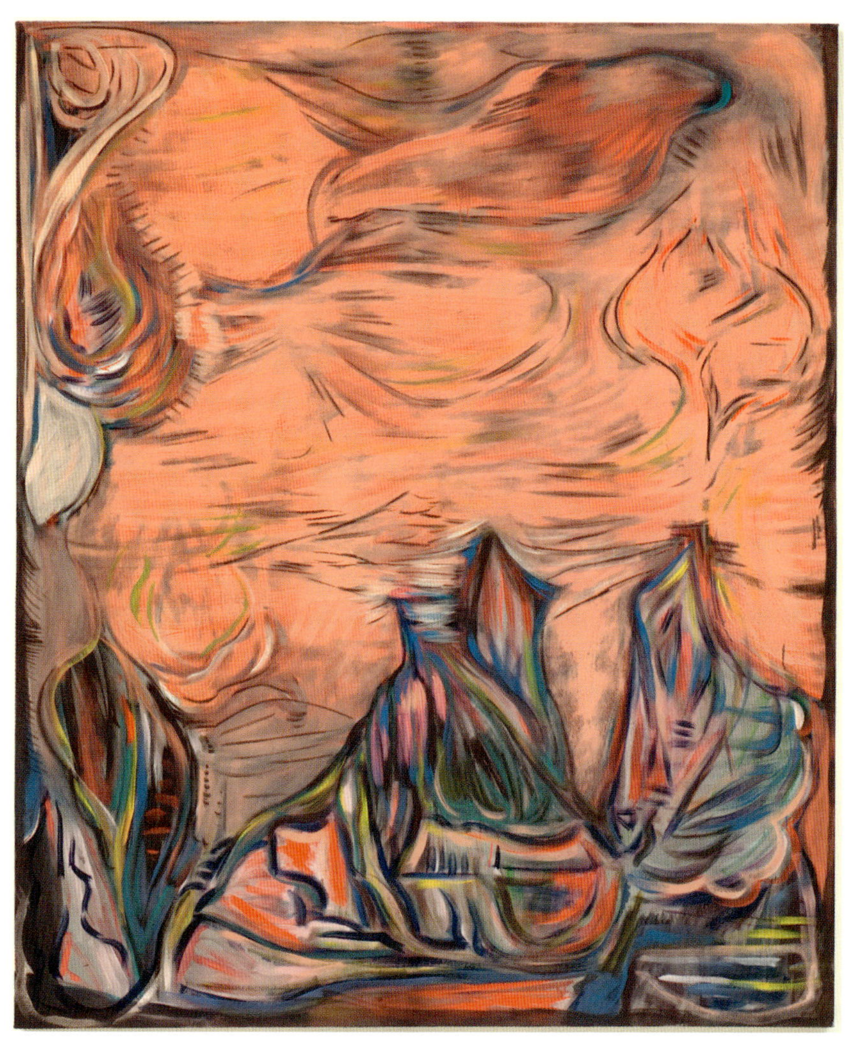

Brian Fahlstrom
Light Low, 2006
Oil on canvas
83 1/4 x 67 in. (211.4 x 170.2 cm)

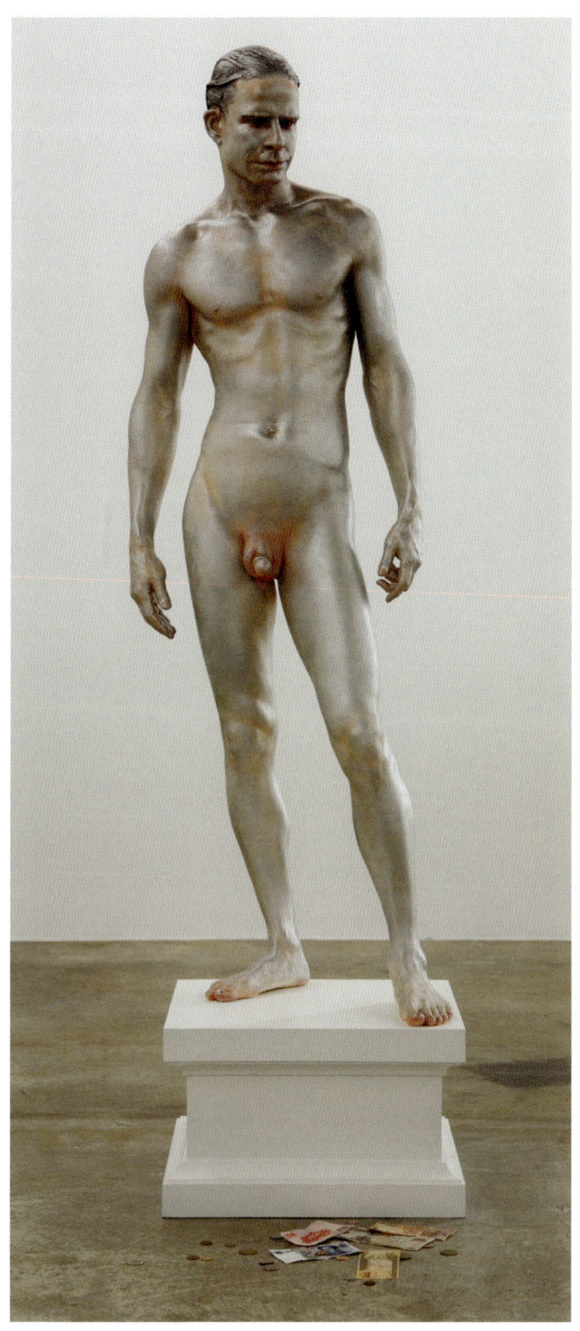

Frank Benson
Human Statue, 2005
Forton MG, oil and acrylic paint, fabric and wood
Ed. of 3 + 1 AP
80 x 21 x 20 in. (203.2 x 53.3 x 50.8 cm)

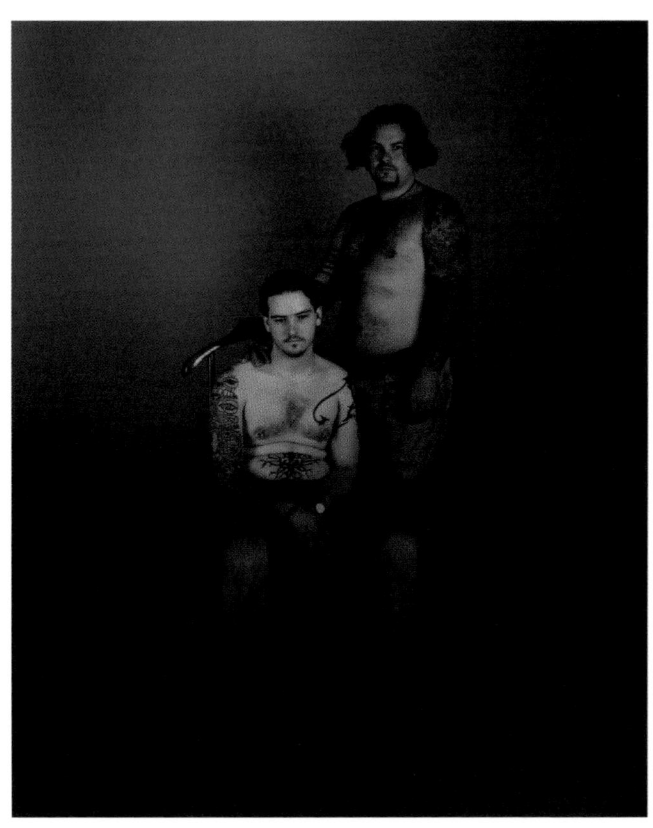

Catherine Opie
John and Scott, 1993
Chromogenic print, Ed. 6/8 + 2 AP
20 x 16 in. (50.8 x 40.6 cm)

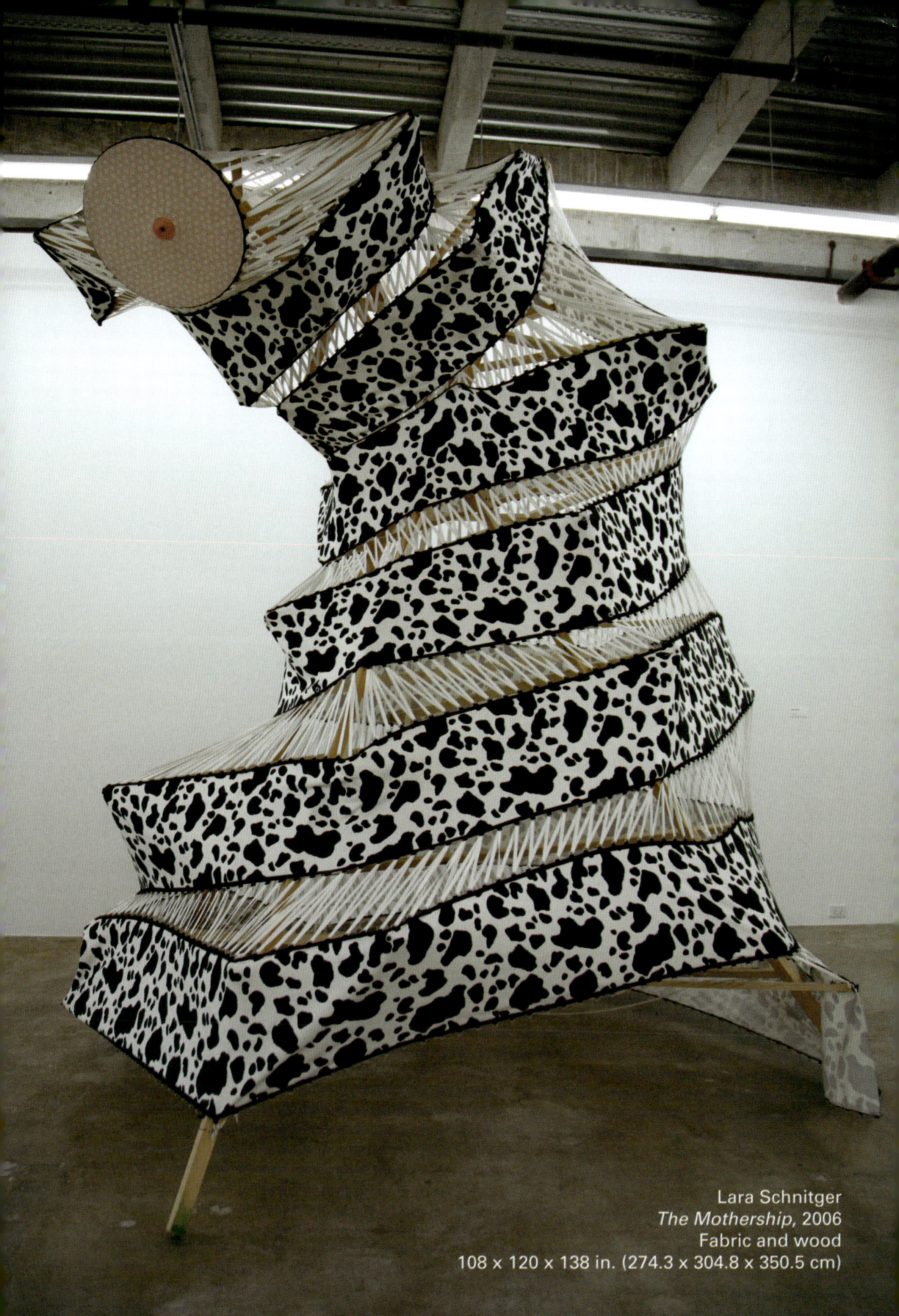

Lara Schnitger
The Mothership, 2006
Fabric and wood
108 x 120 x 138 in. (274.3 x 304.8 x 350.5 cm)

GALLERY 9

MIKE KELLEY

Fresno, 2005
Mixed media with video projection, sound, and photograph
98 x 221 x 185 in. (248.9 x 561.3 x 469.9 cm)

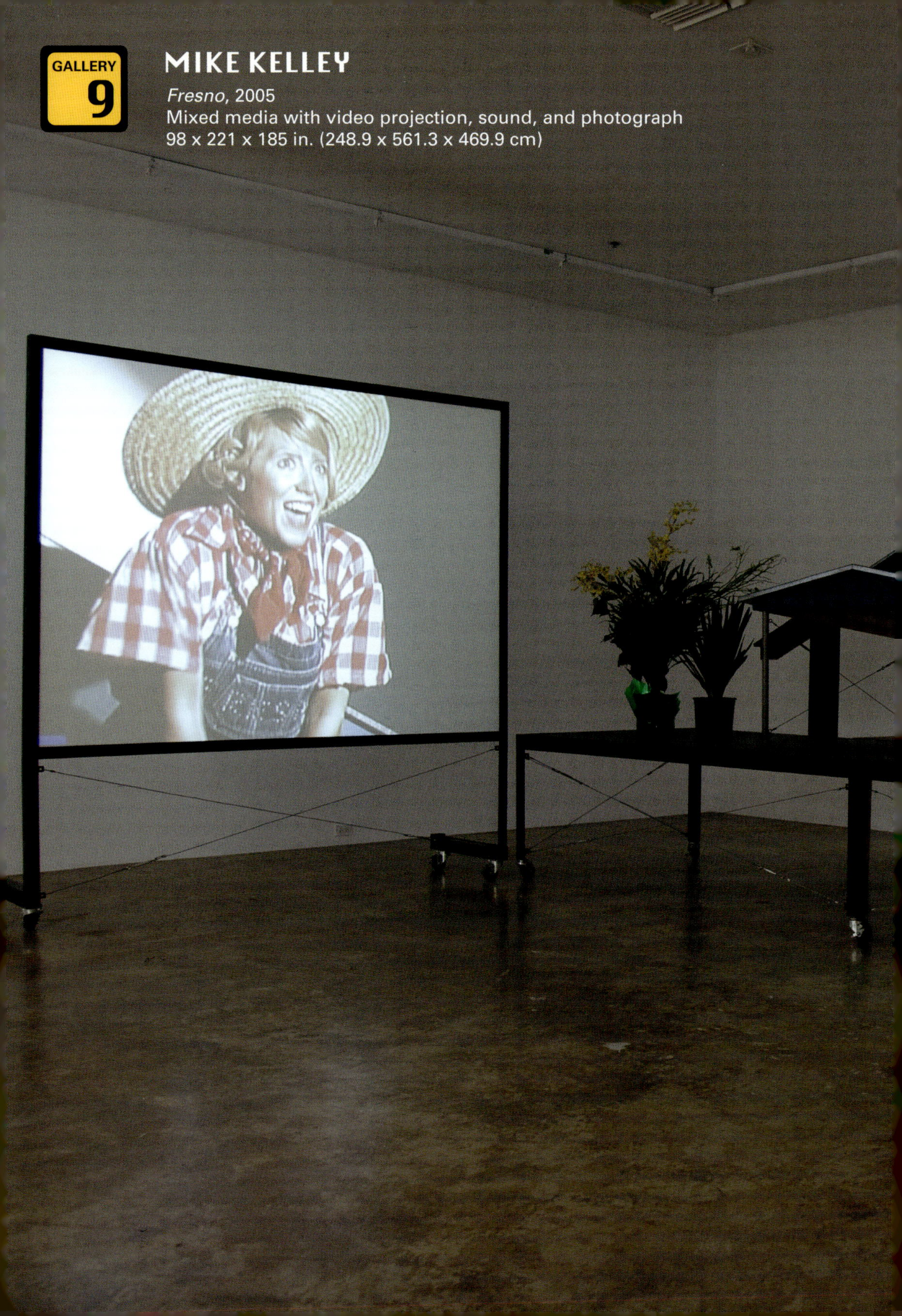

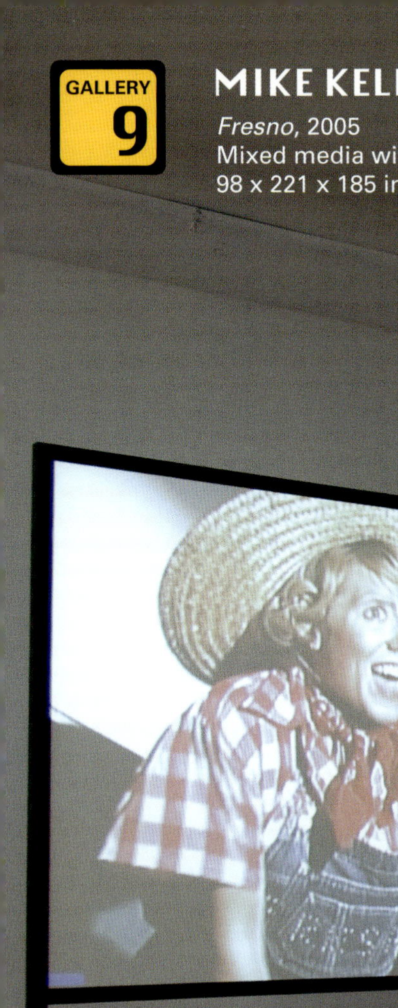

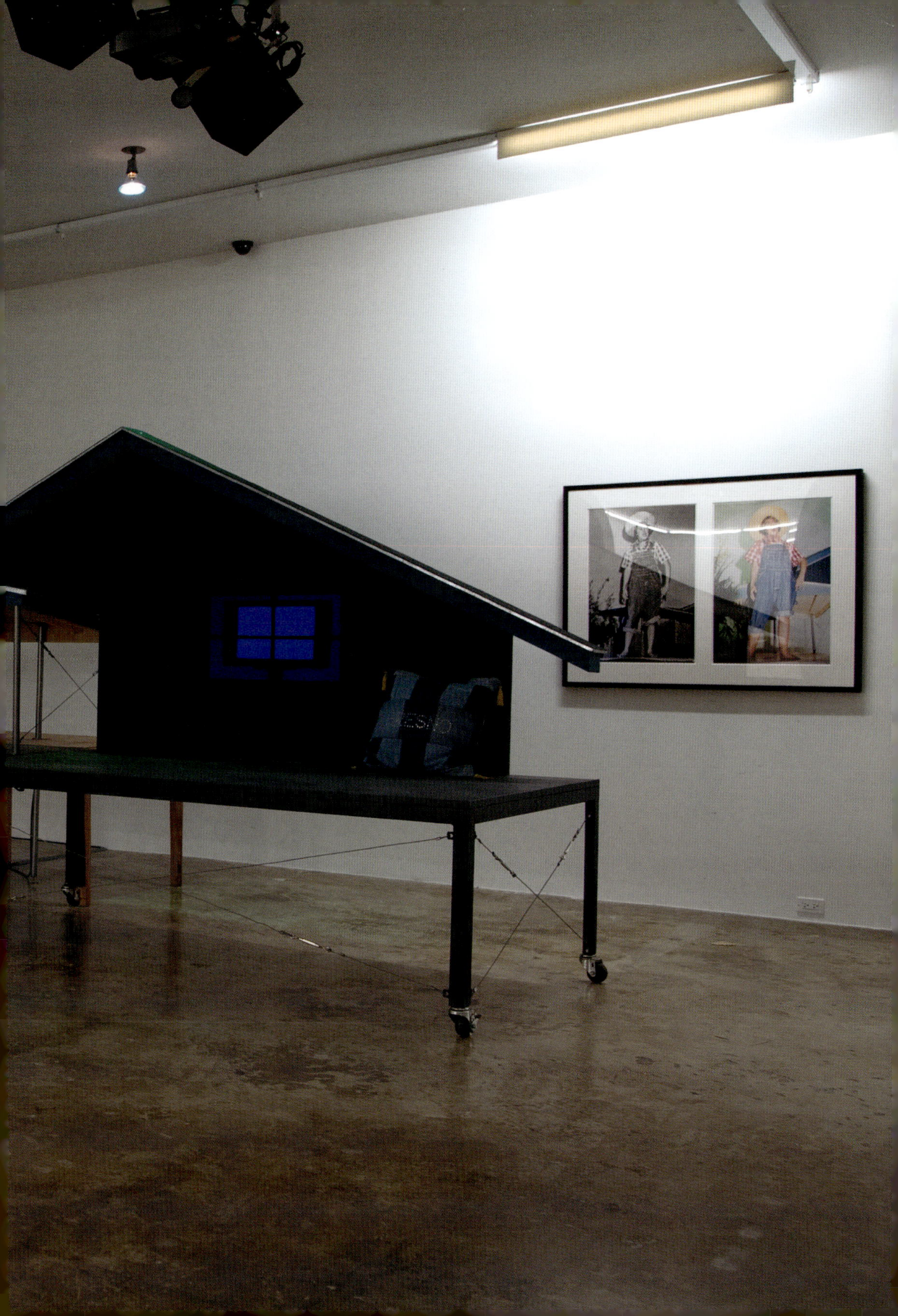

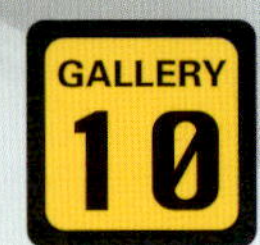

CHARLES RAY

Oh! Charley, Charley, Charley..., 1992
Eight painted cast fiberglass mannequins with wigs
6 x 15 x 15 ft. (183 x 457 x 457 cm)

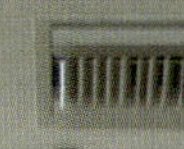

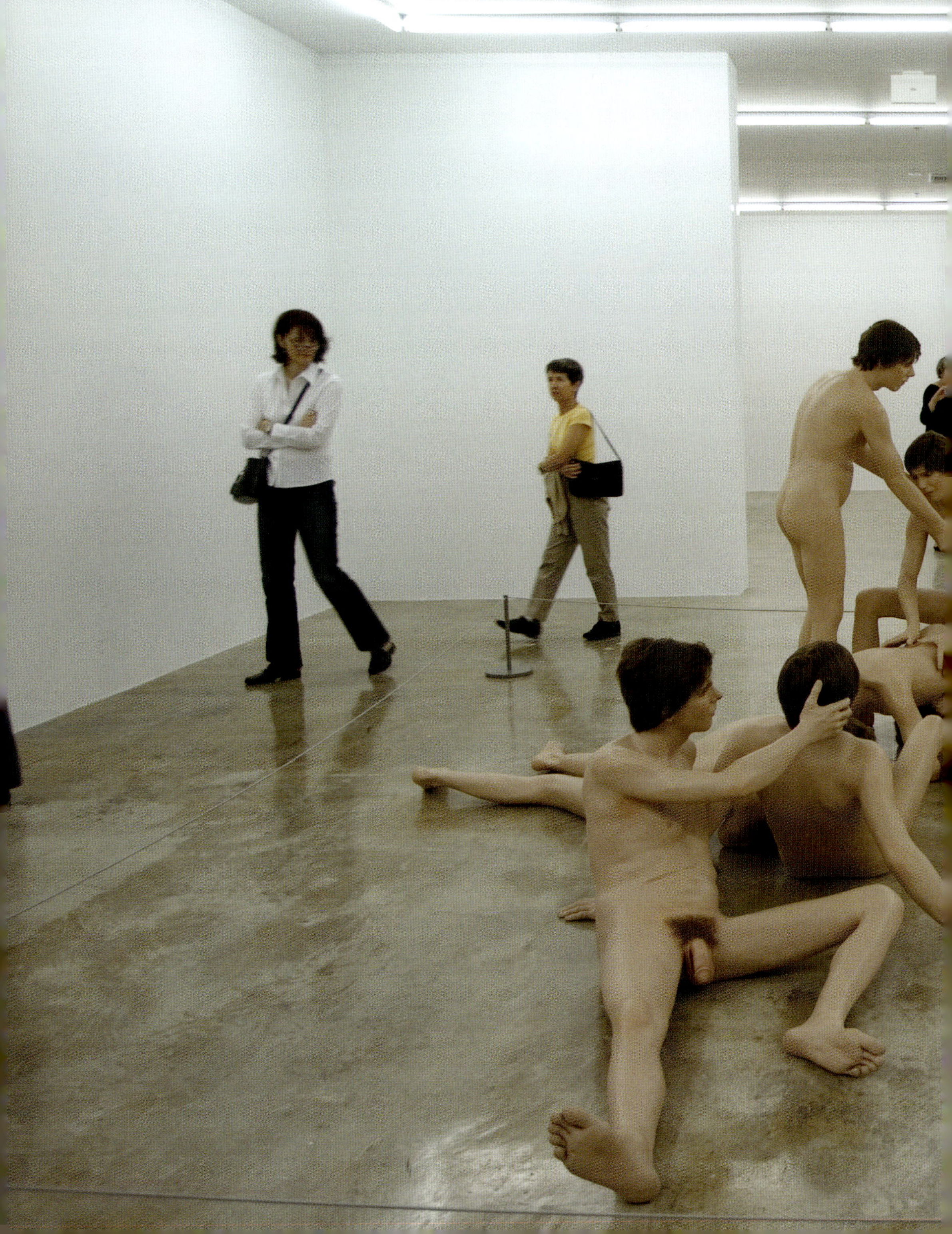

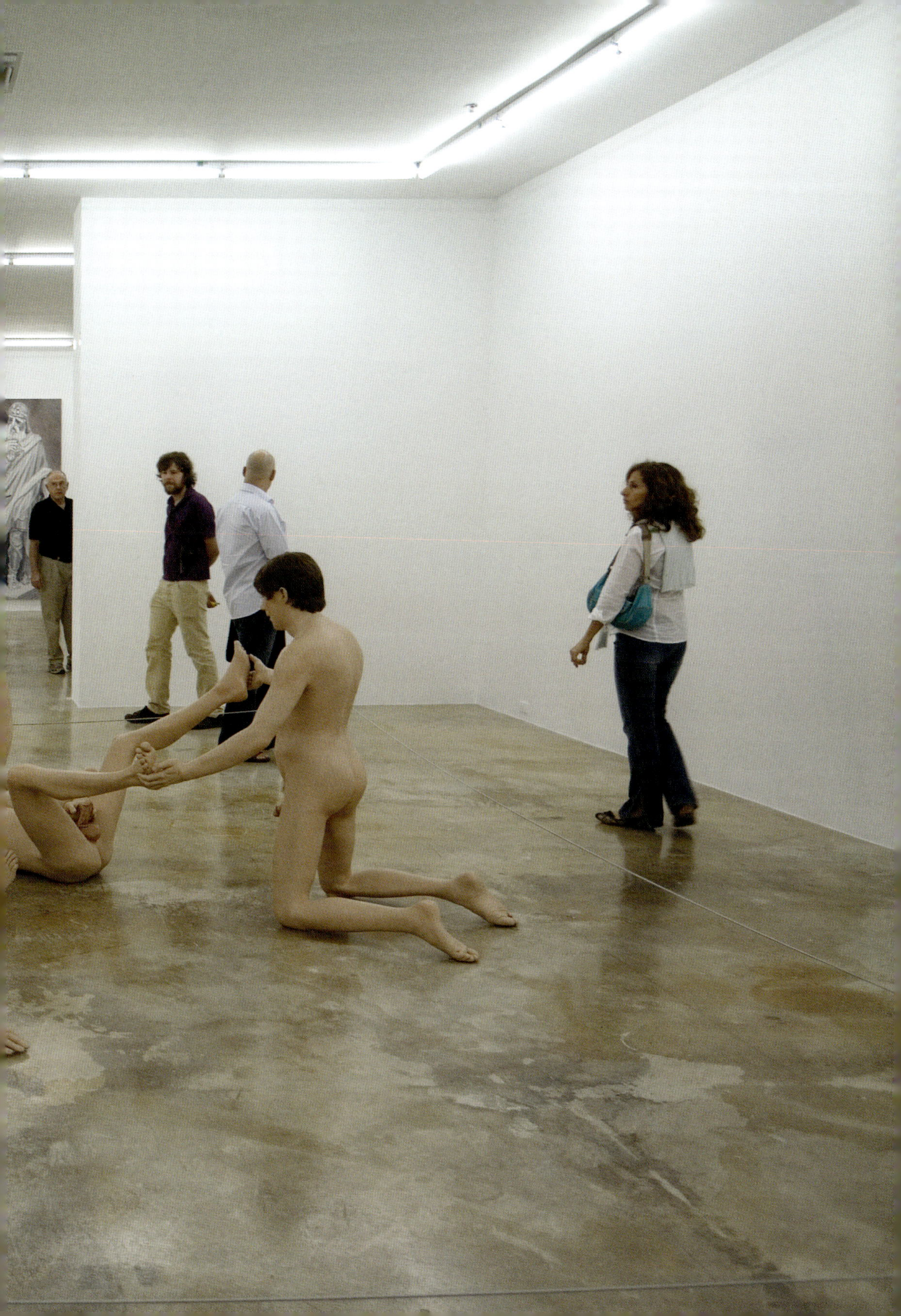

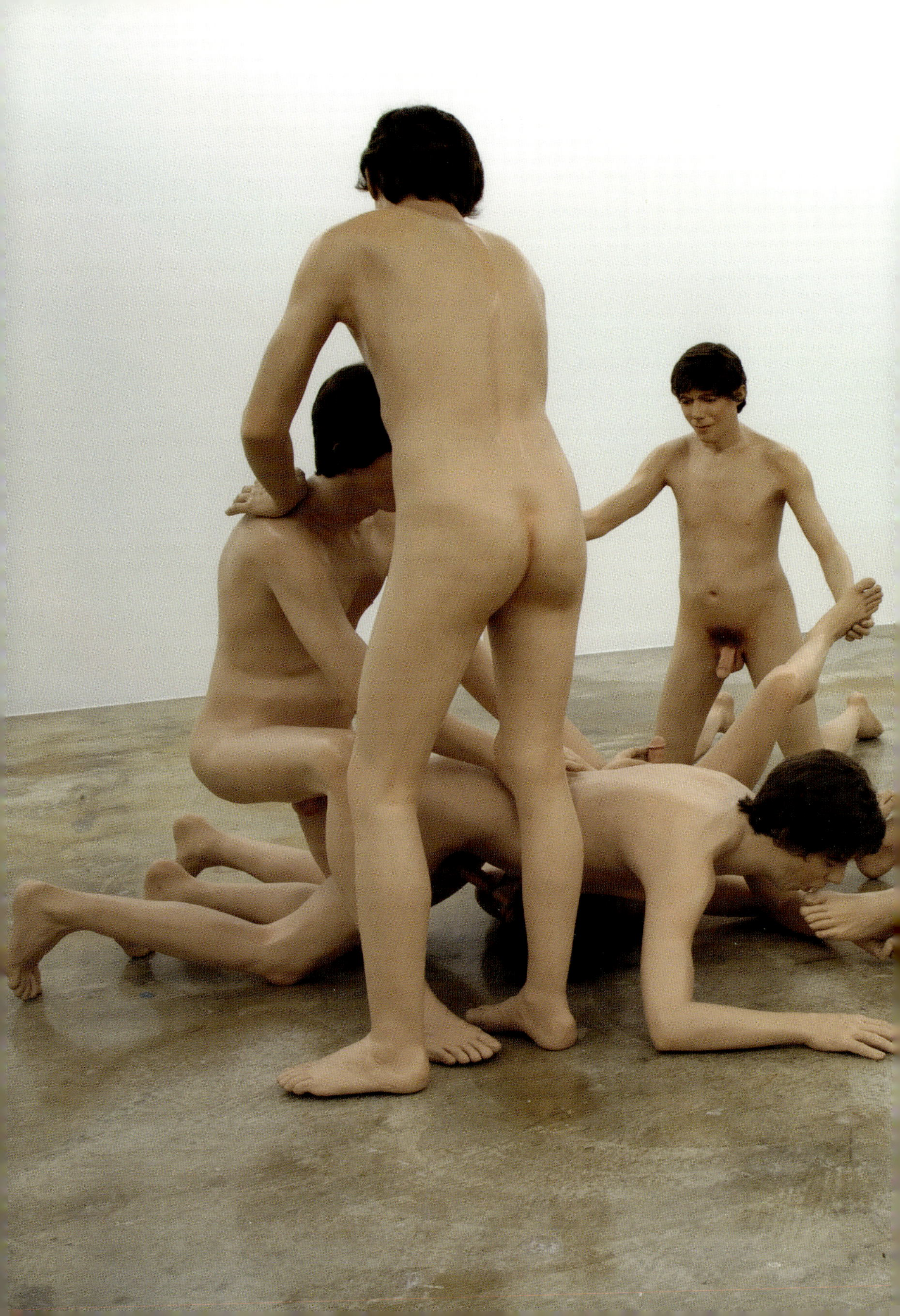

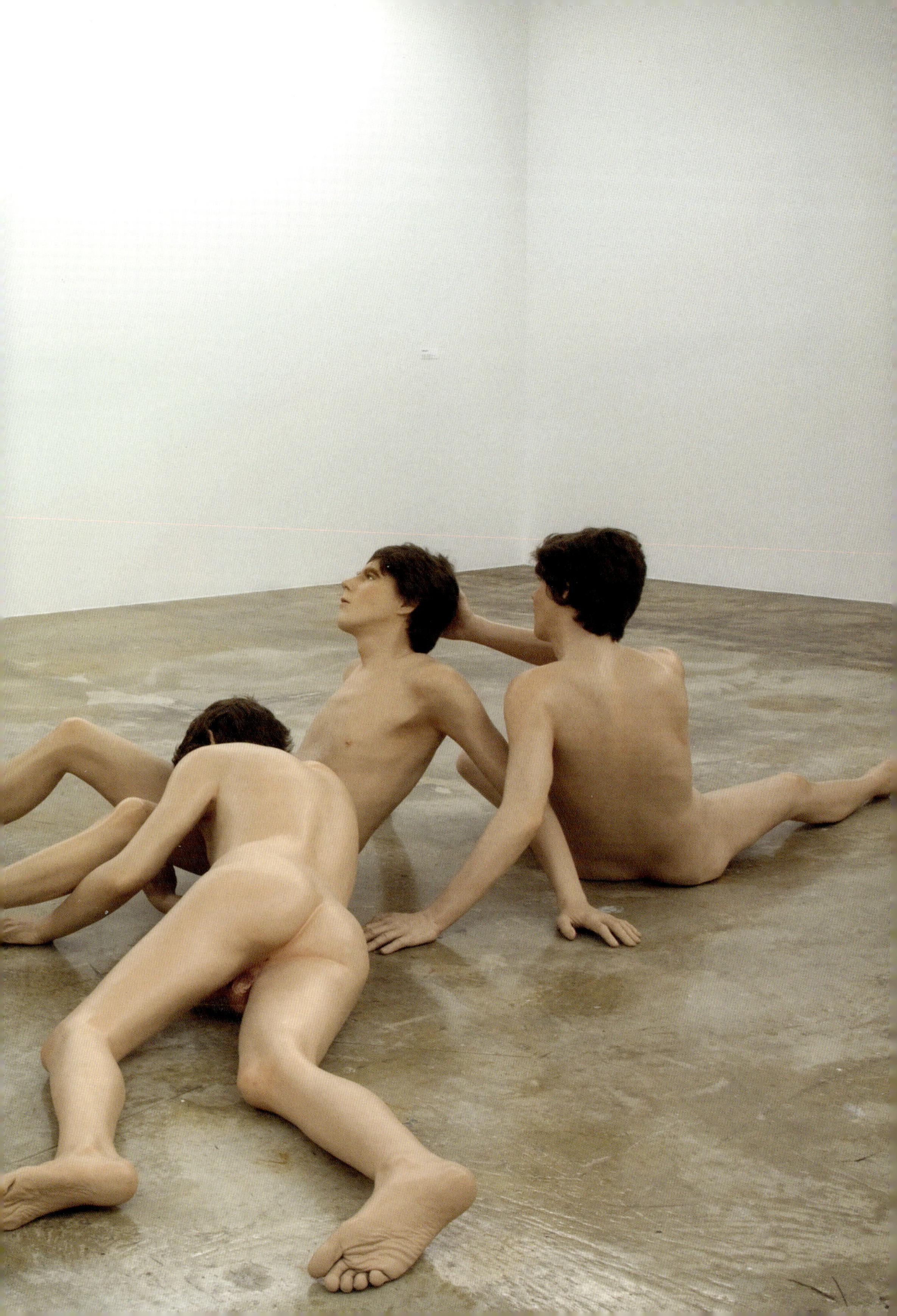

GALLERY 11

INSTALLATION VIEW: AMY BESSONE

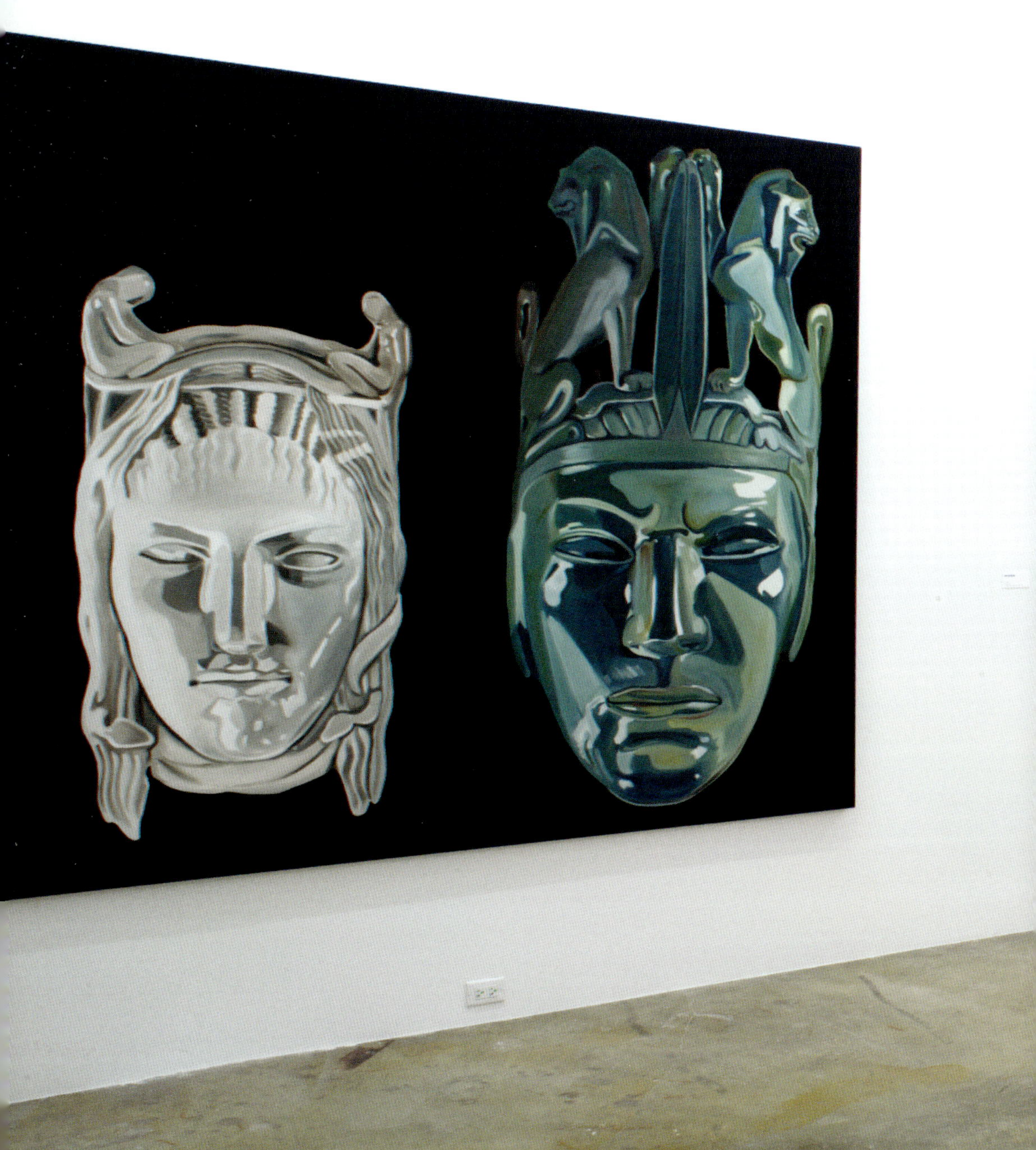

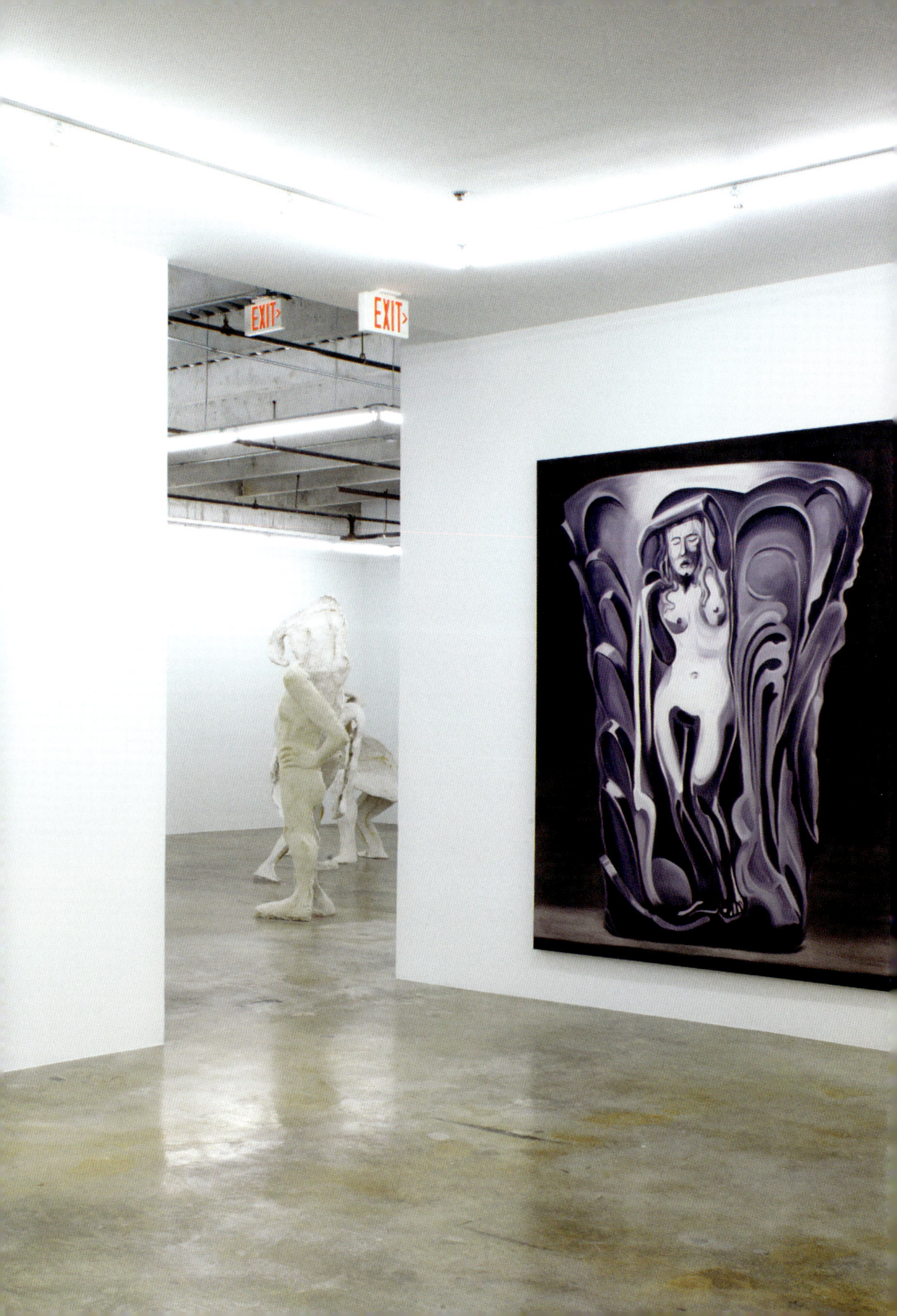
EXIT
EXIT

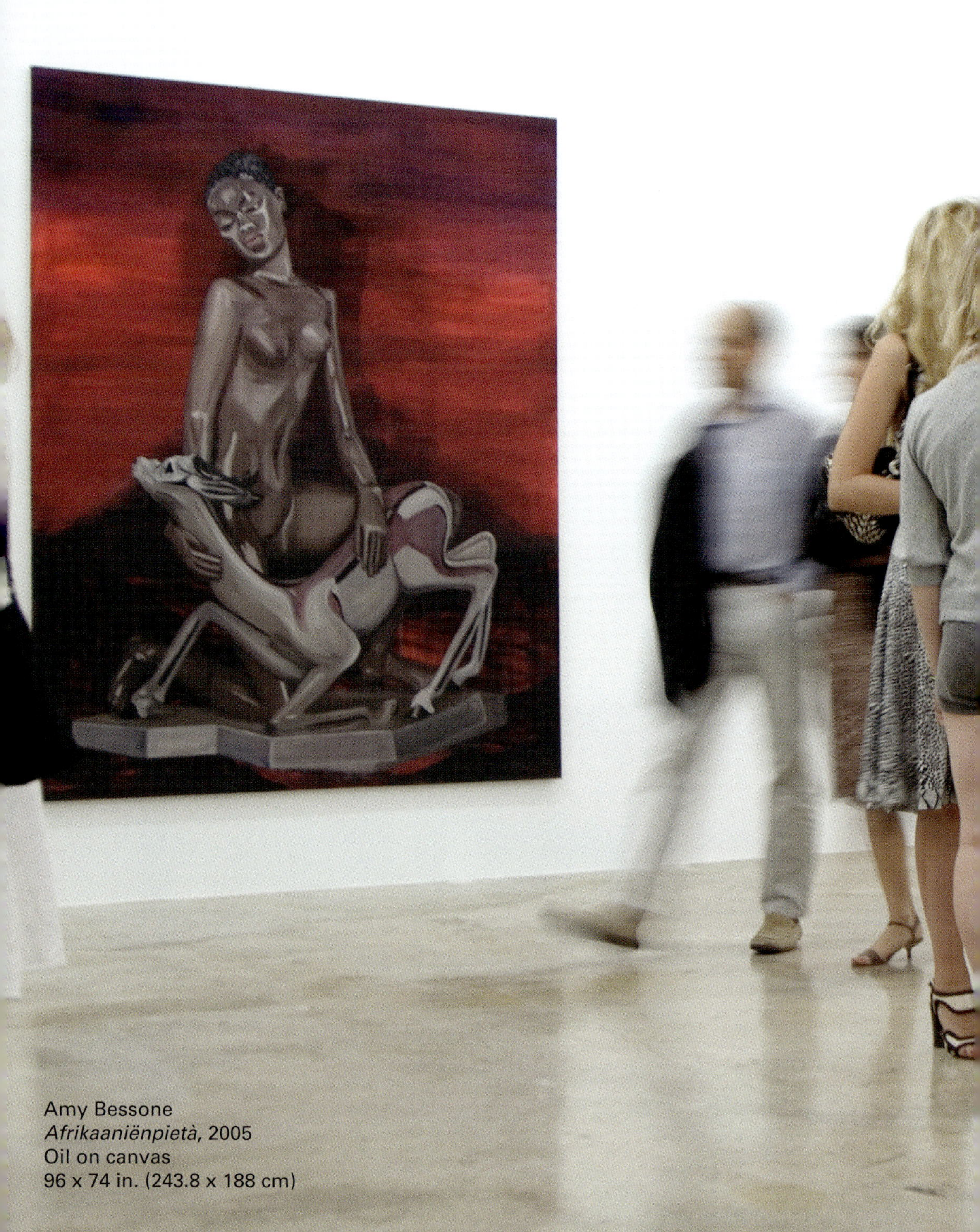

Amy Bessone
Afrikaaniënpietà, 2005
Oil on canvas
96 x 74 in. (243.8 x 188 cm)

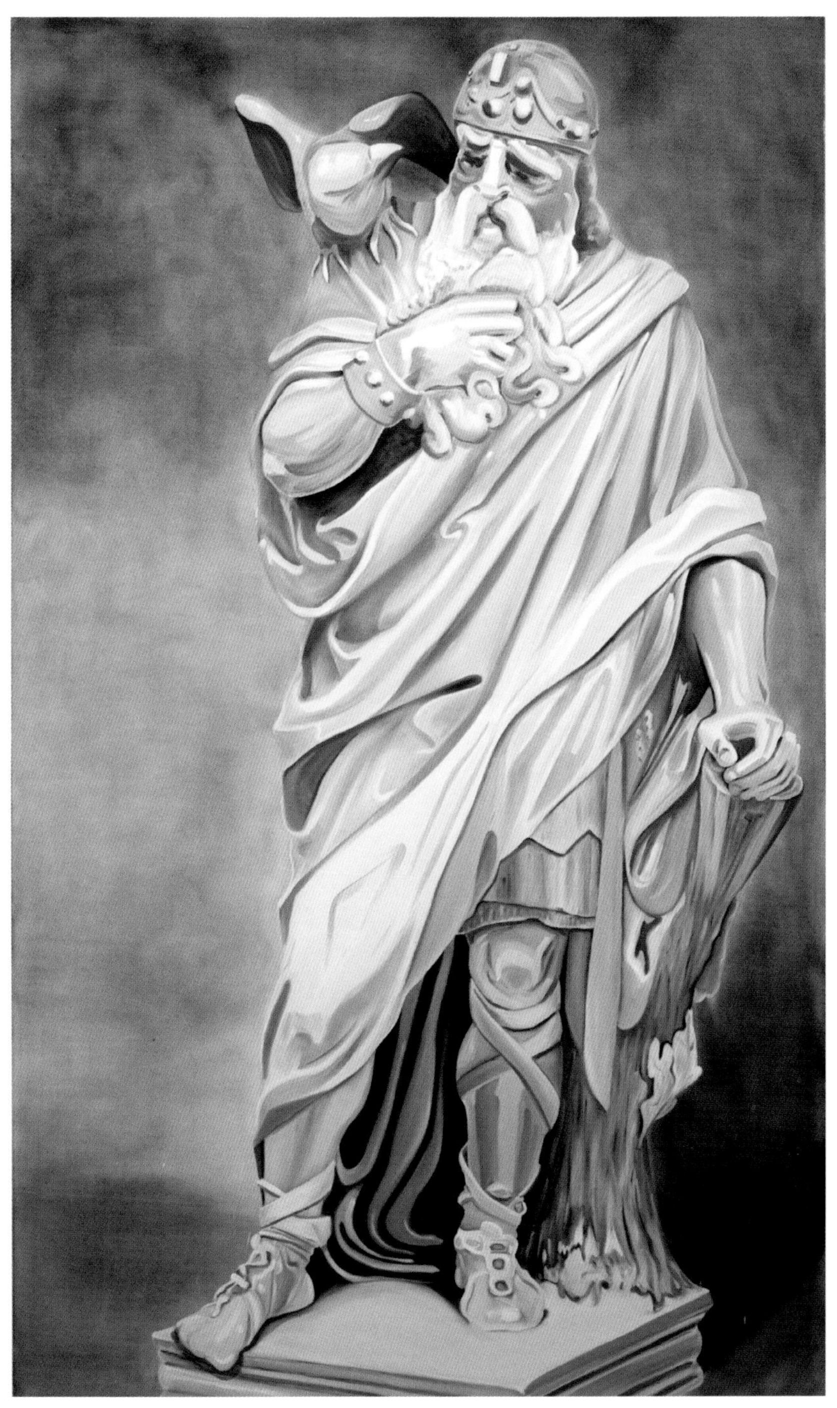

Amy Bessone
German God, 2006
Oil on canvas
110 x 64 in. (279.4 x 162.6 cm)

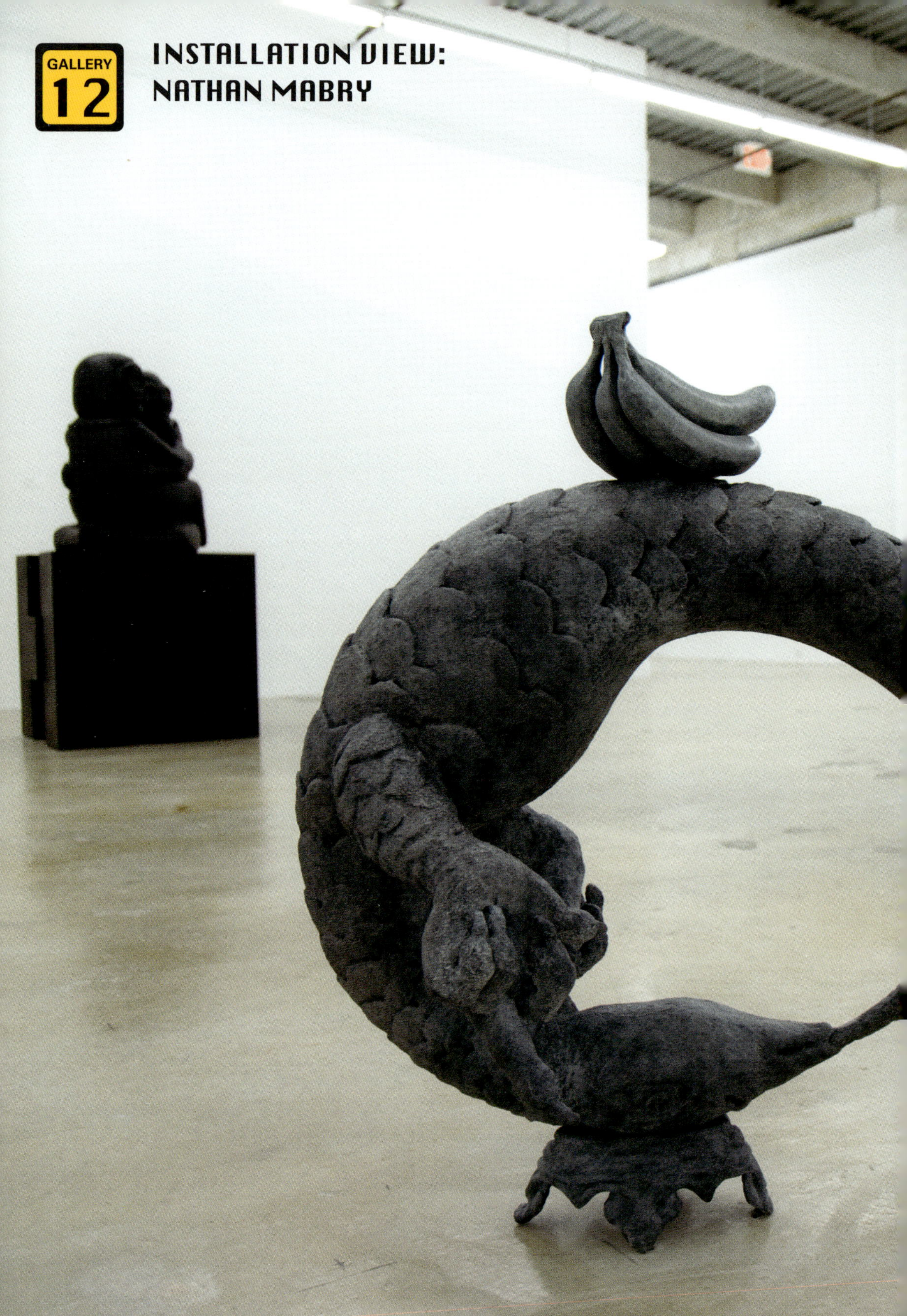

INSTALLATION VIEW: NATHAN MABRY

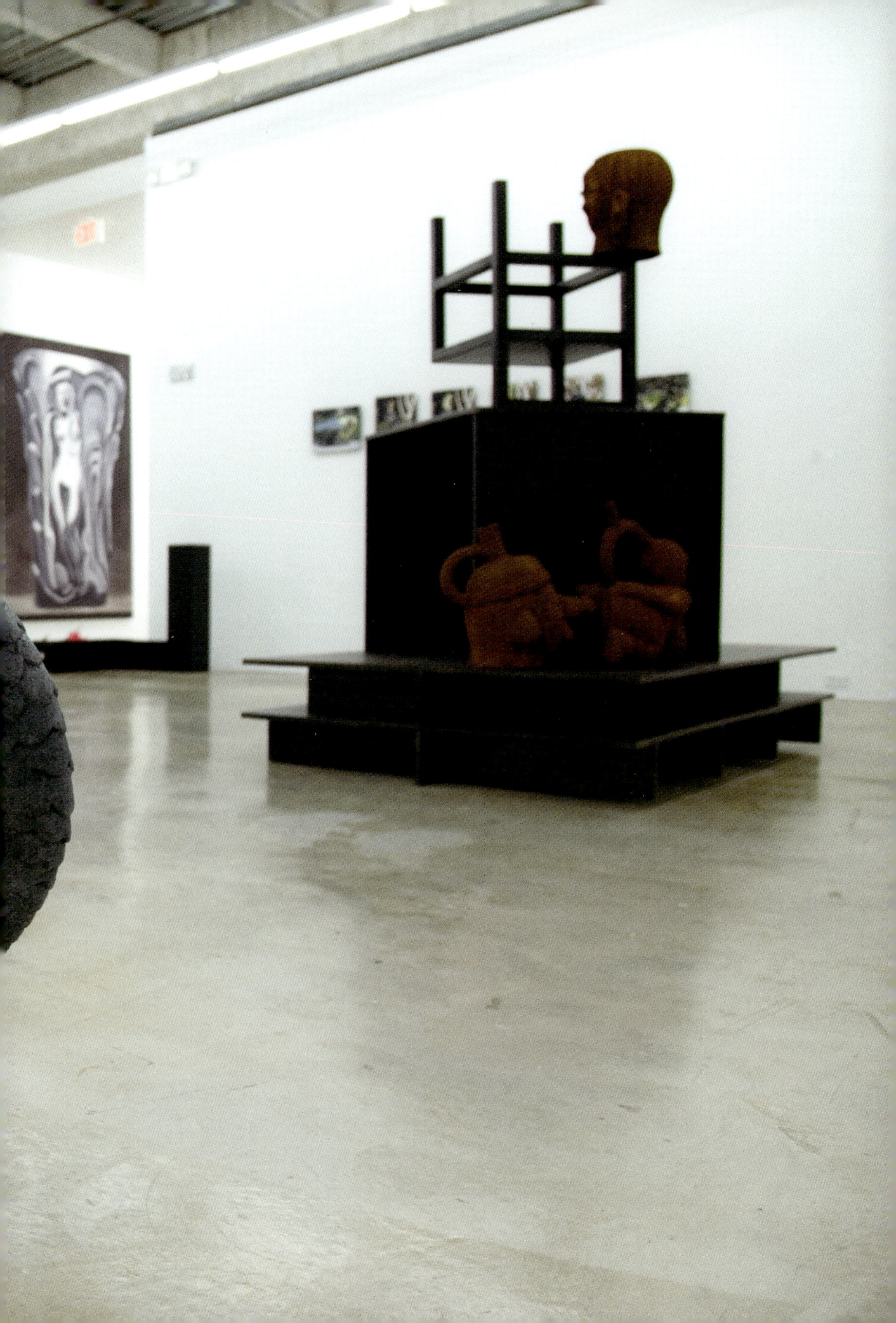

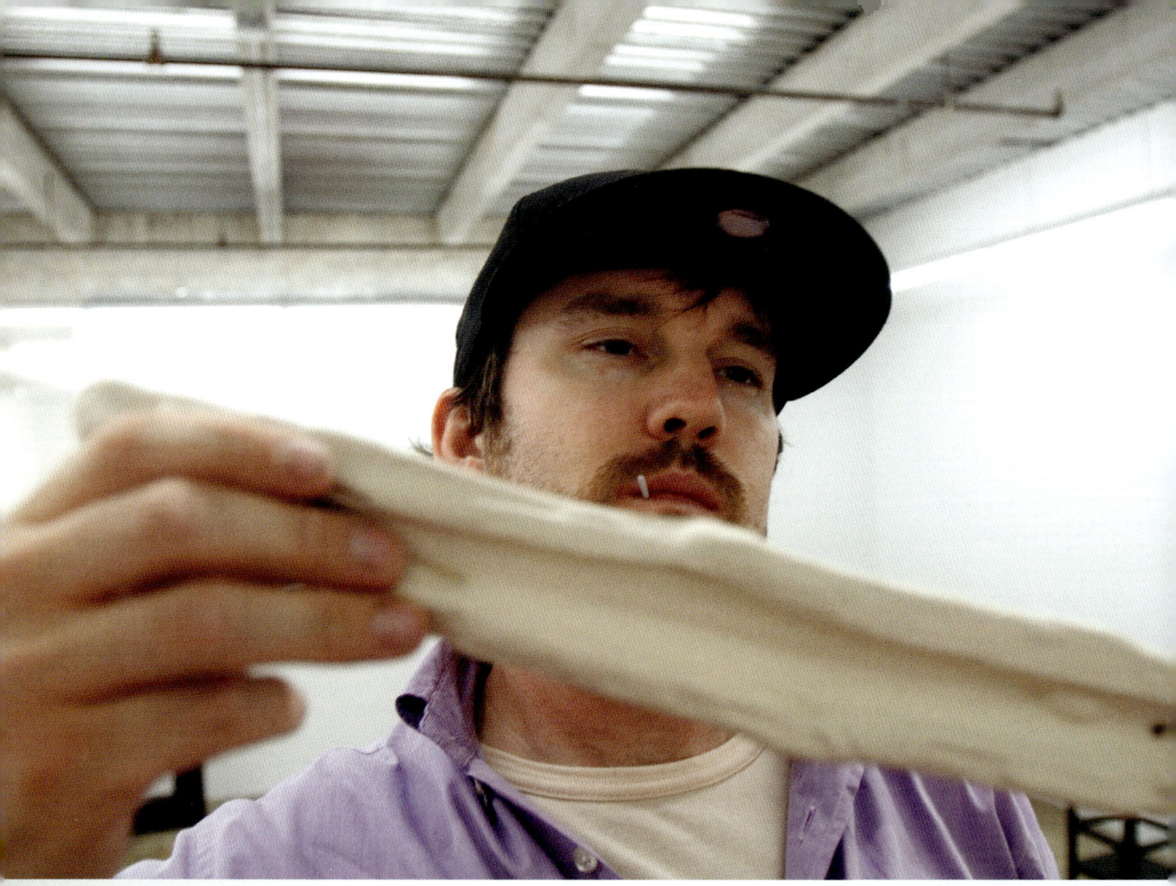

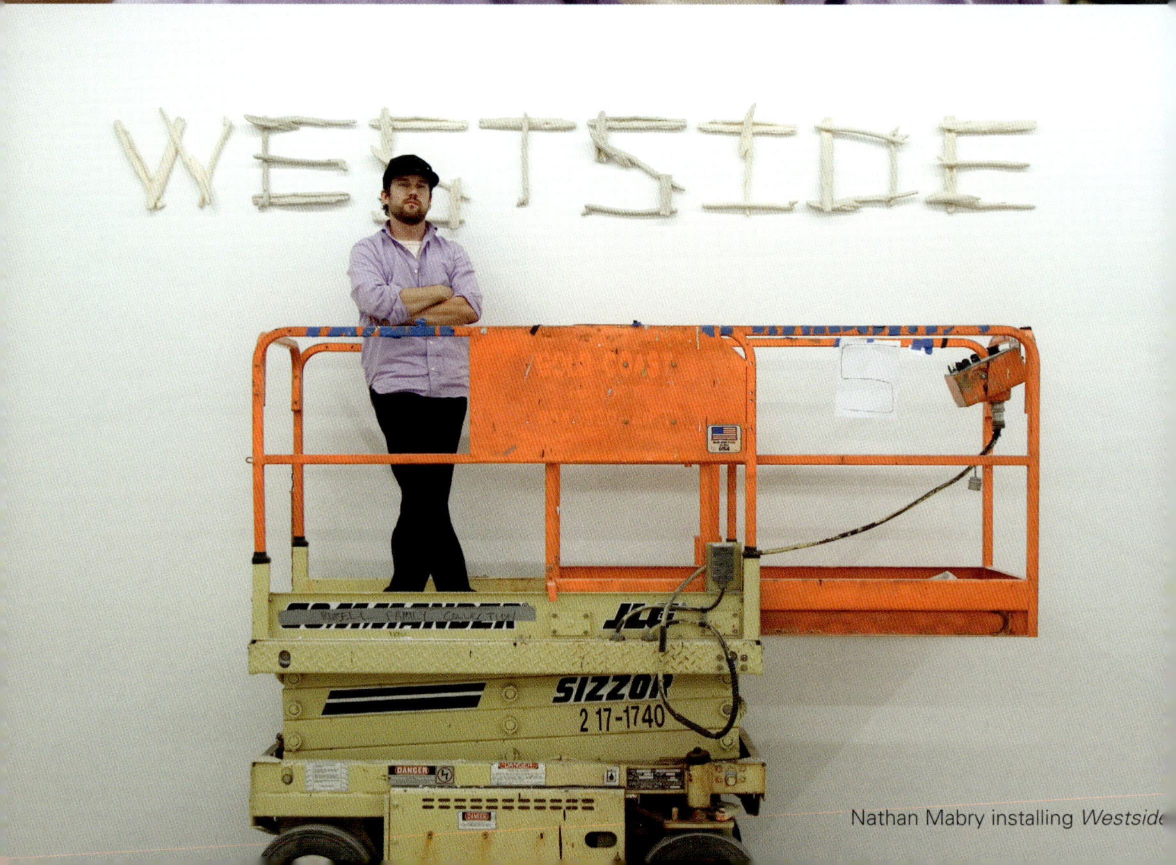

Nathan Mabry installing *Westside*

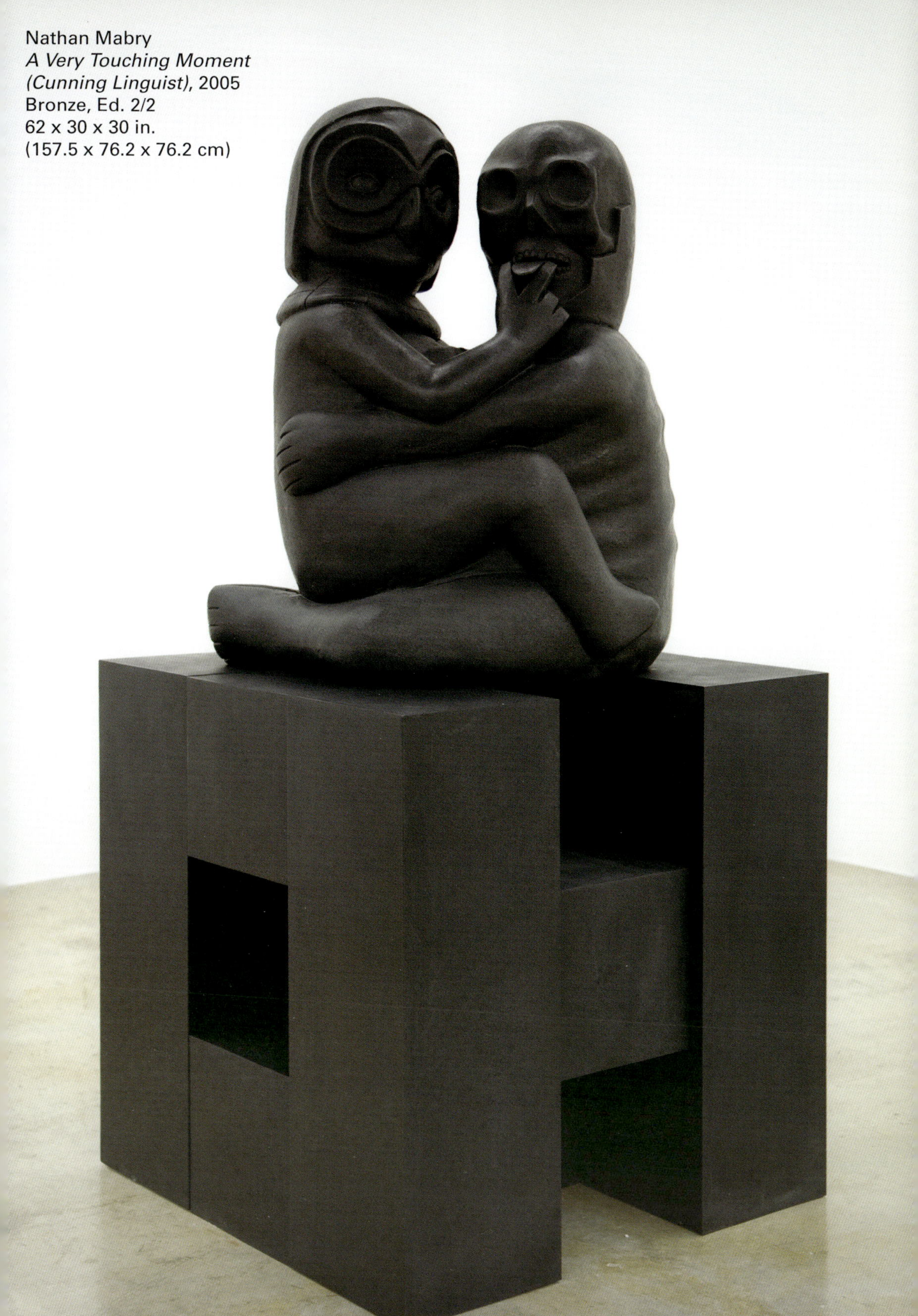

Nathan Mabry
A Very Touching Moment (Cunning Linguist), 2005
Bronze, Ed. 2/2
62 x 30 x 30 in.
(157.5 x 76.2 x 76.2 cm)

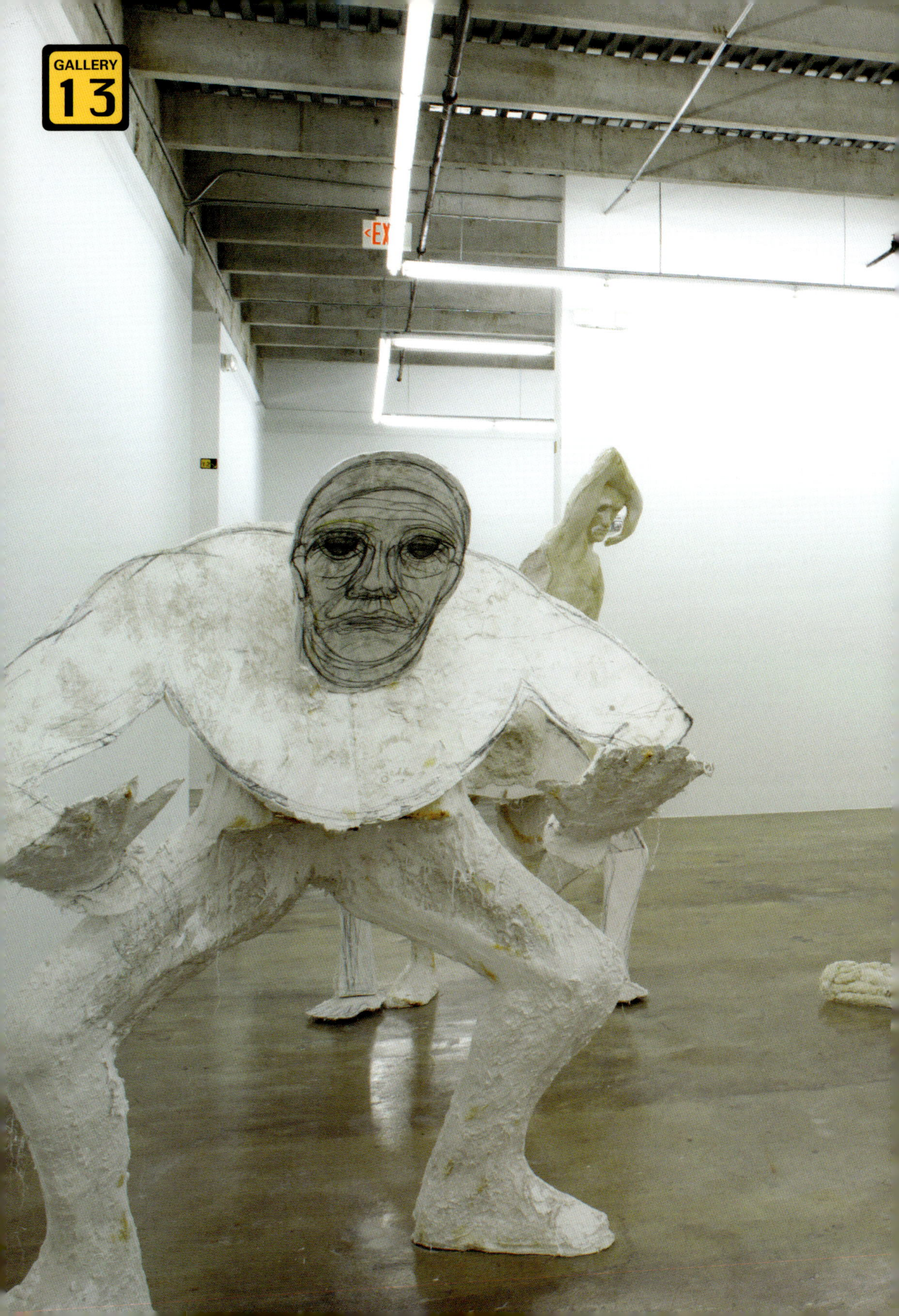
GALLERY
13

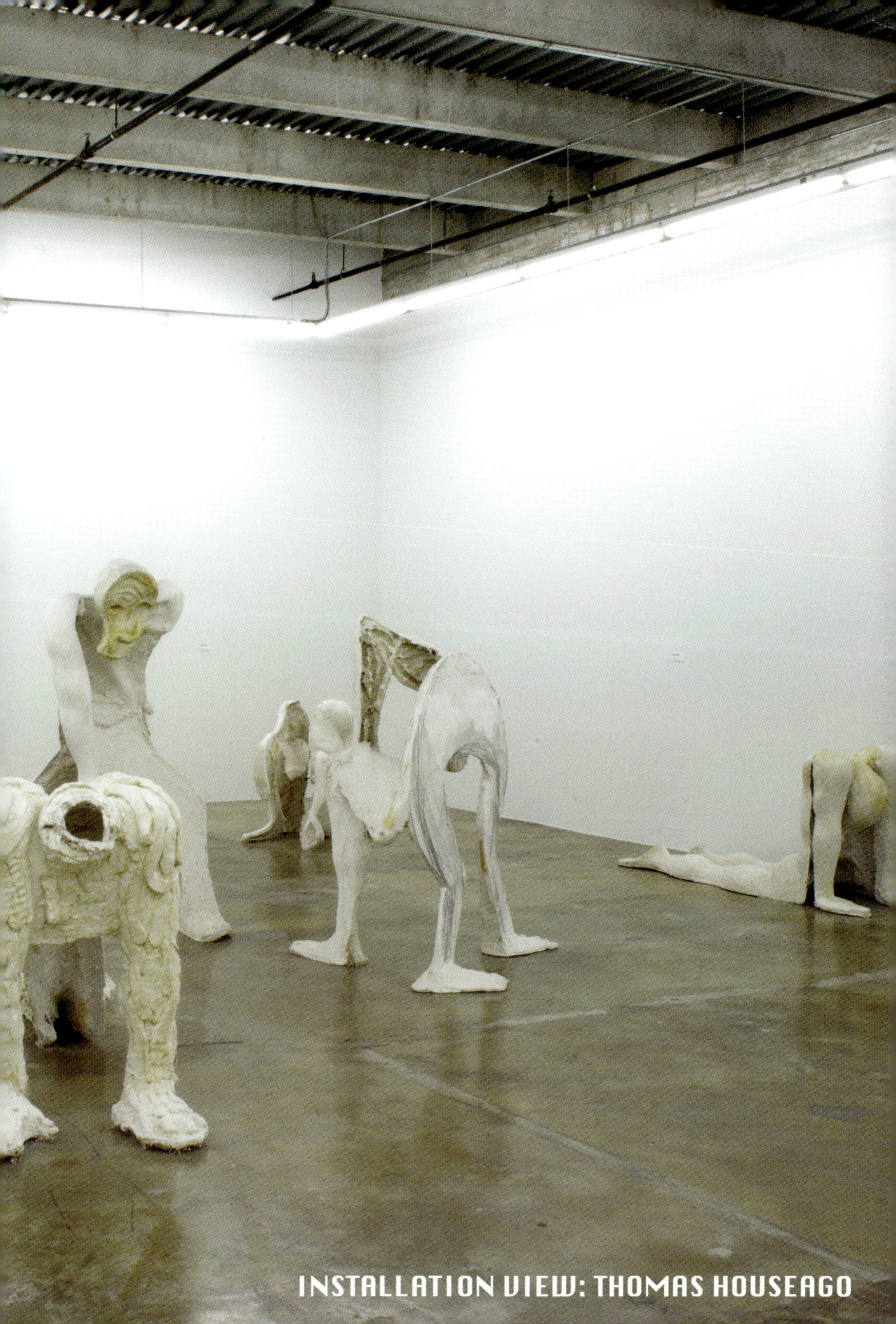

INSTALLATION VIEW: THOMAS HOUSEAGO

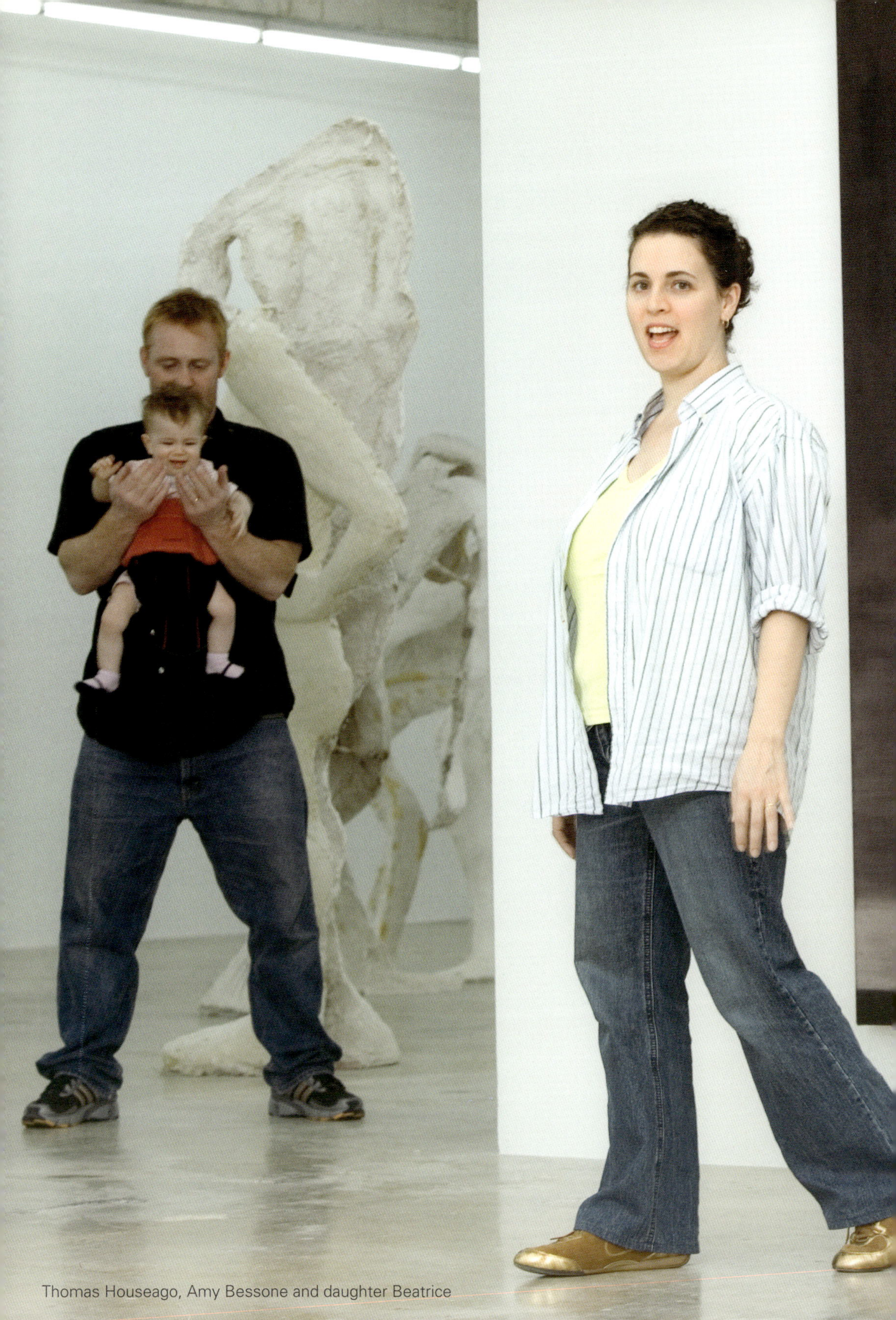

Thomas Houseago, Amy Bessone and daughter Beatrice

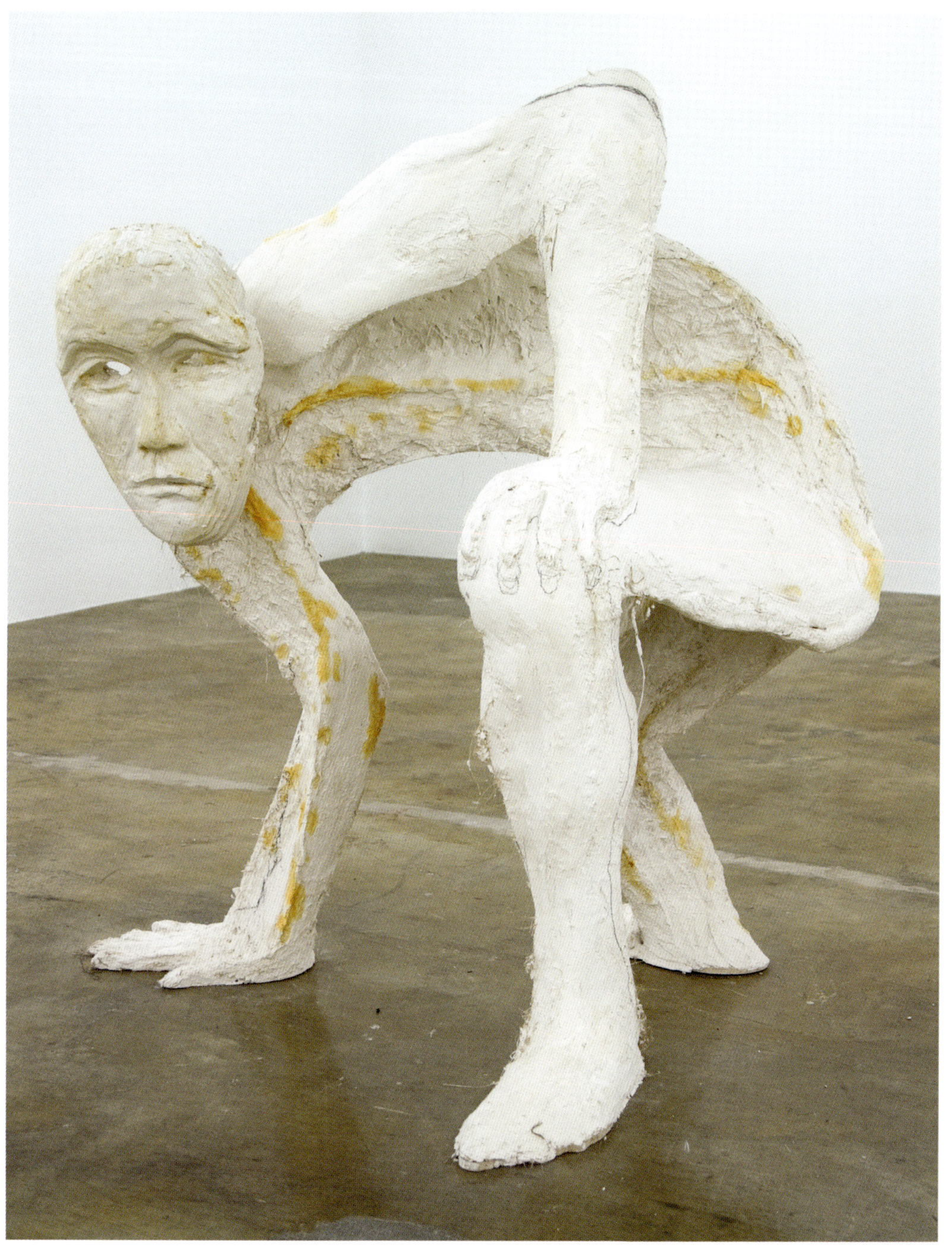

Thomas Houseago
First Light, 2006
Tuf-Cal, hemp, iron, clay and graphite
60 x 53 x 40 in. (152.3 x 134.7 x 101.6 cm)

GALLERY 14

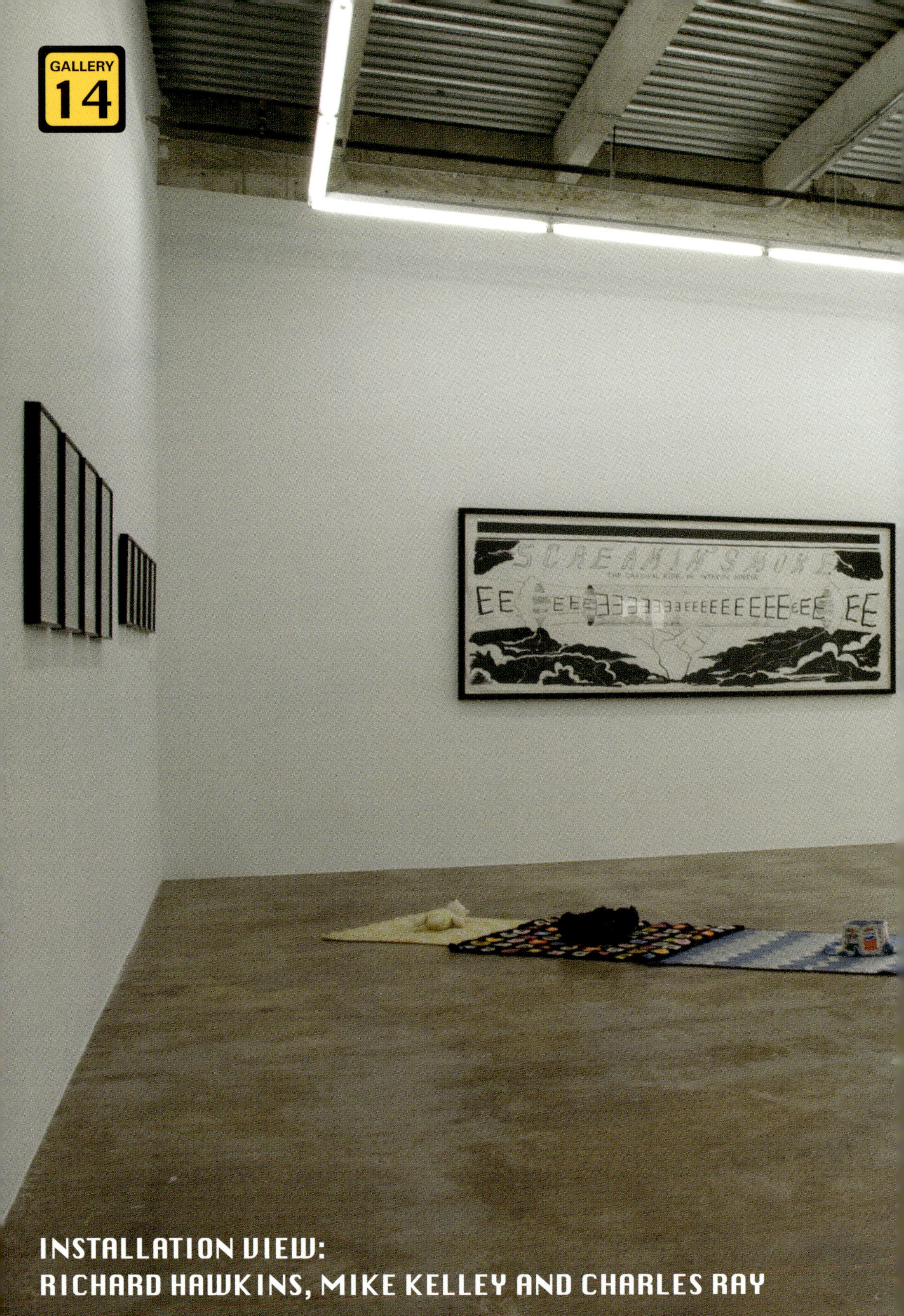

INSTALLATION VIEW:
RICHARD HAWKINS, MIKE KELLEY AND CHARLES RAY

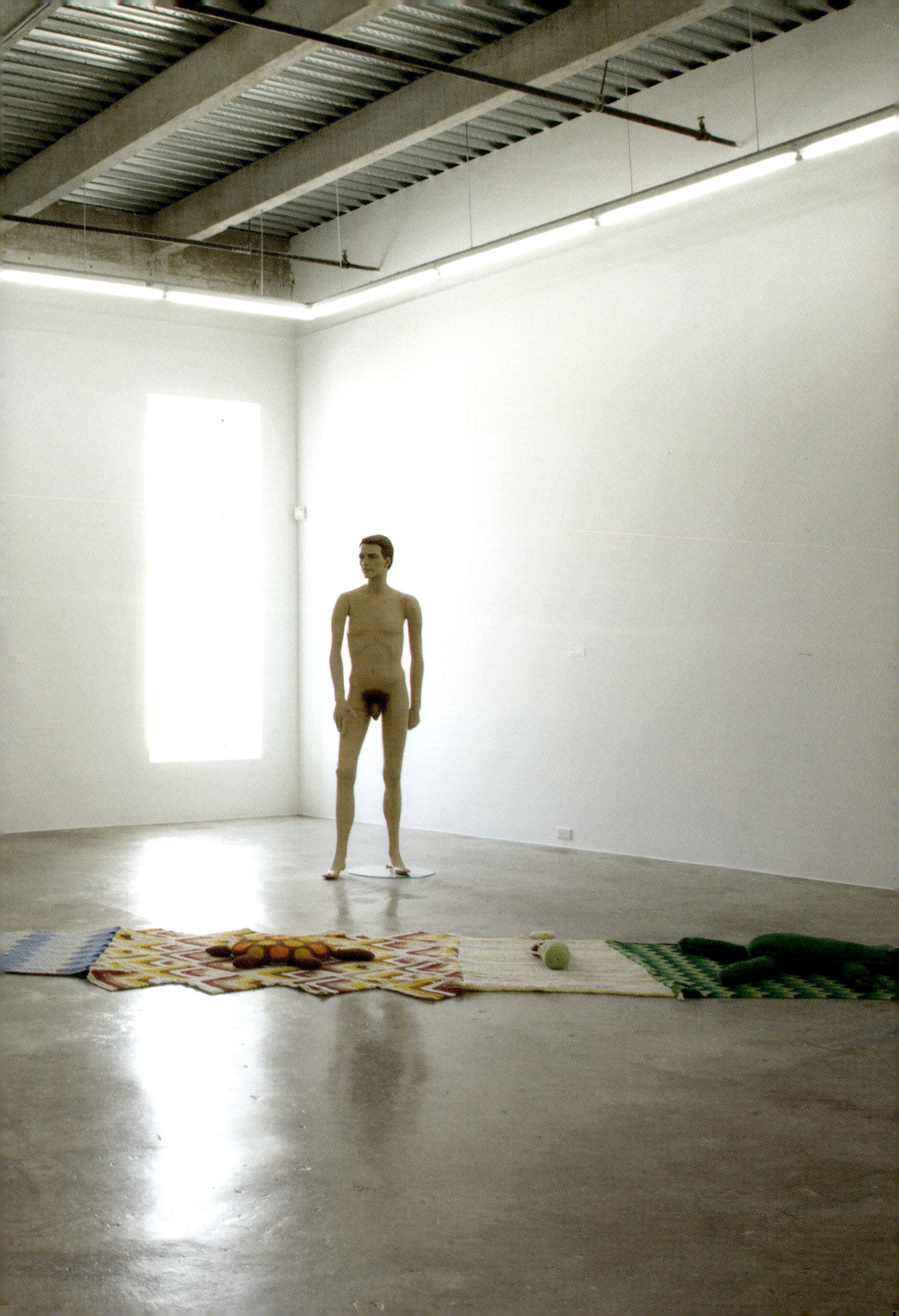

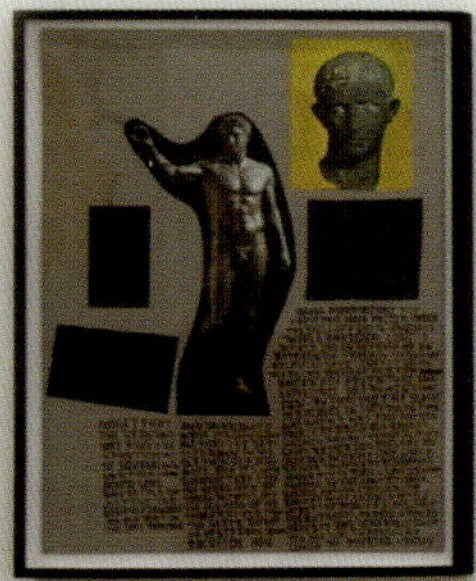

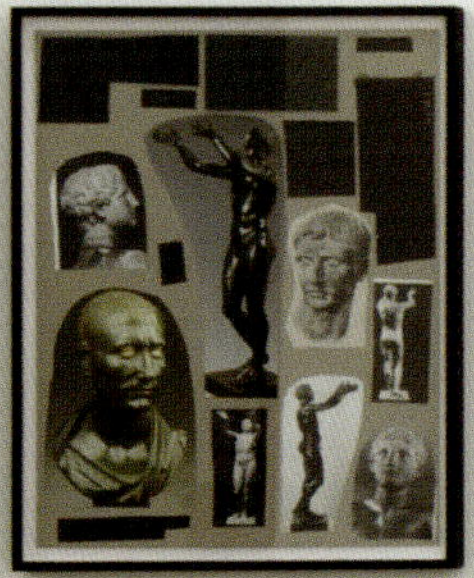

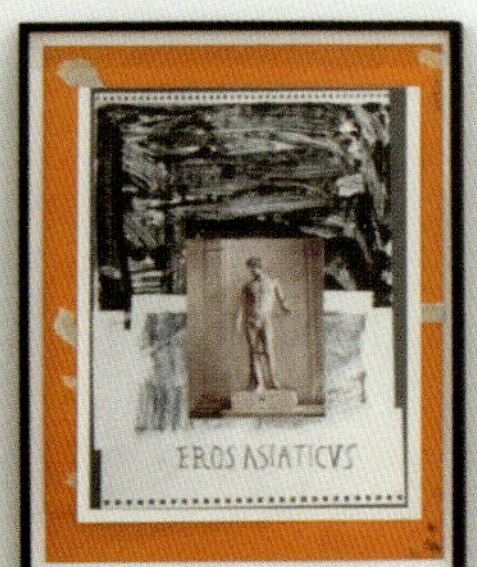

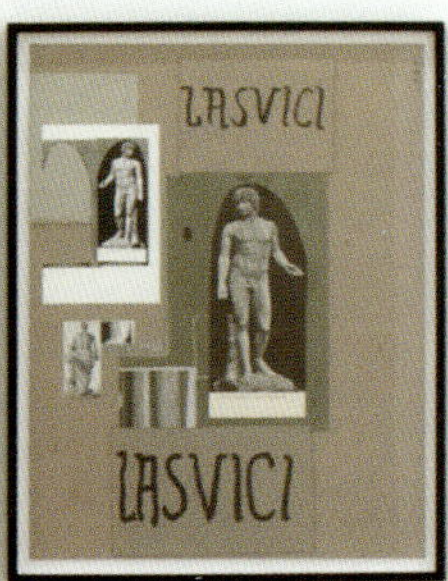

Installation view: Richard Hawkins

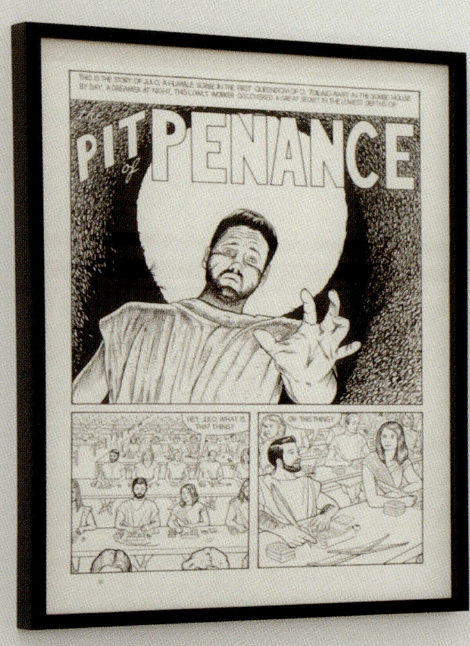

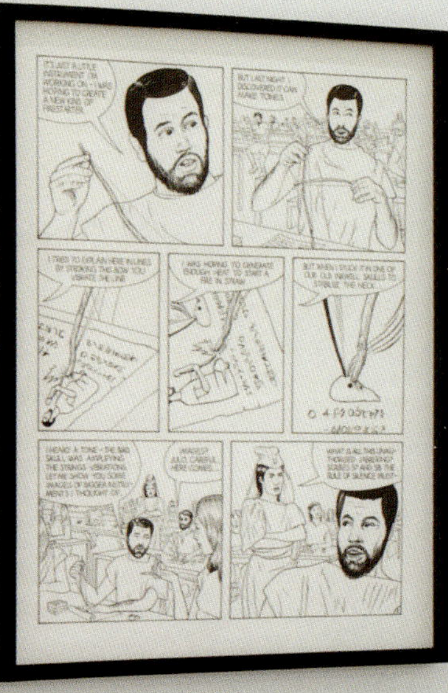

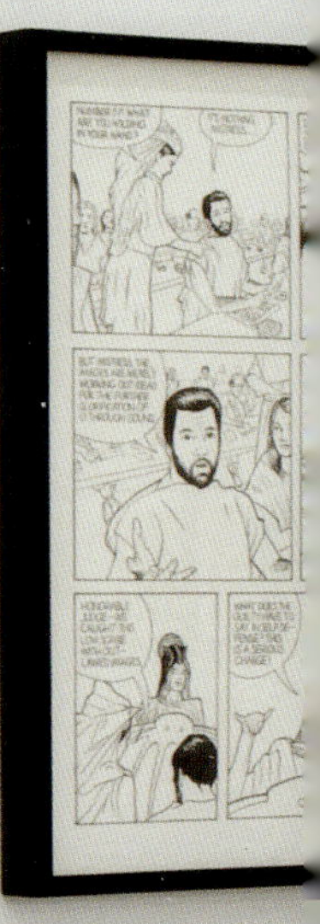

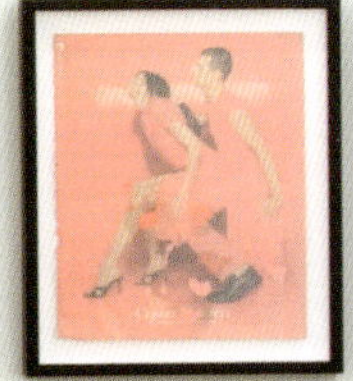
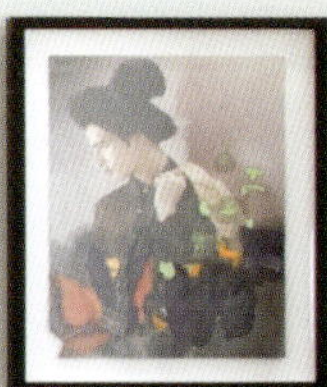
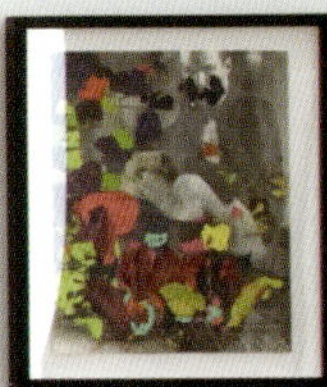
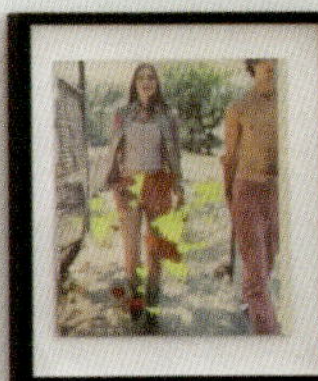
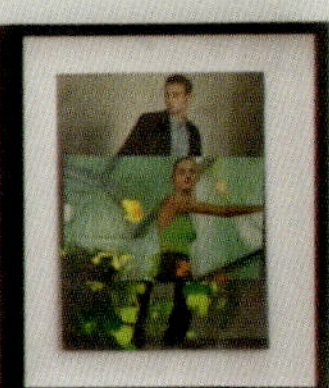

Installation view: Richard Hawkins

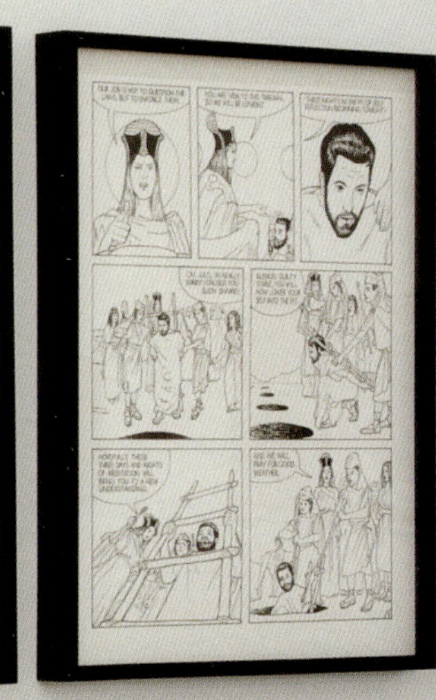
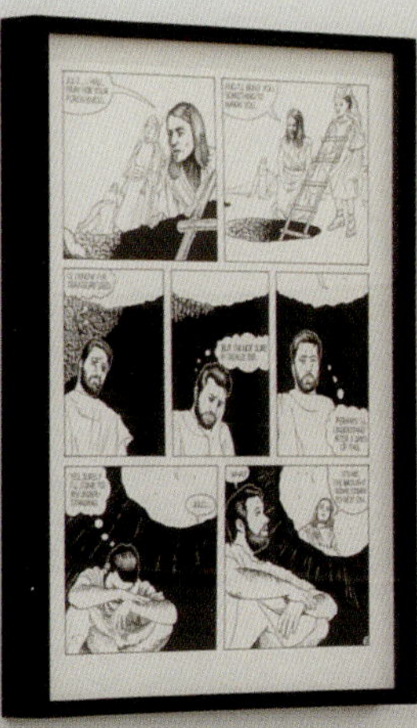
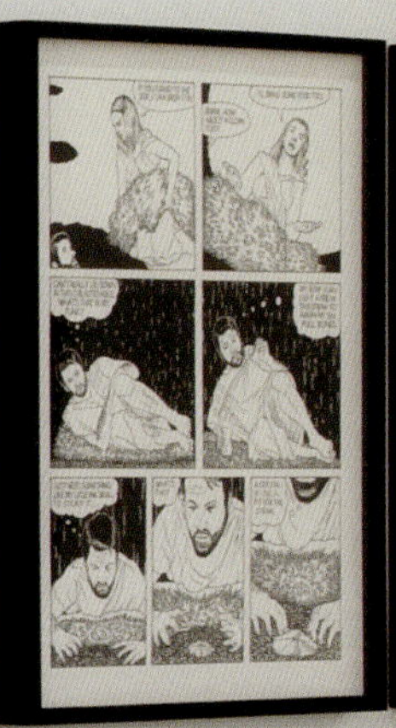
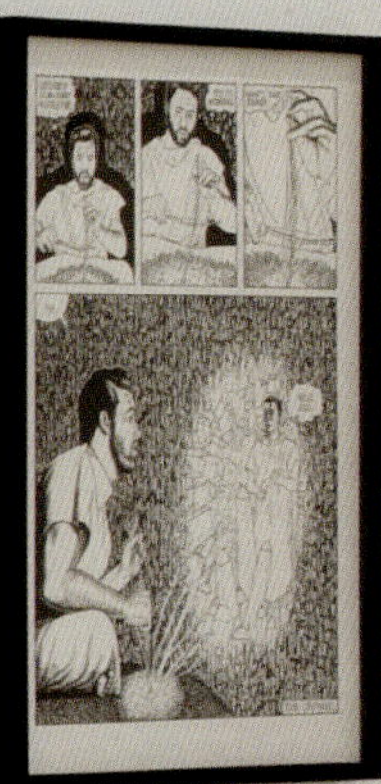

Jim Shaw
Pit of Penance, 2006
Ink on seven sheets of paper
Each: 20 x 15 in. (50.8 x 38.1 cm)

GALLERY 15

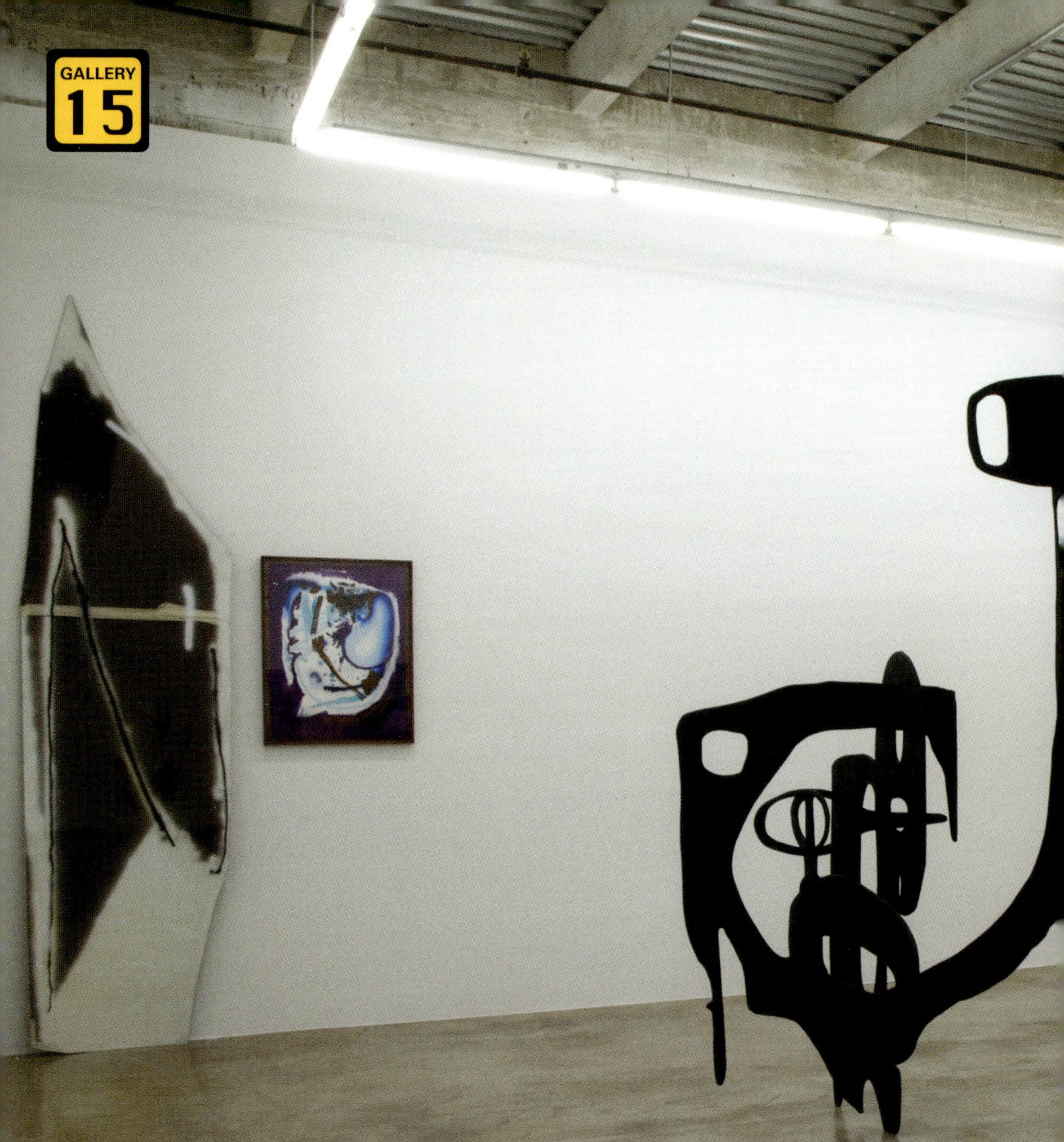

INSTALLATION VIEW: AARON CURRY

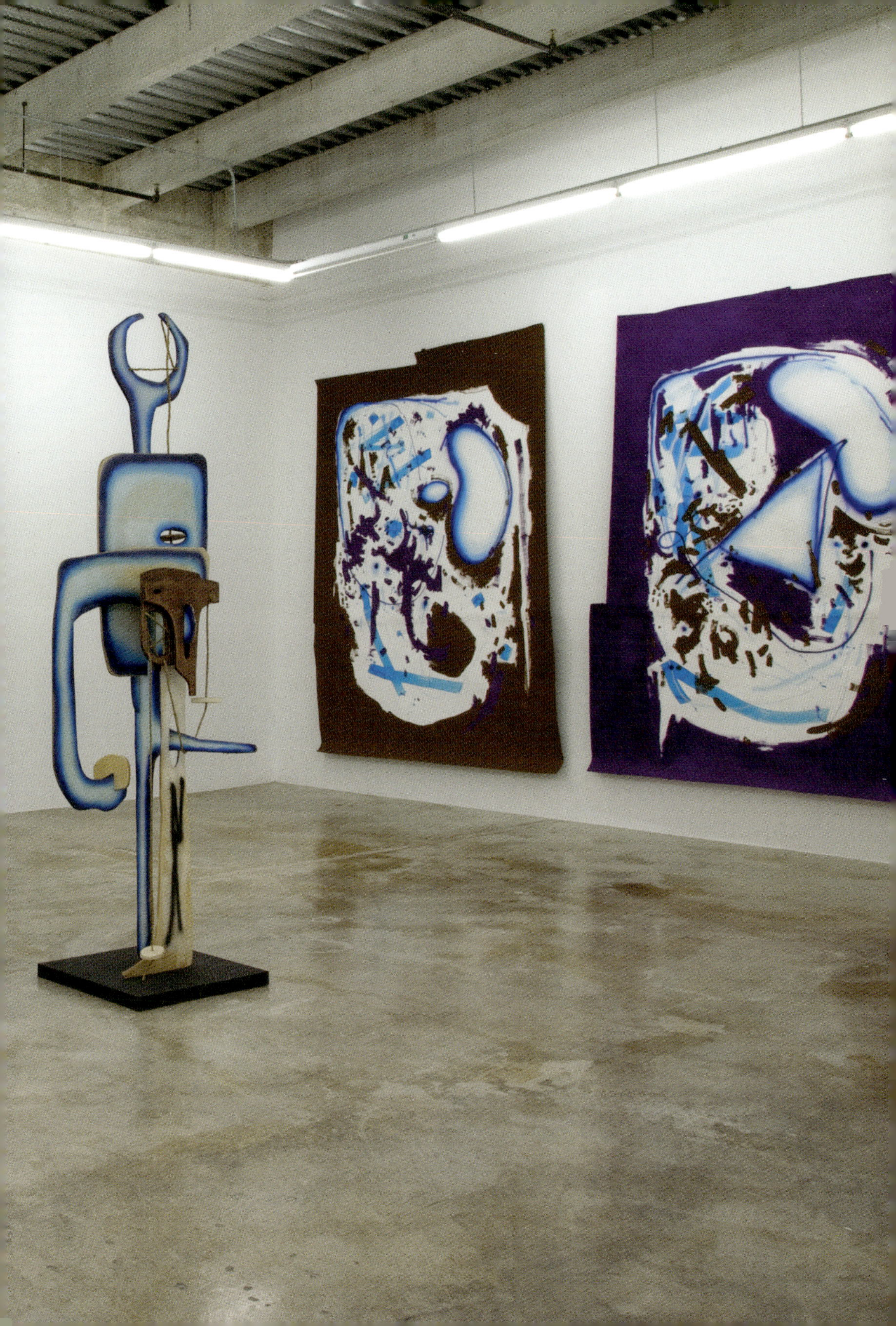

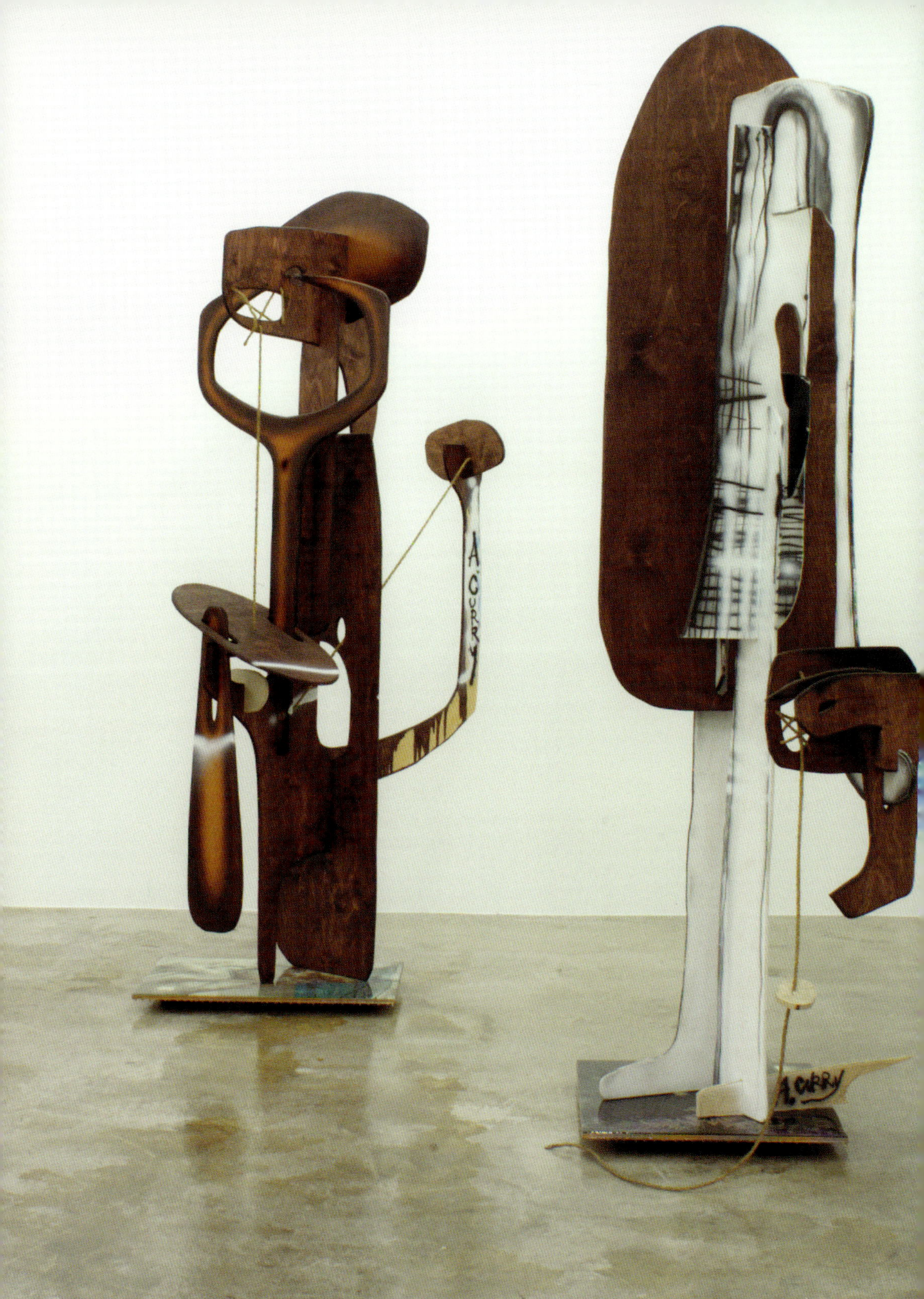

INSTALLATION VIEW: AARON CURRY

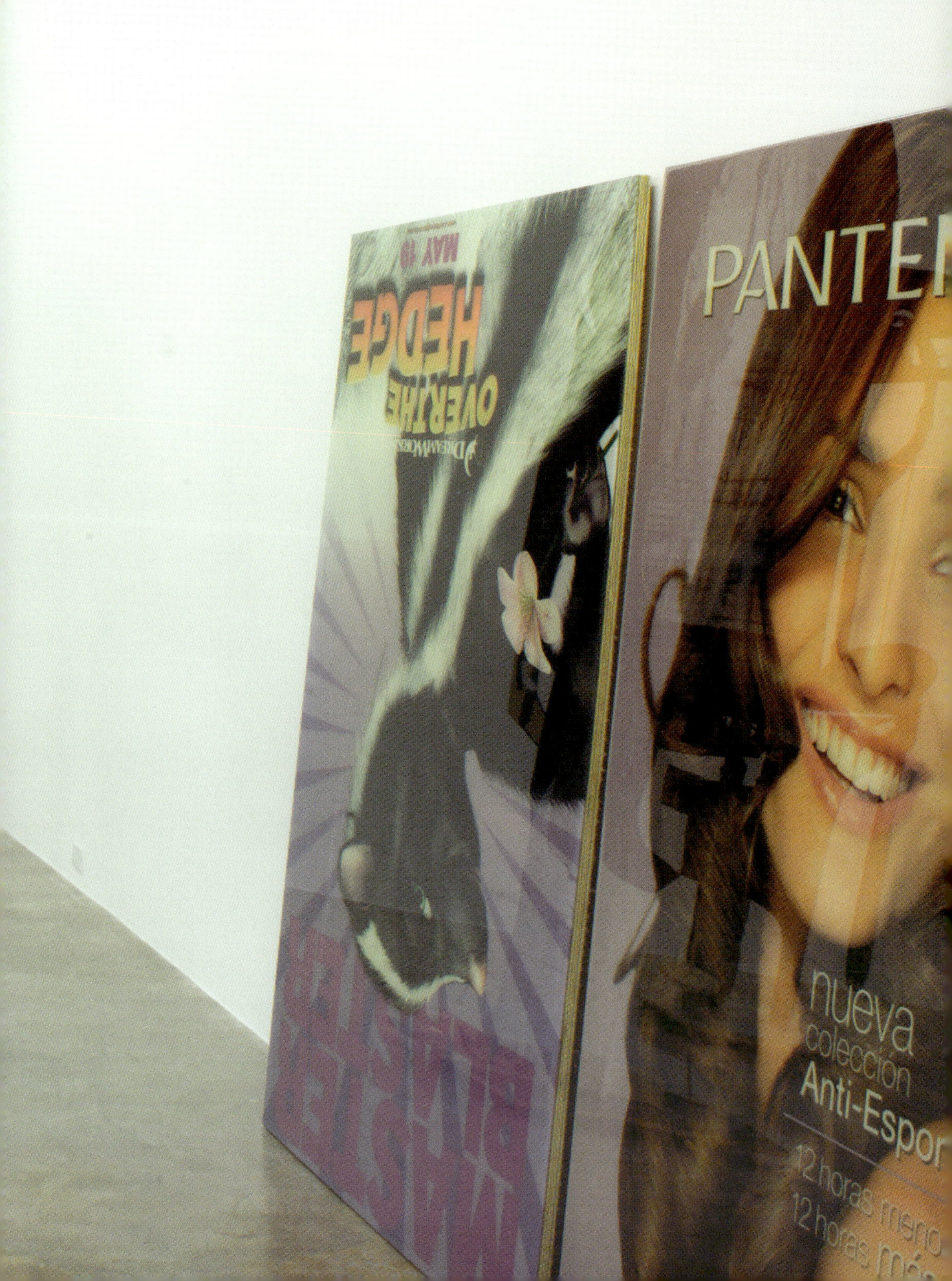
MAY 19
OVER THE
HEDGE
nueva
colección

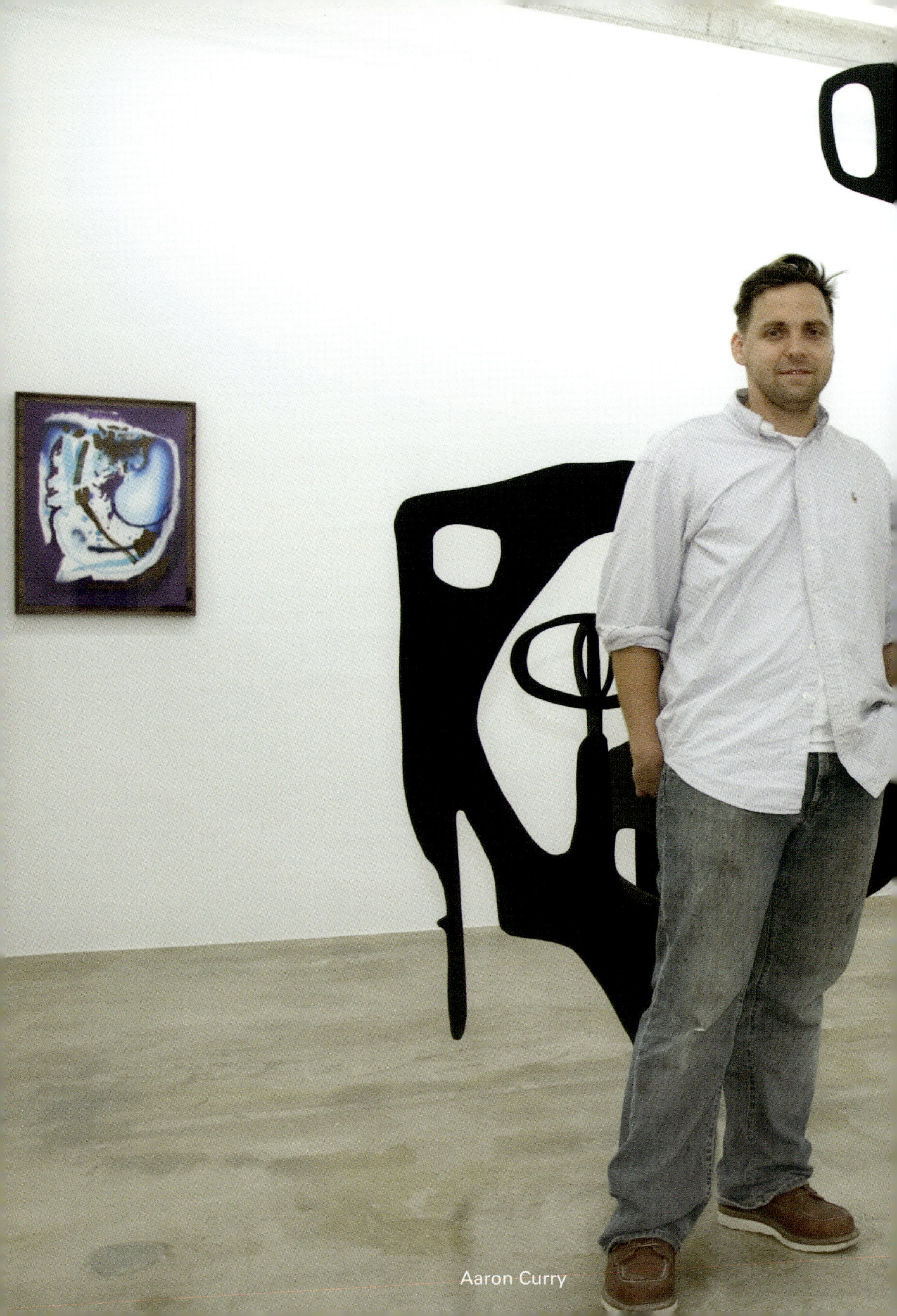

Aaron Curry

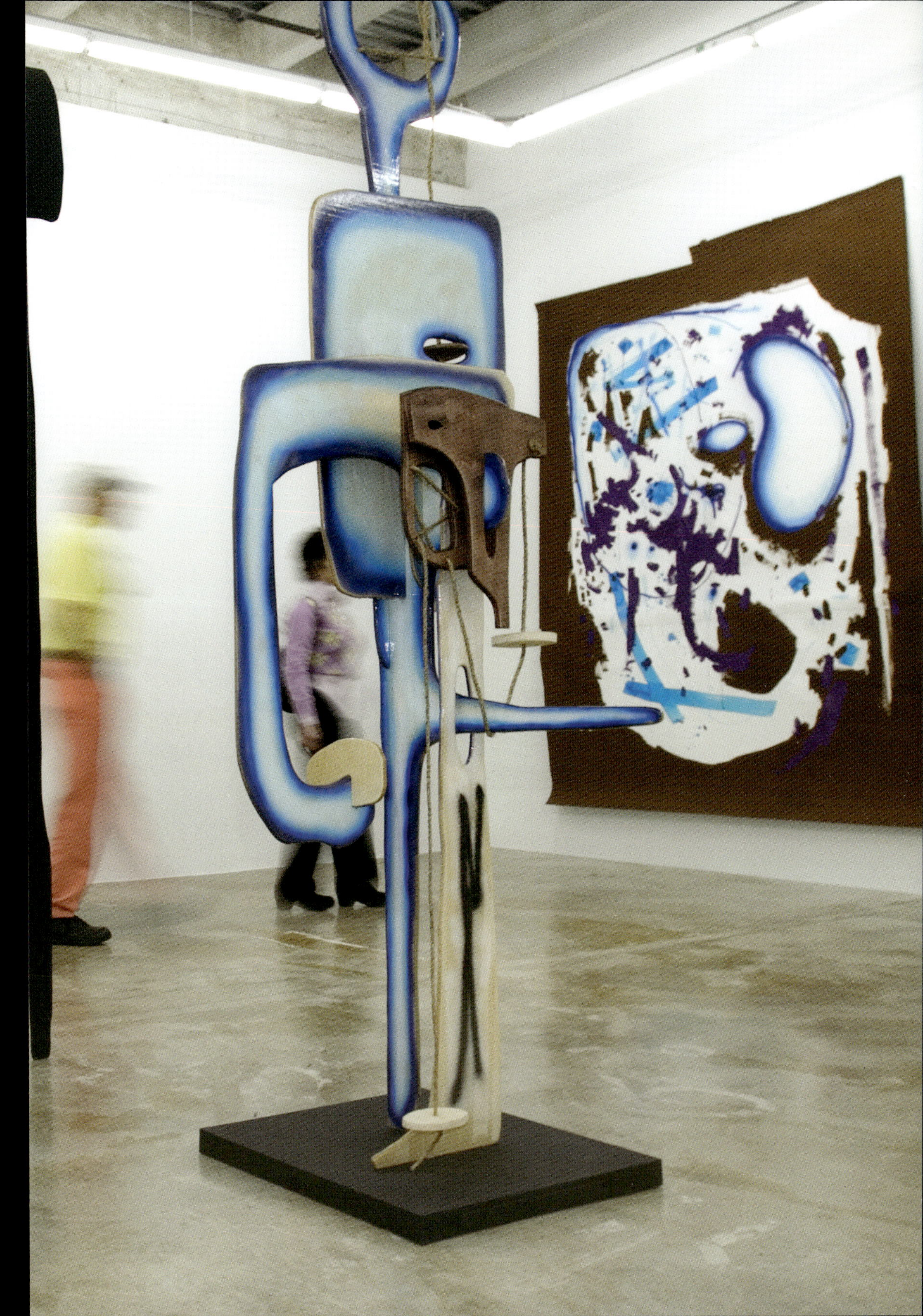

GALLERY 16

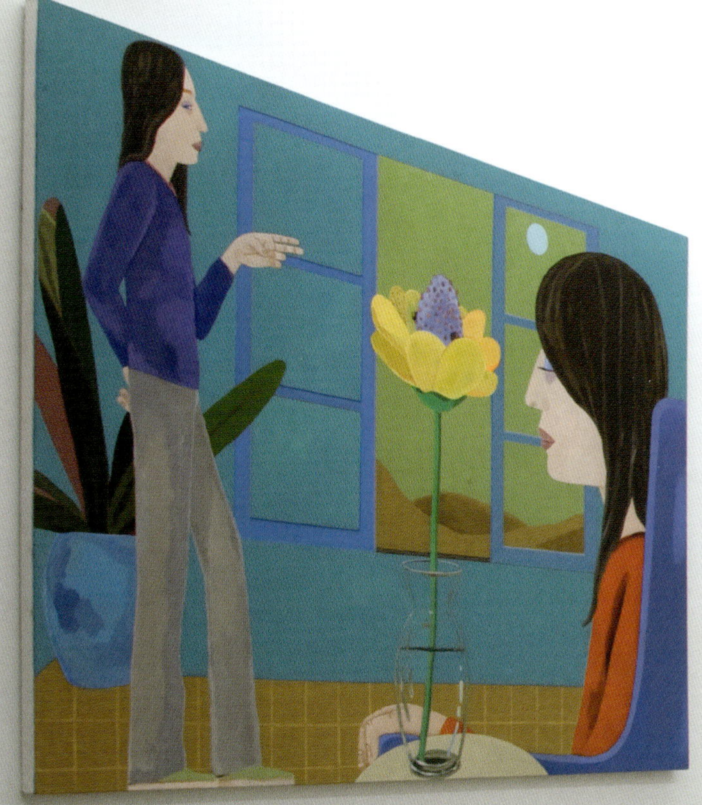

INSTALLATION VIEW:
BRIAN CALVIN AND YUTAKA SONE

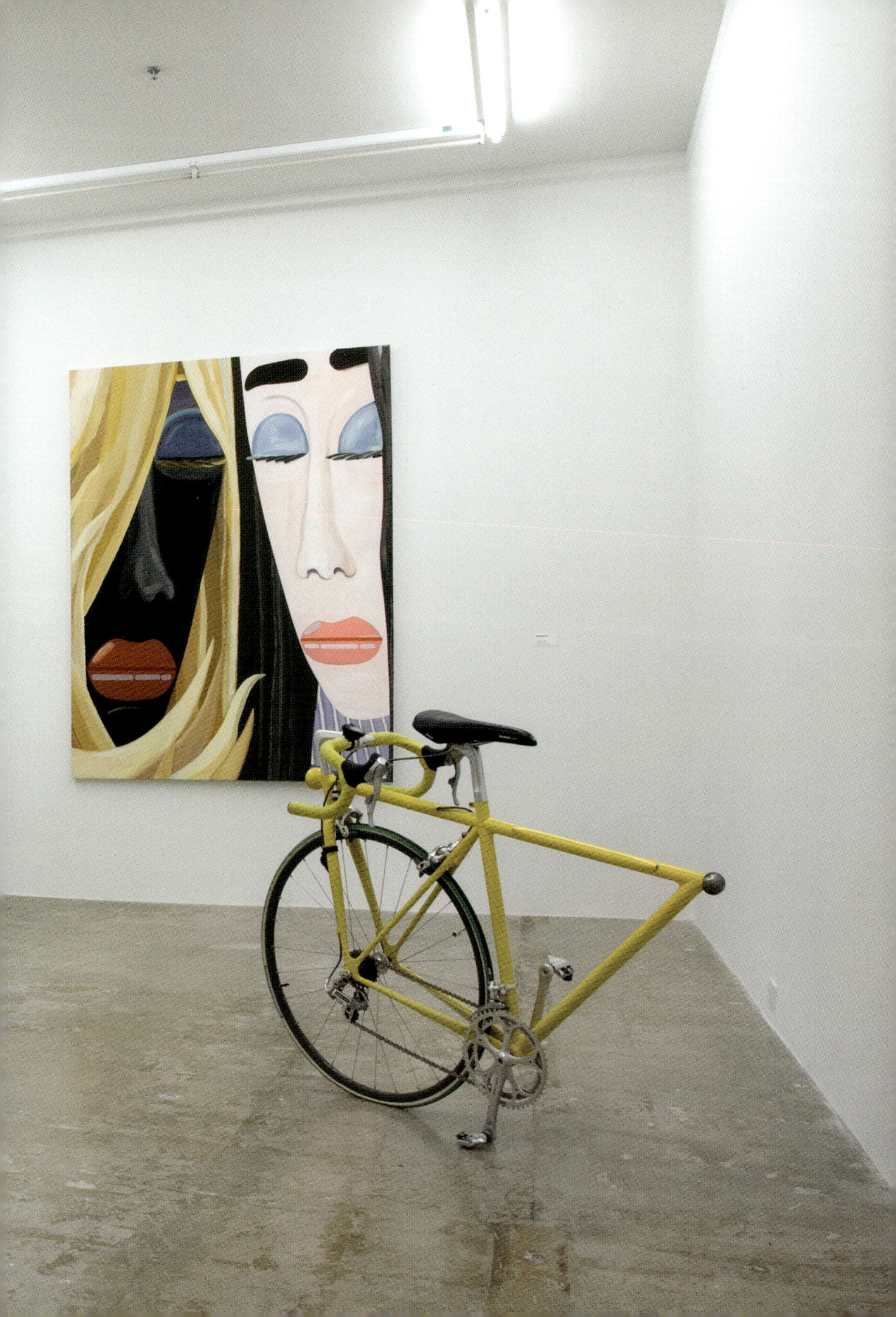

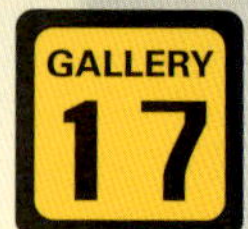

PAUL McCARTHY and MIKE KELLEY

Fresh Acconci (detail), 1995
Fifteen color photographs and video projection with sound, Ed. 5/30
38 x 45 1/2 in. (96.5 x 115.5 cm)

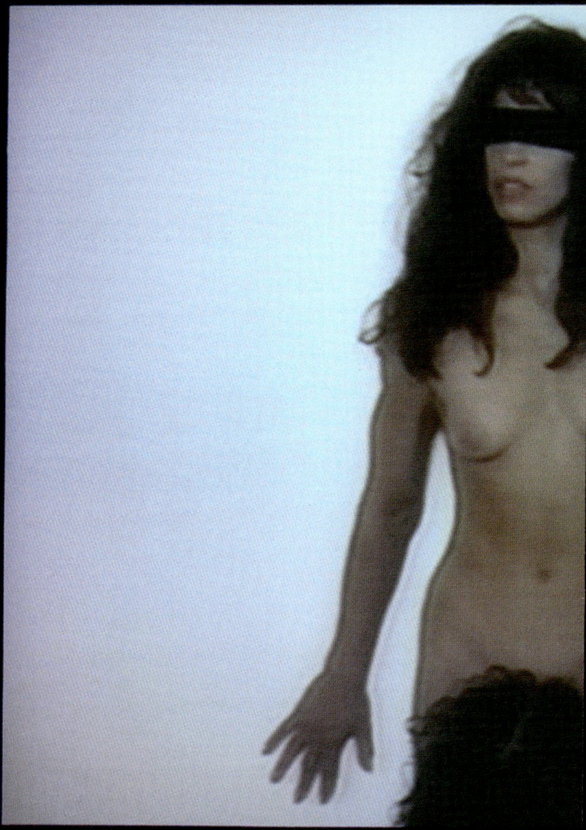

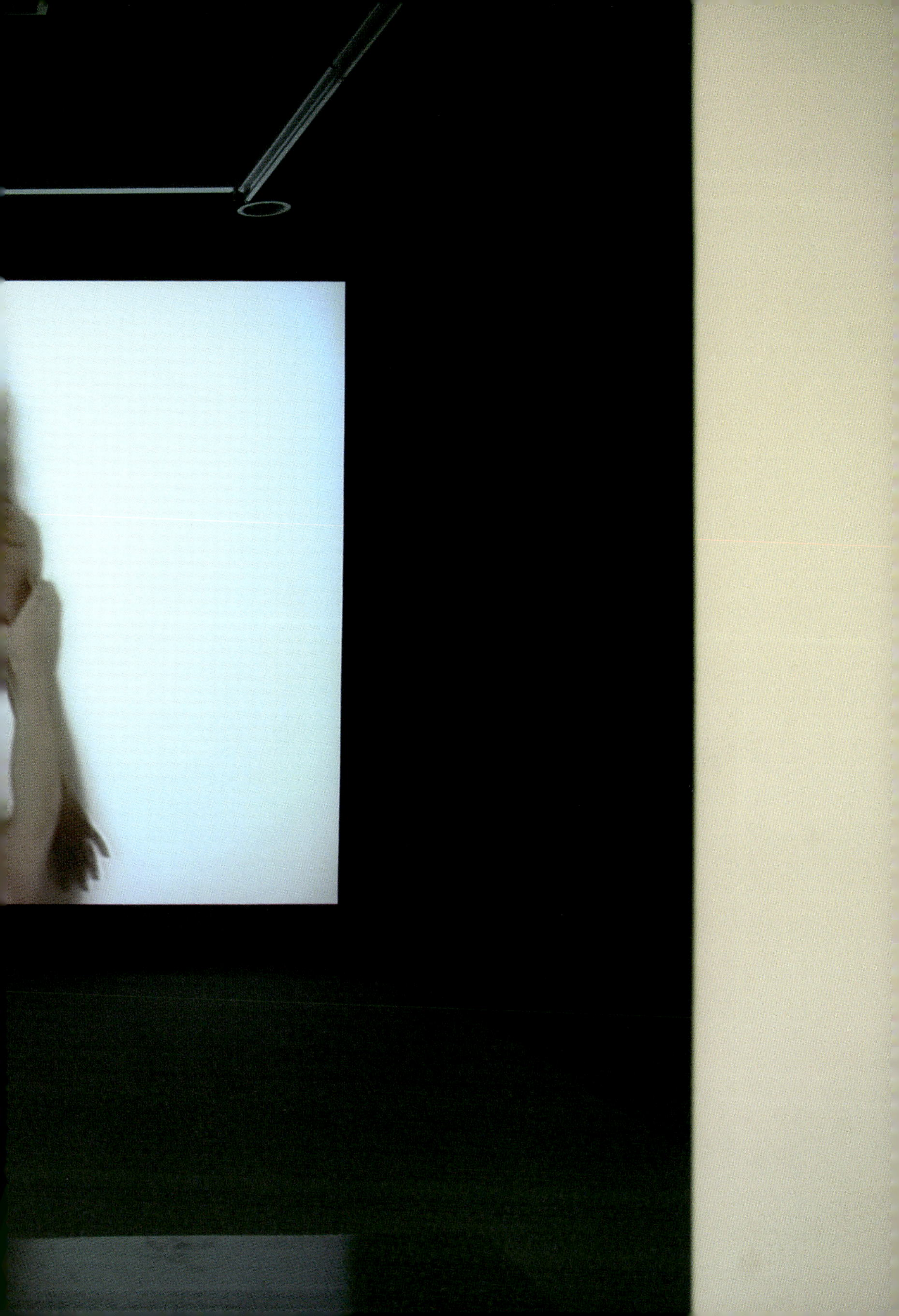

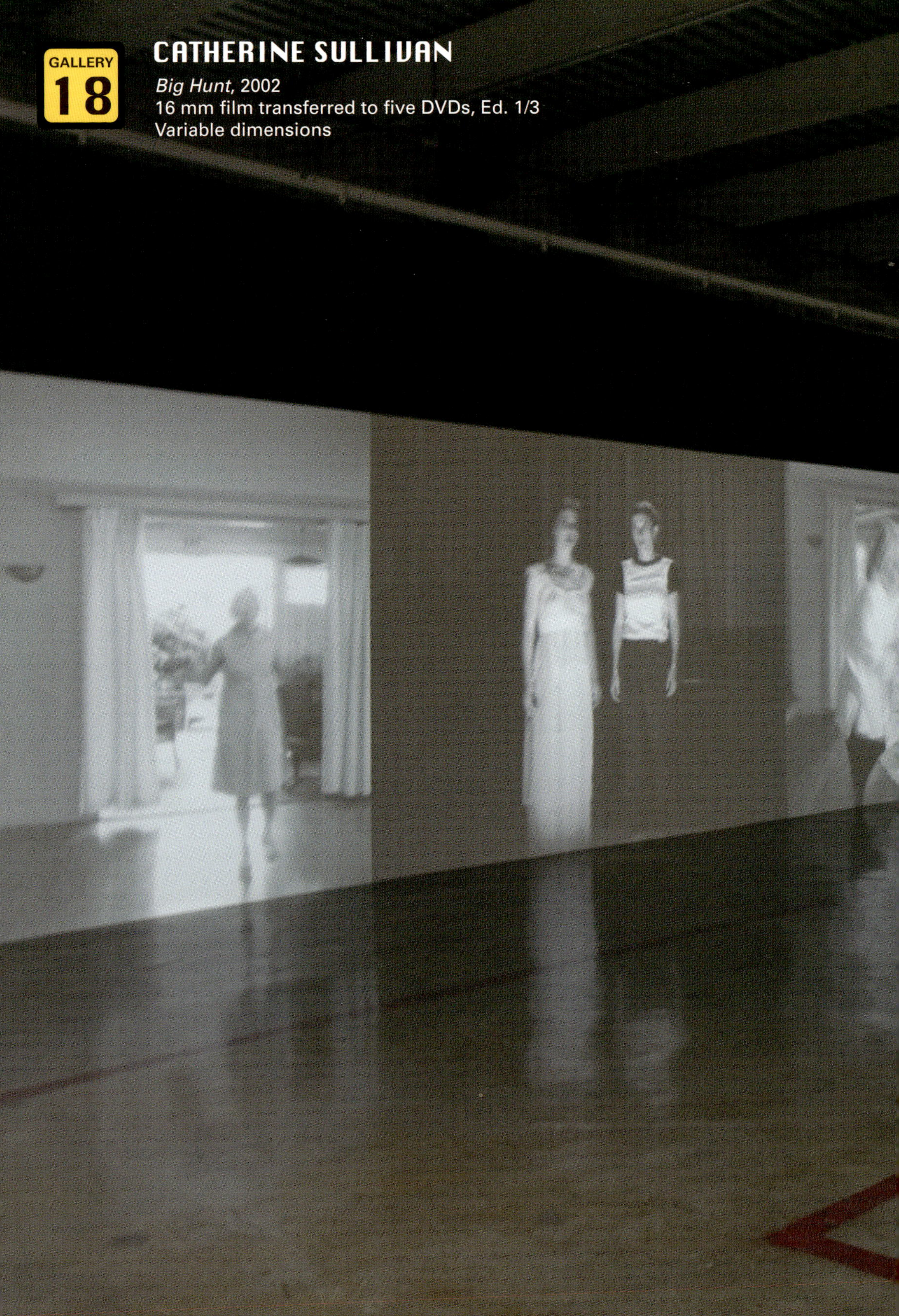

GALLERY 18

CATHERINE SULLIVAN

Big Hunt, 2002
16 mm film transferred to five DVDs, Ed. 1/3
Variable dimensions

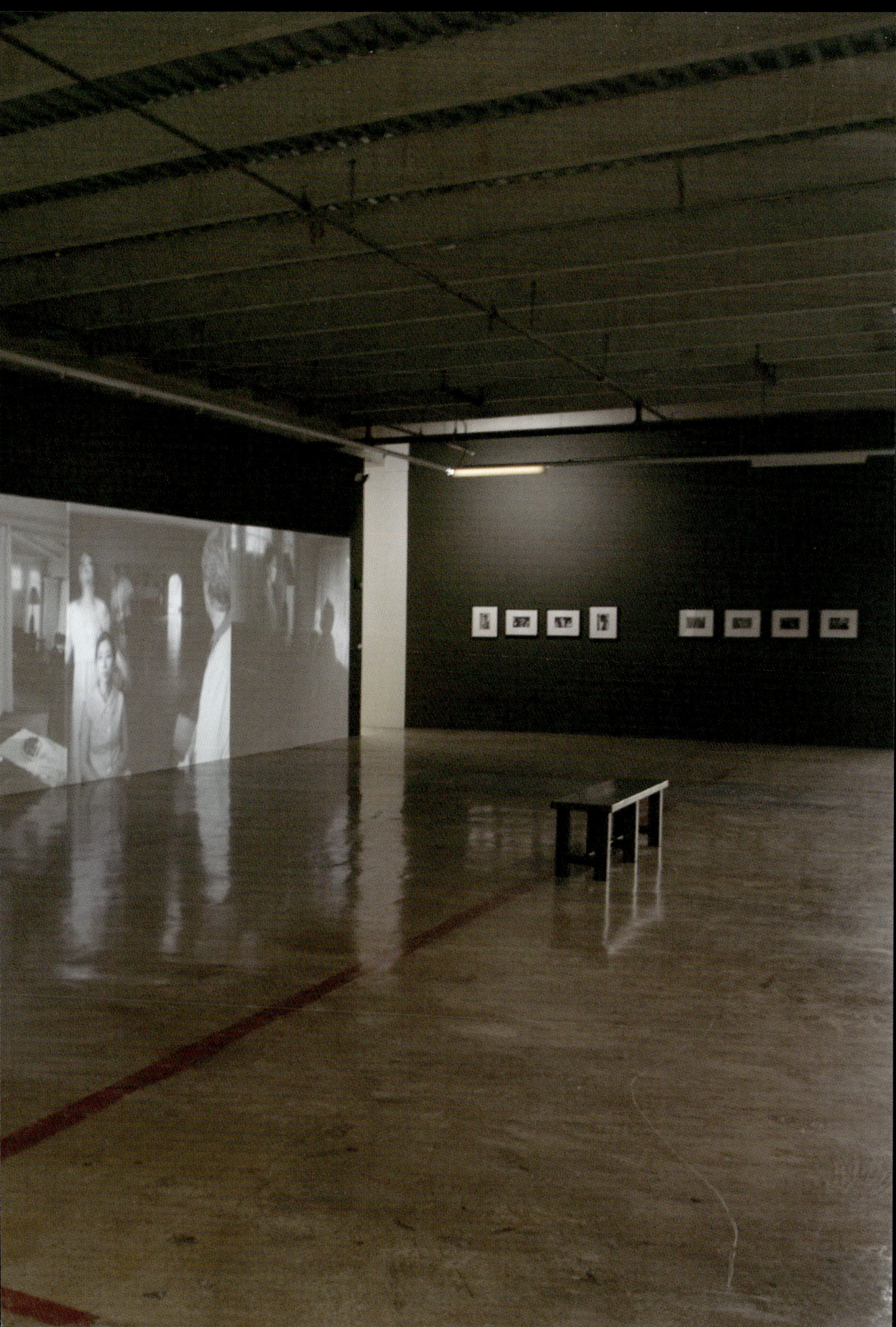

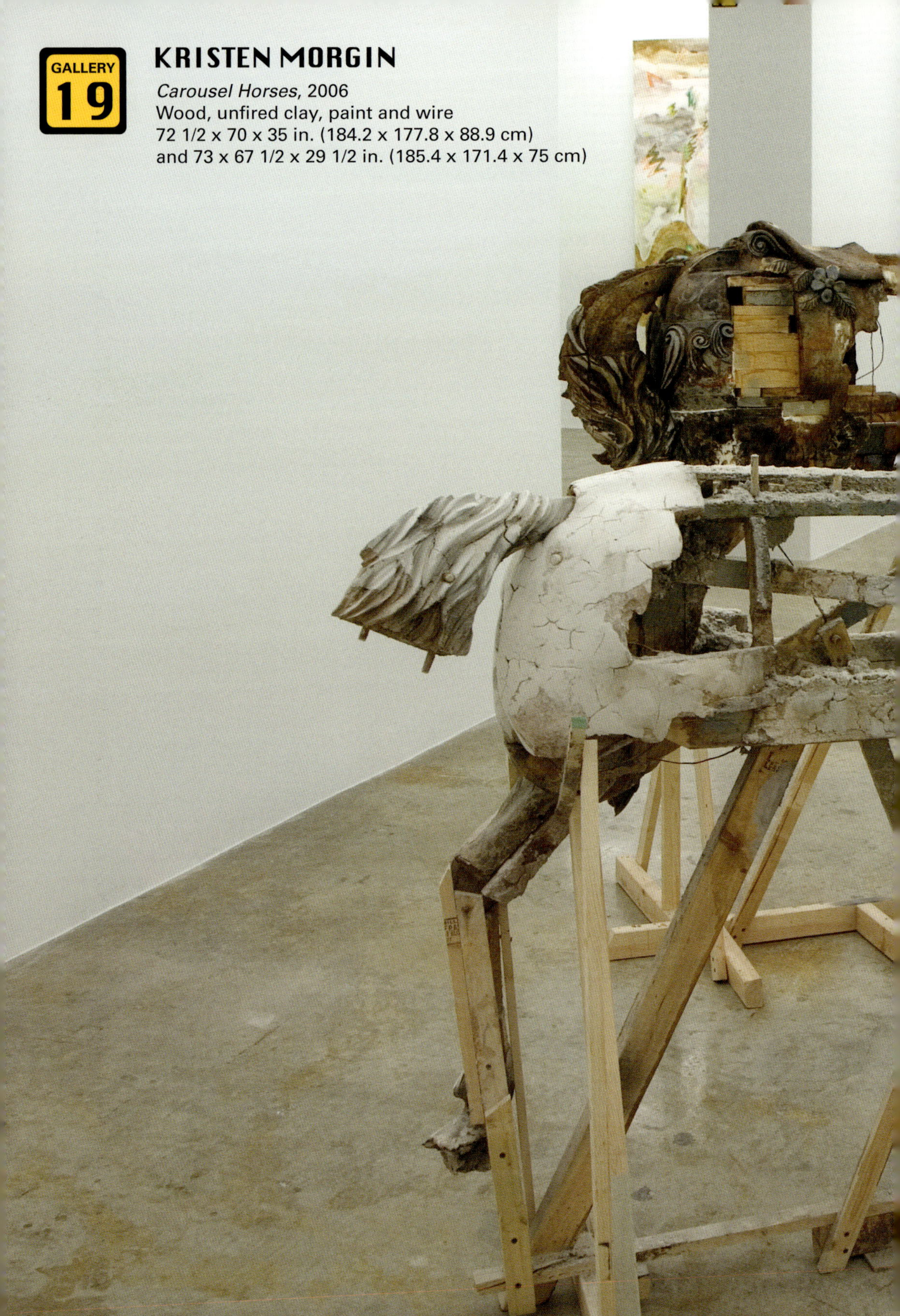

GALLERY 19

KRISTEN MORGIN

Carousel Horses, 2006
Wood, unfired clay, paint and wire
72 1/2 x 70 x 35 in. (184.2 x 177.8 x 88.9 cm)
and 73 x 67 1/2 x 29 1/2 in. (185.4 x 171.4 x 75 cm)

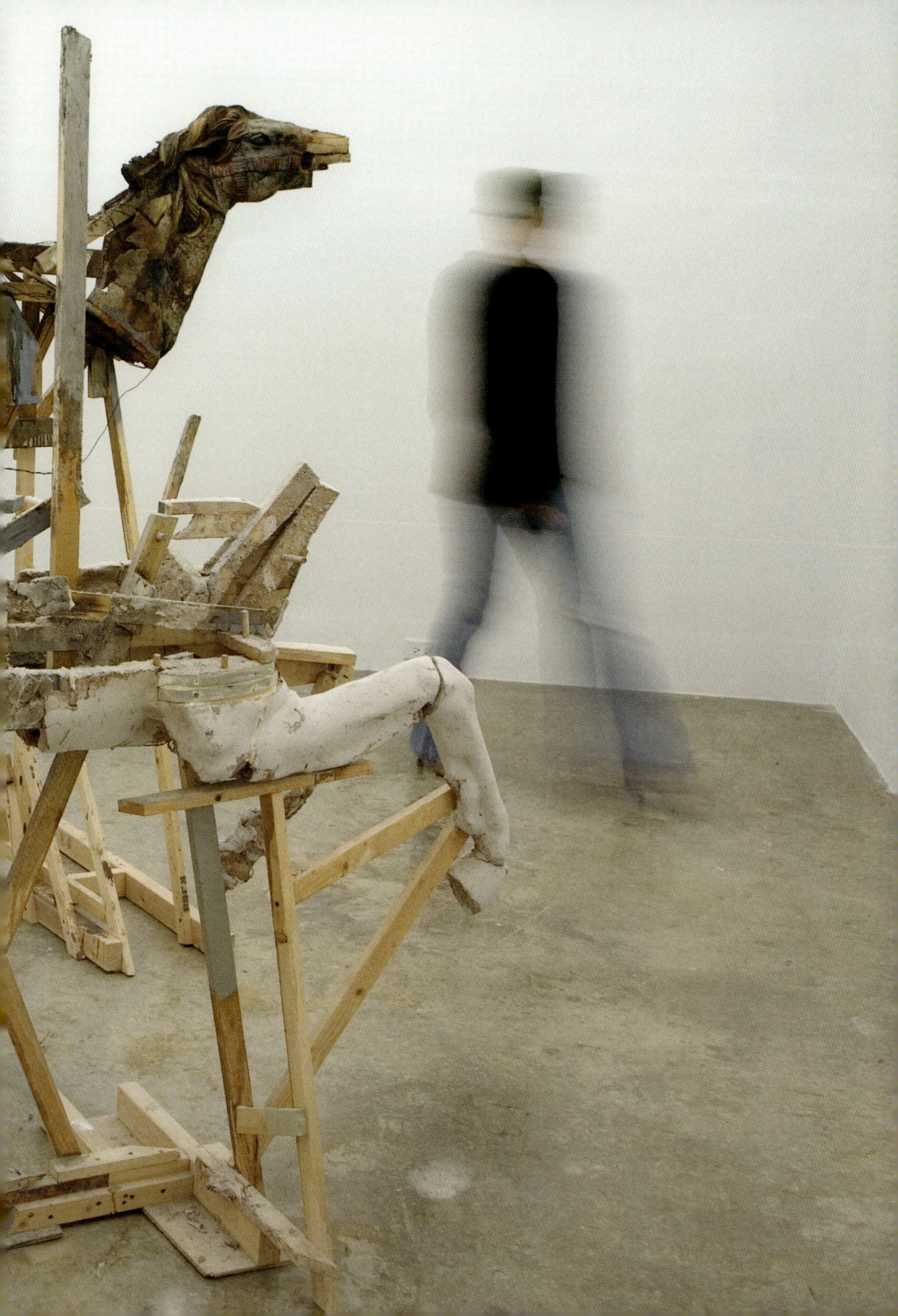

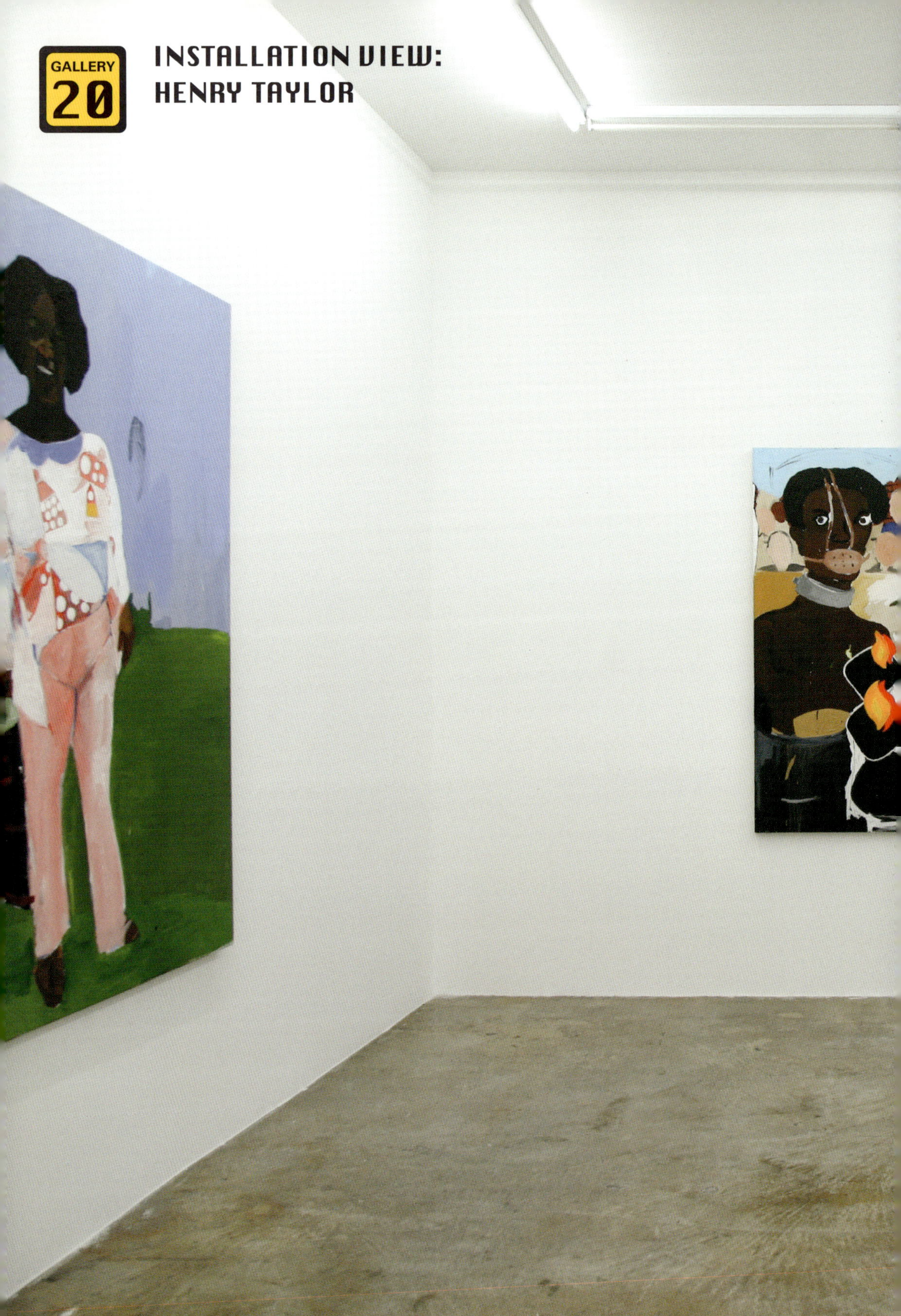
GALLERY
20
INSTALLATION VIEW:
HENRY TAYLOR

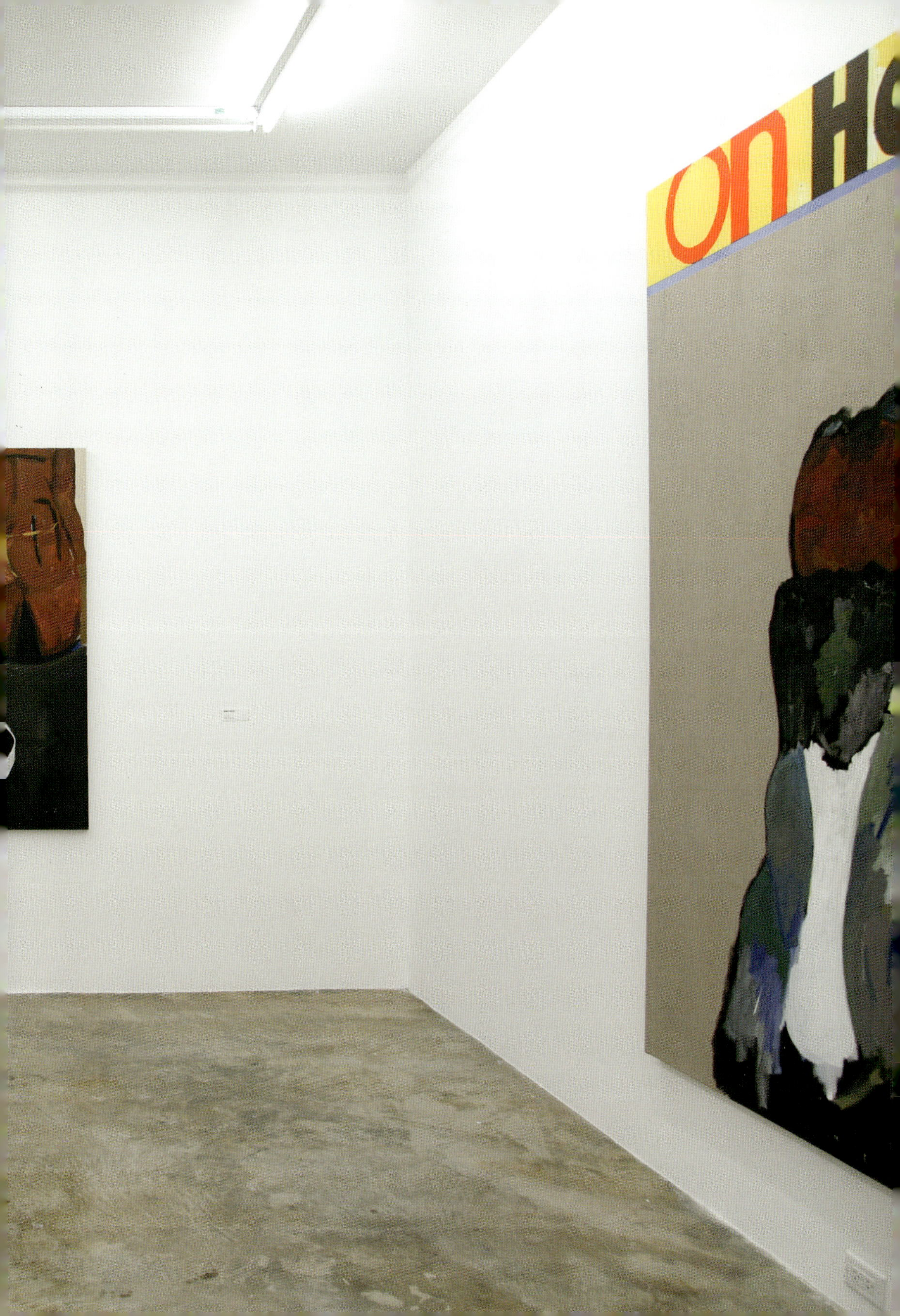
on

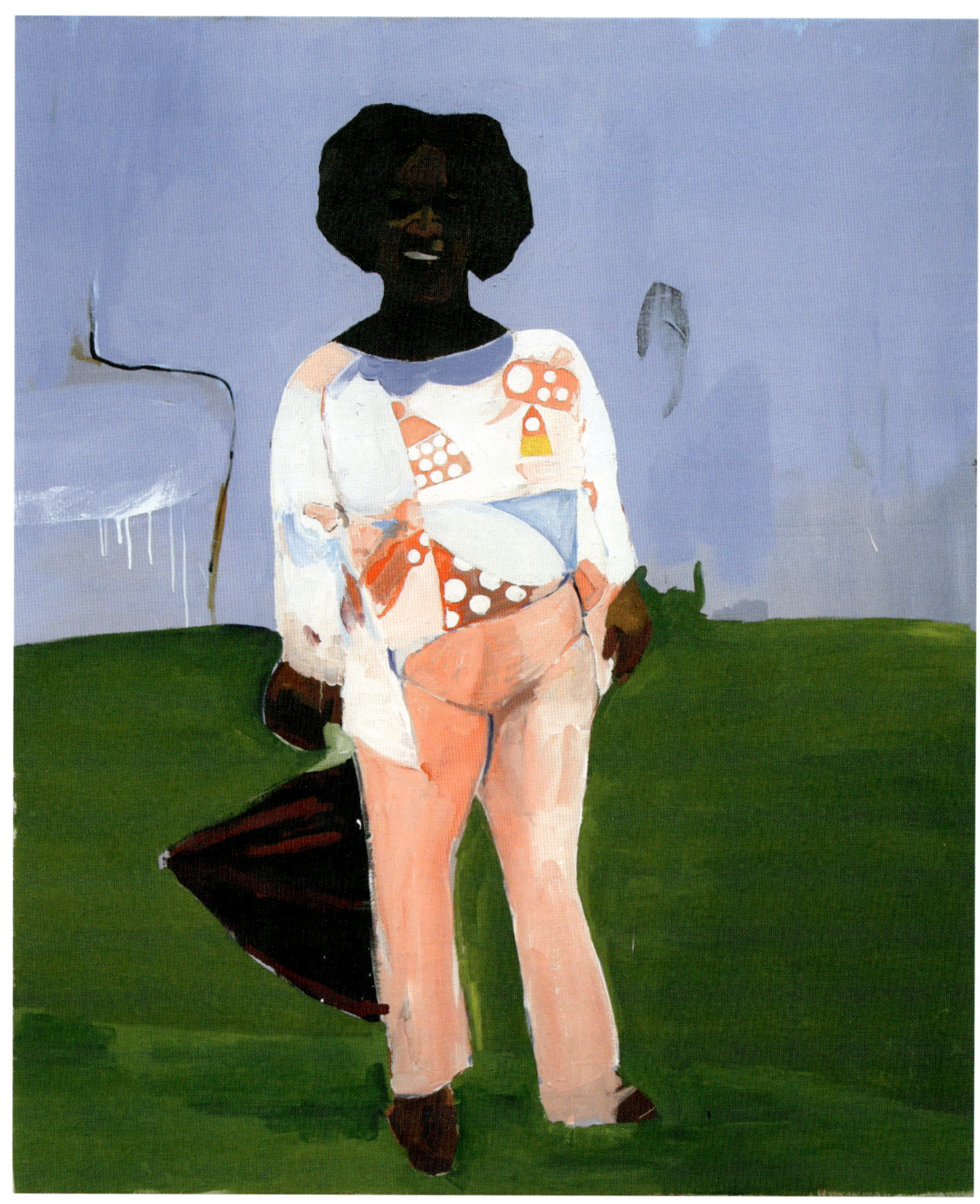

Henry Taylor
Watts County, 2004
Acrylic on canvas
76 x 61 3/4 in. (193 x 157 cm)

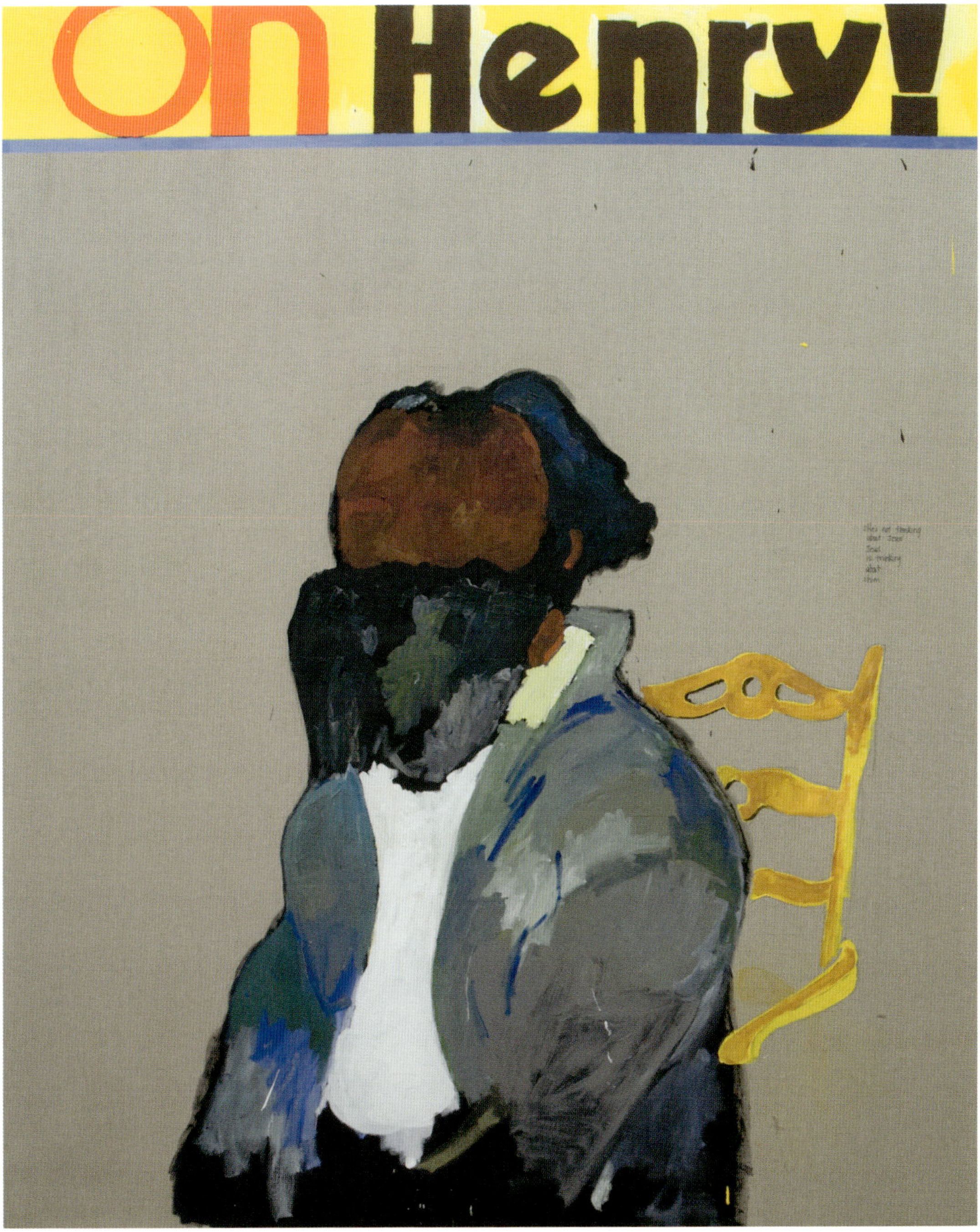

Henry Taylor
On Henry, 2006
Acrylic on canvas
96 3/4 x 75 in. (245.7 x 190.5 cm)

GALLERY 21

INSTALLATION VIEW: RICKY SWALLOW

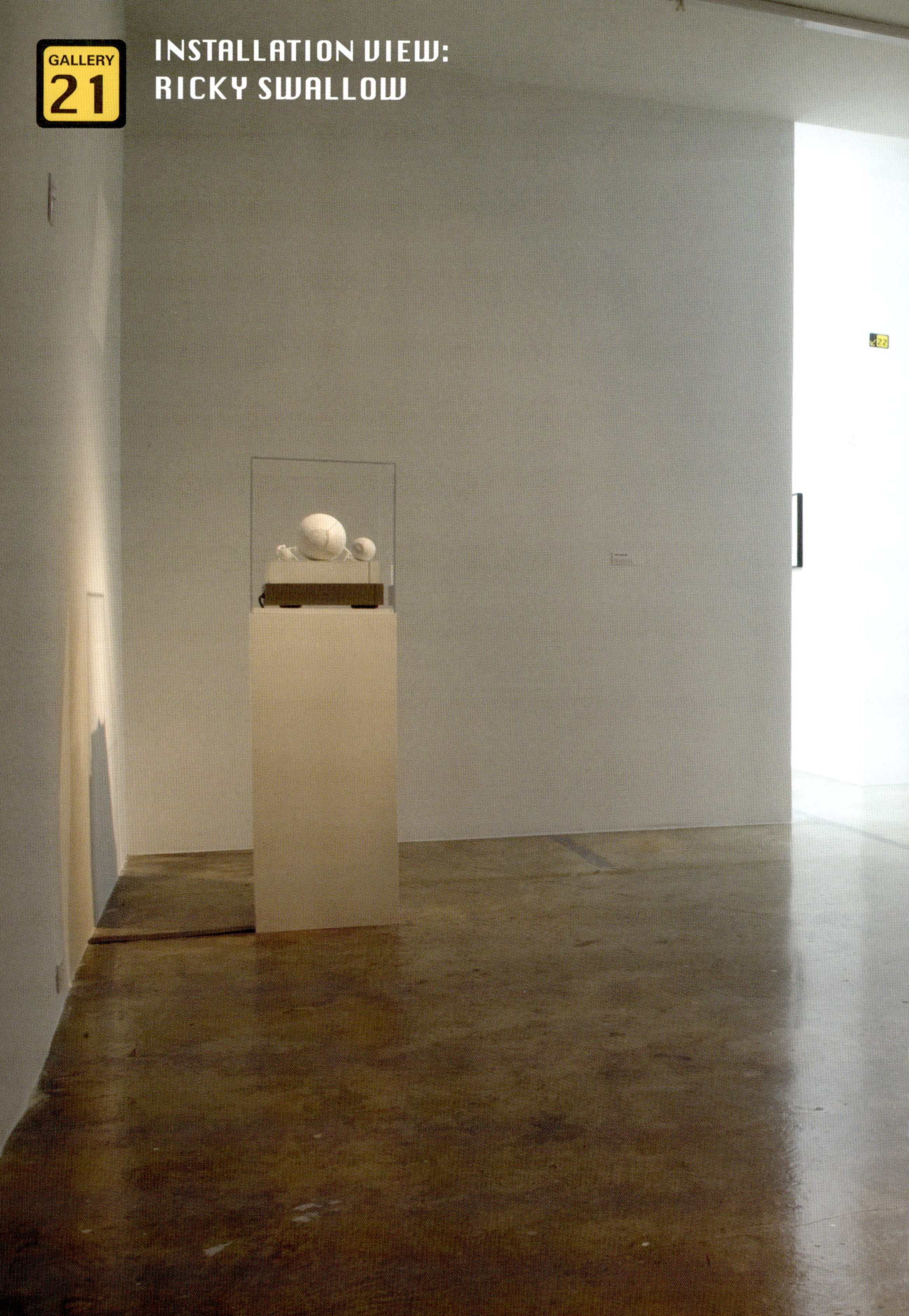

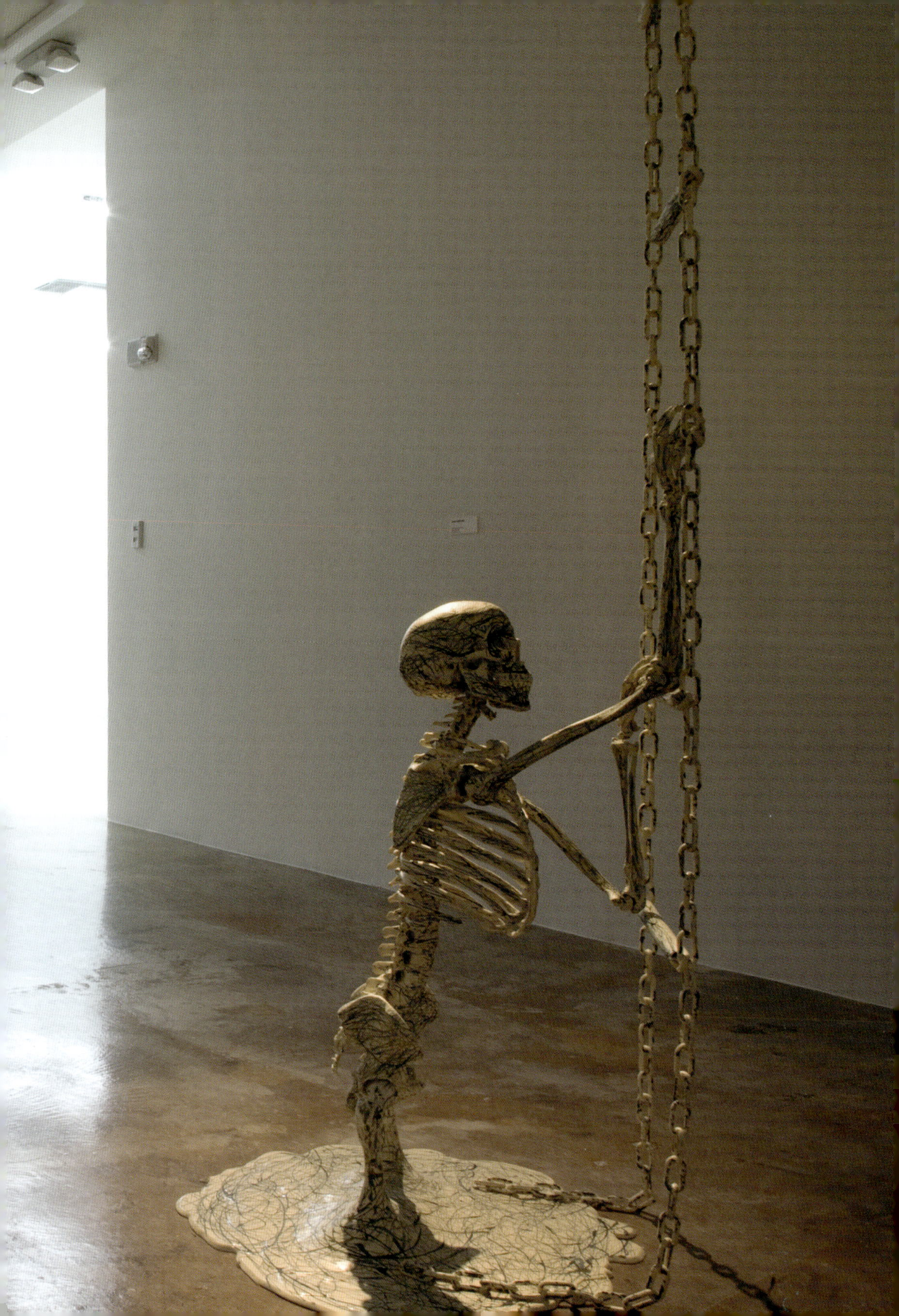

GALLERY 22

INSTALLATION VIEW: LAURA OWENS AND JIM SHAW

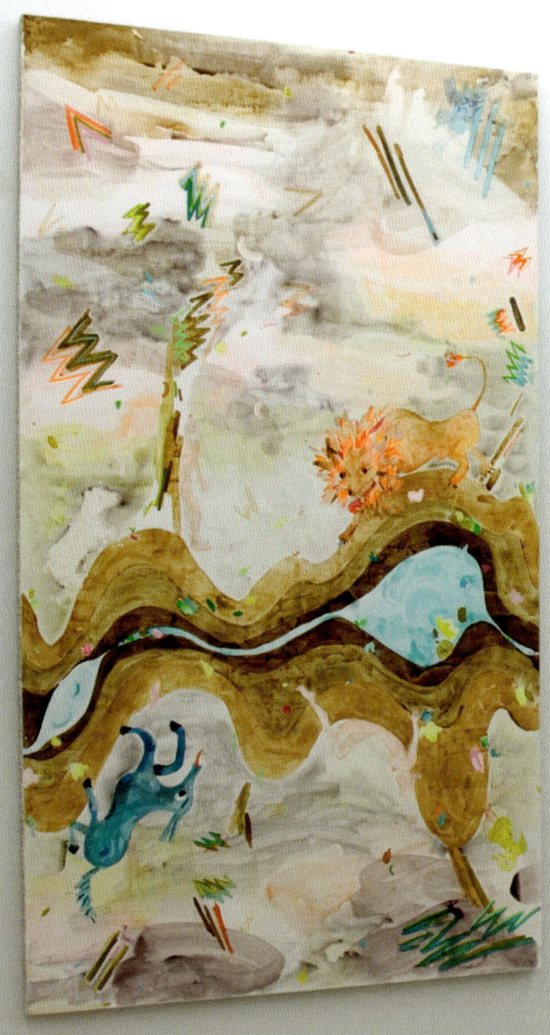

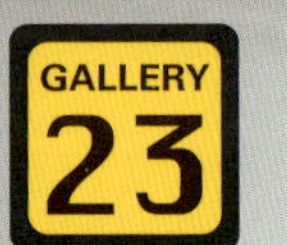

INSTALLATION VIEW:
KAZ OSHIRO AND MARK GROTJAHN

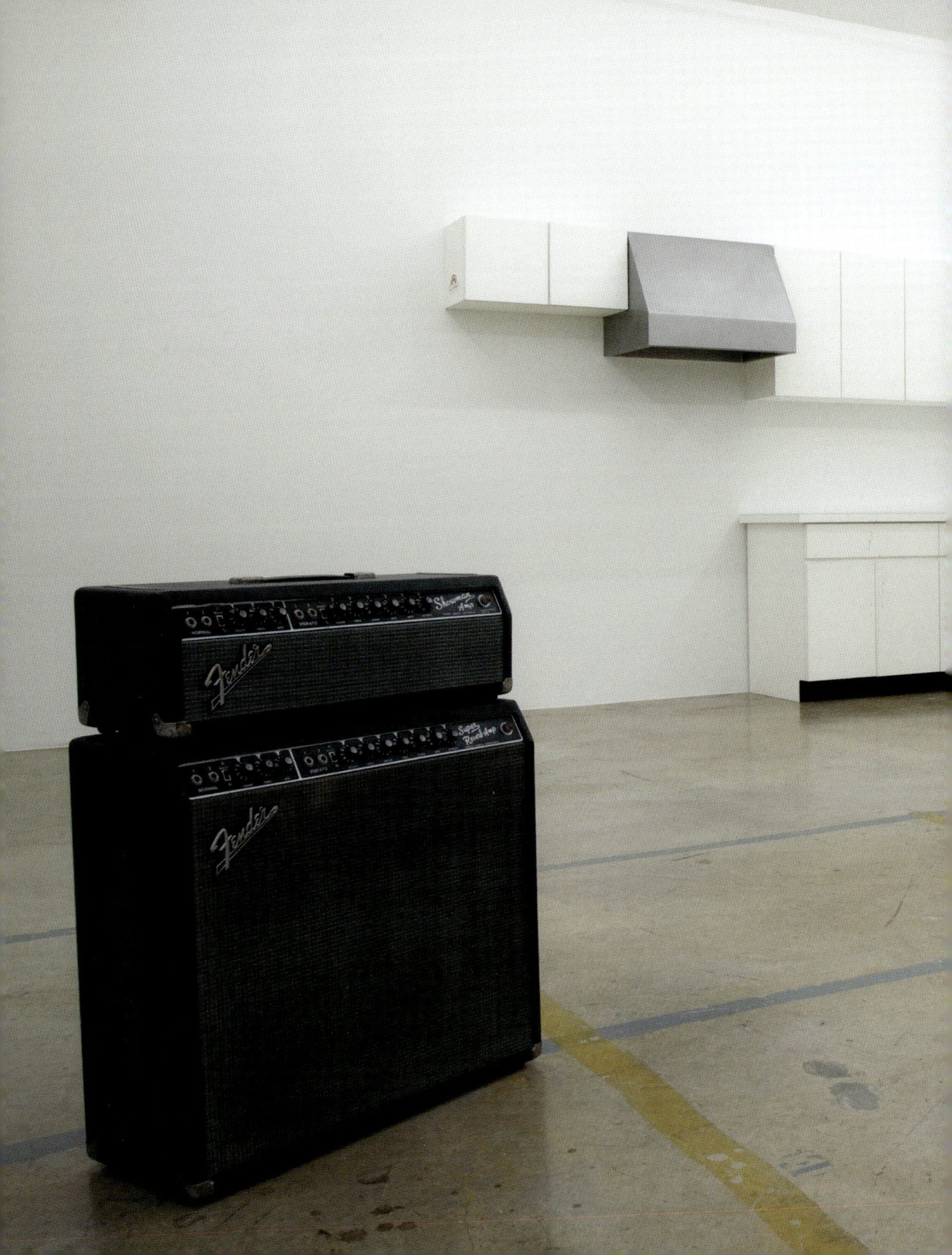

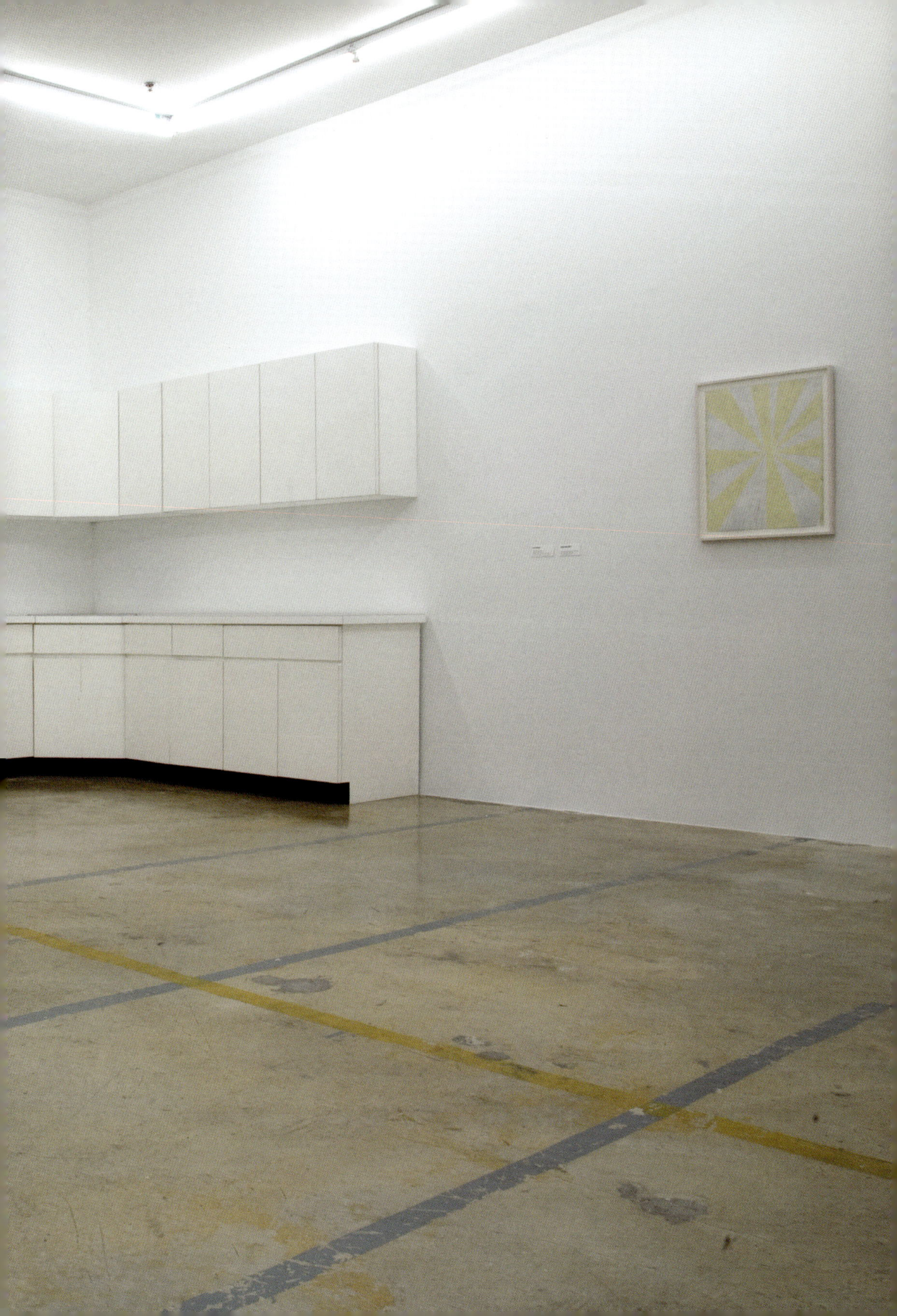

GALLERY 24

INSTALLATION VIEW:
RY ROCKLEN AND VIOLET HOPKINS

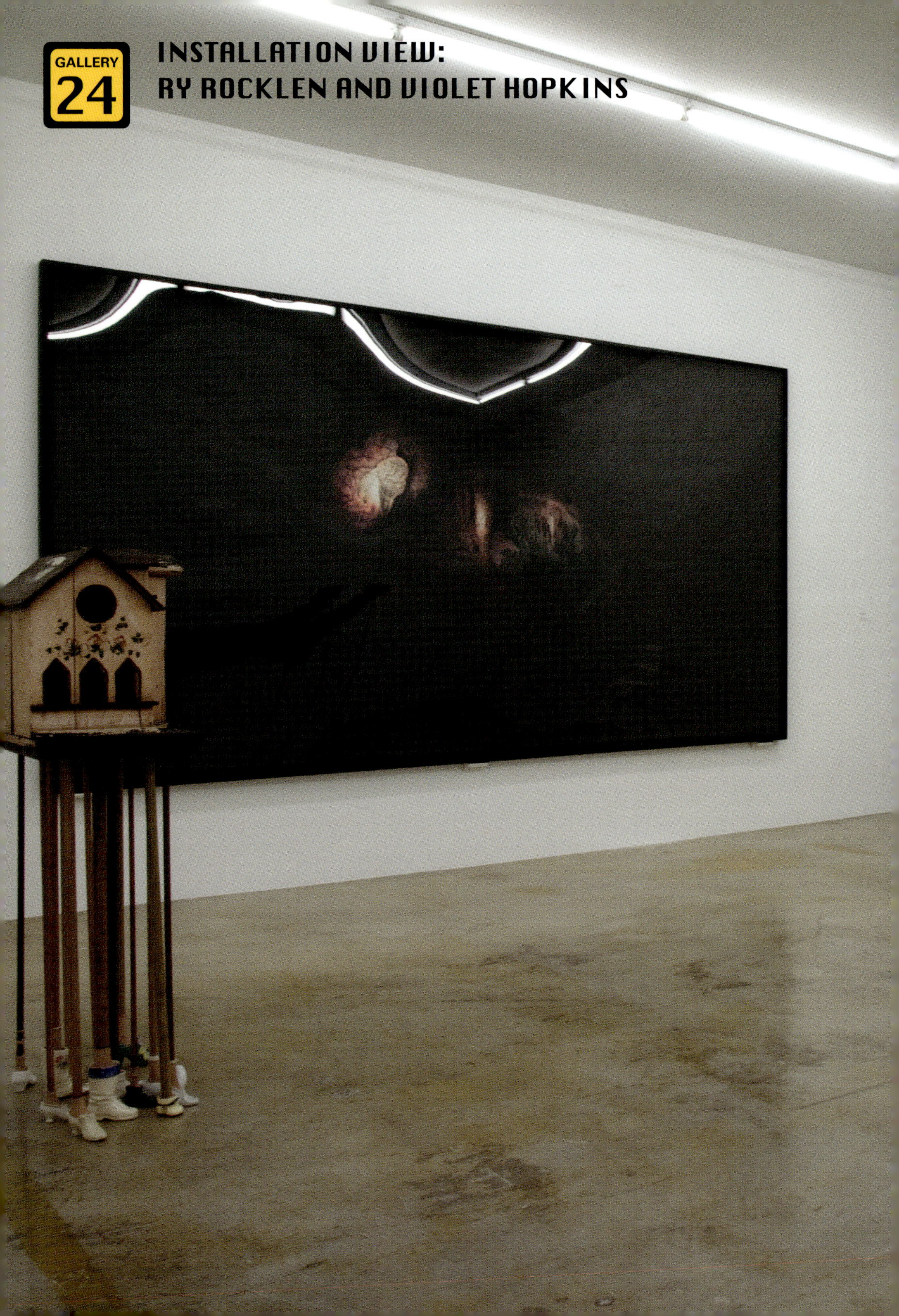

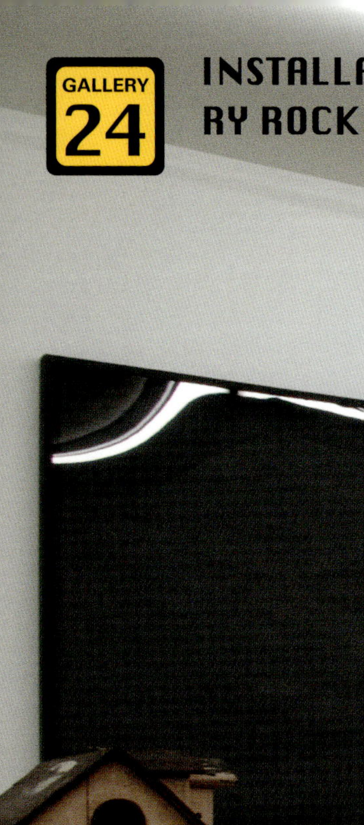

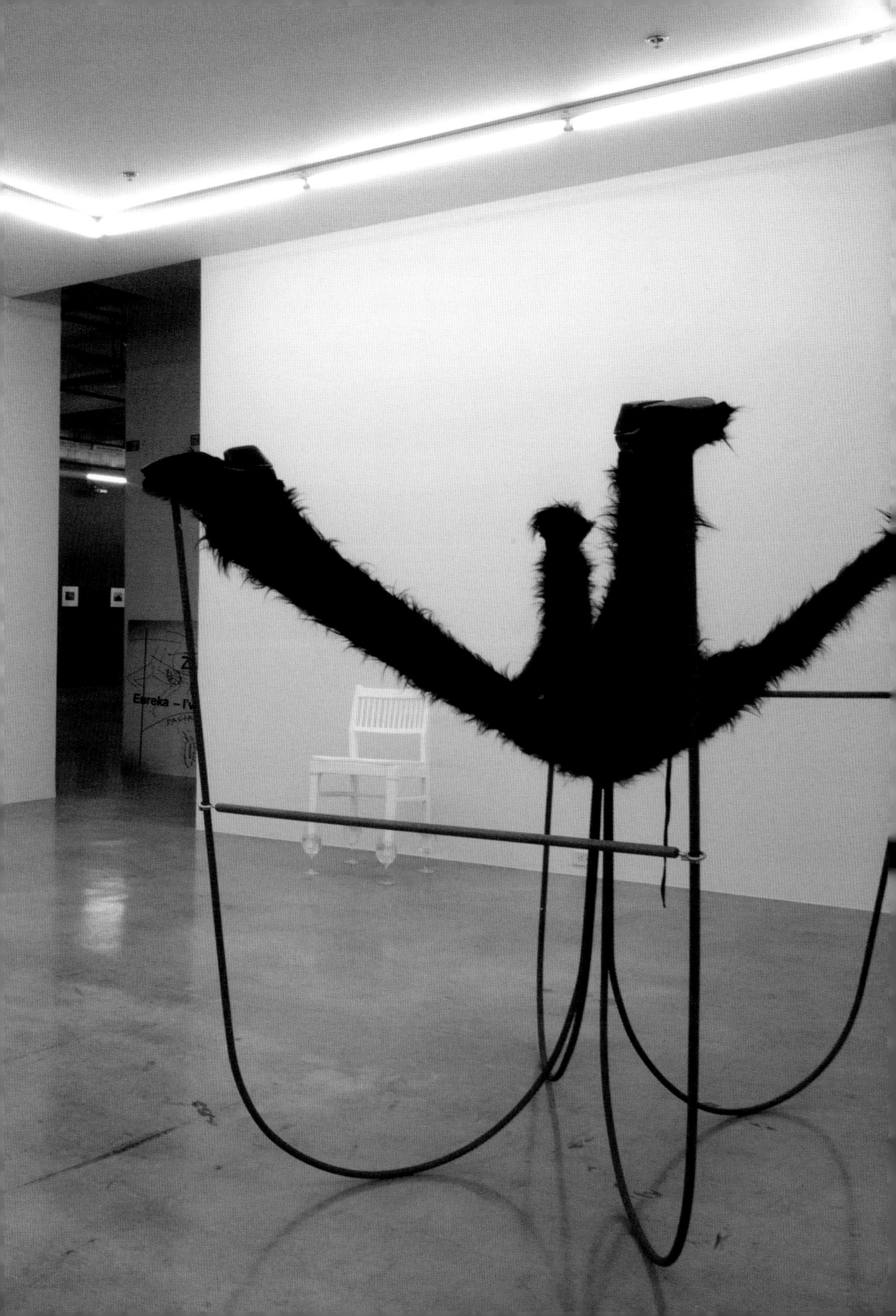
Eureka

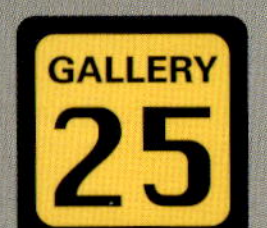

PAUL McCARTHY AND JASON RHOADES

Videos with sound and elements from *Proppposition*, 1999
Mixed media
Variable dimensions

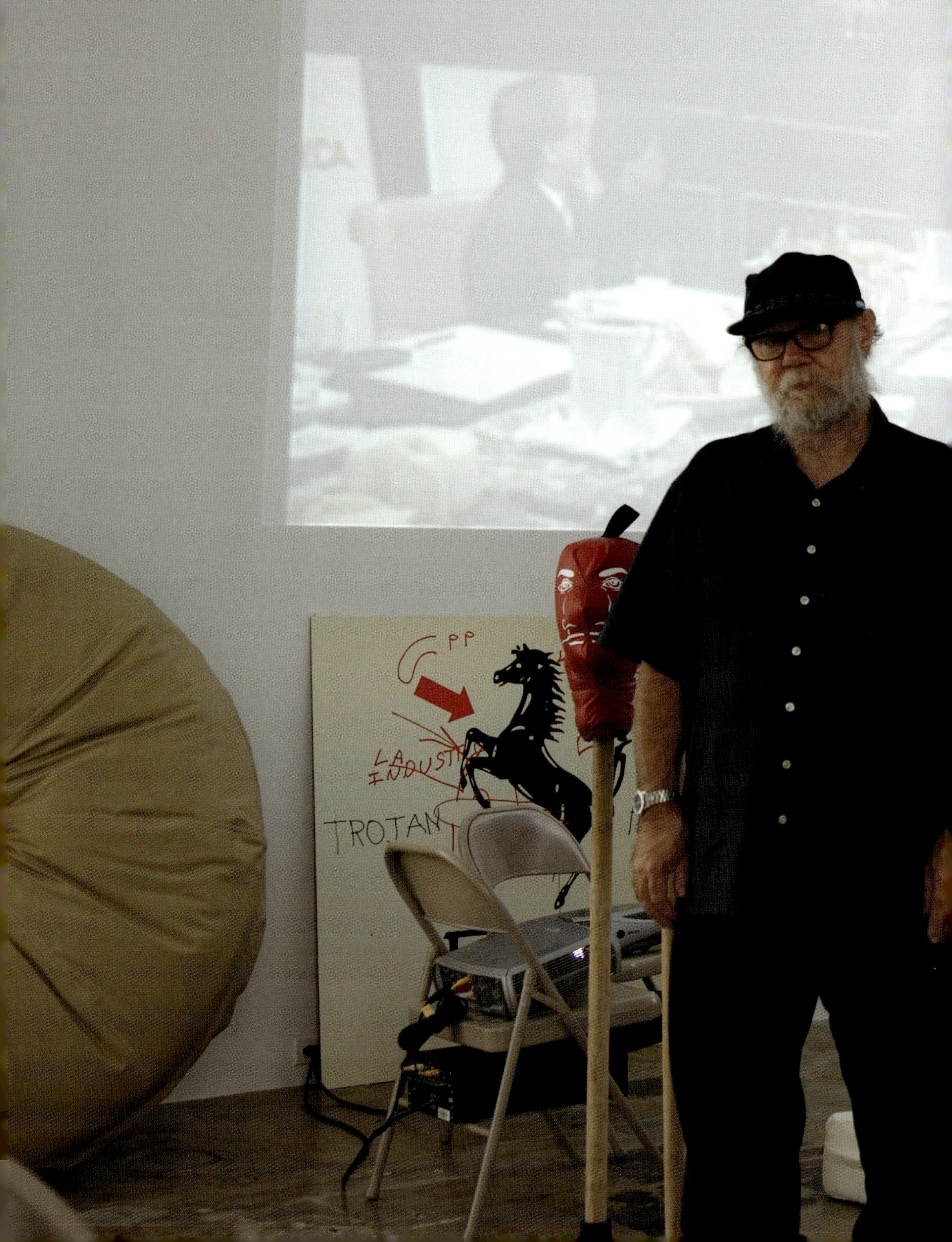

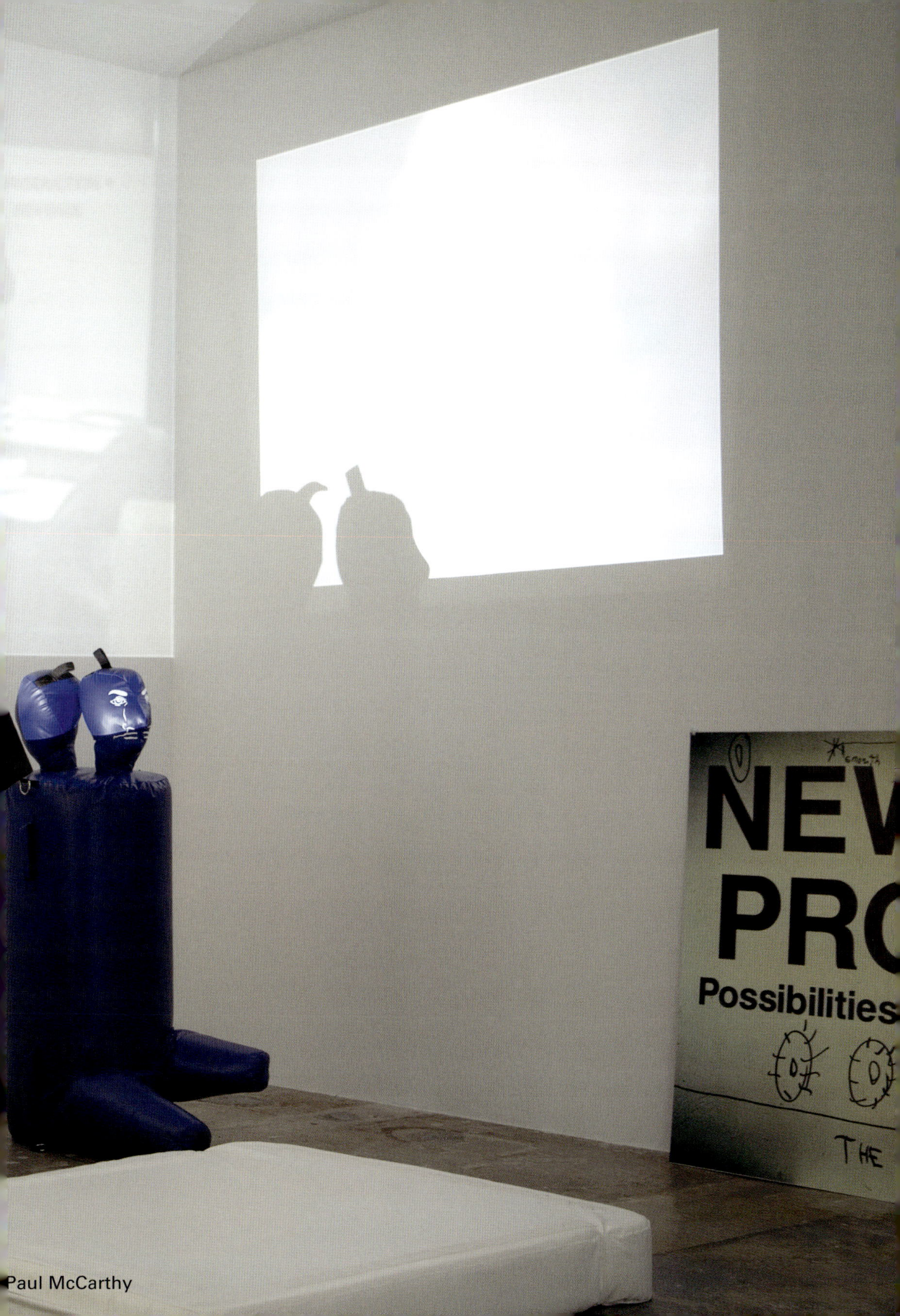

Paul McCarthy

GALLERY 26

INSTALLATION VIEW: JASON MEADOWS AND MARK BRADFORD

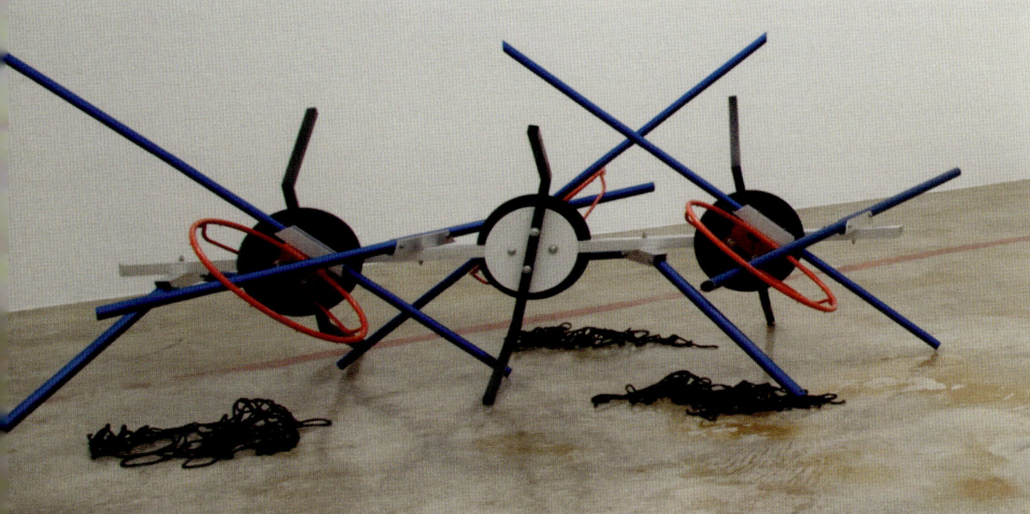

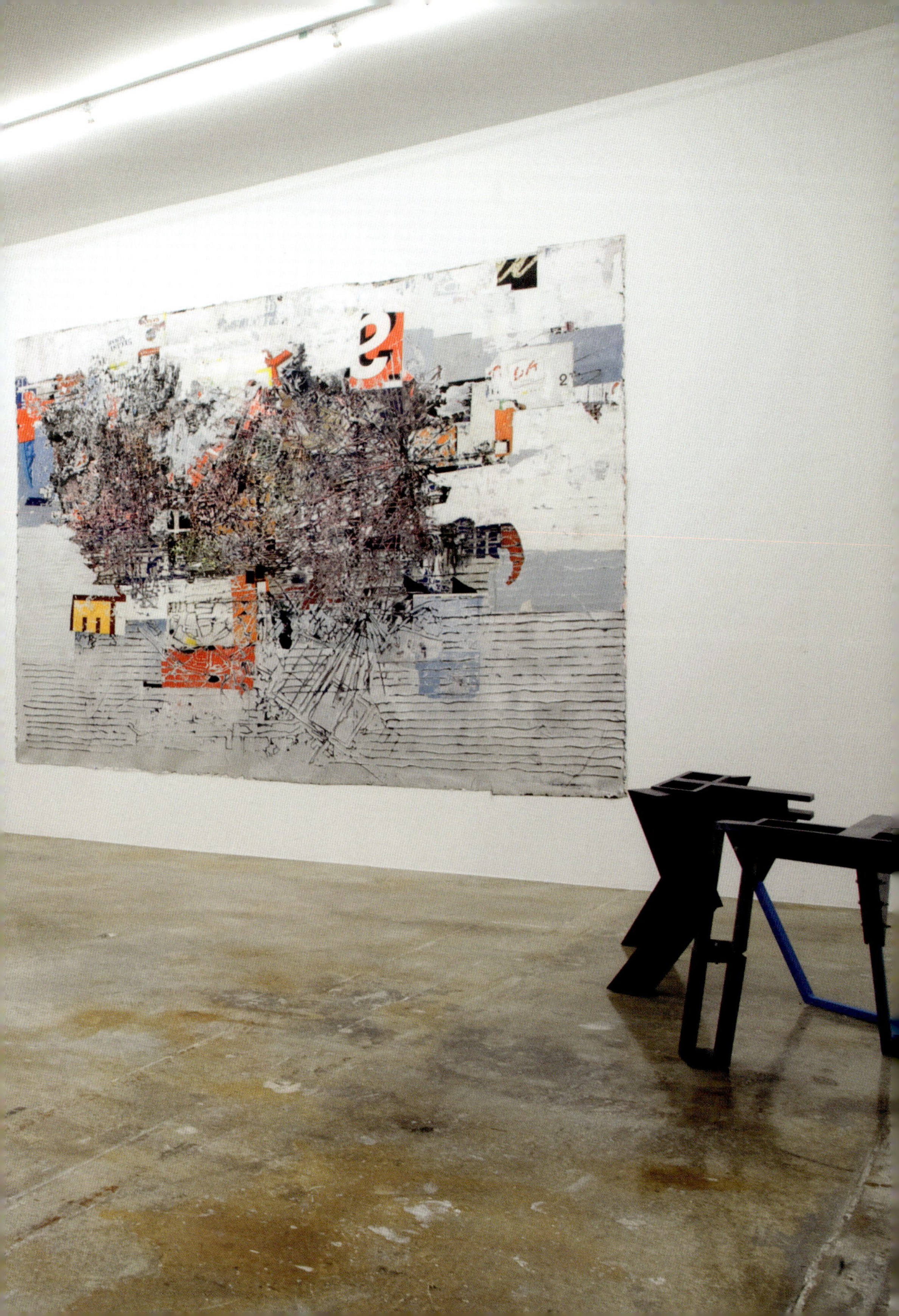

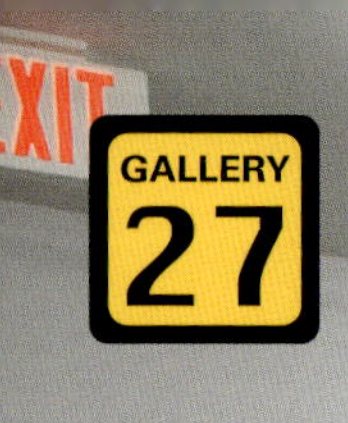

INSTALLATION VIEW: MATTHEW MONAHAN

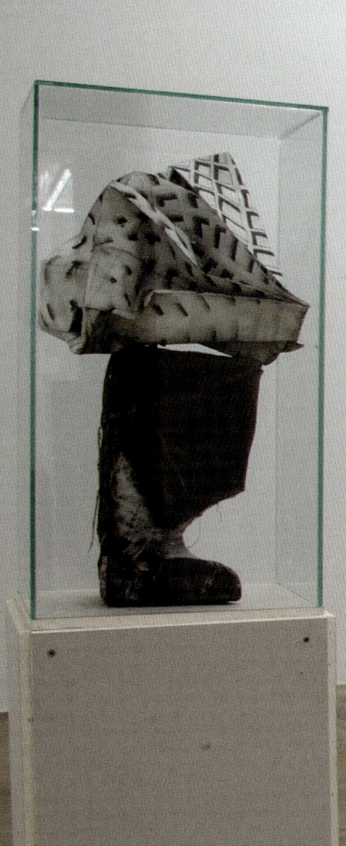

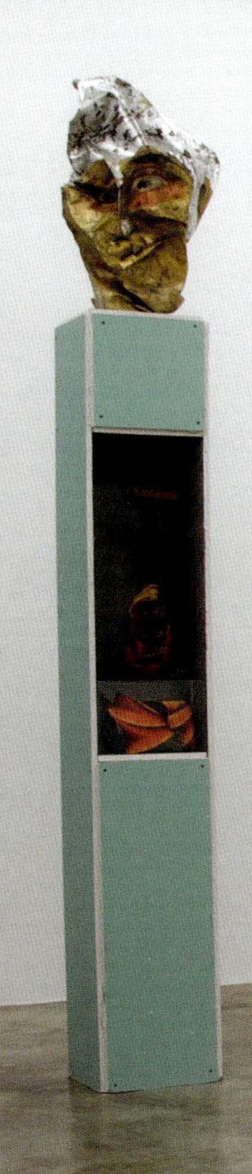

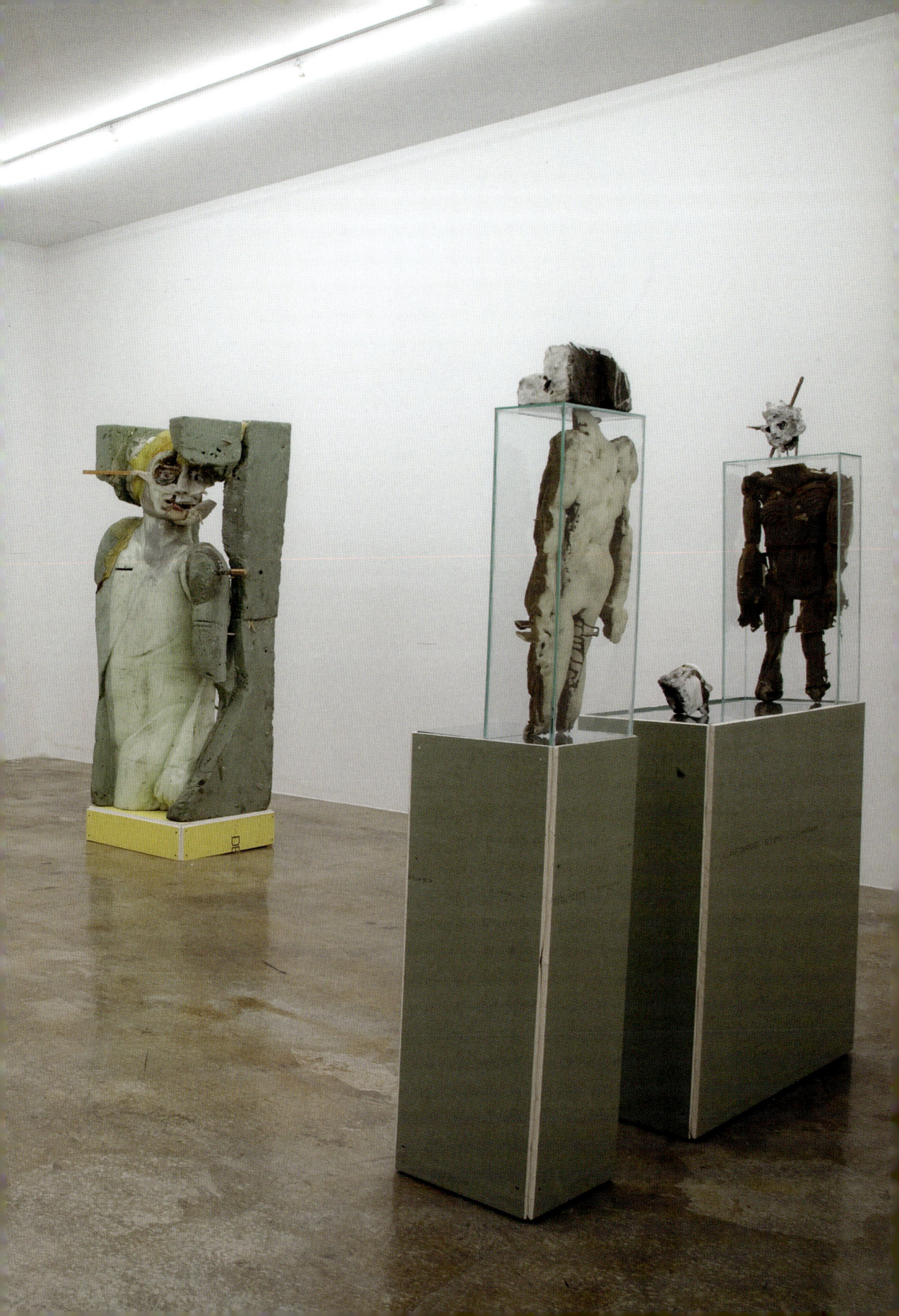

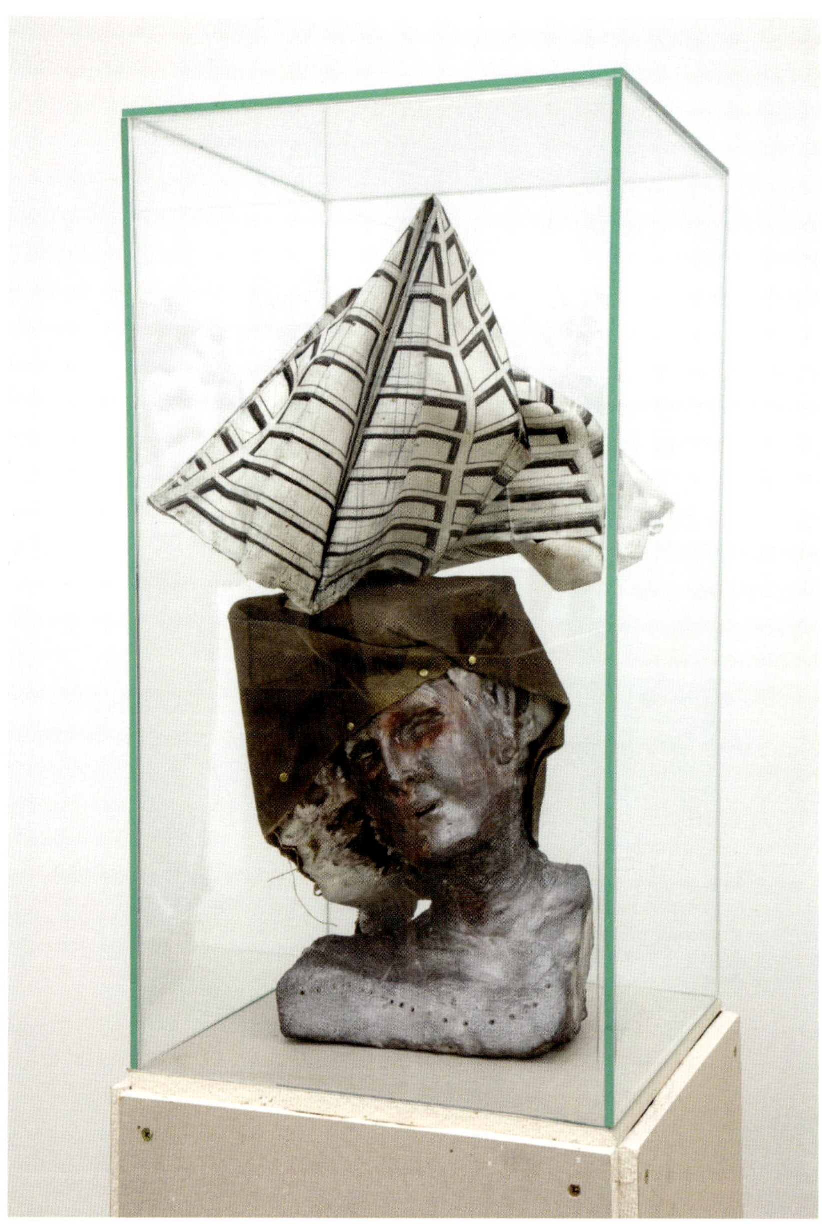

Matthew Monahan
Kopffunk, 2006
Mixed media
60 3/4 x 13 x 13 in. (154.3 x 33 x 33 cm)

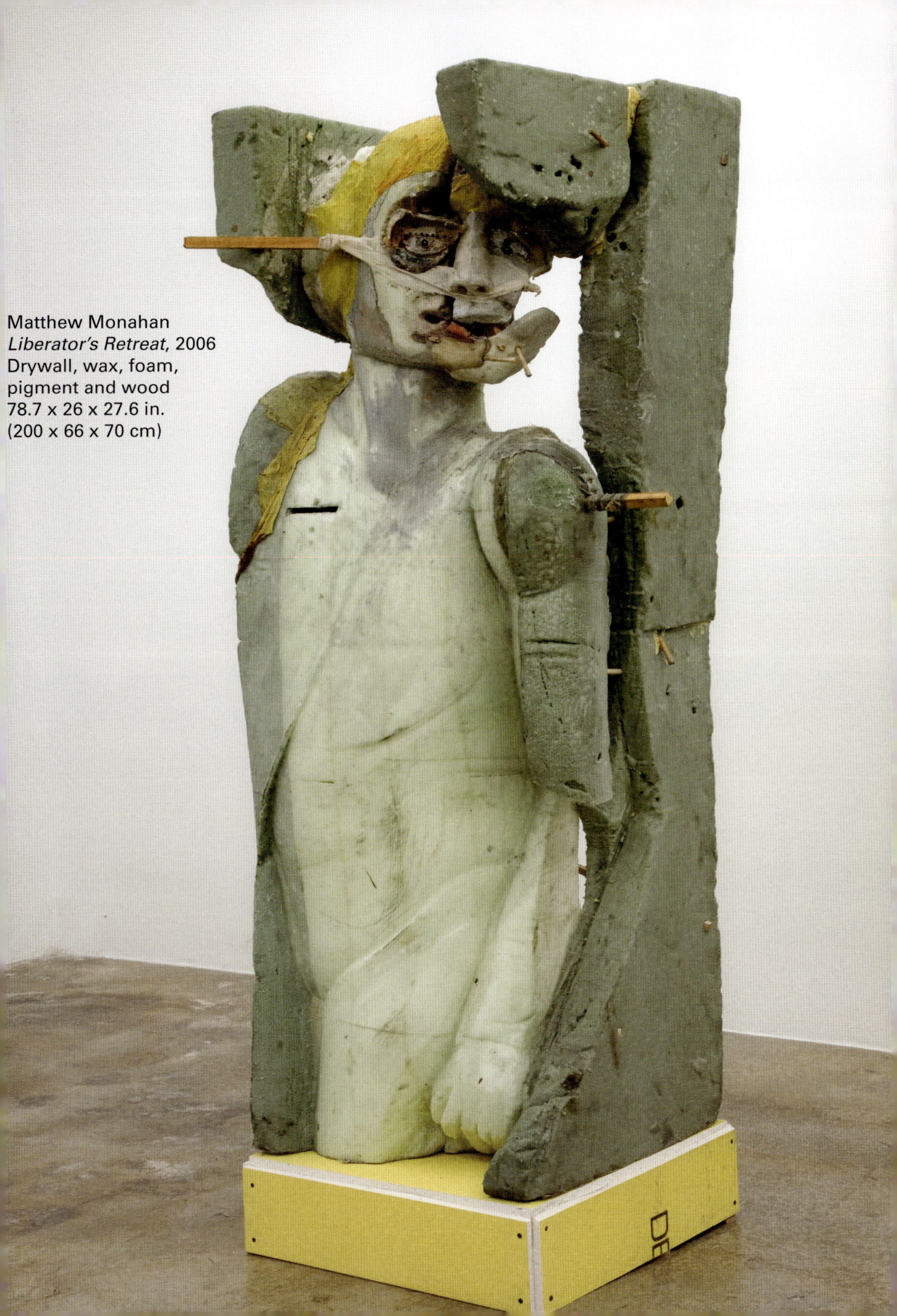

Matthew Monahan
Liberator's Retreat, 2006
Drywall, wax, foam,
pigment and wood
78.7 x 26 x 27.6 in.
(200 x 66 x 70 cm)

©Wyatt Troll

DOUG AITKEN

Born in Redondo Beach, CA, 1968
Lives and works in Los Angeles, CA

Education

1987-1991 B.F.A., Art Center College of Design, Pasadena, CA
1986-1987 One year of coursework, Marymount College, Palos Verdes, CA

Selected Solo Exhibitions

2007 *Sleepwalkers*, The Museum of Modern Art and Creative Time, New York, NY [cat.]
303 Gallery, New York, NY
2006 *Doug Aitken: A Photographic Survey*, Aspen Art Museum, Aspen, CO
2005 Musée d'Art Moderne de la Ville de Paris, Paris, France [cat.]
Regen Projects, Los Angeles, CA
Galerie Eva Presenhuber, Zurich, Switzerland
Doug Aitken: interiors, Henry Art Gallery, University of Washington, Seattle, WA
2004 *This Moment is the Moment*, Taka Ishii Gallery, Tokyo, Japan
2003 *Doug Aitken: I don't exist*, Victoria Miro Gallery, London, England
Kunsthalle Zürich, Zurich, Switzerland
2002 303 Gallery, New York, NY [cat.]
New Ocean (a shifting exhibition), Kunsthaus Bregenz, Bregenz, Austria [cat.]
The Fabric Workshop and Museum, Philadelphia, PA
2001 Serpentine Gallery, London, England [cat.]
I am in you, Kunst-Werke Berlin, Berlin, Germany
2000 *Concentrations 33: Doug Aitken, Diamond Sea*, Dallas Museum of Art, Dallas, TX [cat.]
1997 303 Gallery, New York, NY
1994 303 Gallery, New York, NY

Selected Group Exhibitions

2007 *Uneasy Angel / Imagine Los Angeles*, Monika Sprüth Philomene Magers, Munich, Germany
Mapping the City, Stedelijk Museum, Amsterdam, Netherlands
2006 *Red Eye: L.A. Artists from the Rubell Family Collection*, Rubell Family Collection, Miami, FL [cat.]
Surprise, Surprise, Institute of Contemporary Arts, London, England
Ecotopia, International Center of Photography, New York, NY [cat.]
2005 *Universal Experience: Art, Life, and the Tourist's Eye*, Museum of Contemporary Art Chicago, Chicago, IL; traveled to The Hayward Gallery, London, England [cat.]
2004 *Hard Light*, P.S.1 Contemporary Art Center, Long Island City, NY
2003 *Site Specific*, Museum of Contemporary Art Chicago, Chicago, IL
2002 *Sonic Process: A new geography of sounds*, Centre Georges Pompidou, Paris, France [cat.]
Remix: Contemporary Art & Pop, Tate Gallery, Liverpool, England [cat.]
2001 *Urban Pornography*, Artists Space, New York, NY
Form Follows Fiction, Castello di Rivoli Museo d'Art Contemporanea, Turin, Italy [cat.]
2000 *Whitney Biennial 2000*, Whitney Museum of American Art, New York, NY [cat.]
Work from the Angle Collection: Doug Aitken / Electric Earth, The Museum of Contemporary Art, Nagoya, Japan
1997 *Whitney Biennial 1997*, Whitney Museum of American Art, New York, NY [cat.]
We Gotta Get Out of this Place, Cubitt Gallery, London, England
1996 *29' - 0" / East*, New York Kunsthalle, New York, NY [cat.]
Art in the Anchorage 13, Creative Time, Brooklyn Bridge Anchorage, Brooklyn, NY
1995 *La Belle et la Bête: un choix de jeunes artistes americains*, Musée d'Art de la Ville de Paris, Paris, France [cat.]
1994 *Beyond Belief*, Lisson Gallery, London, England

1993 *Okay Behavior*, 303 Gallery, New York, NY
1991 *Artworks / Artworkers*, AC Project Room, New York, NY

Selected Bibliography

Aitken, Doug. *Doug Aitken: A-Z Book (fractals).* Ostfildern-ruit: Hatje Cantz, 2002.
Aitken, Doug. *Notes for new religions, notes for no religions.* Ostfildern-ruit: Hatje Cantz, 2001.
Alpha. Zurich: JRP / Ringier, 2005.
Baker, Kenneth. "Doug Aitken." ARTnews [Vol. 99, No. 9, Oct. 2000]: 184.
Birnbaum, Daniel, *Chronology.* New York: Lukas & Sternberg, 2005.
Birnbaum, Daniel. *Doug Aitken.* London: Phaidon Press, 2001.
Bonami, Francesco. *Campo 6: il villaggio a spirale.* Milan: Skira, 1996.
Bonami, Francesco. *Unfinished History.* Minneapolis: Walker Art Center, 1998.
Bonami, Francesco, and Doug Aitken. *Doug Aitken: (new ocean).* London: Serpentine Gallery, 2001.
Butler, Cornelia H., and Weng Choy Lee. *Flight Patterns.* Los Angeles: Museum of Contemporary Art, 2000.
Coetzee, Mark. *Not Afraid: Rubell Family Collection.* London: Phaidon Press, 2004.
Coetzee, Mark, ed., *Red Eye: L.A. Artists from the Rubell Family Collection.* Miami: Rubell Family Collection, 2007.
Curiger, Bice, and Christoph Heinrich. *Hypermental Rampant Reality 1950-2000 from Salvador Dali to Jeff Koons.* Ostfildern-Ruit: Hatje Cantz, 2000.
Daniel, Noel. *Broken Screen: 26 Conversations with Doug Aitken.* New York: D.A.P.; London: Thames & Hudson, 2005.
Fresh Cream: Contemporary Art in Culture. London: Phaidon Press, 2000: 58-63.
Gili, Marta, and Doug Aitken. *We're Safe As Long As Everything Is Moving.* Barcelona: Fundacio La Caixa, 2004.
Griffin, Tim. "Doug Aitken." Artforum [Vol. 41, No. 4, Dec. 2002]: 137.
Hall, Emily. *Sleepwalkers.* New York: Museum of Modern Art; Creative Time, 2007.
Kalmár, Stefan, and Doug Aitken. *Diamond Sea: Namib Desert, Southwestern Africa, 70,000 square kilometers, restricted access.* London: Book Works, 2001.
Kuipers, Dean, and Doug Aitken. *I am a bullet: living in accelerated culture.* New York: Crown Publishers, 2000.
Kunz, Martin. *29' – 0" / East: Doug Aitken.* New York: New York Kunsthalle, 1996.
La Belle et la Bête: un choix de jeunes artistes americains. Paris: Musée d'Art de la Ville de Paris, 1995: 36-37, 114-115.
Let's Entertain: Life's Guilty Pleasures, Minneapolis: Walker Art Center, 2000: 210-11.
McDonald, Ewen. *Biennale of Sydney 2000.* Sydney: Biennale of Sydney Ltd., 2000: 32-33.
Metallic sleep. Tokyo: Taka Ishii Gallery, 1998.
Morton, Tom. "Doug Aitken." Modern Painters [Vol. 14, No. 4, Winter 2001]: 102-103.
Parreno, Philippe, and Rachael Thomas. *All Hawaii Entrées / Lunar Reggae.* Dublin: Irish Museum of Modern Art, 2006.
Roberts, James. "Doug Aitken: omega man." Parkett. [No. 57, Dec. 1999]: 20-28.
Romano, Gianni. "Doug Aitken." Flash Art [Vol. 34, No. 216, Jan. – Feb. 2001]: 121-122.
Vanderbilt, Tom. "City of glass: On Doug Aitken at MoMA." Artforum [Vol. 45, No. 5, Jan. 2007]: 45-46.
Weaver, Suzanne. *Concentrations 33: Doug Aitken, Diamond Sea.* Dallas: Dallas Museum of Art, 1999.
Wilsher, Mark. "Doug Aitken." Art Monthly [No. 251, Nov. 2001]: 28-29.

Selected Collections

The Art Institute of Chicago, Chicago IL
Astrup Fearnley Museet for Moderne Kunst, Oslo, Norway
Berkeley Art Museum, University of California, Berkeley, Berkeley, CA
Centre Georges Pompidou, Paris, France
Centre pour l'image contemporaine, Saint-Gervais Genève, Geneva, Switzerland
La Colección Jumex, Mexico City, Mexico
Dallas Museum of Art, Dallas, TX
Foundazione Sandretto Re Rebaudengo per l'Arte, Turin, Italy
Kunstmuseum Wolfsburg, Wolfsburg, Germany
The Metropolitan Museum of Art, New York, NY
Museum of Contemporary Art Chicago, Chicago, IL
The Museum of Contemporary Art, Los Angeles, CA
Rubell Family Collection, Miami, FL
Sammlung Goetz, Munich, Germany
San Francisco Museum of Modern Art, San Francisco, CA
Walker Art Center, Minneapolis, MN
Whitney Museum of American Art, New York, NY

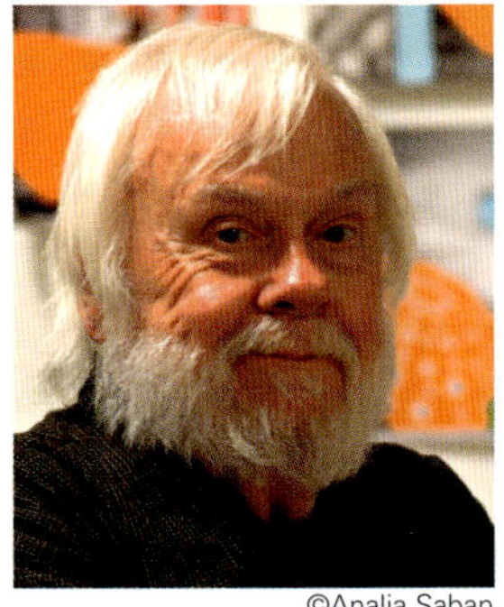

©Analia Saban

JOHN BALDESSARI

Born in National City, CA, 1931
Lives and works in Santa Monica, CA

Education

1957-1959 Los Angeles County Art Institute, Los Angeles, CA
1955-1957 M.A., San Diego State College, San Diego, CA.
1954-1955 University of California, Berkeley, Berkeley, CA
1949-1953 B.A., San Diego State College, San Diego, CA

Selected Solo Exhibitions

2007 *John Baldessari: Music*, Kunstmuseum Bonn, Bonn, Germany; Bonner Kunstverein, Bonn, Germany [cat.]
John Baldessari: Eden: Adam and Eve (With Ear and Nose) Plus Serpent, Portikus, Frankfurt am Main, Germany
2006 *John Baldessari: The Prima Facie Series*, Museum Dhondt-Dhaenens, Deurle, Belgium [cat.]
John Baldessari: Composition for Violin and Voices (Male), 1987, Une oeuvre de la collection, Musée d'Art Contemporain de Lyon, Lyon, France
2005 *John Baldessari: Prima Facie (Fourth State)*, Galerie Meert Rihoux, Brussels, Belgium
John Baldessari: Prima Facie (Third State), Galeria Pepe Cobo, Madrid, Spain
John Baldessari: From Life, Carré d'Art-Musée d'Art Contemporain, Nîmes, France [cat.]
John Baldessari: A Different Kind of Order (Works 1962-1984), Museum Moderner Kunst Stiftung Ludwig Wien, Vienna, Austria [cat.]
2004 *John Baldessari: Somewhere Between Almost Right and Not Quite (With Orange)*, Deutsche Guggenheim, Berlin, Germany [cat.]
2003 *John Baldessari: Vertical / Horizontal Series*, Bernier / Eliades Gallery, Athens, Greece
John Baldessari: Editionen, Einladung zur Eroffnung, Hamburg, Germany
2002 *Overlaps and Intersections*, Marian Goodman Gallery, New York, NY
2001 Museo d'Arte Moderna e Contemporanea di Trento e Rovereto, Trento, Italy
2000 *Baldessari: While something is happening here, something else is happening there: Works 1988-1999*, Sprengel Museum Hannover, Hannover, Germany [cat.]
1999 *John Baldessari: Tetrad Series*, Marian Goodman Gallery, New York, NY [cat.]
Baldessari und Goya, Albertina im Akademiehof, Vienna, Austria
1998 *4 RMS W VU: WALLPAPER, LAMPS AND PLANTS. NEW: A project by John Baldessari*, Witte de With, Center for Contemporary Art, Rotterdam, Netherlands; Migros Museum für Gegenwartskunst, Zurich, Switzerland [cat.]
1995 *John Baldessari: A Retrospective*, Cornerhouse, Manchester, England; traveled to Serpentine Gallery, London, England; Württembergischer Kunstverein Stuttgart, Stuttgart, Germany; Moderna Galerija Ljubljana, Ljubljana, Slovenia; Museet for Samtidskunst, Oslo, Norway; Fundação Calouste Gulbenkian, Lisbon, Portugal [cat.]
1994 *Artist's Choice: John Baldessari*, The Museum of Modern Art, New York, NY
1990 *John Baldessari*, The Museum of Contemporary Art, Los Angeles, CA; traveled to San Francisco Museum of Modern Art, San Francisco, CA; Hirshhorn Museum and Sculpture Garden, Washington, DC; Whitney Museum of American Art, New York, NY; Musée d'Art Contemporain de Montréal, Montreal, Canada
1986 *John Baldessari / MATRIX 94*, Berkeley Art Museum, University of California, Berkeley, Berkeley, CA [cat.]
1985 Le Consortium, Centre d'art Contemporain, Dijon, France
1981 *John Baldessari: Work 1966 - 1980*, New Museum of Contemporary Art, New York, NY; traveled to Contemporary Arts Center, Cincinnati, OH; Contemporary Arts Museum, Houston, Houston, TX [cat.]

Selected Group Exhibitions

2007 *What is Painting? Contemporary Art from the Collection*, The Museum of Modern Art, New York, NY
Learn to Read, Tate Modern, London, England
2006 *Red Eye: L.A. Artists from the Rubell Family Collection*, Rubell Family Collection, Miami, FL [cat.]
2004 *Beyond Geometry: Experiments in Form, 1940s-70s*, Los Angeles County Museum of Art, Los Angeles, CA; traveling to Miami Art Museum, Miami, FL [cat.]
2003 *Utopia Station, 50th Biennale di Venezia*, Venice, Italy
2000 *Departures: 11 Artists at the Getty*, J. Paul Getty Museum, Los Angeles, CA [cat.]
1999 *Crosscurrents: New Art from MoMA*, Hara Museum of Contemporary Art, Tokyo, Japan [cat.]
1997 *47th Biennale di Venezia*, Venice, Italy [cat.]
1991 *Devil on the Stairs; Looking Back at the Eighties*, Institute of Contemporary Art, Philadelphia; traveled to Newport Harbor Art Museum, Newport Beach, CA [cat.]
1985 *Carnegie International*, Carnegie Museum of Art, Pittsburgh, PA
1983 *Whitney Biennial 1983*, Whitney Museum of American Art, New York, NY [cat.]
1982 *Documenta 7*, Kassel, West Germany [cat.]
1972 *Documenta 5*, Kassel, West Germany [cat.]

Selected Bibliography

4 RMS W VU: WALLPAPER, LAMPS AND PLANTS. NEW: A project by John Baldessari. Zurich: Museum fur Gegenwartskunst Zurich, 1998.
Bickers, Patricia. "John Baldessari." Art Monthly [No. 292, Dec. 2005 / Jan. 2006]: 25-27.
Burton, Johanna. "John Baldessari." Artforum [Vol. 43, No. 6, Feb. 2004]: 170-171.
Coetzee, Mark, ed., *Red Eye: L.A. Artists from the Rubell Family Collection*. Miami: Rubell Family Collection, 2007.
Davies, Hugh, and Andrea Hales. *John Baldessari: National City*. San Diego: Museum of Contemporary Art, San Diego, 1996.
Flynn, Tom. "John Baldessari." ArtReview [Vol. 54, May 2004]: 39.
Gea, Politi. "John Baldessari: before day falls." Flash Art [Vol. 37, No. 237, July – Sept. 2004]: 80-84.
Gillick, Liam. "I Will Not Make Any More Boring Art." (Interview) Art Monthly Magazine [No. 187, June 1995]: 3-7.
John Baldessari: Work 1966 - 1980. New York: The New Museum, 1981.
John Baldessari: Somewhere Between Almost Right and Not Quite (With Orange). Lisbon: Centro Cultural de Belem, 2003.
"John Baldessari: Prima Facie." Modern Painters [Sept. 2005]: 110.
Plagens, Peter. "John Baldessari." Artforum [Vol. 40, No. 6, Feb. 2002]: 23.
Richard, Frances. "John Baldessari." Artforum [Vol. 37, No. 8, April 1999]: 121.
Singerman, Howard. "Rereading a fugitive essay." Parkett [No. 29, Sept. 1991]: 30-37.
Smith, Roberta. "Video, in Its Infancy, Had to Crawl Before It Could Walk." The New York Times [Jan. 24, 2003]: B37.
van Bruggen, Coosje. *John Baldessari*. Los Angeles: The Museum of Contemporary Art; New York: Rizzoli, 1990.
Wei, Lilly, and Cecile N. McCann. "Making Art, Making Money." Art in America [Vol. 78, No. 7, July 1990]: 133-134.

Selected Collections

Centre Georges Pompidou, Paris, France
Cincinnati Art Museum, Cincinnati, OH
Deutsche Guggenheim, Berlin, Germany
Hirshhorn Museum and Sculpture Garden, Smithsonian Institution, Washington, DC
Los Angeles County Museum of Art, Los Angeles, CA
The Metropolitan Museum of Art, New York, NY
Museum of Contemporary Art, Chicago, IL
The Museum of Contemporary Art, Los Angeles, CA
The Museum of Fine Arts, Houston, Houston, TX
The Museum of Modern Art, New York, NY
Rubell Family Collection, Miami, FL
San Francisco Museum of Modern Art, San Francisco, CA
Stedelijk Museum, Amsterdam, Netherlands
Tate Modern, London, England
Van Abbemuseum, Eindhoven, Netherlands
Walker Art Center, Minneapolis, MN
Whitney Museum of American Art, New York, NY

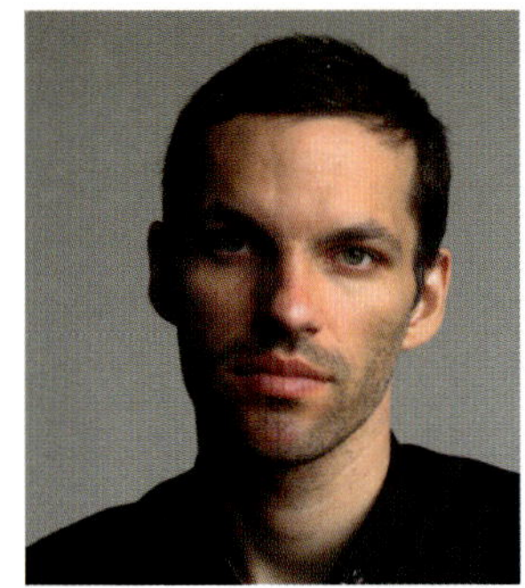
©Xavier Cha

FRANK BENSON

Born in Norfolk, VA, 1976
Lives and works in Brooklyn, NY

Education

2001-2003 M.F.A., University of California, Los Angeles, Los Angeles, CA
2000 Residency, Atlantic Center for the Arts, New Smyrna Beach, FL
1995-1999 B.F.A., Maryland Institute College of Art, Baltimore, MD

Selected Solo Exhibitions

2008 Sadie Coles HQ, London, England
2005 Taxter & Spengemann, New York, NY
2001 *Frank Benson: New Work*, Miami Art Museum, Miami, FL

Selected Group Exhibitions

2006 *Red Eye: L.A. Artists from the Rubell Family Collection*, Rubell Family Collection, Miami, FL [cat.]
New York, Interrupted, PKM Gallery, Beijing, Beijing, China [cat.]
2005 *Uncertain States of America: American Art in the Third Millenium*, Astrup Fearnley Museet for Moderne Kunst, Oslo, Norway; traveled to Center for Curatorial Studies Museum, Bard College, Annandale-on-Hudson, NY; Serpentine Gallery, London, England; Reykjavik Art Museum, Reykjavik, Iceland; Herning Art Museum, Herning, Denmark; Centre for Contemporary Art, Warsaw, Poland; Musée de Sérignan, Sérignan, France; traveling to Galerie Rudolfinum, Prague, Czech Republic; Songzhuang Art Center, Beijing, China [cat.]
Make It Now: New Sculpture in New York, SculptureCenter, New York, NY [cat.]
2004 *Mystery Achievement*, Taxter & Spengemann, New York, NY
Regen Projects, Los Angeles, CA
2003 Grant Selwyn Fine Art, Beverly Hills, CA
2001 *Really*, Artists Space, New York, NY

Selected Bibliography

Birnbaum, Daniel, Gunnar B Kvaran, and Hans-Ulrich Obrist. *Uncertain States of America.* Oslo: Astrup Fearnley Museet for Moderne Kunst, 2005.
Coetzee, Mark, ed., *Red Eye: L.A. Artists from the Rubell Family Collection*. Miami: Rubell Family Collection, 2007.
Cameron, Dan. *New York, Interrupted*. Beijing: PKM Gallery, 2007.
Danto, Arthur C. "Uncertain States of America." Artforum [Vol. 44, Dec. 2005]: 274.
McBride, Nathaniel. "Uncertain States of America and USA Today." Flash Art [Nov. – Dec. 2006]: 50.
Morgan, Anne Bradley. "Miami Supports Miami." Sculpture [Vol. 20, No. 10, Dec. 2001]: 46-51.
Sirmans, Franklin, Mary Ceruti, and Anthony Huberman. *Make it Now: new sculpture in New York*. Long Island City: SculptureCenter, 2005.
Smith, Roberta. "The Many Shades of Now Explored in 3 Dimensions." The New York Times [May 27, 2005]: E17.
Speers, Emily. "Mystery Achievement." www.artforum.com [Oct, 5, 2004].

Selected Collections

Armand Hammer Museum, University of California, Los Angeles, CA
Astrup Fearnley Museet for Moderne Kunst, Oslo, Norway
Collection of Dean Valentine and Amy Adelson, New York, NY
Collection of Martin and Rebecca Eisenberg, New York, NY
Edward and Agnes Lee, London, England
Peter Norton Family Foundation, Santa Monica, CA
Rubell Family Collection, Miami, FL

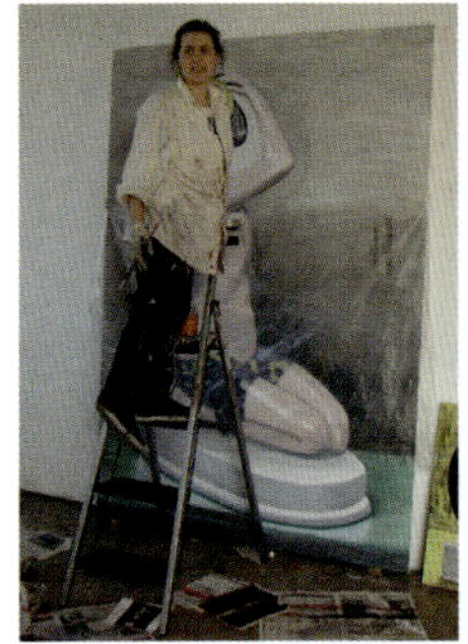
©Ted Mineo

AMY BESSONE

Born in New York, NY, 1970
Lives and works in Los Angeles, CA

Education

1993-1995 Two years of study, de Ateliers, Amsterdam, Netherlands
1989-1993 B.F.A., Parsons Paris, Paris, France
1992 One semester of coursework as exchange student, École nationale supérieure des beaux-arts, Paris, France
1988-1989 One year of coursework, Barnard College, New York, NY

Selected Solo Exhibitions

2008 Salon 94, New York, NY
2007 *Body & Paint*, David Kordansky Gallery, Los Angeles, CA
2000 *Les Salles Étrangères*, Art&Com, Brussels, Belgium
1999 *Amy Bessone – New Paintings*, Buro Empty Gallery, Amsterdam, Netherlands
1997 *Amy Bessone: Schilderijen en tekeningen*, De Nederlandsche Bank, Amsterdam, Netherlands

Selected Group Exhibitions

2006 *Red Eye: L.A. Artists from the Rubell Family Collection*, Rubell Family Collection, Miami, FL [cat.]
Transformers, Donna Beam Fine Art Gallery, University of Nevada Las Vegas, Las Vegas, NV
Hotel California, Glendale College Art Gallery, Glendale Community College, Glendale, CA
2005 *Both Ends Burning*, David Kordansky Gallery, Los Angeles, CA [cat.]
b.a.-ba, un choix dans la collection du Frac Bretagne, Domaine de Kerguéhennec, Bignan, France
2002 Xavier Hufkens, Brussels, Belgium
2001 *Proposition 1 (Peinture)*, Art&Com, Brussels, Belgium
1999 *Archétype*, Kanal 11, Brussels, Belgium
1998 *Aanwinsten 1997,* De Nederlandsche Bank, Amsterdam, Netherlands
1997 *Comité'97*, Jan van Nassau Kazerne, Harderwijk, Netherlands [cat.]
1996 *Young Artists I*, Sabine Wachters Fine Arts, Brussels, Belgium

Selected Bibliography

Both Ends Burning. Los Angeles: David Kordansky Gallery, 2005.
Brooks, Amra. "Must See Art: Amy Bessone, 'Body & Paint' and Matthew Spiegelman,'Officioné'." LA Weekly [Sept. 19, 2007].
Coetzee, Mark, ed., *Red Eye: L.A. Artists from the Rubell Family Collection*. Miami: Rubell Family Collection, 2007.
Garnet, Daisy. "The Collector." The New York Times Magazine [December 3, 2006]: 74.
"Hot Tickets. Exhibitions: Amy Bessone, Thomas Houseago." The Bulletin [September 19, 2002].
Keijer, Kees. "Our little experiment." *Comité'97*. Harderwijk: Jan van Nassau Kazerne, 1997.
Peterson, Kristen. "Good Shows." Las Vegas Sun [December 8, 2006].
Turner, Elisa. "Rubell exhibit explores the West Coast scene." The Miami Herald [April 1, 2007].

Selected Collections

Akzo Nobel Art Foundation, Arnhem, Netherlands
Blake Byrne Collection, Los Angeles, CA
Blondeau Fine Art Services, Geneva, Switzerland
Collection of Susan and Michael Hort, New York, NY

de Ateliers, Amsterdam, Netherlands
De Nederlandsche Bank, Amsterdam, Netherlands
Fonds régional d'art contemporain Bretagne, Châteaugiron, France
The Museum of Contemporary Art, Los Angeles, CA
The Rennie Collection, Vancouver, Canada
Rubell Family Collection, Miami, FL

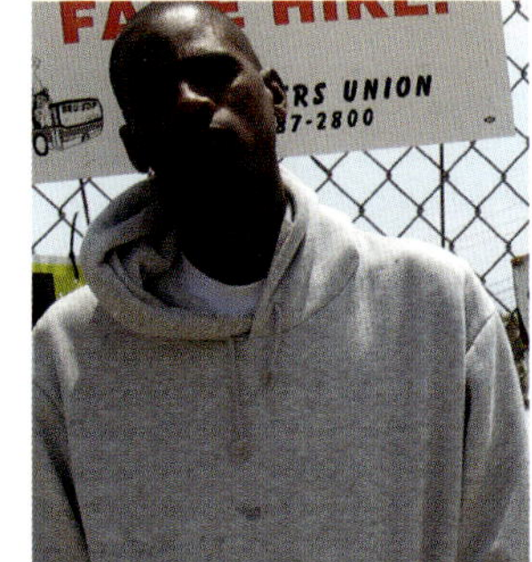

©Juan Carlos Avendano, image courtesy of Sikkema Jenkins & Co.

MARK BRADFORD

Born in Los Angeles, CA, 1961
Lives and works in Los Angeles, CA

Education

1995-1997 M.F.A., California Institute of the Arts, Valencia, CA
1992-1995 B.F.A., California Institute of the Arts, Valencia, CA

Selected Solo Exhibitions

2007 *Mark Bradford: Storefront*, The Fabric Workshop and Museum, Philadelphia, PA
Neither New Nor Correct: New Work by Mark Bradford, Whitney Museum of American Art, New York, NY
2006 *Mark Bradford: The Other Side of Perfect*, World Class Boxing, Miami, FL
2005 *Grace and Measure*, Sikkema Jenkins & Co., New York, NY [cat.]
2003 *Mark Bradford: Very Powerful Lords,* Whitney Museum of American Art, New York, NY

Selected Group Exhibitions

2007 *Eden's Edge: Fifteen LA Artists*, Armand Hammer Museum, University of California, Los Angeles, CA
Street Level: Mark Bradford, William Cordova and Robin Rhode, Nasher Museum of Art at Duke University, Durham, NC [cat.]
2006 *Art on Paper 2006,* Weatherspoon Art Museum, The University of North Carolina at Greensboro, Greensboro, NC
Red Eye: L.A. Artists from the Rubell Family Collection, Rubell Family Collection, Miami, FL [cat.]
Black Alphabet ConTEXTs of Contemporary African American Art, Zacheta National Gallery of Art, Warsaw, Poland
USA TODAY : New American Art from The Saatchi Gallery, Royal Academy of Arts, London, England; traveled to The State Hermitage Museum, St Petersburg, Russia [cat.]
Consider This..., Los Angeles County Museum of Art, Los Angeles, CA
Sisqueiros Project, The Roy and Edna Disney / CalArts Theater, Los Angeles, CA
26th Bienal de São Paulo, São Paulo, Brazil
5th Busan Biennial, Busan, South Korea
Whitney Biennial 2006, Whitney Museum of American Art, New York, NY
2005 *inSite: Art Practices in the Public Domain San Diego Tijuana*, San Diego Museum of Art and the Centro Cultural Tijuana, San Diego, CA and Tijuana, Mexico
African Queen, The Studio Museum in Harlem, New York, NY
2004 *California Biennial*, Orange County Museum of Art, Newport Beach, CA
Bounce: Mark Bradford and Glenn Kaino, The Roy and Edna Disney / CalArts Theater, Los Angeles, CA [cat.]
2003 *Black Belt*, The Studio Museum in Harlem, New York, NY [cat.]
2002 *Mirror Image,* Armand Hammer Museum, University of California, Los Angeles, CA; traveled to Center for Curatorial Studies Museum, Bard College, Annandale-on-Hudson, NY
2001 *Freestyle,* The Studio Museum in Harlem, New York, NY; traveled to Santa Monica Museum of Art, Santa Monica, CA [cat.]
1999 Firenze 1999: Biennale Internazionale dell'Arte Contemporanea, Palazzo degli Affari, Florence, Italy

Selected Bibliography

Amado, Miguel. "Street Level." Artforum.com [May 2007].
Bradford, Mark, et al. *Street Level: Mark Bradford, William Cordova and Robin Rhode*. Durham: Nasher Museum of Art at Duke University, 2007.

Coetzee, Mark, ed., *Red Eye: L.A. Artists from the Rubell Family Collection.* Miami: Rubell Family Collection, 2007.
Colpitt, Frances. "Mark Bradford at Finesilver." Art in America [Vol. 90, No. 11, Nov. 2002]: 165.
Cotter, Holland. "I don't think you ready for this jelly." The New York Times [Nov 9, 2001].
Dambrot, Shana Nys. "Dye Another Day." ARTnews [Vol. 103, No. 10, Nov. 2004]: 141.
Dambrot, Shana Nys. "La La Land: Eden's Edge." ArtReview [Issue 11, May 2007]: 32.
Finkel, Jori. "A Reluctant Fraternity, Thinking Post-Black." The New York Times [June 10, 2007].
Firstenberg, Lauri. "Mark Bradford." Flash Art [Vol. 34, No. 222, Jan. - Feb. 2002]: 95.
Foster, Carter E. *Neither new nor correct: new work by Mark Bradford.* New York: Whitney Museum of American Art; New Haven: Yale University Press, 2007.
Hardy, Ernest. "The Eye of LA." West: The Los Angeles Times [June 11, 2006]: 16-29, 51.
Joo, Eungie. *Bounce: Mark Bradford and Glenn Kaino.* Los Angeles: California Institute of the Arts/REDCAT, 2004.
Klein, Mason. "Mark Bradford." Artforum [Vol. 40, No. 5, Jan. 2002]: 142-143.
Knight, Christopher. "Cultural Evolution in 'Freestyle'." Los Angeles Times [Oct. 2, 2001].
Lindeman, Donald. "Mark Bradford / Sikkema Jenkins." Art in America [April 2006]: 161
Mendelsohn, Meredith. "Mark Bradford / Sikkema Jenkins." ARTnews [March 2006]: 134
Mizota, Sharon. "Mark Bradford at LAXART, Los Angeles." ARTnews [Feb. 2007].
Nelson, Steven. *Mark Bradford.* New York: Sikkema Jenkins & Co., 2006.
Schjeldahl, Peter. "Breaking Away: A Flowering of Young African-American Artists." The New Yorker [June 10, 2001].
Smith, Roberta. "Art in Review: Mark Bradford; Katie Grinnan." The New York Times [Sept. 5, 2003].
Subotnick, Ali. "Snapshot." frieze [Oct. 2001].
Tumlir, Jan. "Snapshot." Artforum [Vol. 40, No. 2, Oct. 2001]: 155.
Valdez, Sarah. "Freestyling." Art in America [Sept. 2001].
Valdez, Sarah. "Mark Bradford at Lombard-Freid." Art in America [Sept. 2003]: 136.

Selected Collections

21c Museum Foundation, Louisville, KY
Armand Hammer Museum, University of California, Los Angeles, CA
The Broad Art Foundation, Santa Monica, CA
Brooklyn Museum of the Arts, Brooklyn, NY
Los Angeles County Museum of Art, Los Angeles, CA
The Museum of Modern Art, New York, NY
Tate Modern, London, England
Rubell Family Collection, Miami, FL
Walker Art Center, Minneapolis, MN
Whitney Museum of American Art, New York, NY

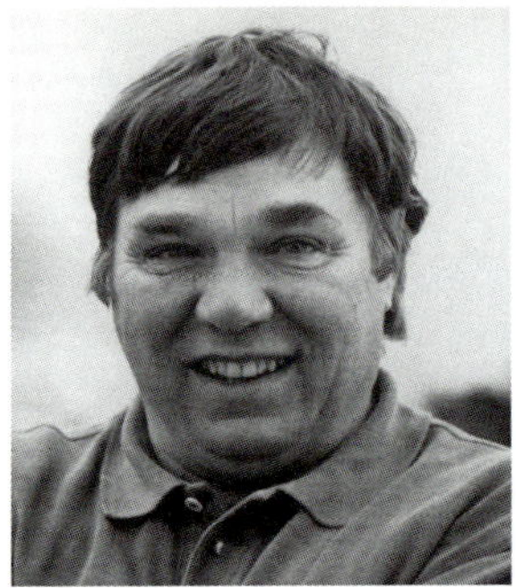

CHRIS BURDEN

Born in Boston, MA, 1946
Lives and works in Los Angeles, CA

Education

1970- 1971 M.F.A., University of California, Irvine, CA
1965-1969 B.F.A., Pomona College, Claremont, CA

Selected Solo Exhibitions

2007 *Yin Yang*, Gagosian Gallery, Beverly Hills, CA
Chris Burden: A Tale of Two Cities, Orange County Museum of Art, Newport Beach, CA
2006 *State of Affairs*, Galleria Massimo De Carlo, Milan, Italy
Chris Burden: Magnolia Double Lamps; Chris Burden: The Flying Steamroller, South London Gallery, London, England
2005 *Bridges and Bullets*, Galerie Krinzinger, Vienna, Austria
2004 *Early Work*, Zwirner & Wirth, New York, NY [cat.]
4th Plinth Project, Trafalgar Square, The National Gallery, London, England
2003 Los Angeles Contemporary Exhibitions, Los Angeles, CA
Bridges and Bullets, Gagosian Gallery, Beverly Hills, CA
2002 *The Bridges (1997-2002)*, BALTIC Centre for Contemporary Art, Gateshead, England
Museum Moderner Kunst Stiftung Ludwig Wien, Vienna, Austria
1996 *Beyond the Limits*, Österreichisches Museum für angewandte Kunst / Gegenwartskunst, Vienna, Austria [cat.]
1995 Centre d'Art Santa Mònica, Barcelona, Spain [cat.]
1994 Galerie Anne de Villepoix, Paris, France [cat.]
Fonds régional d'art contemporain Champagne-Ardenne, Reims, France
1992 Lannan Foundation, Los Angeles, CA
1991 *Chris Burden: Medusa's Head*, Brooklyn Museum, Brooklyn, NY
1989 Carnegie Mellon Art Gallery, Pittsburgh, PA
The Institute of Contemporary Art, Boston, MA
1989 *All the Submarines of the United States of America*, Christine Burgin Gallery, New York, NY
1988 *Chris Burden: A Twenty-Year Survey*, Newport Harbor Art Museum, Newport Beach, CA [cat.]
1986 *Chris Burden / Matrix 86*, Wadsworth Atheneum Museum of Art, Hartford, CT
1985 *Chris Burden: The Artist and His Models*, Lowe Art Museum, University of Miami, Miami, FL [cat.]
1983 Ronald Feldman Fine Arts, New York, NY
1980 *The Big Wheel*, Ronald Feldman Fine Arts, New York, NY
1977 *C.B.T.V. (Chris Burden Television)*, Ronald Feldman Fine Arts, New York, NY
1976 *Relics*, Ronald Feldman Fine Arts, New York, NY
1975 *White Light / White Heat*, Ronald Feldman Fine Arts, New York, NY

Selected Group Exhibitions

2006 *Red Eye: L.A. Artists from the Rubell Family Collection*, Rubell Family Collection, Miami, FL [cat.]
Los Angles 1955-1985: The Birth of an Art Capital, Centre Georges Pompidou, Paris, France [cat.]
2001 *7th International Istanbul Biennial*, Istanbul, Turkey [cat.]
A Room of Their Own: From Rothko to Rauschenberg, The Museum of Contemporary Art, Los Angeles, CA
2000 *Made in California: Art, Image, and Identity, 1900-2000*, Los Angeles County Museum of Art, Los Angeles, CA [cat.]
1999 *48th Biennale di Venezia*, Venice, Italy [cat.]
1998 *Out of Actions: Between Performance and Object, 1949-1979*, The Museum of Contemporary Art, Los Angeles, CA [cat.]
1997 *Sunshine & Noir: Art in L.A.1960-1997,* Louisiana Museum for Moderne Kunst, Humlebaek, Denmark;

traveled to Kunstmuseum Wolfsburg, Wolfsburg, Germany; Castello di Rivoli Museo d'Arte Contemporanea, Turin, Italy; The Armand Hammer Museum of Art and Culture Center, University of California, Los Angeles, CA [cat.]
4e Biennale de Lyon, Lyon, France [cat.]
Whitney Biennial 1997, Whitney Museum of American Art, New York, NY [cat.]
1996 *Blurring the Boundaries*, Museum of Contemporary Art San Diego, San Diego, CA [cat.]
1994 *Hors Limites*, Centre Georges Pompidou, Paris, France [cat.]
1993 *Whitney Biennial 1993*, Whitney Museum of American Art, New York, NY [cat.]
1992 *Helter Skelter: L.A. Art of the 1990s*, The Museum of Contemporary Art, Los Angeles, CA [cat.]
1991 *Dislocations*, The Museum of Modern Art, New York, NY [cat.]
1990 *New Works for New Spaces: Into the Nineties*, Wexner Center for the Visual Arts, The Ohio State University, Columbus, OH [cat.]
Seven Obsessions, Whitechapel Gallery, London, England [cat.]
1989 *Whitney Biennial 1989*, Whitney Museum of American Art, New York, NY [cat.]
1986 *Individuals: A Selected History of Contemporary Art 1945-1986*, The Museum of Contemporary Art, Los Angeles, CA [cat.]
1985 *NO! Contemporary American Dada*, Henry Art Gallery, University of Washington, Seattle, WA [cat.]
1982 *Eight Artists: The Anxious Edge*, Walker Art Center, Minneapolis, MN [cat.]
1981 *The Museum as Site: Sixteen Projects*, Los Angeles County Museum of Art, Los Angeles, CA [cat.]
1977 *Documenta 6*, Kassel, Germany [cat.]
Whitney Biennial 1977, Whitney Museum of American Art, New York, NY [cat.]

Selected Bibliography

Ayres, Anne, and Paul Schimmel. *Chris Burden: A twenty-year survey*. Newport Beach: Newport Harbor Art Museum, 1988.
Burden, Chris. "Chris Burden." Flash Art [No. 70-71, Jan. – Feb. 1977]: 40-43.
Chris Burden. Vienna: Galerie Krinzinger, 1992.
Chris Burden: The Artist and His Models. Coral Gables: The Lowe Art Museum. 1985.
Chris Burden France 1994-1995. Paris: Galerie Anne de Villepoix, 1996.
Chris Burden: octubre 1995-gener 1996. Barcelona: Centre d'Art Santa Mònica, 1995.
Chris Burden: un livre du survie. Paris: Blocnotes, 1995.
Coetzee, Mark, ed., *Red Eye: L.A. Artists from the Rubell Family Collection*. Miami: Rubell Family Collection, 2007.
Harvey, Doug. "Lightening up." ArtReview. [No. 2, Aug. 2006]: 111-121.
Hoffman, Fred. *Chris Burden*. Newcastle: Locus +, 2007.
Le Feuvre, Lisa. "Chris Burden." Artforum. [Vol. 44, No. 3, Nov. 2003]: 267.
Morris, Frances. *Chris Burden: When Robots Rule: The Two Minute Airplane Factory*. London: Tate Gallery, 1999.
Noever, Peter. *Chris Burden: Beyond the Limits*. Vienna: Österreichisches Museum für angewandte Kunst, 1996.
Selwyn, Marc. "Chris Burden." Flash Art [No. 144, Jan. – Feb. 1989]: 90-94.
Tumlir, Jan. "First Break: Chris Burden." Artforum [Vol. 40, No. 4, Dec. 2001]: 23.
Ward, Frazer. "Gray zone: watching Shoot." October [No. 95, Winter 2001]: 114-130.
Wrange, Måns. *Chris Burden: Februari - Maj 1999*. Stockholm: Magasin 3 Stockholm Konsthall, 1999.

Selected Collections

Albertina, Vienna, Austria
The Art Museum of South Texas, Corpus Christi, TX
The Broad Art Foundation, Santa Monica, CA
Dallas Museum of Art, Dallas, TX
Los Angeles County Museum of Art, Los Angeles, CA
Musée de Marseilles, Marseilles, France
Museum of Contemporary Art Chicago, Chicago, IL
The Museum of Contemporary Art, Los Angeles, CA
Museum of Contemporary Art San Diego, San Diego, CA
The Museum of Modern Art, New York, NY
Orange County Museum of Art, Newport Beach, CA
Österreichisches Museum für angewandte Kunst / Gegenwartskunst, Vienna, Austria
Rubell Family Collection, Miami, FL
Wexner Center for the Visual Arts, The Ohio State University, Columbus, OH
Whitney Museum of American Art, New York, NY
Yale University, New Haven, CT

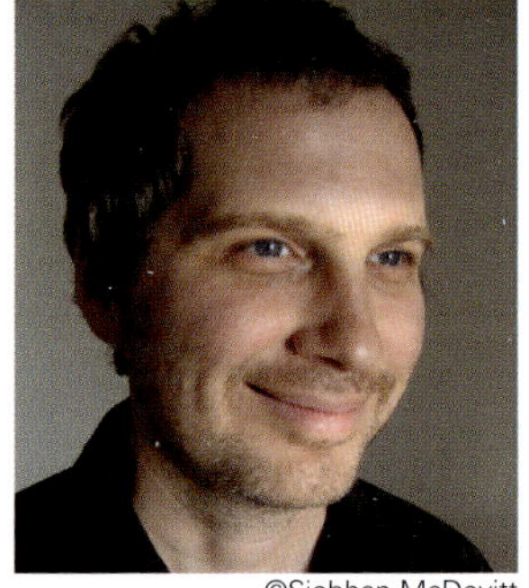
©Siobhan McDevitt

BRIAN CALVIN

Born in Visalia, CA, 1969
Lives and works in Los Angeles, CA

Education

1992-1994 M.F.A., The School of the Art Institute of Chicago, Chicago, IL
1987-1991 B.A., University of California, Berkeley, Berkeley, CA

Selected Solo Exhibitions

2007 Corvi-Mora, London, England
MARC FOXX, Los Angeles, CA
2006 Anton Kern, New York, NY
2005 Corvi-Mora, London, England
MARC FOXX, Los Angeles, CA
2004 Anton Kern, New York, NY
2003 Corvi-Mora, London, England
The Conversation, MARC FOXX, Los Angeles, CA
2002 Gallery Side 2, Tokyo, Japan
MARC FOXX, Los Angeles, CA
2001 Corvi-Mora, London, England
2000 *Days*, MARC FOXX, Los Angeles, CA
1999 Gallery Side 2, Tokyo, Japan
1998 Gallery Side 2, Tokyo, Japan
1996 *God's Plot & John Wilkes Booth*, Zolla / Lieberman Gallery, Chicago, IL

Selected Group Exhibitions

2007 *Good Morning, Midnight*, Casey Kaplan, New York, NY
If Everybody Had an Ocean. Brian Wilson: An Art Exhibition, Tate St. Ives, St. Ives, England; traveled to CAPC Musée d'Art Contemporain de Bordeaux, Bordeaux, France [cat.]
Very Abstract and Hyper Figurative, Thomas Dane Gallery, London, England
2006 *Red Eye: L.A. Artists from the Rubell Family Collection*, Rubell Family Collection, Miami, FL
2004 *California Biennial*, Orange County Museum of Art, Newport Beach, CA
2003 *Prague Biennale 1: Lazarus Effect*, Veletrzní Palác, Prague, Czech Republic
Baja to Vancouver: The West Coast in Contemporary Art, Seattle Art Museum, Seattle, WA; Museum of Contemporary Art San Diego, San Diego, CA; Vancouver Art Gallery, Vancouver, Canada; CCA Wattis Institute for Contemporary Arts, California College of the Arts, San Francisco, CA [cat.]
Ishtar, Midway Contemporary Art, Minneapolis, MN [cat.]
The Great Drawing Show: 1550-2003 AD, Michael Kohn Gallery, Los Angeles, CA
The Fourth Sex: Adolescent Extremes, Stazione Leopolda, Florence, Italy
Painting Pictures, Kunstmuseum Wolfsburg, Wolfsburg, Germany
2002 *youngsters* Skulpturen und andere Arbeiten aus Los Angeles & New York / youngsters* Sculptures and other works from Los Angeles & New York *Sammlung Köhn,* Krinzinger Projekte, Vienna, Austria [cat.]
Grey Gardens, Michael Kohn Gallery, Los Angeles, CA
The Galleries Show: Contemporary Art in London, Royal Academy of Arts, London, England
Paintings, MARC FOXX, Los Angeles, CA
Dear Painter, Paint me, Centre Georges Pompidou, Paris, France; traveled to Kunsthalle Wien, Vienna; Schirn Kunsthalle Frankfurt, Frankfurt am Main, Germany [cat.]
2001 *The Americans. New Art*, Barbican Art Gallery, London, England [cat.]
The Devil Is In The Details, Allston Skirt Gallery, Boston, MA

2000 MARC FOXX, Los Angeles, CA
1999 Gallery Side 2, Tokyo, Japan
1996 *Brian Calvin, Suzanne Doremus, Edward Henderson & Deborah Orapallo*, Foster Gallery, University of Wisconsin-Eau-Claire, Eau-Claire, Wisconsin
1995 *X-sightings*, UB Anderson Gallery, University at Buffalo, The State University of New York, Buffalo, New York, NY
1994 *Created Here: a Salon d'Ecole*, Richard Himmel Gallery, Chicago, IL
Recent Paintings, Gallery 2, The School of the Art Institute of Chicago, Chicago, IL
Don Baum's Grab Bag, Hyde Park Art Center, Chicago, IL
Discontents & Debutantes: Brian Calvin & Mike Cockrill, Center for the Visual Arts, Illinois State University, Normal, IL
1993 *Whose Broad Stripes & Bright Stars: Death, Reverence & the Struggle for Equality in America*, Betty Rymer Gallery, The School of the Art Institute of Chicago, Chicago, IL

Selected Bibliography

Bankowsky, Jack. "Best of 2004." Artforum [Vol. 43, No. 4, Dec. 2004]: 162-163.
Campagnola, Sonia. "Focus Los Angeles: a survey of contemporary Los Angeles art." Flash Art. [Vol. 39, No. 246, Jan. / Feb. 2006]: 69-75.
Coetzee, Mark, ed., *Red Eye: L.A. Artists from the Rubell Family Collection.* Miami: Rubell Family Collection, 2007.
Comer, Stuart. "Teenage fan club." Art Review [Vol. 54, Sept. 2003]: 58-63.
Farquharson, Alex. *Brian Wilson: An Art Book*, London: Four Corners, 2005.
"Focus painting part one: contemporary painting today." Flash Art [Vol. 34, No. 226, Oct. 2002]: 78-85.
Garrett, Craig. "Raf Simons." Flash Art [Vol. 37, No. 235, March - April 2004]: 65-67.
Gingeras, Alison. "Subversion du kitsch: conjectures on conceptual uses of figurative realism." Art Press [December 2000]: 28-36.
Hainley, Bruce. "Openings: Brian Calvin." Artforum [Vol. 39, No. 6, Feb. 2001]: 140-141.
Herbert, Martin. "The states of art." Art Review [Vol. 53, Oct. 2001]: 48-51.
Higgie, Jennifer. "Brian Calvin." frieze [Issue 61, Sept. 2001]: 89, 96.
Kraus, Chris, and Jane McFadden, et al. *LA Artland: Contemporary Art from Los Angeles*, London: Black Dog, 2005.
Mullins, Charlotte. *Painting people: figure painting today*. New York: D.A.P., 2006.
Pagel, David. "Sober, steady, yet electrifying." The Los Angeles Times [May 13, 2005]: E24.
Pagel, David. "The unmemorable now unforgettable." The Los Angeles Times [May 9, 2003]: E21.
Smith, Roberta. "The Staying Power (and It's Not a Freeze Frame) of Paint." The New York Times [July 21, 2002]: 25, 27.
Wilson, Michael. "Brian Calvin." Artforum [Vol. 43, No. 4, Dec. 2004]: 195.

Selected Collections

Hudson Valley Center for Contemporary Art, Peekskill, NY
The Museum of Contemporary Art, Los Angeles, CA
Orange County Museum of Art, Newport Beach, CA
Rubell Family Collection, Miami, FL

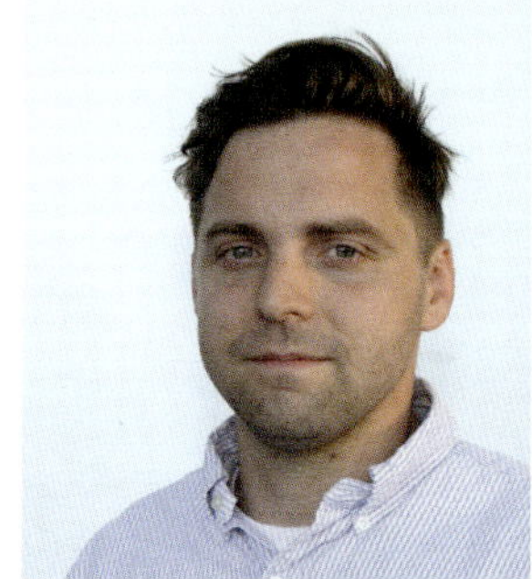
©Simon Hare Photography 2006

AARON CURRY

Born in San Antonio, TX, 1972
Lives and works in Los Angeles, CA

Education

2003-2005 M.F.A., Art Center College of Design, Pasadena, CA
1991-1994, 2000-2002 B.F.A., The School of the Art Institute of Chicago, Chicago, IL

Selected Solo Exhibitions

2008 Michael Werner Gallery, New York, NY
Galerie Daniel Buchholz, Cologne, Germany
2007 Michael Werner Gallery (Temporary), London, England
2006 *Bank Robber*, David Kordansky Gallery, Los Angeles, CA

Selected Group Exhibitions

2007 *Unmonumental: The Object in the 21st Century*, New Museum of Contemporary Art, New York, NY [cat.]
Post Rose: Artists In and Out of the Hazard Park Complex, Galerie Christian Nagel, Berlin, Germany
Sculptors' Drawings: Ideas, Studies, Sketches, Proposals, and More, Angles Gallery, Santa Monica, CA
L.A. Desire (Part 1), Galerie Dennis Kimmerich, Dusseldorf, Germany
Stuff: Internatonal Contemporary Art from the Collection of Burt Aaron, Museum of Contemporary Art Detroit, Detroit, MI
Aspects, Forms, and Figures, Bellwether Gallery, New York, NY
Material Photographs, Shane Campbell Gallery, Oak Park, IL [cat.]
2006 *Red Eye: L.A. Artists from the Rubell Family Collection,* Rubell Family Collection, Miami, FL [cat.]
L.A. Trash & Treasure, Milliken Gallery, Stockholm, Sweden
Untitled (for H. C. Westermann), The Contemporary Museum, Honolulu, Honolulu, HI [cat.]
Cloudbreak, Hiromi Yoshii, Tokyo, Japan
The Figs Play Fox Dead, David Kordansky Gallery, Los Angeles, CA
2005 *Southern Exposure*, New Wight Gallery, University of California, Los Angeles, Los Angeles, CA
Autonomy, Foxy Production, New York, NY
2004 *Group Show*, Worth Ryder Gallery, University of California, Berkeley, Berkeley, CA

Selected Bibliography

Bartels, Daghild. "Jeder Penny fur die Kunst." Parnass [Jan. 2007]: 77.
Brooks, Amra. "Must See Art." LA Weekly [Nov. 15, 2006].
Brooks, Amra. "Los Angeles Roundup: A Report on Current Gallery, Museum Shows." Artinfo.com [April 2006].
Coetzee, Mark, ed., *Red Eye: L.A. Artists from the Rubell Family Collection*. Miami: Rubell Family Collection, 2007.
Cotter, Holland. "Art in Review: Aspects, Forms, and Figures." The New York Times [March 2, 2007]. E30.
Cotter, Holland. "Autonomy." The New York Times [Sept. 30, 2005].
Cotter, Holland. "The World Tour Rolls Into Town, Sprawling but Tidy (Art Review: The Armory Show)." The New York Times [March 10, 2006]: E29, E41.
Garnet, Daisy. "The Collector: Why the Collector Mera Rubell Keeps it All in the Family." The New York Times Magazine [Dec. 3, 2006]: 74.
Holte, Michael Ned. "Openings." Artforum [Summer 2007]: 481-483.
Kino, Carol. "ART; Welcome to the Museum of My Stuff." The New York Times [Feb. 18, 2007]: Section 2, 30.
Pearson, Anthony. *Material Photographs*. Oak Park: Shane Campbell Gallery, 2007.
Rochette, Anne, and Wade Saunders. "Place Matters: Los Angeles Sculpture Today." Art in America [Nov. 2006]: 174.

Rooks, Michael. *Dreaming of a Speech Without Words: The Paintings and Early Objects of H.C. Westermann.* Honolulu: The Contemporary Museum, 2006.
Smith, Roberta. "Michael Queenland: Bread & Balloons." The New York Times [March 9, 2007].
Smith, Roberta. "More Than You Can See: Storm of Art Engulfs Miami." The New York Times [Dec. 9, 2005].
Tumlir, Jan. "Sci-fi Historicism Part 3: Character Animation in Contemporary Los Angeles Art." Flash Art [July-Sept. 2007]: 120-124.
Tumlir, Jan. "Sci-fi Historicism." Flash Art [May-June 2007]: 118-121.

Selected Collections

Armand Hammer Museum, University of California, Los Angeles, CA
Blake Byrne Collection, Los Angeles, CA
Collection of Dean Valentine and Amy Adelson, Los Angeles, CA
Collection of Gaby and Wilhelm Schürmann, Aachen, Germany
Collection of Martin and Rebecca Eisenberg, New York, NY
The Rachofsky Collection, Dallas, TX
The Rennie Collection, Vancouver, Canada
Rubell Family Collection, Miami, FL
Collection of Susan and Michael Hort, New York, NY

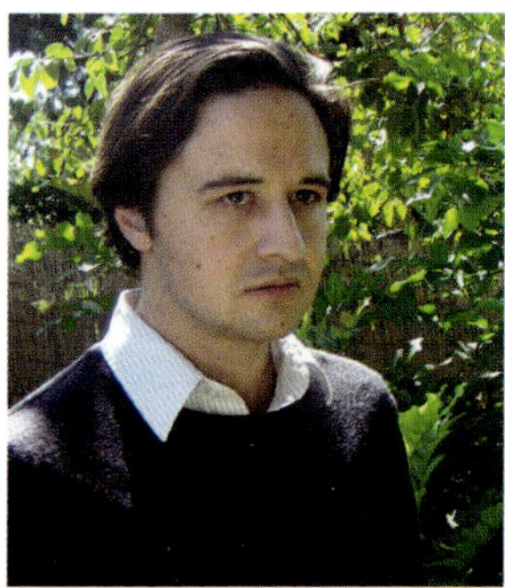

BRIAN FAHLSTROM

Born in Kansas City, MO, 1978
Lives and works in Los Angeles, CA

Education

2001- 2003 M.F.A., Art Center College of Design, Pasadena, CA
1997- 2000 B.F.A., Kansas City Art Institute, Kansas City, MO

Selected Solo Exhibitions

2007 Suzie Q, Zurich, Switzerland
2006 MARC FOXX, Los Angeles, CA
gallery.sora, Tokyo, Japan
2005 MARC FOXX, Los Angeles, CA

Selected Group Exhibitions

2007 *Abstract America*, The Saatchi Gallery, London, England
Modern Lovers, Glendale College Art Gallery, Glendale College, Glendale, CA
Poker, Galleria Monica de Cardenas, Milan, Italy
2006 *Homecoming*, JCCC Gallery of Art, Johnson County Community College, Overland Park, KS
Red Eye: L.A. Artists from the Rubell Family Collection, Rubell Family Collection, Miami, FL [cat.]
2006 *2006 California Biennial*, Orange County Museum of Art, Newport Beach, CA [cat.]
2005 MARC FOXX, Los Angeles, CA
2004 *An Arc, Another, and So On,* Fine Arts Gallery, California State University, Los Angeles, CA
The Next Wave: New Abstract Painting in Los Angeles, Black Dragon Society, Los Angeles, CA

Selected Bibliography

Balaschak, Chris. "Brian Fahlstrom." frieze [March 2007]: 200-201.
Coetzee, Mark, ed., *Red Eye: L.A. Artists from the Rubell Family Collection*. Miami: Rubell Family Collection, 2007.
Dailey, Meghan, and Norman Rosenthal. *USA TODAY: New American Art from the Saatchi Gallery*, London: Royal Academy of Arts; New York: Harry N. Abrams, 2006.
Holte, Michael Ned. "Richard Aldrich, Olivia Booth, Brian Fahlstrom, et al." www.artforum.com [March 12, 2005].
Pagel, David. "Brian Fahlstrom at Marc Foxx: Layer upon layer of references." The Los Angeles Times, [July 29, 2005]: E25.
Pence, Elizabeth. "The Next Wave: New Abstract Painting in Los Angeles" Artweek [May 2004]: 21-22.
Timberg, Scott. "Affordable Art? Right This Way." The Los Angeles Times [August 25, 2007].
Tumlir, Jan. *2006 California Biennial Catalogue.* Newport Beach: Orange County Museum of Art, 2006.

Selected Collections

The Capital Group Companies, Inc., Los Angeles, CA
Creative Artists Agency, Los Angeles, CA
Nerman Museum of Contemporary Art, Johnson County Community College, Overland Park, KS
Orange County Museum of Art, Newport Beach, CA
Rubell Family Collection, Miami, FL
Saatchi Collection, London, England
The UBS Art Collection, Zurich Switzerland

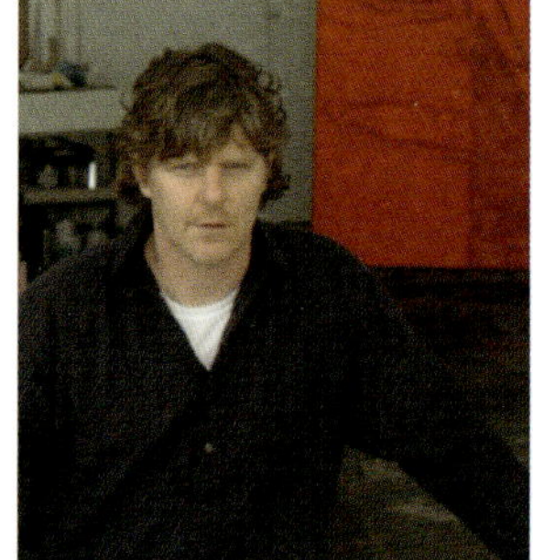

MARK GROTJAHN

Born in Pasadena, CA, 1968
Lives and works in Los Angeles, CA

Education

1995 Skowhegan School of Painting and Sculpture, Skowhegan, ME
1994-1995 M.F.A., Department of Art Practice, University of California, Berkeley, Berkeley, CA
1986-1990 B.F.A., Department of Art Practice, University of Colorado, Boulder, CO

Selected Solo Exhibitions

2007 *Mark Grotjahn*, Kunstmuseum Thun, Thun, Switzerland
Mark Grotjahn. Blue Paintings, Light to Dark, One through Ten, Anton Kern Gallery, New York, NY
2006 *Mark Grotjahn*, Whitney Museum of American Art, New York, NY
2005 Blum & Poe, Los Angeles, CA
Stephen Friedman Gallery, London, England
Mark Grotjahn: Drawings, The Armand Hammer Museum of Art and Culture Center, University of California, Los Angeles, CA
2003 Anton Kern Gallery, New York, NY
2002 Blum & Poe, Santa Monica, CA
2000 Blum & Poe, Santa Monica, CA
1998 Blum & Poe, Santa Monica, CA

Selected Group Exhibitions

2007 *Like Color in Pictures*, Aspen Art Museum, Aspen, CO
Hammer Contemporary Collection Part I, The Armand Hammer Museum of Art and Culture Center, University of California, Los Angeles, CA
L.A. Desire, Part 1, Galerie Dennis Kimmerich, Dusseldorf, Germany
Painting as Fact – Fact as Fiction, de Pury & Luxembourg, Zurich, Switzerland [cat.]
Zbigniew Rogalski, Galerie Almine Rech, Paris, France
2006 *Red Eye: L.A. Artists from the Rubell Family Collection*, Rubell Family Collection, Miami, FL [cat.]
Painting in Tongues, The Museum of Contemporary Art, Los Angeles, CA
Whitney Biennial, Whitney Museum of American Art, New York, NY
Delete / How to Make a Perfect Ghost, Anton Kern Gallery, NY
Shane Campbell Gallery, Chicago, IL
Gone Formalism, Institute of Contemporary Art, Philadelphia, PA
Figures in the Field: Figurative Sculpture and Abstract Painting from Chicago Collections, Museum of Contemporary Art Chicago, Chicago, IL
The Last Time They Met, Stephen Friedman Gallery, London, England
The Monty Hall Problem, Blum & Poe, Santa Monica, CA
Dark Matter, White Cube, London, England
Modern Primitivism, Shane Campbell Gallery, Chicago, IL
2005 *The Painted World*, P.S. 1 Contemporary Art Center, Long Island City, NY
New Work/New Acquisitions, The Museum of Modern Art, New York, NY
Think Blue, Blum & Poe, Santa Monica, CA
Tête à Tête, Greenberg Van Doren Gallery, New York, NY
Plip, Plip, Plipty!, Richard Telles Fine Art, Los Angeles, CA
2004 *54th Carnegie International,* Carnegie Museum of Art, Pittsburgh. PA
Now is a Good Time, Andrea Rosen Gallery, New York, NY
I, Assassin, Wallspace, New York, NY
Colored Pencil, KS Art, New York, NY
The Thought That Counts, sister, Los Angeles, CA
2003 Blum & Poe, Los Angeles, CA

2002 *L.A. On My Mind: Recent Acquisitions from MOCA's Collection*, The Museum of Contemporary Art, Los Angeles, CA

2001 *Jennifer Bornstein, Mark Grotjahn, Dave Muller, Florian Maier-Aichen*, Blum & Poe, Santa Monica, CA
Sharing Sunsets, Museum of Contemporary Art, Tucson, AZ
Out of Bounds: Working Off Paper, Luckman Gallery, California State University, Los Angeles, CA

2000 *'00*, Gladstone Gallery, New York, NY
Works on Paper From Los Angeles, Studio Guenzani, Milan, Italy
Young and Dumb, Acme, Los Angeles, CA

1998 *Entropy at Home*, Neuer Aachener Kunstverein, Aachen, Germany
Selections Winter 1998, The Drawing Center, New York, NY
Group Show, Derek Eller Gallery, New York, NY

1997 Gallery 16, San Francisco, CA
Helmut Federle, Gunter Umberg, Mark Grotjahn, Ingo Meller, Anthony Meier Fine Arts, San Francisco, CA

1996 Four Walls, San Francisco, CA

Selected Bibliography

Baker, Kenneth. "Access." San Francisco Chronicle [May 9, 1995].
"Best of the Rest" New York Magazine [Sept. 4-11, 2006].
Brown, Delia. "Artforum Top Ten." Artforum [Vol. 41, No. 5, Jan. 2003]: 41.
Burton, Johanna. "Mark Grotjahn – Anton Kern." Artforum [Vol. 42, No. 4, Dec. 2003]: 146-7.
Coetzee, Mark, ed., *Red Eye: L.A. Artists from the Rubell Family Collection.* Miami: Rubell Family Collection, 2007.
Conner, Justin. "Mark Grotjahn - Abstractionists Are Flexing More Than Their Muscles." Interview [Sept. 2006]: 96.
Coomer, Martin. "The Butterfly Effect." ArtReview [No. 3, Sept. 2006]: 74-77.
Fazzolari, Bruno. "Backroads with Doug McConnell." Artweek [May 1996].
Goodbody, Bridget. "Mark Grotjahn at Anton Kern Gallery." The New York Times [Feb. 16, 2007].
Grosz, David. "Butterflies by a Graphite-Stained Hand." The New York Sun [Oct. 26, 2006].
"Group Show at Gorney, Bravin + Lee." The New Yorker [Feb. 5, 2001]: 18.
Hankwitz, Molly. "Backroads with Doug McConnell." Art Papers [July 1996].
Haus, Mary. "Sign here!" ARTnews [Vol. 103, No. 7, Summer 2004]: 162-165.
Helfand, Glen. "Mark Grotjahn, Brent Petersen, Paul Sietsema." Bay Area Guardian [Aug. 13, 1997].
Holte, Michael Ned. "Mark Grotjahn." Artforum [Vol. 44, No. 3 Nov. 2005]: 259-260.
Kimmelman, Michael. "Biennial 2006 Short on Pretty, Long on Collaboration." The New York Times [March 13, 2006].
Knight, Christopher. "A Global Cacophony." Los Angeles Times [Dec. 5, 2004].
Knight, Christopher. "Mark Grotjahn at The Hammer Museum." Los Angeles Times [Feb. 18, 2004].
Knight, Christopher. "Painting can speak in many tongues." Los Angeles Times [Feb. 4, 2006].
Kunitz, Daniel. "Whitney Biennial 2006-2006 - Day for Night." ArtReview [May / June, 2006]: 123.
Kuspit, Donald. "Mark Grotjahn." Artforum [Vol. 45, No. 5, Jan. 2007]: 253.
Lavitt, Lauren. "Focus Los Angeles." Flash Art [Vol. 39, No. 246, Jan. – Feb. 2006].
Miles, Christopher. "Working Variables, Switching Games: Mark Grotjahn." Artext, [No. 72, Fall 2002]: 44-51.
Pagel, David. "Trying to Fit In." Los Angeles Times [Nov. 20, 1998]: F32.
Saltz, Jerry. "The Parallax View." Village Voice [Oct. 24, 2006].
Smith, Roberta. "Mark Grotjahn at Whitney." The New York Times [Sept. 22, 2006].
Trainor, James. "Rates of Exchange." frieze [No. 78, Oct. 2003]: 116-117.
Tumlir, Jan. "Big Nose Baby and the Moose." Flash Art [Vol. 40, No. 252, Feb. 2007]: 82.

Selected Collections

Carnegie Museum of Art, Pittsburgh, PA
The Museum of Contemporary Art, Los Angeles, CA
The Museum of Modern Art, New York, NY
Rubell Family Collection, Miami, FL
San Francisco Museum of Modern Art, San Francisco, CA
Solomon R. Guggenheim Museum, New York, NY
Whitney Museum of American Art, New York, NY

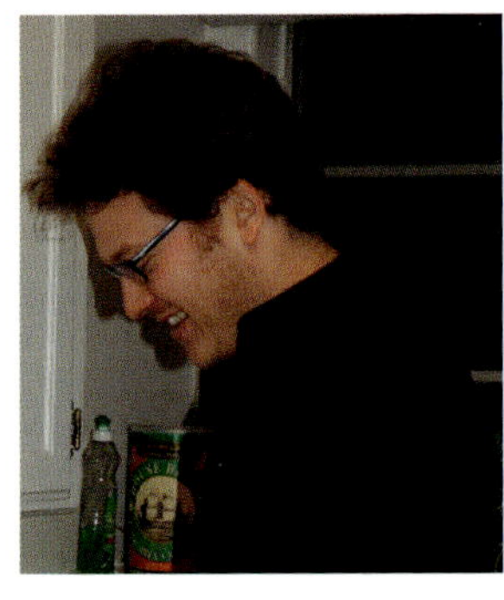

KARL HAENDEL

Born in Great Neck, NY, 1976
Lives and works in Los Angeles, CA

Education

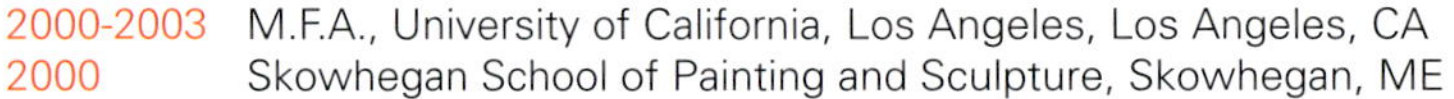

2000-2003 M.F.A., University of California, Los Angeles, Los Angeles, CA
2000 Skowhegan School of Painting and Sculpture, Skowhegan, ME
1998-1999 Whitney Museum Independent Study Program, Whitney Museum of American Art, New York, NY
1994-1998 B.A., Art Semiotics and Art History, Brown University, Providence, RI

Selected Solo Exhibitions

2007 *I Need Work*, Harris Lieberman, New York, NY
Last Fair Deal Gone Down, Anna Helwing Gallery, Los Angeles, CA
2006 *MOCA Focus: Karl Haendel*, The Museum of Contemporary Art, Los Angeles, CA [cat.]
Makes a Long Time Man Feel Bad, Sommer Contemporary Art, Tel Aviv, Israel
Make Me Down a Pallet on Your Floor, Sorcha Dallas, Glasgow, Scotland
2005 *Grits Ain't Groceries (All Around the World)*, Anna Helwing Gallery, Los Angeles, CA
2003 Anna Helwing Gallery, Los Angeles, CA

Selected Group Exhibitions

2007 *Lines, Grids, Stains, Words*, The Museum of Modern Art, New York, NY [cat.]
Hammer Contemporary Collection: Part I, Armand Hammer Museum, University of California, Los Angeles, CA
HB – Works on Paper, Studio Guenzani, Milan, Italy
The Price of Everything…, The Amie and Tony James Gallery, The Graduate Center, The City University of New York, New York, NY [cat.]
The New Authentics: Artists of the Post-Jewish Generation, Spertus Museum, Spertus Institute of Jewish Studies, Chicago, IL; traveling to Rose Art Museum of Brandeis University, Brandeis University, Waltham, MA [cat.]
2006 *Red Eye: L.A. Artists from the Rubell Family Collection*, Rubell Family Collection, Miami, FL [cat.]
Transforming Chronologies: An Atlas of Drawings, Part Two, The Museum of Modern Art, New York, NY [cat.]
Particulate Matter, Mills College Art Museum, Mills College, Oakland, CA [cat.]
Pierre Bismuth, Ryan Gander, Karl Haendel, T.Kelly Mason, Cohan and Leslie, New York, NY
A Brighter Day, James Cohan Gallery, New York, NY [cat.]
Down by Law, Whitney Biennial 2006, Whitney Museum of American Art, New York, NY [cat.]
2005 *Hunch and Flail*, Artists Space, New York, NY
Drive Time, Wignall Museum / Gallery, Chaffey College, Rancho Cucamonga, CA
Rogue Wave, LA Louver, Venice, CA [cat.]
Uncertain States of America: American Art in the Third Millenium, Astrup Fearnley Museet for Moderne Kunst, Oslo, Norway; traveled to Center for Curatorial Studies Museum, Bard College, Annandale-on-Hudson, NY; Serpentine Gallery, London, England; Reykjavik Art Museum, Reykjavik, Iceland; Herning Art Museum, Herning, Denmark; Centre for Contemporary Art, Warsaw, Poland; Musée de Sérignan, Sérignan, France; traveling to Galerie Rudolfinum, Prague, Czech Republic; Songzhuang Art Center, Beijing, China [cat.]
2004 *2004 California Biennial*, Orange County Museum of Contemporary Art, Newport Beach, CA [cat.]
Gio Ponti: Furnished Settings & Figuration, ACME, Los Angeles, CA
2002 *Emily Jacir, Karl Haendel, Kevin Hooyman*, La Panaderia, Mexico City, Mexico

Selected Bibliography

Bluhm, Erik. "Karl Haendel." artUS [Issue 13, May / June 2006]: 5.

Coetzee, Mark, ed., *Red Eye: L.A. Artists from the Rubell Family Collection.* Miami: Rubell Family Collection, 2007.

Jones, Leslie. "Karl Haendel at Anna Helwing Gallery." Art on Paper [Vol. 9, No. 6, July / Aug. 2005]: 65.

Searle, Adrian. "Rebels without a cause." The Guardian Unlimited [Sept. 12, 2006]: G2, 18-20.

Smith, Roberta. "Chelsea Is a Battlefield: Galleries Muster Groups." The New York Times [July 28, 2006]: B25 / B31.

Smith, Roberta. "Endgame Art? It's Borrow, Sample and Multiply in an Exhibition at Bard College." The New York Times [July 7, 2006]: B23, B27.

Sutton, Gloria, and Gabriel Ritter. *MOCA Focus: Karl Haendel.* Los Angeles: Museum of Contemporary Art, 2006.

Szakacs, Dennis, and Elizabeth Armstrong. *2004 California Biennial.* Newport Beach: Orange County Museum of Art, 2004.

Thompson, Susannah, "Karl Haendel." Contemporary Magazine [No. 83, 2006]: 60-63.

Zellan, Jody. "Karl Haendel." Art Press [No. 309, Feb. 2005]: 69.

Selected Collections

Armand Hammer Museum, University of California, Los Angeles, CA
Astrup Fearnley Museet for Moderne Kunst, Oslo, Norway
Frank Cohen Museum of Contemporary Art, Manchester, England
The Israel Museum, Jerusalem, Israel
Michael Rabkin and Chip Tom Collection, Los Angeles, CA
The Museum of Contemporary Art, Los Angeles, CA
The Museum of Modern Art, New York, NY
Orange County Museum of Art, Newport Beach, CA
Rubell Family Collection, Miami, FL
Whitney Museum of American Art, New York, NY

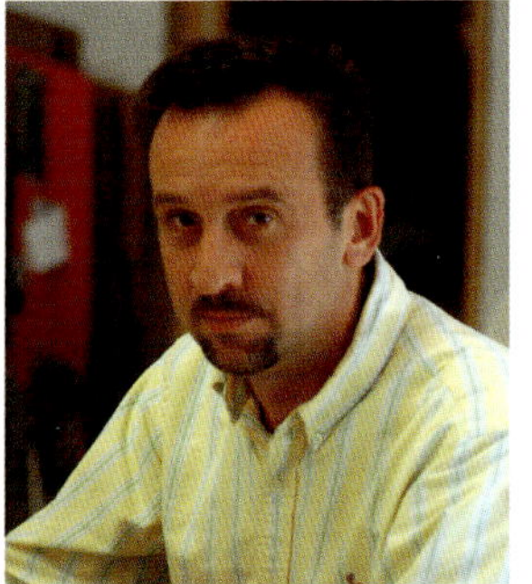

RICHARD HAWKINS

Born in Mexia, TX, 1961
Lives in and works in Los Angeles, CA

Education

1986-1988 M.F.A., California Institute of the Arts, Valencia, CA
1980-1984 B.F.A., The University of Texas at Austin, Austin, TX

Selected Solo Exhibitions

2007 Richard Telles Fine Art, Los Angeles, CA
Of Two Minds, Simultaneously, de Appel, Amsterdam, Netherlands [cat.]
2006 Corvi-Mora, London, England
Urbis Paganus Part I + III, Galerie Daniel Buchholz, Cologne, Germany
Greene Naftali, New York, NY
2004 Richard Telles Fine Art, Los Angeles, CA
Corvi-Mora, London, England
Galerie Daniel Buchholz, Cologne, Germany
2003 Kunstverein Heilbronn, Heilbronn, Germany [cat.]
Galerie Praz-Delavallade, Paris, France
Richard Telles Fine Art, Los Angeles, CA
2002 Corvi-Mora, London, England
2001 Galerie Praz-Delavallade, Paris, France
2000 Richard Telles Fine Art, Los Angeles, CA
Corvi-Mora, London, England
Galerie Daniel Buchholz, Cologne, Germany
1999 Galerie Praz-Delavallade, Paris, France
1997 Richard Telles Fine Art, Los Angeles, CA
1996 *Richard Hawkins: new work*, Feature Inc., New York, NY
Richard Telles Fine Art, Los Angeles, CA
1995 *c. 1975-76: wiley wiggins, frail 8th grade oddity / freshman-year glam [w / matt dillon as my boyfriend at the time]*, Richard Telles Fine Art, Los Angeles, CA
1993 *Into the Heart of China*, Richard Telles Fine Art, Los Angeles, CA
New Work by Richard Hawkins, Feature Inc., New York, NY
1992 Roy Boyd Gallery, Santa Monica, CA

Selected Group Exhibitions

2007 *If Everybody Had an Ocean: Brian Wilson: an Art Exhibition*, Tate St. Ives, St. Ives, England; traveled to CAPC Musée d'Art Contemporain de Bordeaux, Bordeaux, France [cat.]
RAW Among the Ruins, Marres Centrum voor Contemporaine Cultuur, Maastricht, Netherlands [cat.]
2006 *Red Eye: L.A. Artists from the Rubell Family Collection*, Rubell Family Collection, Miami, FL [cat.]
Galerie Daniel Buchholz, Köln, at Metro Pictures, Metro Pictures Gallery, New York, NY
3° Attese Biennale di Ceramica nell'Arte Contemporanea, Albissola Marina, Italy; Vado Ligure, Italy [cat.]
2005 *The Blake Byrne Collection*, The Museum of Contemporary Art, Los Angeles, CA [cat.]
2003 *Ishtar*, Midway Contemporary Art, Minneapolis, MN [cat.]
2002 *Mirror Image*, Armand Hammer Museum, University of California, Los Angeles, Los Angeles, CA [cat.]
2000 *Unraveling Desire*, Center for Curatorial Studies Museum, Bard College, Annandale-on-Hudson, NY [cat.]
1999 *Richard Hawkins & Champion Studios*, Richard Telles Fine Art, Los Angeles, CA
Persuasion: Tales of Commerce and the Avant-Garde, UB Art Galleries, University at Buffalo, The State University of New York, Buffalo, NY [cat.]

1998 *The Unreal Person: Portraiture in the Digital Age*, Huntington Beach Art Center, Huntington Beach, CA [cat.]
In Your Face, The Andy Warhol Museum, Pittsburgh, PA
1997 *Scene of the Crime*, Armand Hammer Museum, University of California, Los Angeles, Los Angeles, CA [cat.]
1995 *In a Different Light*, Berkeley Art Museum and Pacific Film Archive, University of California at Berkeley, Berkeley, CA [cat.]
Narcissistic Disturbance, Ben Maltz Gallery, Otis College of Art and Design, Los Angeles, CA [cat.]
It's Only Rock & Roll: Rock & Roll Currents in Contemporary Art, Phoenix Art Museum, Phoenix, AZ; traveled to Contemporary Arts Center, Cincinnati, OH; Lakeview Museum of Arts and Sciences, Peoria, IL; Virginia Beach Center for the Arts, Virginia Beach, VA; Tacoma Art Museum, Tacoma, WA; Museum of Contemporary Art Jacksonville, Jacksonville, FL; Bedford Gallery, Lesher Center for the Arts, Walnut Creek, CA; Lowe Art Museum, University of Miami, Coral Gables, FL; Milwaukee Art Museum, Milwaukee, WI; Arkansas Arts Center, Little Rock, AR [cat.]
1994 *The Use of Pleasure*, Terrain Gallery, San Francisco, CA [cat.]
Mechanical Reproduction, Galerie van Gelder, Amsterdam, Netherlands [cat.]
1993 *Commodity Image*, International Center of Photography, New York, NY; traveled to National Museum of American Art, Washington, DC; Laguna Art Museum, Laguna Beach, CA; Mary and Leigh Block Museum of Art, Northwestern University, Evanston, IL
1992 *Hollywood, Hollywood: Identity Under the Guide of Celebrity*, Alyce de Roulet Williamson Gallery, Art Center College of Design, Pasadena, CA [cat.]
The Mud Club, Winchester Cathedral & Lake Nairobi, William E. Gahlberg Gallery, McAninch Arts Center, College of DuPage, Glen Ellyn, IL [cat.]
1991 *Situation: Perspectives on Lesbian and Gay Artists*, New Langton Arts, San Francisco, CA [cat.]
Presenting Rearwards, Rosamund Felsen Gallery, Santa Monica, CA [cat.]

Selected Bibliography

Coetzee, Mark, ed., *Red Eye: L.A. Artists from the Rubell Family Collection*. Miami: Rubell Family Collection, 2007.
Eichler, Dominic. "Variety Shows." AfterAll [Spring / Summer 2007]: 35-52.
Farquharson, Alex. "Different Strokes." frieze [Issue 97, March 2006].
Farquharson, Alex. "Richard Hawkins." frieze [Issue 54, Sept. – Oct. 2000]. 121-122.
Ferguson, Russell. "Richard Hawkins." Artforum [Oct. 2004].
Hainley, Bruce. "Message to Michael from Bruce Hainley." frieze [No. 48, Sept. - Oct. 1999]: 72-77.
Hainley, Bruce. "Richard Hawkins." Artforum [Vol. 36, No. 7, March 1998]: 106.
Handel, Susan. *Cream: Contemporary Art Culture*. London: Phaidon Press, 1999: 172- 175.
Knight, Christopher. *Last Chance for Eden: Selected Art Criticism by Christopher Knight*. Malin Wilson, ed. Los Angeles: Art Issues Press, 1995: 309-312.
Miles, Christopher. "Richard Hawkins." Artforum [Vol. 43, No. 6, Feb. 2005]: 178-179.
Myers, Terry. "Richard Hawkins." Modern Painters [Feb. 2005]: 107.
Rehberg, Vivian. "Le Voyage Intérieur." Flash Art [Issue 98, April 2006]: 54.

Selected Collections

Astrup Fearnley Museet for Moderne Kunst, Oslo, Norway
Armand Hammer Museum, University of California, Los Angeles, Los Angeles, CA
Michael Rabkin and Chip Tom Collection, Los Angeles, CA
The Museum of Contemporary Art, Los Angeles, CA
The Museum of Modern Art, New York, NY
Rubell Family Collection, Miami, FL
University of San Francisco, San Francisco, CA

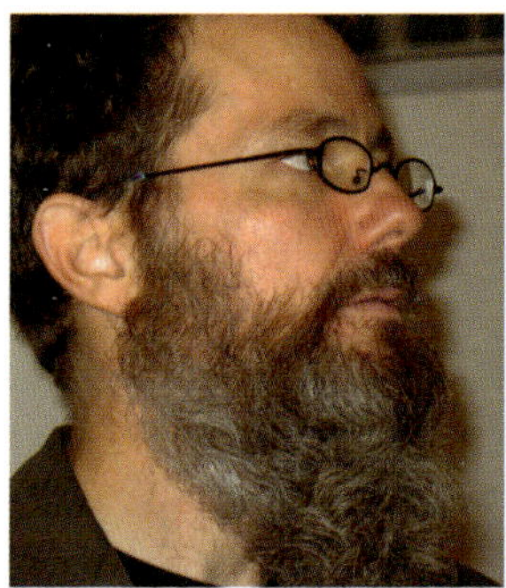
©Aristide Gagliardi

EVAN HOLLOWAY

Born in La Mirada, CA, 1967
Lives and works in Los Angeles, CA

Education

1995-1997 M.F.A., University of California, Los Angeles, CA
1986-1989 B.A., University of California, Santa Cruz, CA

Selected Solo Exhibitions

2007 *Scripted and Scored*, Galleria Raucci / Santamaria, Naples, Italy
for REE, MARC FOXX, Los Angeles, CA
2006 *$ocial Epi$temology*, Harris Lieberman Gallery, New York, NY
2005 *A Voyage to Laputa*, Xavier Hufkens, Brussels, Belgium
Analog Counterrevolution, The Approach, London, England
2004 *I Don't Exist*, MARC FOXX, Los Angeles, CA
2003 *A White Hunter*, MARC FOXX, Los Angeles, CA
2002 Xavier Hufkens, Brussels, Belgium
Galleria Raucci / Santamaria, Naples, Italy
2001 *New Sculptures*, The Approach, London, England
MARC FOXX, Los Angeles, CA
1999 MARC FOXX, Los Angeles, CA
1997 *Black Cabinet*, MARC FOXX, Santa Monica, CA

Selected Group Exhibitions

2007 *Ensemble*, Institute of Contemporary Art, University of Pennsylvania, Philadelphia, PA
Designomite, Black Dragon Society, Los Angeles, CA
Time Difference, Initial Access, Wolverhampton, England
2006 *Red Eye: L.A. Artists from the Rubell Family Collection*, Rubell Family Collection, Miami, FL [cat.]
The Uncertainty of Objects and Ideas: Recent Sculpture, Hirshhorn Museum and Sculpture Garden, Smithsonian Institution, Washington, DC [cat.]
Gone Formalism, Institute of Contemporary Art, University of Pennsylvania, Philadelphia, PA
2005 *Drunk vs. Stoned 2*, Gavin Brown's enterprise, New York, NY
Think Blue, Blum & Poe, Los Angeles, CA
Sculptures d'Appartement, Musée Départemental d'Art Contemporain de Rochechouart, Rochechouart, France [cat.]
Rogue Wave '05: 19 Artists from Los Angeles, LA Louver, Los Angeles, CA [cat.]
A Walk to Remember, Los Angeles Contemporary Exhibitions, Los Angeles, CA
We Disagree, Andrew Kreps Gallery and The Wrong Gallery, New York, NY
2004 *New Work: Evan Holloway / Dave Muller*, San Francisco Museum of Modern Art, San Francisco, CA [cat.]
Painting on Sculpture, Tanya Bonakdar Gallery, New York, NY
for nobody knows himself if he is only himself and not another at the same time, MARC FOXX, Los Angeles, CA
Baja to Vancouver: The West Coast and Contemporary Art, Seattle Art Museum, Seattle, WA; traveled to Museum of Contemporary Art San Diego, San Diego, CA; Vancouver Art Gallery, Vancouver, Canada; CCA Wattis Institute for Contemporary Arts, California College of the Arts, San Francisco, CA [cat.]
Warped Space, CCA Wattis Institute for Contemporary Arts, California College of the Arts, San Francisco, CA

2003 *Evan Holloway / Gary Webb*, The Approach, London, England
Evan Holloway, Matthew Ronay, Hiroshi Sugito, MARC FOXX, Los Angeles, CA
The Moderns, Castello di Rivoli Museo d'Art Contemporanea, Turin, Italy [cat.]
Guided by Heroes, Z33, Hasselt, Belgium [cat.]
Youngstars, Krinzinger Projekte, Vienna, Austria
2002 *2002 Whitney Biennial*, Whitney Museum of American Art, New York, NY [cat.]
A Show That Will Show That a Show Is Not Only a Show, The Project, Los Angeles, CA
2002 California Biennial, Orange County Museum of Art, Newport Beach, CA [cat.]
My Head Is On Fire But My Heart Is Full Of Love, Charlottenburg Museum, Copenhagen, Denmark
Officina America, Galleria d'Arte Moderna di Bologna, Bologna, Italy [cat.]
2001 *The Americans: New Art*, The Barbican, London, England [cat.]
Mise en Scène: New L.A. Sculpture, Santa Monica Museum of Art, Santa Monica, CA [cat.]
2000 *SHOCKWAVE*, Galleria Raucci / Santamaria, Naples, Italy
1999 *Standing Still & Walking In Los Angeles*, Gagosian Gallery, Los Angeles, CA [cat.]
Caught, 303 Gallery, New York, NY
1998 *Play Mode*, The University Art Gallery, University of California, Irvine, CA; traveled to Jean Paul Slusser Gallery, University of Michigan, Ann Arbor, MI [cat.]
Plaats, W139, Amsterdam, Netherlands
Low, MARC FOXX, Los Angeles, CA
1997 *Work & Progress*, Los Angeles Contemporary Exhibitions, Los Angeles, CA

Selected Bibliography

Adler, Dan. "Evan Holloway at Marc Foxx." Art in America [May 2005]: 177.
Coetzee, Mark, ed., *Red Eye: L.A. Artists from the Rubell Family Collection*. Miami: Rubell Family Collection, 2007.
Ellegood, Anne. *The uncertainty of objects and ideas: recent sculpture*, Washington: Hirshhorn Museum and Sculpture Garden, 2006.
Hainley, Bruce. "Evan Holloway at Marc Foxx." Artforum [Jan. 1998]: 106.
Ice Cream: Contemporary Art in Culture, London: Phaidon Publishing, 2007.
Intra, Giovanni. "Evan Holloway: when bad attitude becomes form." artext [No. 72, Feb. - April 2001]: 52-55.
Kraus, Chris, and Jane McFadden, et al. *LA Artland: Contemporary Art from Los Angeles*, London: Black Dog, 2005.
Kuo, Michelle. "Review: The Uncertainty of Objects and Ideas." Artforum [Feb. 2007].
Myers, Terry R. *Standing Still & Walking in Los Angeles*, Beverly Hills: Gagosian Gallery, 1999.
Pagel, David. "A Group's Power to Unsettle Us." The Los Angeles Times [Oct. 22, 2004]: E20.
Rappolt, Mark. "The man who sold the world." I-D [Issue 264, March 2006].
Sholis, Brian. "Review at Marc Foxx, Los Angeles." www.artforum.com [Nov. 5, 2004].
Smith, Roberta. "Evan Holloway: Social Epistemology." The New York Times [Nov. 17, 2006].

Selected Collections

Armand Hammer Museum, University of California, Los Angeles, CA
Hirshhorn Museum and Sculpture Garden, Smithsonian Institution, Washington, DC
Laguna Art Museum, Laguna Beach, CA
Los Angeles County Museum of Art, Los Angeles, CA
Rubell Family Collection, Miami, FL
Whitney Museum of American Art, New York, NY

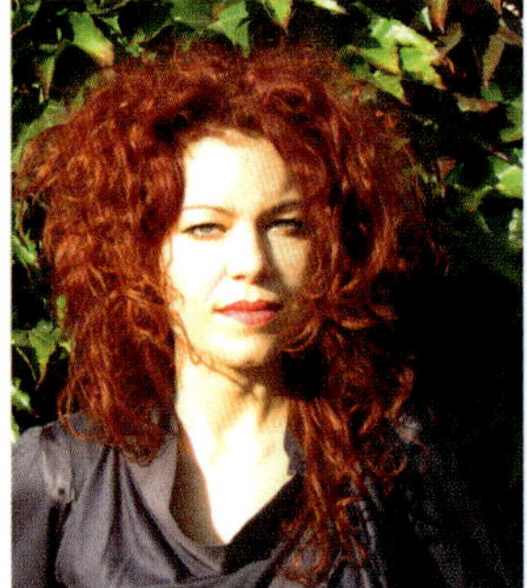
©Ted Mineo

VIOLET HOPKINS

Born in El Paso, TX, 1973
Lives and works in Los Angeles, CA

Education

2000-2002 M.F.A., California Institute of the Arts, Valencia, CA
1991-1996 B.F.A., The University of Texas at Austin, Austin, TX

Selected Solo Exhibitions

2008 gallery.sora, Tokyo, Japan
2007 *Bultungin,* Galerie Balice Hertling, Paris, France
2006 *Entoptically Yours*, Foxy Production, New York, NY
Chromatophoric, David Kordansky Gallery, Los Angeles, CA
2004 *Fauna*, Golinko Kordansky Gallery, Los Angeles, CA
2002 *Illuminated Echoes*, lemon sky: projects + editions, Los Angeles, CA
At the Brimming, Lime Gallery, California Institute of the Arts, Valencia, CA
2001 *Glow*, Lime Gallery, California Institute of the Arts, Valencia, CA

Selected Group Exhibitions

2006 *Against The Sky,* Stuart Shave / Modern Art, London, England
Red Eye: L.A. Artists from the Rubell Family Collection, Rubell Family Collection, Miami, FL [cat.]
Art On Paper 2006, Weatherspoon Art Museum, The University of North Carolina at Greensboro, Greensboro, NC [cat.]
LAXed: Paintings from the Other Side, Peres Projects, Berlin, Germany
Hotel California, Glendale College Art Gallery, Glendale Community College, Glendale, CA
2005 *Drawn Out*, Gallery 400, College of Architecture and the Arts, University of Illinois at Chicago, Chicago, IL
Rogue Wave '05: 19 Artists from Los Angeles, LA Louver, Los Angeles, CA [cat.]
The Seventh Annual Altoids Curiously Strong Collection, Consolidated Works, Seattle, WA; traveled to Blue Star Contemporary Art Center, San Antonio, TX; Soo Visual Arts Center, Minneapolis, MN; New Museum of Contemporary Art, New York, NY; Luckman Gallery, California State University, Los Angeles, CA
2004 *Origins of Harold*, Deitch Projects, New York, NY
Paper, Patricia Faure Gallery, Santa Monica, CA
Happy Days Are Here Again, David Zwirner, New York, NY
Private, CRG Gallery, New York, NY
Tapestry From An Asteroid, Golinko Kordansky Gallery, Los Angeles, CA
Cave Canem, John Connelly Presents, New York, NY
2003 *Inaugural Exhibition*, Golinko Kordansky Gallery, Los Angeles, CA
Study, Taka Ishii Gallery, Tokyo, Japan
2002 *Das Spyder-Män*, Los Angeles Contemporary Exhibitions, Los Angeles, CA
2001 *Free One Oh Three Retrospective*, Good / Bad Art Collective, New York, NY
Renegade, California Institute of the Arts, Valencia, CA
2000 *Beautiful Stranger*, Stevenson Blanche Devereaux Gallery, California Institute of the Arts, Valencia, CA

Selected Bibliography

Brooks, Amra. "Violet Hopkins." Artforum [Vol. 45, No. 1, Sept. 2006]: 385-386.
Coetzee, Mark, ed., *Red Eye: L.A. Artists from the Rubell Family Collection*. Miami: Rubell Family Collection, 2007.

Cotter, Holland. "Dealers Gather at the River, Convenient to Lofts With Bare Walls." The New York Times [March 11, 2005].
Doll, Nancy, and Xandra Eden. *Art on Paper 2006: The 39th exhibition of Art on Paper, November 12, 2006 - January 21, 2007,* Greensboro: University of North Carolina at Greensboro, 2006.
Finkel, Jori. "First Come the Dealers and Then the Diplomas." The New York Times [July 3, 2005]: 22-23.
Johnson, Ken. "Happy Days Are Here Again." The New York Times [July 23, 2004].
Knight, Christopher. "Watercolors with an air of mystery." Los Angeles Times calendarlive.com [May 19, 2006].
"L.A. Louver Catches Rogue Wave." Santa Monica Mirror [June 29 – July 5, 2005]: 13.
Lasarow, Bill. "Rogue Wave." ArtScene [July/Aug. 2005].
Myers, Holly. "Turning Impulses Into Works of Art." Los Angeles Times [Aug. 16, 2002].
Ollman, Leah. "Showing the power of synergy." Los Angeles Times [May 28, 2004]: E28.
Pagel, David. "Summer sampler has a dark side." Los Angeles Times [July 8, 2005].
Pence, Elizabeth. "Violet Hopkins at Golinko Kordansky Gallery." Artweek [Issue 35 No.6, July – Aug. 2004]: 23.
Robinson, Walter. "Weekend Update." artnet.com [July 20, 2004].
Spiegler, Marc. "L.A. art is here to stay." The Art Newspaper [Dec. 8, 2006].

Selected Collections

Blake Byrne Collection, Los Angeles, CA
Collection of Dean Valentine and Amy Adelson, Los Angeles, CA
Collection of Eileen Harris Norton, Santa Monica, CA
Foundation Louis Vuitton, Paris, France
Collection of Martin & Rebecca Eisenberg, New York, NY
The Museum of Modern Art, New York, NY
New Museum of Contemporary Art, New York, NY
Rubell Family Collection, Miami, FL
Sender Collection, New York, NY

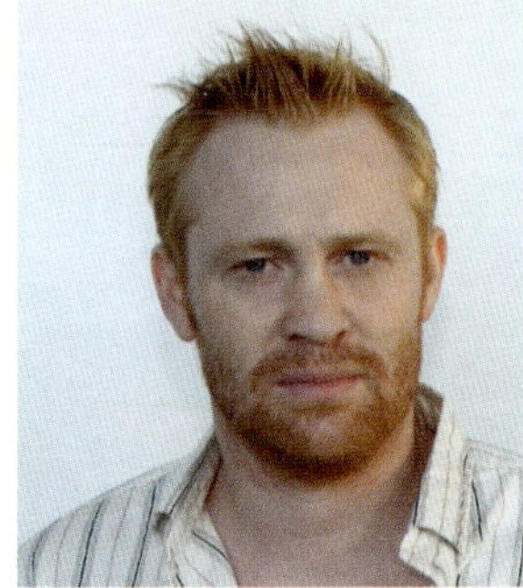
©Simon Hare Photography 2006

THOMAS HOUSEAGO

Born in Leeds, England, 1972
Lives and works in Los Angeles, CA

Education

1994-1996 Two years of study, de Ateliers, Amsterdam, Netherlands
1991-1994 B.F.A., Central St. Martins College of Art and Design, London, England
1990-1991 Foundation Diploma, Jacob Kramer College, Leeds College of Art and Design, Leeds, England

Selected Solo Exhibitions

2008 Xavier Hufkens, Brussels, Belgium
David Kordansky Gallery, Los Angeles, CA.
Herald St., London, England
2007 The Modern Institute / Toby Webster Ltd., Glasgow, Scotland
2003 *Thomas Houseago, I Am Here, Selected Sculptures 1995-2003,* Stedelijk Museum voor Actuele Kunst, Ghent, Belgium
2000 *Something to be*, Galerie Fons Welters, Amsterdam, Netherlands
1996 Stedelijk Museum Bureau Amsterdam, Stedelijk Museum, Amsterdam, Netherlands

Selected Group Exhibitions

2008 *Sonsbeek 2008*, Arnhem, Netherlands
2007 *Strange things permit themselves the luxury of occurring*, Camden Arts Centre, London, England
Sculptors' Drawings: Ideas, Studies, Sketches, Proposals, And More, Angles Gallery, Santa Monica, CA.
Personal Belongings – Contemporary Sculpture from Los Angeles, Sabine Knust Galerie Maximilian Verlag, Munich, Germany
2006 *Red Eye: L.A. Artists from the Rubell Family Collection,* Rubell Family Collection, Miami, FL [cat.]
Transformers, Donna Beam Fine Art Gallery, University of Nevada, Las Vegas, NV
The Glass Bead Game, Vilma Gold Project Space, Berlin, Germany
2005 *Both Ends Burning*, David Kordansky Gallery, Los Angeles, CA
2003 *Passie in Beeld, ruimtelijk werk uit de collectie van de Nederlandsche Bank*, Maliebeeld, Den Haag, Netherlands
Galerie Fons Welters, Amsterdam, Netherlands
2002 Xavier Hufkens, Brussels, Belgium
2001 *Rondom Jheronimous Bosch*, Museum Boijmans Van Beuningen, Rotterdam, Netherlands
1999 *Glad IJs*, Stedelijk Museum, Amsterdam, Netherlands
Werk boven de bank, Archipel, Apeldoorn, Netherlands
1998 *Morning Glory*, de Ateliers, Amsterdam, Netherlands [cat.]
Summer Show, Xavier Hufkens, Brussels, Belgium
Acquisitions 1997, De Nederlandsche Bank, Amsterdam, Netherlands
Mum's tattoo, Si en La, Antwerp, Belgium

Selected Bibliography

Akbar, Arifa. "Saatchi's New Stars: Collector Prepares for New Gallery Opening." The Independent [July 23, 2007].
Bartels, Daghild. "Ein Fulltimejob fur die kunst." Handelsblatt [March 2-4, 2007].
Bartels, Daghild. "Jeder Penny fur die Kunst." Parnass [Jan. 2007]: 78.
Both Ends Burning. Los Angeles: David Kordansky Gallery, 2005.

Coetzee, Mark, ed., *Red Eye: L.A. Artists from the Rubell Family Collection*. Miami: Rubell Family Collection, 2007.
"Glad IJs." De Standaard [Oct. 6, 1999].
"Hot Tickets, Exhibitions: Amy Bessone, Thomas Houseago." The Bulletin [Sept. 19, 2002].
Keijer, Kees. "Onvoltooid voorkomen." Het Parool [Nov. 3, 2000].
Lambrecht, Luk. "Dissonante Schoonheid." De Morgen [Aug 7, 1998].
Lutticken, Sven. "Groteske monsters van gips." Het Parool [Sept 13, 1996].
Mason, Christopher. "It's what's on the inside that counts: New acquisitions in some familiar territory." Art Basel Miami Beach 2006 [Dec. 2006]: 98B.
"Outstanding." Gemeente Haarlemmermeer [2004]: 20-23.
Peterson, Kristen. "Good Shows." Las Vegas Sun [Dec. 8, 2006].
Pontzen, Rutger. "Glad IJs: viezige keuzen van Fuchs." Vrij Nederland [Oct. 9, 1999].
Pontzen, Rutiger. "De vuile handen van Thomas Houseago." Vrij Nederland [Oct. 28, 2000].
Rochette, Anne and Wade Saunders. "Place Matters: Los Angeles Sculpture Today." Art in America [No. 10, Nov. 2006]: 168-191.
Segade, Alex. "Nothing Up The Sleeve." artUS [No. 15, Oct. / Nov. 2006]: 16-17.
Sherwin, Skye. "Future Greats." ArtReview [No. 9, March 2007]: 78-79, 101.
Smallenburg, Sandra. "Thomas Houseago." NRC Handelsblad [Nov. 10, 2000].
Smith, Roberta. "Art in Review: Michael Queenland." The New York Times [March 9, 2007].
Smith, Roberta. "More Than You Can See: Storm of Art Engulfs Miami." The New York Times [Dec. 9, 2005]: A21.
Spiegler, Marc. "American Renaissance." The Art Newspaper Art Basel Daily Edition [June 14, 2006]: 6.
Spiegler, Marc. "LA art is here to stay." The Art Newspaper [Dec. 8, 2006]: 1-8.
Suto, Wilma. "De aap die naar een stropdas verlangt." de Volkskrant [Oct. 4, 1996].
van den Boogerd, Dominic. "De Frankenstein factor." HP/De Tijd [Nov. 3, 2000].
Veugen, Christine. "De energie van gips en klei." Kunstbeeld [No. 14, Nov. 2000].

Selected Collections

Blake Byrne Collection, Los Angeles, CA
De Nederlandsche Bank, Amsterdam, Netherlands
Museum Boijmans Van Beuningen, Rotterdam, Netherlands
The Rennie Collection, Vancouver, Canada
Rubell Family Collection, Miami, FL
Stedelijk Museuem voor Actuele Kunst, Ghent, Belgium
Saatchi Collection, London, England
Stedelijk Museum, Amsterdam, Netherlands
Collection of Susan and Michael Hort, New York, NY

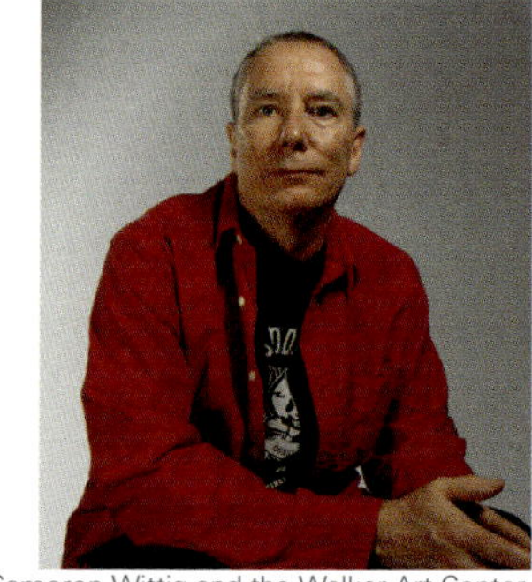

©Cameron Wittig and the Walker Art Center, Minneapolis, MN, 2003

MIKE KELLEY

Born in Detroit, MI, 1954
Lives and works in Los Angeles, CA

Education

1976-1978 M.F.A., California Institute of the Arts, Valencia, CA
1972-1976 B.F.A., University of Michigan, Ann Arbor, MI

Selected Solo Exhibitions

2007 *Mike Kelley: Kandors,* Jablonka Galerie, Berlin, Germany
Mike Kelley: Hermaphrodite Drawings, Gagosian Gallery, London, England
2006 *Mike Kelley: Profondeurs Vertes*, Musée du Louvre, Paris, France
Mike Kelley: Liquid Diet and Related Works, Galerie Ghislaine Hussenot, Paris, France
2005 *Mike Kelley: Day Is Done,* Gagosian Gallery - 24th Street, New York, NY
2004 *Mike Kelley: The Uncanny*, Tate Liverpool, Liverpool, England; Museum Moderner Kunst Stiftung Ludwig Wien, Vienna, Austria [cat.]
Mike Kelley, Galerie Ghislaine Hussenot, Paris, France
2003 *Mike Kelley: Memory Ware, Wood Grain, Carpet*, Galleria Emi Fontana, Milan, Italy [cat.]
2002 *Mike Kelley: Black Out*, Patrick Painter Inc., Santa Monica, CA
Reversals, Recyclings, Completions, and Late Additions, Metro Pictures, New York, NY
2001 *Mike Kelley: Memory Ware*, Jablonka Galerie, Cologne, Germany [cat.]
2000 *Mike Kelley: Sublevel, Framed and Frame, Test Room/ re:view*, Migros Museum für Gegenwartskunst, Zurich, Switzerland [cat.]
1999 *Mike Kelley*, Magasin - Centre National d'Art Contemporain, Grenoble, France [cat.]
1997 *Mike Kelley: 1985-1996*, Museu d'Art Contemporani de Barcelona, Spain; traveled to Rooseum Center for Contemporary Art, Malmö, Sweden; Van Abbemuseum, Eindhoven, Netherlands [cat.]
1996 *Land-O-Lakes*. Wako Works of Art, Tokyo, Japan [cat.]
1995 *Mike Kelley: Toward a Utopian Arts Complex*, Metro Pictures, New York, NY
1993 *Mike Kelley: Catholic Tastes,* Whitney Museum of American Art, New York, NY; traveled to Los Angeles County Museum of Art, Los Angeles, CA; Moderna Museet, Stockholm, Sweden; Haus der Kunst, Munich, Germany [cat.]
1992 *Mike Kelley*, Kunsthalle Basel, Basel, Switzerland; traveled to Institute of Contemporary Arts, London, England; CAPC Musée d'Art Contemporain de Bordeaux, Bordeaux, France [cat.]
1991 *Mike Kelley: Half a Man,* Hirshhorn Museum and Sculpture Garden, Smithsonian Institution, Washington, DC
1990 Galerie Ghislaine Hussenot, Paris, France
1988 *Three Projects: Half a Man, From My Institution to Yours, Pay for Your Pleasure,* The Renaissance Society at The University of Chicago, Chicago, IL [cat.]
1987 *Half a Man,* Rosamund Felsen Gallery, Los Angeles, CA
1985 *Plato's Cave, Rothko's Chapel, Lincoln's Profile*, Rosamund Felsen Gallery, Los Angeles, CA
1983 *The Sublime,* Hallwalls Contemporary Arts Center, Buffalo, New York, NY
1982 *Monkey Island and Confusion,* Metro Pictures, New York, NY

Selected Group Exhibitions

2007 *Skulptur Projekte Münster 07,* Münster, Germany [cat.]
2006 *Los Angeles: 1955-1985*, Centre Georges Pompidou, Paris, France [cat.]
2nd Bienal Internacional de Arte Contemporáneo de Sevilla, Fundacion BIACS, Seville, Spain [cat.]
2005 *Translation*, Palais de Tokyo, Paris, France [cat.]
2004 *Monument To Now*: Deste Foundation Center for Contemporary Art, Athens, Greece [cat.]
2002 *2002 Biennial Exhibition*, Whitney Museum of American Art, New York, NY [cat.]

Sod and Sodie Sock, 7th Biennale d'art contemporain de Lyon, le Musée d'art contemporain, Lyon, France
2001 *Artists Take on Detroit,* Detroit Institute of Arts, Detroit, MI
Bienal de Valencia, Generalitat Valenciana, Valencia, Spain
2000 *Apocalypse: Beauty and Horror in Contemporary Art,* Royal Academy of Arts, London, England [cat.]
1999 *The American Century: Art and Culture 1950-2000*, Whitney Museum of American Art, New York, NY
1997 *The Poetics Project: 1977-1997(a collaboration between Tony Oursler and Mike Kelley),* Documenta X, Kassel, Germany [cat.]
1995 *Whitney Biennial 1995*, Whitney Museum of American Art, New York, NY [cat.]
1994 *Radical Scavenger(s): The Conceptual Vernacular in Recent American Art,* Museum of Contemporary Art Chicago, Chicago, IL [cat.]
1992 *Documenta IX,* Kassel, Germany [cat.]
1991 *Whitney Biennial 1991*, Whitney Museum of American Art, New York, NY [cat.]
1989 *A Forest of Signs: Art in the Crisis of Representation,* The Museum of Contemporary Art, Los Angeles, CA [cat.]
Whitney Biennial 1989, Whitney Museum of American Art, New York, NY [cat.]
1988 *43rd Biennale di Venezia,* Venice, Italy
1987 *Avant-Garde in the Eighties,* Los Angeles County Museum of Art, Los Angeles, CA [cat.]
1985 *Whitney Biennial 1985,* Whitney Museum of American Art, New York, NY [cat.]
1984 *The Fifth Biennale of Sydney,* Art Gallery of New South Wales, Sydney, Australia [cat.]
1980 *By-Products: Mike Kelley, Tony Oursler, Mitchell Syrop,* Los Angeles Contemporary Exhibitions, Los Angeles, CA

Selected Bibliography

Aupetitallot, Yves. "Grenoble: Mike Kelley." Art Press [No. 250, Oct. 1999]: 14-17.
Coetzee, Mark. *Not Afraid: Rubell Family Collection.* London: Phaidon Press, 2004.
Coetzee, Mark, ed., *Red Eye: L.A. Artists from the Rubell Family Collection.* Miami: Rubell Family Collection, 2007.
Diederichsen, Diedrich. "America: yet another discovery – Mike Kelley in video." Parkett [No. 31, March 1992]: 74-79.
Hainley, Bruce. "Mike Kelley." Artforum [Vol. 41, No. 2, Oct. 2002]: 180.
Kellein, Thomas, and Mike Kelley. *Mike Kelley.* Basel: Edition Cantz, 1992.
Kelley, Mike. "Day is Done." Artforum [Vol. 44, No. 2, Oct. 2005]: 233-235.
Kelley, Mike. *Foul Perfection: Essays & Criticism.* Cambridge: MIT Press, 2003.
Kelley, Mike. *Mike Kelley: 1985-1996.* Barcelona: Museu d'Art Contemporani de Barcelona, 1997.
Kelley, Mike. *The Uncanny.* Cologne, London: Walther König, 2004.
Miles, Christopher. "Mike Kelley." Artforum [Vol. 37, No. 8, April 1999]: 127.
Sussman, Elizabeth. *Mike Kelley: Catholic Tastes.* New York: Whitney Museum of American Art; Harry N. Abrams Inc., 1993.
Taylor, Paul. "Mike Kelley." Flash Art [No. 154, Oct. 1990]: 141-143.
Welchman, John C., et al. *Mike Kelley.* London: Phaidon, 1999.
Welchman, John C. *Minor Histories.* Cambridge: MIT Press, 2004.

Selected Collections

Carnegie Museum of Art, Pittsburgh, PA
Centre Georges Pompidou, Paris, France
Detroit Institute of Art, Detroit, MI
Los Angeles County Museum of Art, Los Angeles, CA
Metropolitan Museum of Art, New York, NY
Museum Moderner Kunst, Vienna, Austria
Museum of Contemporary Art, Chicago, IL
Museum of Contemporary Art, Los Angeles, CA
Museum of Fine Arts, Boston, MA
Museum of Modern Art, New York, NY
Rubell Family Collection, Miami, FL
Solomon R. Guggenheim Museum, New York, NY
The Art Institute of Chicago, Chicago, IL
Van Abbe Museum, Eindhoven, Netherlands
Walker Art Center, Minneapolis, MN
Whitney Museum of American Art, New York, NY

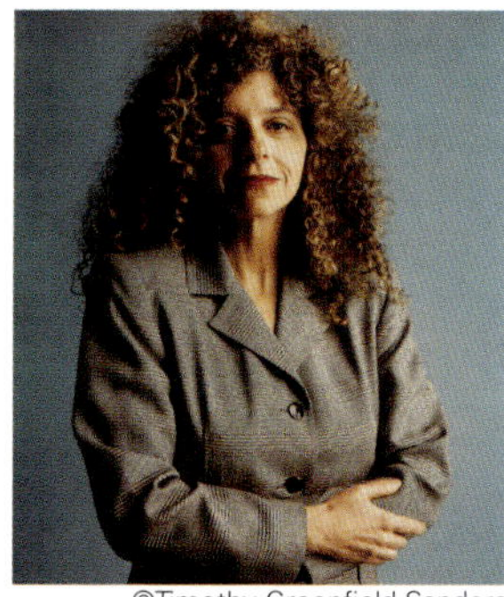
©Timothy Greenfield-Sanders

BARBARA KRUGER

Born in Newark, NJ, 1945
Lives and works in New York, NY and Los Angeles, CA

Education

Syracuse University, Syracuse, NY
Parsons School of Design, New York, NY

Selected Solo Exhibitions

2007 Mary Boone Gallery, New York, NY
2006 Kestner Gesellschaft, Hannover, Germany [cat.]
2005 Gallery of Modern Art, Glasgow, Scotland
Tramway, Glasgow, Scotland [cat.]
Museum of Contemporary Art San Diego, San Diego, CA
Australian Centre for Contemporary Art, Melbourne, Australia
2004 *Twelve*, Mary Boone Gallery, New York, NY
2000 Whitney Museum of American Art, New York, NY
1999 Galerie Yvon Lambert, Paris, France [cat.]
The Museum of Contemporary Art, Los Angeles, CA [cat.]
1997 *Power Pleasure Desire Disgust*, 18 Wooster Street / Deitch Projects, New York, NY
1996 Museum of Modern Art at Heide, Bulleen, Australia [cat.]
1994 Mary Boone Gallery, New York, NY
1992 Magasin - Centre National d'Art Contemporain, Grenoble, France
1991 Mary Boone Gallery, New York, NY [cat.]
1990 Kölnischer Kunstverein, Cologne, Germany
1987 Mary Boone Gallery, New York, NY [cat.]
1986 *Barbara Kruger / Matrix 100*, Berkeley Art Museum, University of California, Berkeley, CA [cat.]
Slices of Life: The Work of Barbara Kruger, Krannert Art Museum, University of Illinois at Urbana-Champaign, Champaign, IL [cat.]
1985 Los Angeles County Museum of Art, Los Angeles, CA
Striking Poses, Contemporary Arts Museum Houston, Houston, TX
1983 *We won't play nature to your culture*, Institute of Contemporary Arts, London, England; traveled to Watershed Media Centre, Bristol, England; Nouveau Musée, Villeurbanne, France; Kunsthalle Basel, Basel, Switzerland [cat.]

Selected Group Shows

2007 *Panic Attack: Art in the Punk Years*, Barbican Art Gallery, London, England [cat.]
2006 *Red Eye: L.A. Artists from the Rubell Family Collection*, Rubell Family Collection, Miami, FL [cat.]
A Short History of Performance – Part IV, Whitechapel Gallery, London, England [cat.]
2005 *51st Biennale di Venezia*, Italian Pavilion, Venice, Italy
1999 *The American Century: Art and Culture, 1900-2000: Part II, 1950-2000*, Whitney Museum of American Art, New York, NY [cat.]
1998 *Read My Lips: Jenny Holzer, Barbara Kruger, Cindy Sherman*, National Gallery of Australia, Canberra, Australia [cat.]
1996 *Thinking Print: Books to Billboards, 1980-95*, The Museum of Modern Art, New York, NY [cat.]
1994 *Wall to Wall*, Serpentine Gallery, London, England; traveled to Southampton City Art Gallery, Southampton, England; Leeds City Art Gallery, Leeds, England [cat.]
1992 *More Than One Photography: Works Since 1980 From the Collection*, The Museum of Modern Art, New York, NY [cat.]
1991 *Devil on the Stairs: Looking Back on the Eighties*, Institute of Contemporary Art, Philadelphia, PA [cat.]
1990 *Art et Publicité: 1890-1990*, Centre Georges Pompidou, Paris, France [cat.]

1989 *A Forest of Signs: Art in the Crisis of Representation*, The Museum of Contemporary Art, Los Angeles, CA [cat.]
Magiciens de la Terre, Centre Georges Pompidou, Paris, France [cat.]
Image World: Art and Media Culture, Whitney Museum of American Art, New York, NY [cat.]
1988 *11th Biennale of Sydney*, Sydney, Australia [cat.]
1987 *Whitney Biennial 1987*, Whitney Museum of American Art, New York, NY [cat.]
Documenta 8, Kassel, West Germany [cat.]
1986 *Jenny Holzer, Barbara Kruger*, The Israel Museum, Jerusalem, Israel [cat.]
1985 *Whitney Biennial 1985*, Whitney Museum of American Art, New York, NY [cat.]
1983 *Whitney Biennial 1983*, Whitney Museum of American Art, New York, NY [cat.]
1982 *Documenta 7*, Kassel, West Germany [cat.]
40th Biennale di Venezia, Venice, Italy [cat.]
1981 *Nineteen Artists: Emergent Americans*, Solomon R. Guggenheim Museum, New York, NY [cat.]

Selected Bibliography

Barbara Kruger. Wellington: National Art Gallery, 1988.
Brenson, Michael. "Barbara Kruger." The New York Times [May 15, 1987]: C26.
Coetzee, Mark, ed., *Red Eye: L.A. Artists from the Rubell Family Collection*. Miami: Rubell Family Collection, 2007.
Deitcher, David. "Barbara Kruger: Resisting Arrest." Artforum [Vol. 29, No. 6, Feb. 1991]: 84-91.
Frankel, David. "Barbara Kruger." Artforum [Vol. 36, No. 6, Feb. 1998]: 88.
Frankel, David. "Barbara Kruger." Artforum [Vol. 42, No. 9, May 2004]: 208.
Goodeve, Thyrza Nichols. "The Art of Public Address." Art in America [Vol. 85, No. 11, Nov. 1997]: 92-99.
Johnson, Ken. "Barbara Kruger: 'Twelve'." The New York Times [April 23, 2004]: E31.
Johnson, Ken. "Theater of Dissent." Art in America [Vol. 79, No. 3, March 1991]: 128-131.
Knight, Christopher. "MOCA's Flag Mural: It's a Wrap." Los Angeles Times [July 4, 1990]: F1, F5-F6.
Kruger, Barbara, Ann Goldstein, and Rosalyn Deutsche. *Barbara Kruger*. Los Angeles: Museum of Contemporary Art, 1999.
Landau, Suzanne. *Jenny Holzer, Barbara Kruger*. Jerusalem: Israel Museum, 1986.
Linker, Kate. *Love For Sale: The Words and Pictures of Barbara Kruger*. New York: Harry N. Abrams, 1990.
Siegel, Jeanne. "Barbara Kruger: Pictures and Words." Arts Magazine [June 1987]: 17-20.
Smith, Roberta. "Barbara Kruger examines images of terror." The New York Times [March 18, 1994]: C23.
Smith, Roberta. "Barbara Kruger's Large-Scale Self-Expression." The New York Times [Jan. 11, 1991]: C12.
Squiers, Carol. "Barbara Kruger." Aperture [No. 138, Feb. 1995]: 58-67.
Squiers, Carol. "Diversionary (Syn)tactics / Barbara Kruger has a Way with Words." ARTnews [Feb. 1987]: 76-85.
Stephanson, Anders. "Barbara Kruger." Flash Art [No. 136, Oct. 1987]: 55-59.

Selected Collections

Art Gallery of Ontario, Toronto, Canada
Baltimore Museum of Art, Baltimore, MD
The Broad Art Foundation, Santa Monica, CA
Daros Collection, Zurich, Switzerland
Denver Art Museum, Denver, CO
Deste Foundation Centre for Contemporary Art, Athens, Greece
Henry Art Gallery, University of Washington, Seattle, WA
John and Mable Ringling Museum of Art, Florida State University, Sarasota, FL
Los Angeles County Museum of Art, Los Angeles, CA
Mildred Lane Kemper Art Museum, Washington University, St. Louis, MO
Museum Ludwig, Cologne, Germany
Museum of Contemporary Art Chicago, Chicago, IL
The Museum of Contemporary Art, Los Angeles, CA
Museum of Fine Arts, Boston, MA
The Museum of Modern Art, New York, NY
Rubell Family Collection, Miami, FL
Saint Louis Art Museum, Saint Louis, MO
Solomon R. Guggenheim Museum, New York, NY
Walker Art Center, Minneapolis, MN
Whitney Museum of American Art, New York, NY
Ydessa Hendeles Art Foundation, Toronto, Canada
Yokohama Museum of Art, Yokohama, Japan

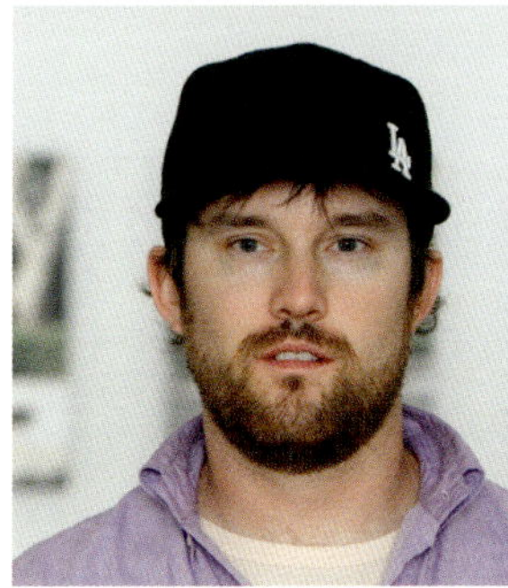

©Simon Hare Photography 2006

NATHAN MABRY

Born in Durango, CO, 1978
Lives and works in Los Angeles, CA

Education

2001-2004 M.F.A., University of California, Los Angeles, CA
1997-2001 B.F.A., Kansas City Art Institute, Kansas City, MO

Selected Solo Exhibitions

2006 *Nathan Mabry: Old Fashioned Fourth of July Celebration and Parade*, Aspen Art Museum, Aspen, CO
Cherry and Martin, Los Angeles, CA
2000 Filter Gallery, Kansas City, MO

Selected Group Exhibitions

2006 *Red Eye: L.A. Artists from the Rubell Family Collection*, Rubell Family Collection, Miami, FL [cat.]
The Beginning of the End of the Beginning, Bucket Rider Gallery, Chicago, IL
2005 *THING: New Sculpture from Los Angeles, The Armand Hammer Museum of Art and Cultural Center, University of California, Los Angeles, CA.* [cat.]
Rogue Wave '05: Nineteen Artists from Los Angeles, LA Louver, Venice, CA [cat.]
WivesHusbands, domestic setting, Los Angeles, CA
2004 *Cornceptual Popstraction,* cherrydelosreyes, Los Angeles, CA [cat.]
cherrydelosreyes, Los Angeles, CA
Supersonic, The Wind Tunnel, Art Center College of Design, Pasadena, CA [cat.]
2003 *I Am Human And I Deserve To Be Loved,* Overtones Gallery, Los Angeles, CA
2001 The Cube at Beco, Kansas City, MO
Jan Weiner Gallery, Kansas City, MO
H&R Block Art Space, Kansas City Art Institute, Kansas City, MO
2000 The Gordon Gallery, Yountville, CA

Selected Bibliography

Coetzee, Mark, ed., *Red Eye: L.A. Artists from the Rubell Family Collection*. Miami: Rubell Family Collection, 2007.
Elaine, James, Aimee Chang and Christopher Miles. *THING: new sculpture from Los Angeles*. Los Angeles: Hammer Museum; Fellows of Contemporary Art, 2005.
Finkel, Jori. "Nathan Mabry at Cherry and Martin." ARTnews [Vol. 105, No. 5, 2006]: 177.
Freeman, Tommy. "Nathan Mabry at Cherry and Martin." Artweek [Vol. 37, Issue 4, May 2006]: 19.
Freeman, Tommy. "Summer Group Show at cherrydelosreyes." Artweek [Vol. 35, No. 8, 2004]: 20-21.
Harvey, Doug. "Young Outsiders at Overtones." LA Weekly [Aug. 2003].
Herbert, Simon. "Thing: New Sculpture from Los Angeles." Art Monthly [No. 286, May 2005]: 29-30.
Holte, Michael Ned. "West Coast Thing." www.artforum.com [Feb. 10, 2005].
Knight, Christopher. "Come and Gather Around the Llama for an Intimate Chat." The Los Angeles Times [Nov. 25, 2005].
Knight, Christopher. "The next big 'Thing' in L.A." The Los Angeles Times [Feb. 9, 2005].
Mack, Joshua. "Thing: New Sculpture from Los Angeles." Modern Painters [April 2005]: 104-105.
Miles, Christopher. "The Idolater's Revenge." Flash Art [Vol. 38, No. 242, May – June 2005]: 104-108
Myers, Terry R. "Nathan Mabry: A Very Touching Moment." Modern Painters [May 2006]: 113.
Nathan Mabry. Los Angeles: Cherry and Martin, 2006.
Ollman, Leah. "A Sculptor Who Loves To Play Tricks." The Los Angeles Times [March 10, 2006].

Pagel, David. "Summer Sampler has a Dark Side." The Los Angeles Times [July 8, 2005].
Rogue Wave '05. Los Angeles: LA Louver, 2005.
Roug, Louise. "Object Lessons." The Los Angeles Times [Jan. 2, 2005].
Spiegler, Marc. "American Renaissance." The Art Newspaper [June 14, 2006]: 6.

Selected Collections

Armand Hammer Museum, University of California, Los Angeles, CA
Michael Rabkin and Chip Tom Collection, Los Angeles, CA
Rubell Family Collection, Miami, FL
Vanhaerents Art Collection, Brussels, Belgium
Whitney Museum of American Art, New York, NY
Zabludowicz Collection, London, England

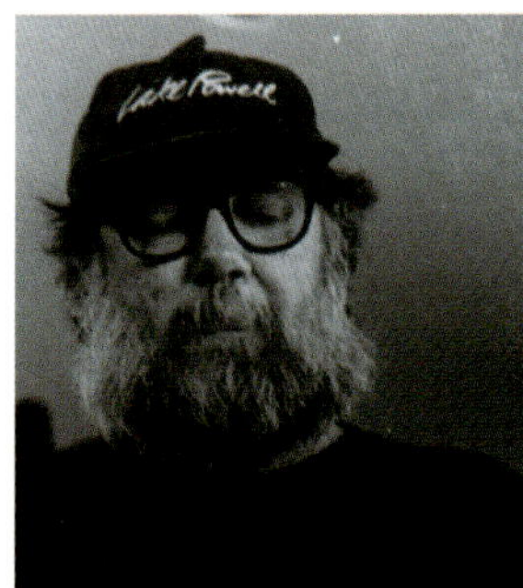

©Mara McCarthy, 2001. Courtesy the artist and Hauser & Wirth Zürich London

PAUL McCARTHY

Born in Salt Lake City, UT, 1945
Lives and works in Altadena, CA

Education

1970-1973 M.F.A., University of Southern California, Los Angeles, CA
1968-1969 B.F.A., San Francisco Art Institute, San Francisco, CA
1966-1968 University of Utah, Salt Lake City, UT

Selected Solo Exhibitions

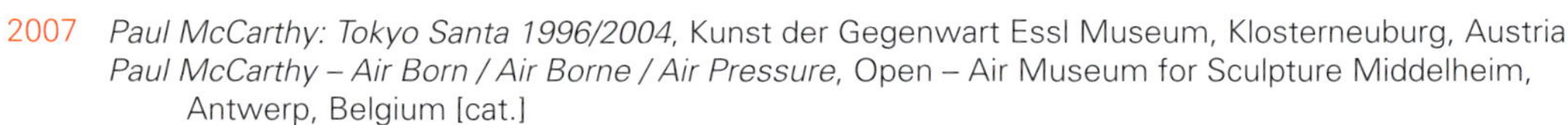

2007 *Paul McCarthy: Tokyo Santa 1996/2004*, Kunst der Gegenwart Essl Museum, Klosterneuburg, Austria
Paul McCarthy – Air Born / Air Borne / Air Pressure, Open – Air Museum for Sculpture Middelheim, Antwerp, Belgium [cat.]
Paul McCarthy / Damon McCarthy. Portfolios, Hauser & Wirth, Zurich, Switzerland
2006 *Paul McCarthy: Between Beauty and the Beast. Sculptures, Drawings and Photographs*, Nyehaus, New York, NY [cat.]
Paul McCarthy: Head Shop / Shop Head, Moderna Museet, Stockholm, Sweden; traveled to Stedelijk Museum voor Actuele Kunst, Ghent, Belgium [cat.]
2005 *Paul McCarthy: LaLa Land Parody Paradise*, Whitechapel Art Gallery, London, England [cat.]
Paul McCarthy: LaLa Land Parodie Paradies, Haus der Kunst, Munich, Germany [cat.]

Selected Group Exhibitions

2007 *There is Never a Stop and Never a Finish. In Memoriam Jason Rhoades, Werke aus der Friedrich Christian Flick Collection im Hamburger Bahnhof*, Hamburger Bahnhof - Museum für Gegenwart, Berlin, Germany [cat.]
Panic Attack! Art in the Punk Years, Barbican Art Gallery, London, England [cat.]
Traum & Trauma. Werke aus der Sammlung Dakis Joannou, Athens, Kunsthalle Wien and Museum Moderner Kunst Stiftung Ludwig Wien, Vienna, Austria [cat.]
2006 *Red Eye: L.A. Artists from the Rubell Family Collection*, Rubell Family Collection, Miami, FL [cat.]
Transforming Chronologies: An Atlas of Drawings, Part Two, The Museum of Modern Art, New York, NY
Into Me / Out of Me, P.S.1 Contemporary Art Center, Long Island City, NY; traveled to KW Institute for Contemporary Art, Berlin, Germany; Museo d'Arte Contemporanea Roma, Rome, Italy [cat.]
Of Mice and Men, 4th Berlin Biennial for Contemporary Art, Berlin, Germany [cat.]
Los Angeles – Paris, Centre Georges Pompidou, Paris, France [cat.]
2005 *Viennese Actionism*, Museum Moderner Kunst Stiftung Ludwig Wien, Vienna, Austria
Speaking with Hands, Guggenheim Museum Bilbao, Bilbao, Spain; traveled to Museum Folkwang, Essen, Germany; Solomon R. Guggenheim Museum, New York, NY
Mythologies, Walker Art Center, Minneapolis, MN
Les Grands Spectacles: 120 Years of Art and Mass Culture, Museum der Moderne Salzburg, Salzburg, Austria
Dionysiac, Centre Georges Pompidou, Paris France [cat.]
John McCracken / Paul McCarthy, Hauser & Wirth, Zurich, Switzerland

Selected Bibliography

Avgikos, Jan. "Paul McCarthy." Artforum [Vol. 41, No. 5, Jan. 2003]: 137-138.
Coetzee, Mark. *Not Afraid: Rubell Family Collection*. London: Phaidon Press, 2004.

Coetzee, Mark, ed., *Red Eye: L.A. Artists from the Rubell Family Collection*. Miami: Rubell Family Collection, 2007.
Holert, Tom. "Schooled for scandal." Artforum [Vol. 39, No. 3, Nov. 2000]: 134-141.
McCarthy, Paul. *Tokyo Santa*, New York: Distributed Art Publishers, 2004.
Meyer-Hermann, Eva. *Paul McCarthy „Dimensions of the Mind" The Denial and the Desire in the Spectacle*, Cologne: Oktagon, 2000.
Meyer-Hermann, Eva, and Van Abbemuseum Eindhoven. *Paul McCarthy. Brain Box Dream Box*, Düsseldorf: Richter Verlag, 2004.
Muchnic, Suzanne. "Paul McCarthy." ARTnews [Vol. 100, No. 2, Feb. 2001]: 160.
Paul McCarthy at Tate Modern, London: Tate Publishing, 2003.
Petersens, Magnus af, and Paul McCarthy. *Head Shop / Shop Head*, Stockholm: Moderna Museet; Göttingen: Steidl.
Piccadilly Circus. Bunker Basement, Göttingen: Steidl; London: Thames & Hudson, 2008.
Rosenthal, Stephanie. *LaLa Land Parody Paradise*, Ostfildern-Ruit: Hatje Cantz, 2005.
Sigler, Jeremy. "Facsimile of the original manuscript / Faksimile des Orginalmanuskripts." Parkett [No. 73, 2005]: 120-134.
Turner, Grady. "Paul McCarthy: inside and outside." Flash Art [Vol. 34, No. 217, March – April 2001]: 86-91.
Unterdörfer, Michaela, and Matthias Winzen. *(In the Search of) The Perfect Lover*, Ostfildern-Ruit: Hatje Cantz, 2003: 96-125.
Weissman, Benjamin. "The Autobiography of Paul McCarthy." Modern Painters [July – Aug. 2005]: 58-63.
Yaa-Hoo, Cologne: Verlag der Buchhandlung Walther König, 1998.

Selected Collections

Collection of Benedikt Taschen, Cologne, Germany
Collection of Dimitri Daskalopoulos, Athens, Greece
Collection of Pier Luigi Mazzari, Milan, Italy
Collection of Sandra Simpson, Toronto, Canada
De Hallen Haarlem, Haarlem, Netherlands
Deste Foundation Centre for Contemporary Art, Athens, Greece
Fondazione Sandretto Re Rebaudengo per l'Arte, Turin, Italy
Fonds Régional d'Art Contemporain Languedoc-Roussillon, Montpellier, France
Fonds Régional d'Art Contemporain Poitou-Charentes, Angoulème, France
Frans Hals Museum, Haarlem, Netherlands
Friedrich Christian Flick Collection, Berlin, Germany
Jumex Foundation, Mexico City, Mexico
Kunsthaus Zürich, Zurich, Switzerland
The Marieluise Hessel Collection, Bard College, Annandale-on-Hudson, New York
Museum Moderner Kunst Stiftung Ludwig Wien, Vienna, Austria
The Museum of Contemporary Art, Los Angeles, CA
The Museum of Modern Art, New York, NY
Peter Norton Family Foundation, Santa Monica, CA
The Patchett Collection, Museum of Contemporary Art, San Diego, San Diego, CA
Rubell Family Collection, Miami, FL
Sammlung Hauser & Wirth, St. Gallen, Switzerland
Solomon R. Guggenheim Foundation, New York, NY
Tate Modern, London, England
Walker Art Center, Minneapolis, MN
Whitney Museum of American Art, New York, NY
Ydessa Hendeles Art Foundation, Toronto, Canada

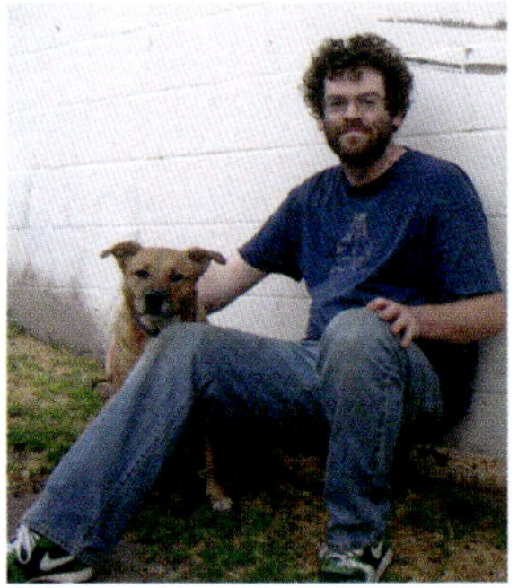

JASON MEADOWS

Born in Indianapolis, IN, 1972
Lives and works in Los Angeles, CA

Education

1996-1998 M.F.A., University of California, Los Angeles, CA
1990-1994 B.F.A., School of the Art Institute of Chicago, Chicago, IL

Selected Solo Exhibitions

2008 MARC FOXX, Los Angeles, CA
2007 *Frame Narrative*, Tanya Bonakdar, New York, NY
Jason Meadows: A Light in the Attic, Corvi-Mora, London, England
2006 *Life on Mars*, MARC FOXX, Los Angeles, CA
2005 *Light Year / Clear Spot*, Tanya Bonakdar Gallery, New York, NY
2004 Corvi-Mora, London, England
2003 *Order in the Court*, MARC FOXX, Los Angeles, CA
Corvi-Mora, London, England

Selected Group Exhibitions

2007 *Eight Sculptors from Los Angeles*, Galerie Sabine Knust, Munich, Germany
2006 *Red Eye: L.A. Artists from the Rubell Family Collection*, Rubell Family Collection, Miami, FL [cat.]
Untitled (for H. C. Westermann), The Contemporary Museum, Honolulu, HI [cat.]
2005 *Monuments for the USA*, White Columns, New York, NY
Sculptures d'Appartement, Musée Départemental d'Art Contemporain de Rochechouart, Rochechouart, France [cat.]
2004 *Expander*, Royal Academy of Arts, London, England [cat.]
Gallery Artists, MARC FOXX, Los Angeles, CA
I, Assassin, Wallspace, New York, NY
2003 *Painting on Sculpture*, Tanya Bonakdar Gallery, New York, NY
2000 *Mise en Scène: New L.A. Sculpture*, Santa Monica Museum of Art, Santa Monica, CA [cat.]

Selected Bibliography

Campagnola, Sonia. "Focus Los Angeles: Jason Meadows." Flash Art [Vol 39, No. 246, Jan. – Feb. 2006]: 68-75.
Charlesworth, J.J. *Expander*. London: Royal Academy of Arts, 2004.
Coetzee, Mark. *Not Afraid: Rubell Family Collection*. London: Phaidon Press, 2004.
Coetzee, Mark, ed., *Red Eye: L.A. Artists from the Rubell Family Collection*. Miami: Rubell Family Collection, 2007.
Cooper, Dennis. "Jason Meadows." Artforum [Vol. 36, No. 9, May 1998]: 136-137.
Dykstra, Jean. "Painting on Sculpture at Tanya Bonakdar Gallery." ArtReview [Vol 54, March 2004]: 102.
Farquharson, Alex. "Jason Meadows." Art Monthly [No. 246, May 2001]: 33-35.
Hainley, Bruce. "Jason Meadows." Artforum [Vol. 44, No. 9, May 2006]: 297.
Hainley, Bruce. "Jason Meadows." Artforum [Vol. 41, No. 6, Feb. 2003]: 145.
Iannaccone, Carmine. "Mise en Scene: New L.A. Sculpture." artext [No. 71, Nov. 2000 – Jan. 2001]: 84-85.
Kerr, Merrily. "Jason Meadows." Flash Art [Vol. 34, No. 225, July – Sept. 2002]:117.
Knight, Christopher. "Art off and on its Pedestal." Los Angeles Times [July 9, 2004]: E30.

Mise en Scène: New L.A. Sculpture. Santa Monica: Santa Monica Museum of Art, 2000.
Rochette, Anne and Wade Saunders. "Place Matters: Los Angeles Sculpture Today." Art in America [No. 10, Nov. 2006]: 168-191, 224.
Sculptures d' Appartement. Rochechouart: Musée Départemental d'Art Contemporain de Rochechouart, 2005.
Turvey, Lisa. "Jason Meadows at Tanya Bonakdar." Artforum [Sept. 2007]: 469-470.
Wilson, Michael, "I, Assassin at Wallspace." frieze [May 2004].

Selected Collections

Armand Hammer Museum, University of California, Los Angeles, CA
Laguna Art Museum, Laguna Beach, CA
Los Angeles County Museum of Art, Los Angeles, CA
The Museum of Contemporary Art, Los Angeles, CA
The Museum of Modern Art, New York, NY
Rubell Family Collection, Miami, FL
South Coast Repertory, Costa Mesa, CA
Tate Modern, London, England

MATTHEW MONAHAN

Born in Eureka, CA, 1972
Lives and works in Los Angeles, CA

Education

2002 Three month travel and residence at Chinese European Art Center, Xiamen, China
1999-2000 Residence in Kitakyushu, Japan
1994-1996 Two years of study, de Ateliers, Amsterdam, Netherlands
1993 Gerrit Rietveld Academy, Amsterdam, Netherlands
1990-1994 B.F.A., The Cooper Union for the Advancement of Science and Art, New York, NY

Selected Solo Exhibitions

2007 *MOCA Focus: Matthew Monahan*, The Museum of Contemporary Art, Los Angeles, CA [cat.]
The Douglas Hyde Gallery, Dublin, Ireland [cat.]
2006 Stuart Shave / Modern Art, London, England
2005 Anton Kern Gallery, New York, NY
Galerie Fons Welters, Amsterdam, Netherlands
2002 *Nameless Man From Not-Even-Anywhere*, Galerie Fons Welters, Amsterdam, Netherlands
1999 *Artist's Proof*, Buro Leeuwarden, Fries Museum, Leeuwarden, Netherlands
1998 *Figuring out*, Galerie Fons Welters, Amsterdam, Netherlands
Fools Gold, De Nederlandsche Bank, Amsterdam, Netherlands
1996 *Zeno's Quiver*, Stedelijk Museum, Amsterdam, Netherlands

Selected Group Exhibitions

2007 *Hammer Contemporary Collection*, Armand Hammer Museum, University of California, Los Angeles, CA
Eden's Edge: Fifteen LA Artists, Armand Hammer Museum, University of California, Los Angeles, CA
Eight Sculptors from Los Angeles, Sabine Knust Galerie, Munich, Germany
Uneasy Angel / Imagine Los Angeles, Monika Sprüth Philomene Magers, Munich, Germany
2006 *Red Eye: L.A. Artists from the Rubell Family Collection*, Rubell Family Collection, Miami, FL [cat.]
4th Berlin Biennial for Contemporary Art, Berlin, Germany [cat.]
Whitney Biennial 2006, Whitney Museum of American Art, New York, NY [cat.]
2005 *Both Ends Burning*, David Kordansky Gallery, Los Angeles, CA
2004 *MB: the Mary Blair Story (with My Barbarian),* The Roy and Edna Disney / CalArts Theater, Los Angeles, CA
2002 *Civilized Special Zone*, Chinese European Art Center, Xiamen, China
Matthew Monahan & Georg Herold, Anton Kern Gallery, New York, NY
2001 *Free-standing,* Beaver College Art Gallery, Arcadia University, Glenside, PA
2000 *Exorcism Aesthetic Terrorism,* Museum Boijmans Van Beuningen, Rotterdam, Netherlands [cat.]
Gozaimas, Stedelijk Museum Bureau Amsterdam, Stedelijk Museum, Amsterdam, Netherlands
1999 *Glad Ijs / Thin Ice*, Stedelijk Museum Bureau Amsterdam, Stedelijk Museum, Amsterdam, Netherlands
ArtLovers, Liverpool Biennial 1999, Liverpool, England
1998 *Morning Glory*, de Ateliers, Amsterdam, Netherlands [cat.]

Selected Bibliography

Campagnola, Sonia. "Focus Los Angeles: a survey of contemporary Los Angeles art." Flash Art [Vol. 39, No. 246, Jan. – Feb. 2006]: 68-75.
Coetzee, Mark, ed., *Red Eye: L.A. Artists from the Rubell Family Collection*. Miami: Rubell Family Collection, 2007.

Eleey, Peter. "Matthew Monahan." frieze [Issue 94, Oct. 2005]: 214.
Harris, Gareth. "Going along for the ride." The Art Newspaper [Vol. 15, No. 171, July – Aug. 2006]: 33.
Goodbody, Bridget L. "Matthew Monahan." ArtReview [Vol. 56, Aug. 2005]: 108.
Griffin, Jonathan. "Matthew Monahan: Sculpture and anthropology from the school of hard knocks." frieze [Issue 110, Oct. 2007]
Kimmelman, Michael. "Biennial 2006: Short on Pretty, Long on Collaboration." The New York Times [March 13, 2006].
Matthew Monahan. Dublin: Douglas Hyde Gallery, 2007.
"Matthew Monahan and Georg Herold." The New York Times [Feb. 8, 2002].
"Matthew Monahan and Tabwa Masks." The New York Times [Sept. 19, 1997].
Monahan, Matthew, Ari Wiseman, and Elizabeth Hamilton. *Matthew Monahan: five years, ten years, maybe never*. Los Angeles: Museum of Contemporary Art, 2005.
Schambelan, Elizabeth. "Matthew Monahan." Artforum [Vol. 44, No. 2, Oct. 2005]: 264-265.
Schambelan, Elizabeth "Matthew Monahan and Georg Herold at Anton Kern." Art in America [Vol. 90, No. 7, July 2002]: 92.
Smith, Roberta. "Art in Review: Matthew Monahan." The New York Times [July 8, 2005].

Selected Collections

Akzo Nobel Art Foundation, Arnhem, Netherlands
Bernard Nadal-Ginard, Boston, MA
Centraal Utrecht Museum, Utrecht, Netherlands
Collection of Dean Valentine, Los Angeles, CA
Chris Dercon, Rotterdam, Netherlands
de Ateliers, Amsterdam, Netherlands
Fries Museum, Leeuwarden, Netherlands
Georg Herold, Cologne, Germany
Luc Tuymans, Antwerp, Belgium
Museum Boijmans Van Beuningen, Rotterdam, Netherlands
The Museum of Contemporary Art, Los Angeles, CA
The Museum of Modern Art, New York, NY
The Museum of Old and New Art, State Collection of the Tasmanian Museum and Art Gallery, Tasmania, Australia
Rubell Family Collection, Miami, FL
Saatchi Collection, London, England
Stedelijk Museum, Amsterdam, Netherlands
Tate Modern, London, England
Willem Oorbeek, Brussels, Belgium

KRISTEN MORGIN

Born in Brunswick, GA, 1968
Lives and works in Long Beach, CA

Education

1995-1997 M.F.A., New York State College of Ceramics School of Art & Design, Alfred University, Alfred, NY
1990-1993 B.A., California State University, Hayward, CA

Selected Solo Exhibitions

2006 Marc Selwyn Fine Art, Los Angeles, CA
2004 *The Third Movement*, Viento y Agua Gallery, Long Beach, CA
2001 *The Ticking Elephant and Other Surviving Excerpts of the Hope Symphony*, Cuesta College Art Gallery, Cuesta College, San Luis Obispo, CA

Selected Group Exhibitions

2007 *Sculptors' Drawings: Ideas, Studies, Sketches, Proposals, and More*, Angles Gallery, Santa Monica, CA
Hammer Contemporary Collection: Part II, Armand Hammer Museum, University of California, Los Angeles, CA
2006 *Red Eye: L.A. Artists from the Rubell Family Collection*, Rubell Family Collection, Miami, FL [cat.]
RAW: Unfired Clay Installations, Northern Clay Center, Minneapolis, MN
2005 *The 3RD World Ceramic Biennale 2005 Korea, Trans-Ceramic-Art, Beyond Medium,* Icheon World Ceramic Center, Icheon, Korea
THING: New Sculpture from Los Angeles The Armand Hammer Museum of Art and Cultural Center, University of California, Los Angeles, CA [cat.]
61st Ceramic Annual, Ruth Chandler Williamson Gallery, Scripps College, Claremont, CA [cat.]
2004 *Unscenery*, Raid Projects, Los Angeles, CA
Because the EARTH IS 1/3 DIRT, CU Art Museum, University of Colorado at Boulder, Boulder, CO [cat.]
Play Pause, SCA Project Gallery, Pomona, CA
2003 *Unscenery*, Cypress College Fine Arts Gallery, Cypress College, Cypress, CA
2002 *Faculty Biennial*, University Art Museum, California State University, Long Beach, CA
The Body Minded Problem, Max L. Gatov Gallery, Long Beach, CA
New Territory, Belger Arts Center, Kansas City, MO
2001 *To Be Continued*, Cerritos College Art Gallery, Cerritos College, Norwalk, CA
2000 *Menagerie*, Kirkland Arts Center, Kirkland, WA; traveled to Covivant Gallery, Tampa, FL; Gaston College Galleries, Gaston College, Dallas, NC
1999 *Common Threads*, Diane Nelson Fine Art Gallery, Laguna Beach, CA
1998 *Five Sculptors / Figurative Work*, Diane Nelson Fine Art Gallery, Laguna Beach, CA
Igal and Diane Silber Collection of International Contemporary Ceramics, Laguna Art Museum, Laguna Beach, CA [cat.]
1997 Fosdick-Nelson Gallery, Alfred University, Alfred, NY

Selected Bibliography

because the EARTH IS 1/3 DIRT. Bolder: CU Art Museum, University of Colorado at Boulder, 2004.
Brumer, Andy. "Where clay gets a chance to make a big impression." The Los Angeles Times [Jan. 27, 2005]: E21.
Ceramic Annual 2005: Scripps College 61st Ceramic Exhibition. Newent: Perpetua Press, 2005.
Coetzee, Mark, ed., *Red Eye: L.A. Artists from the Rubell Family Collection*. Miami: Rubell Family Collection, 2007.
Elaine, James, Aimee Chang, and Christopher Miles. *Thing: new sculpture from Los Angeles*, Los Angeles: Armand Hammer Museum, 2005.

Harvey, Doug. "Good Thing: Emerging L.A. sculptors at the Hammer." LA Weekly [Feb. 4-10, 2005]: 32-33.
Knight, Christopher. "The next big 'Thing' in L.A." The Los Angeles Times [Feb. 9, 2005]: E1, E6.
Miles, Christopher. "The Idolaters' Revenge." Flash Art [Vol. 38, No. 242, May – June 2005]: 104-108.
Roug, Louise. "The (quirky) object's the thing for a fresh crop of sculptors." The Los Angeles Times [Jan. 2, 2005]: E41, E48-E49.

Selected Collections

Alfred University, Alfred, NY
Armand Hammer Museum, University of California, Los Angeles, CA
Collection of Dean Valentine and Amy Adelson, Los Angeles, CA
Diane and Igal Silber Collection, Laguna Beach, CA
Rubell Family Collection, Miami, FL

©Photo by Daphne Fitzpatrick, 2000

CATHERINE OPIE

Born in Sandusky, Ohio, 1961
Lives and works in Los Angeles, CA

Education

1986-1988 M.F.A., California Institute of the Arts, Valencia, CA
1981-1985 B.F.A., San Francisco Art Institute, San Francisco, CA

Solo Exhibitions

2006 *Catherine Opie: 1999 & In and Around Home*, The 2004 Larry Aldrich Award Exhibition, The Aldrich Contemporary Art Museum, Ridgefield, CT; traveled to Orange County Museum of Art, Newport Beach, CA; Museum of Contemporary Art Cleveland, Cleveland OH; Weatherspoon Art Museum, The University of North Carolina at Greensboro, Greensboro, NC [cat.]
Catherine Opie: Chicago (American Cities), Museum of Contemporary Art Chicago, Chicago, IL [cat.]
American Cities, Gladstone Gallery, New York, NY
2004 *Children*, Studio Guenzani, Milan, Italy
Surfer Series, Stephen Friedman Gallery, London, England
Surfers, Regen Projects, Los Angeles, CA
2002 *Catherine Opie: Icehouses*, Regen Projects, Los Angeles, CA; Studio Guenzani, Milan, Italy
Catherine Opie: Skyways and Icehouses, Walker Art Center, Minneapolis, MN [cat.]
2001 *Wall Street*, Stephen Friedman Gallery, London, England
2000 *currents 82*: *Catherine Opie: In between here and there*, Saint Louis Art Museum, St. Louis, MO
Altered States of America: Catherine Opie, The Photographers' Gallery, London, England; traveled to the Museum of Contemporary Art Chicago, Chicago, IL [cat.]
1999 *Domestic*, Regen Projects, Los Angeles, CA
1997 *Focus Series: Catherine Opie*, The Museum of Contemporary Art, Los Angeles, CA [cat.]
1996 *Houses and Landscapes*, Regen Projects, Los Angeles, CA
Houses and Freeways, Jay Gorney Modern Art, New York, NY
Freeways, Feigen Gallery, Chicago, IL
1995 *Portraits and Freeways*, Richard Foncke Gallery, Ghent, Belgium
1994 *Portraits*, Regen Projects, Los Angeles, CA
Catherine Opie: Photographs from the Freeway Series, Jack Hanley Gallery, San Francisco, CA

Selected Group Exhibitions

2007 *All the More Real: Portrayals of Intimacy and Empathy*, The Parrish Art Museum, Southampton, NY [cat.]
Global Feminisms Remix, Elizabeth A. Sackler Center for Feminist Art, Brooklyn Museum, Brooklyn, NY [cat.]
Pretty Baby, Modern Art Museum of Fort Worth, Fort Worth, TX [cat.]
Family Pictures, Solomon R. Guggenheim Museum, New York, NY
Hammer Contemporary Collection, Part II, Armand Hammer Museum, University of California, Los Angeles, CA
2006 *Red Eye: L.A. Artists from the Rubell Family Collection*, Rubell Family Collection, Miami, FL [cat.]
The Unhomely: Phantom Scenes in Global Society, 2nd International Biennial of Contemporary Art of Seville, Seville, Spain [cat.]
The Eighth Square: Gender, Life and Desire in the Arts since 1960, Museum Ludwig, Cologne, Germany [cat.]
Still Points of the Turning World, Sixth International Biennial Exhibition, 2006, SITE Santa Fe, Santa Fe, NM [cat.]
2005 *Literally and Figuratively. Photographic Portraits*, The Montreal Museum of Fine Arts, Montreal, Canada
Ideal Worlds: New Romanticism in Contemporary Art, Schirn Kunsthalle Frankfurt, Frankfurt, Germany [cat.]
2004 26th Bienal de São Paulo, São Paulo, Brazil
Whitney Biennial 2004, Whitney Museum of American Art, New York, NY [cat.]

2003 *Art, Lies and Videotape: Exposing Performance*, Tate Liverpool, Liverpool, England [cat.]
2001 *Open City: Street Photographs Since 1950*, Modern Art Oxford, Oxford, England; traveled to The Lowry, Manchester, England; Museo de Bellas Artes de Bilbao, Bilbao, Spain; Hirshhorn Museum and Sculpture Garden, Smithsonian Institution, Washington, DC [cat.]
2000 *Made in California: Art, Image and Identity, 1900 - 2000*, Los Angeles County Museum of Art, Los Angeles, CA [cat.]
1999 *The American Century: Art and Culture, Part II, 1950-2000*, Whitney Museum of American Art, New York, NY [cat.]
Melbourne International Biennial 1999, Melbourne, Australia [cat.]
1998 *Love's Body, Rethinking Naked and Nude in Photography*, Tokyo Metropolitan Museum of Photography, Tokyo, Japan [cat.]
Lost Paradise: Catherine Opie, Ellen Cantor, Joachim Koester, Presença Gallery, Porto, Portugal
From the Corner of the Eye, Stedelijk Museum, Amsterdam, Netherlands [cat.]
1997 *Sunshine & Noir: Art in L.A.: 1960-1997,* Louisiana Museum for Moderne Kunst, Humlebaek, Denmark; traveled to Kunstmuseum Wolfsburg, Wolfsburg, Germany; Castello di Rivoli, Museo d'Arte Contemporanea, Turin, Italy; Armand Hammer Museum, University of California, Los Angeles, CA [cat.]
1996 *Inbetweener*, Centre for Contemporary Arts, Glasgow, Scotland
Gender, Fucked, Center on Contemporary Art, Seattle, WA [cat.]
1995 *Whitney Biennial 1995*, Whitney Museum of American Art, New York, NY [cat.]
1994 *Persona Cognita*, Museum of Modern Art at Heide, Melbourne, Australia [cat.]
1992 *Wasteland: Landscape from Now On*, Fotografie Biënnale Rotterdam III, Rotterdam, Netherlands [cat.]

Selected Bibliography

Avgikos, Jan. "Catherine Opie." Artforum [Vol. 45, No. 3, Nov. 2006]: 297.
Campbell, Clayton. "Catherine Opie." Flash Art [Vol. 37, No. 235, March – April 2004]: 108.
Catherine Opie: Skyways & Icehouses, Minneapolis: Walker Art Center, 2002.
Coetzee, Mark, ed., *Red Eye: L.A. Artists from the Rubell Family Collection*. Miami: Rubell Family Collection, 2007.
Ferguson, Russell, and Catherine Opie. *Catherine Opie: The Photographers' Gallery, London*, London: Photographers' Gallery, 2000.
Hainley, Bruce. "Catherine Opie." Artforum [Vol. 42, No. 8, April 2004]: 164-165.
Myers, Terry R. "Catherine Opie: In and around home." ArtReview [No. 3, Sept. 2006]: 142.
Nico, Israel. "Catherine Opie." Artforum [Vol. 38, No. 10, Summer 2000]: 183.
Reilly, Maura. "The Drive to Describe: an interview with Catherine Opie." Art Journal [Vol. 60, No. 2, Sept. 2001]: 82-95.
Sheets, Hilarie M. "Catherine Opie." ARTnews [Vol. 105, No. 10, Nov. 2006]: 180.
Smith, Elizabeth A.T. *Catherine Opie: Chicago (American cities)*, Chicago: Museum of Contemporary Art, 2006.
Steiner, Rochelle, and Catherine Opie. *Catherine Opie: in between here and there*, St. Louis: Saint Louis Art Museum, 2000.

Selected Collections

Albright-Knox Art Gallery, Buffalo, NY
Centro Cultural de Arte Contemporáneo, Mexico City, Mexico
Fondazione Sandretto Re Rebaudengo per l'Arte, Turin, Italy
Groninger Museum, Groningen, Holland
The Israel Museum, Jerusalem, Israel
Long Beach Museum of Art, Long Beach, CA
Los Angeles County Museum of Art, Los Angeles, CA
Miami Art Museum, Miami, FL
The Museum of Contemporary Art, Los Angeles, CA
Museum of Contemporary Art, Chicago, IL
Museum of Fine Arts, Boston, MA
The Museum of Modern Art, New York, NY
Orange County Museum of Art, Newport Beach, CA
Rubell Family Collection, Miami, FL
San Francisco Museum of Modern Art, San Francisco, CA
Solomon R. Guggenheim Museum, New York, NY
Walker Art Center, Minneapolis, MN
Whitney Museum of American Art, New York, NY

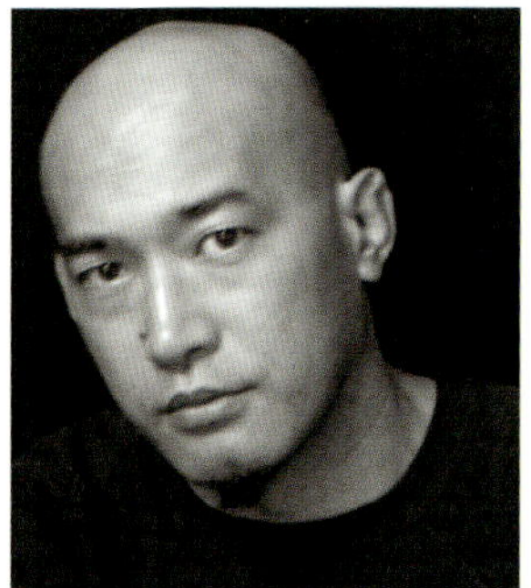

KAZ OSHIRO

Born in Okinawa, Japan, 1967
Lives and works in Los Angeles, CA

Education

1999-2002 M.F.A., California State University, Los Angeles, CA
1991-1998 B.A., California State University, Los Angeles, CA

Selected Solo Exhibitions

2009 Rosamund Felsen Gallery, Santa Monica, CA
2007 *Room Acoustics*, Tokyo Institute of Technology, Tokyo, Japan
Common Noise, galerie frank elbaz, Paris, France
Paintings and Works on Paper, 1999-2006, Las Vegas Art Museum, Las Vegas, NV
Yvon Lambert Gallery, New York, NY
2006 *Driving with Dementia,* Rosamund Felsen Gallery, Santa Monica, CA
Subpar, Steven Wolf Fine Arts, San Francisco, CA
2005 *Project Series 27: Kaz Oshiro*, Pomona College Museum of Art, Montgomery Art Center, Claremont, CA [cat.]
Drone, Rosamund Felsen Gallery, Santa Monica, CA
2004 *Out-n-In*, Rosamund Felsen Gallery, Santa Monica, CA
2002 *Pop Tatari (Curse of Pop Music)*, Rosamund Felsen Gallery, Santa Monica, CA

Selected Group Exhibitions

2007 *Humor Us*, Municipal Art Gallery, Los Angeles, CA
Sculptors' Drawings: Ideas, Studies, Sketches, Proposals, and More, Angles Gallery, Santa Monica, CA
If Everybody Had an Ocean. Brian Wilson: An Art Exhibition, Tate St. Ives, St. Ives, England; traveled to CAPC Musée d'Art Contemporain de Bordeaux, Bordeaux, France [cat.]
Beneath the Underdog, Gagosian Gallery, New York, NY
Forged Realities, UniversalStudios-beijing, Beijing, China
Endless Western Sunset, Leo Castelli Gallery, New York, NY
2006 *Red Eye: L.A. Artists from the Rubell Family Collection*, Rubell Family Collection, Miami, FL [cat.]
One Way or Another: Asian American Art Now, Asia Society, New York, NY; traveled to Berkeley Art Museum, University of California, Berkeley, CA; Blaffer Gallery, University of Houston, Houston, TX; traveling to Japanese American National Museum, Los Angeles, CA [cat.]
Banquet: A Feast for the Senses, Pacific Asia Museum, Pasadena, CA
DEAF: "From the audible to the visible," galerie frank elbaz, Paris, France
2005 *THING: New Sculpture from Los Angeles, The Armand Hammer Museum of Art and Cultural Center, University of California, Los Angeles, CA.)* [cat.]
Pan / Sonic, Northern Illinois University Art Museum, College of Visual and Performing Arts, Northern Illinois University, Chicago, IL
2004 *ROCK*, Mark Moore Gallery, Los Angeles, CA
Giggles, Angstrom Gallery, Dallas, TX
Nothing Compared to This: ambient, incidental and new minimal tendencies in current art, Contemporary Arts Center, Cincinnati, OH
2004 California Biennial, Orange County Museum of Art, Newport Beach, CA [cat.]
2003 *2003 Summer Program*, Apex Art, New York, NY
Redux: Selected Works by Recent Cal State L.A. M.F.A. Alumni, Luckman Gallery, California State University, Los Angeles, CA
2002 Rosamund Felsen Gallery, Santa Monica, CA

Selected Bibliography

Bockus, Kim."Drone-ing On." NY Arts [Vol. 11, No. 1 / 2, Jan.-Feb. 2006].
Bockus, Kim. "Spin Cycle." NY Arts [Vol. 11, No 3 / 4, March-April 2006].
Campagnola, Sonia. "Focus Los Angeles: a survey of contemporary Los Angeles art." Flash Art [Vol. 39. No. 246, Jan.-Feb. 2006]: 68-75.
Coetzee, Mark, ed., *Red Eye: L.A. Artists from the Rubell Family Collection.* Miami: Rubell Family Collection, 2007.
Elaine, James, Aimee Chang and Christopher Miles. *THING: new sculpture from Los Angeles.* Los Angeles: Hammer Museum; Fellows of Contemporary Art, 2005.
Harvey, Doug."Good Thing: Emerging L.A. Sculptors at the Hammer." L.A. Weekly [Feb. 4-10, 2005]: 32-33.
Helfand, Glen."Kaz Oshiro at Steven Wolf Fine Arts." Artforum [Vol. 44, No. 9, May 2006]: 296.
Herbert, Simon. "Thing: New Sculpture from Los Angeles." Art Monthly [No. 286, May 2005]: 29-30.
Hettig, Frank-Alexander. "Thing. Neue Skulpturen aus Los Angeles. Armand Hammer Museum of Art, Los Angeles." Kunstforum International [No. 175, April-May 2005]: 356-358.
Holte, Michael Ned. "Los Angeles Critics' Pick." www.artforum.com [April 2004].
Kaz Oshiro. Claremont: Pomona College Museum of Art, 2005.
Peterson, Kristen. "Master of the Mundane." Las Vegas Sun [April 10, 2007].
Peterson, Kristen. "They came, they saw, they were impressed and perplexed." Las Vegas Sun [June 8, 2007].
Robinett, Rae Anne. "Kaz Oshiro." ArtAsiaPacific [No. 42, Fall 2004]: 80.
Szakacs, Dennis, and Elizabeth Armstrong. *2004 California Biennial.* Newport Beach: Orange County Museum of Art, 2004.

Selected Collections

Frederick R. Weisman Art Foundation, Los Angeles, CA
Michael Rabkin and Chip Tom Collection, Los Angeles, CA
Nora Eccles Harrison Museum of Art, Utah State University, Logan, UT
Peter Norton Family Foundation, Santa Monica, CA
Rubell Family Collection, Miami, FL
Saatchi Collection, London, England
Zabludowicz Collection, London, England

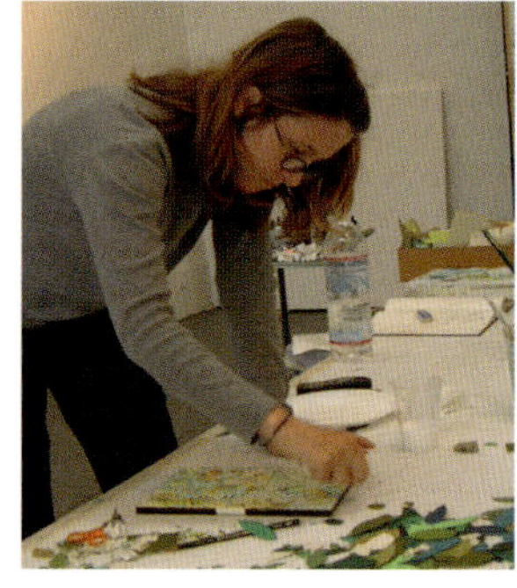

LAURA OWENS

Born in Euclid, OH, 1970
Lives and works in Los Angeles, CA

Education

1994-1996 M.F.A., California Institute of the Arts, Valencia, CA
1994 Skowhegan School of Painting and Sculpture, Skowhegan, ME
1988-1992 B.F.A., Rhode Island School of Design, Providence, RI

Solo Exhibitions

2006 *Red Eye: L.A. Artists from the Rubell Family Collection*, Rubell Family Collection, Miami, FL [cat.]
Laura Owens, Kunsthalle Zürich, Zurich, Switzerland; traveled to Camden Arts Centre, London, England; Ausstellungshalle zeitgenössische Kunst Münster, Münster, Germany; Bonnefantenmuseum Maastricht, Netherlands [cat.]
Laura Owens, The Douglas Hyde Gallery, Dublin, Ireland [cat.]
Sadie Coles HQ, London, England
2005 *Laura Owens*, Shiseido Gallery, Tokyo, Japan [cat.] Schirn Kunsthalle
2004 Museum of Contemporary Art, North Miami, FL
Galerie Gisela Capitain, Cologne, Germany
Fabric Workshop and Museum, Philadelphia, PA
Gavin Brown's enterprise, New York, NY
Crown Point Press Gallery, San Francisco, CA [cat.]
2003 *Laura Owens*, Museum of Contemporary Art, Los Angeles, CA; traveled to Aspen Art Museum, Aspen, CO [cat.]
Laura Owns, Milwaukee Art Museum, Milwaukee, WI
2001 *Laura Owens*: *New Work at The Isabella Stewart Gardner Museum*, The Isabella Stewart Gardner Museum Boston, MA [cat.]
Laura Owens, ACME, Los Angeles, CA

Group Exhibitions

2006 *The Garden Party*, Deitch Projects, New York, NY
2005 *The Fluidity of Time: Selections from the MCA Collection*, Museum of Contemporary Art, Chicago, IL
After Cézanne, Museum of Contemporary Art, Los Angeles, CA
Ideal Worlds: New Romanticism in Contemporary Art, Schirn Kunsthalle Frankfurt, Frankfurt, Germany [cat.]
Extreme Abstraction, Albright-Knox Art Gallery, Buffalo, NY [cat.]
Drunk vs. Stoned, Passerby, New York, NY
2004 *The Undiscovered Country, The Armand Hammer Museum of Art and Culture Center,* University of California, Los Angeles, CA [cat.]
Huts, The Douglas Hyde Gallery, Dublin, Ireland [cat.]
Paintings' Edge. IdyllwildArts, Idyllwild, CA
2004 Whitney Biennial, Whitney Museum of American Art, New York, NY [cat.]
2002 *Drawing Now: Eight Propositions*, Museum of Modern Art, New York, NY [cat.]
Painting on the move, Kunstmuseum Basel and Museum für Gegenwartskunst, Basel, Switzerland [cat.]
Urgent Painting, Musée d'Art Moderne de la Ville de Paris, Paris, France [cat.]
Cavepainting: Peter Doig, Chris Ofili, and Laura Owens, Santa Monica Museum of Art, Santa Monica, CA [cat.]

Selected Bibliography

Avgikos, Jan. "Laura Owens." Artforum [Vol. 37, No. 5, Jan. 1999]: 119-120.
Cavalchini, Pieranna, ed. *Laura Owens*, Boston: Isabella Stewart Gardner Museum; Milan: Charta, 2001.
Coetzee, Mark, ed., *Red Eye: L.A. Artists from the Rubell Family Collection*. Miami: Rubell Family Collection, 2007.
Ferguson, Russell. "Laura Owens paints a picture / Laura Owens malt ein Bild." Parkett [No. 65, 2002]: 58-73.
Fresh cream: contemporary art in culture, London: Phaidon Publishers, 2000.
Gleeson, David. "Laura Owens." Art Monthly [No. 301, Nov. 2006]: 23-24.
Hutchinson, John, ed. *Laura Owens*, Dublin: Douglas Hyde Gallery, 2006.
Miller, Francine Koslow. "Laura Owens." Artforum [Vol. 40, No. 5, Jan. 2006]: 144.
Moreno, Gean. "Laura Owens: never the same twice." Flash Art [Vol. 36, No. 232, Oct. 2003]: 94-96.
Morgan, Susan, and Laura Owens. "A thousand words." (Interview) Artforum [Vol. 37, No. 10, Summer 1999]: 130-131.
Muchnic, Suzanne. "Laura Owens." ARTnews [Vol. 102, No. 10, Nov. 2003]: 162.
O'Reilly, Sally. "Laura Owens." ArtReview [No. 2, Aug. 2006]: 136.
Ruf, Beatrix, and Irene Aeberli. *Laura Owens. [12. Juni - 13. August 2006]*. Zurich: Kunsthalle Zurich; JRP Ringier, 2006.Schimmel, Paul. *Laura Owens*, Los Angeles: Museum of Contemporary Art, 2003.
Singerman, Howard. "Laura Owens." Artforum [Vol. 41, No. 9, May 2003]: 163.

Selected Collections

The Art Institute of Chicago, Chicago, IL
Carnegie Museum of Art, Pittsburgh, PA
Centre Georges Pompidou, Paris, France
Joslyn Art Museum, Omaha, NE
Los Angeles County Museum of Art, Los Angeles, CA
Metropolitan Museum of Art, New York, NY
Museum für Gegenwartskunst, Basel, Switzerland
Museum of Contemporary Art Chicago, Chicago, IL
The Museum of Contemporary Art, Los Angeles, CA
Rubell Family Collection, Miami, FL
San Francisco Museum of Modern Art, San Francisco, CA
Solomon R. Guggenheim Museum, New York, NY
Whitney Museum of American Art, New York, NY

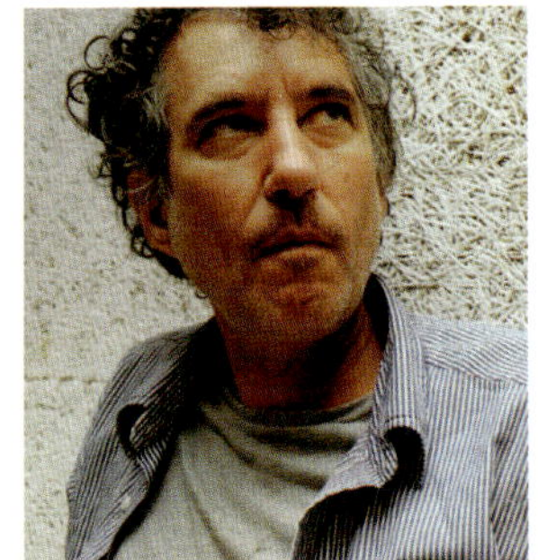

RAYMOND PETTIBON

Born in Tucson, Arizona, 1957
Lives and works in Hermosa Beach, CA

Education

1974-1977 B.A., University of California, Los Angeles, Los Angeles, CA

Selected Solo Exhibitions

2007 *Raymond Pettibon: Here's Your Irony Back (The Big Picture)*, David Zwirner, New York, NY
Raymond Pettibon: V-Boom, Kestner Gesellschaft, Hannover, Germany
2006 *Raymond Pettibon: Whatever It Is You're Looking For You Won't Find It Here*, Kunsthalle Wien, Vienna, Austria
Raymond Pettibon, Centro de Arte Contemporáneo de Málaga, Malaga, Spain
2005 *Raymond Pettibon: Untitled*, Whitney Museum of American Art, New York, NY
Raymond Pettibon, Contemporary Fine Arts, Berlin, Germany [cat.]
2004 *Raymond Pettibon*, David Zwirner, New York, NY
2003 *Raymond Pettibon*, Galerie Meyer Kainer, Vienna, Austria
Raymond Pettibon: Drawings, Museion-Museo d'Arte Moderno e Contemporanea, Bolzano, Italy; traveled to Galleria d'Arte Moderna Bologna, Bologna, Italy [cat.]
2002 *Raymond Pettibon*, Contemporary Fine Arts, Berlin, Germany
Raymond Pettibon, plots laid thick, Museu d'Art Contemporani de Barcelona, Barcelona, Spain; traveled to Tokyo Opera City Art Gallery, Tokyo, Japan; Gemeentemuseum den Haag, The Hague, Netherlands
2001 Gesellschaft für Moderne Kunst am Museum Ludwig, Cologne, Germany
Raymond Pettibon, Whitechapel Art Gallery, London, England
2000 *Raymond Pettibon: Plots on Loan I - Plots on Loan II*, Galerie Tanit, Munich, Germany
Raymond Pettibon: The Books, Contemporary Fine Arts, Berlin, Germany; traveled to MAK-Österreichisches Museum für angewandte Kunst, Vienna, Austria; David Zwirner, New York, NY; Santa Monica Museum of Art, Santa Monica, CA [cat.]
1998 *Raymond Pettibon*, The Renaissance Society at The University of Chicago, Chicago, IL; traveled to The Drawing Center, New York, NY; Philadelphia Museum of Art, Philadelphia, PA; The Museum of Contemporary Art, Los Angeles, CA [cat.]
1996 *Raymond Pettibon*, Tramway, Glasgow, Scotland
1993 *Raymond Pettibon*, Jack Hanley Gallery, San Francisco, CA
1992 *Raymond Pettibon / Matrix 151*, Berkeley Art Museum, University of California, Berkeley, CA
Galerie Rüdiger Schöttle, Munich, Germany
1991 Robert Berman Gallery, Santa Monica, CA
1990 *Raymond Pettibon: Readings*, Feature Inc., New York, NY
A Long Parenthesis, Richard/Bennett Gallery, Los Angeles, CA
1989 *Raymond Pettibon*, Feature Inc., New York, NY

Selected Group Exhibitions

2007 *Sympathy for the Devil: Art and Rock and Roll Since 1967*, Museum of Contemporary Art Chicago, Chicago, IL
52nd Biennale di Venezia, Venice, Italy
2006 *Red Eye: L.A. Artists from the Rubell Family Collection*, Rubell Family Collection, Miami, FL [cat.]
Art in Los Angeles between 1960 and 1990, Kunstverein Braunschweig e.V., Braunschweig, Germany
Los Angeles 1955-1985: The Birth of an Art Capital, Centres Georges Pompidou, Paris, France, [cat.]
2005 *Les Grands Spectacles*, Museum der Moderne Salzburg, Salzburg, Austria
Big Bang: Destruction and Creation in 20th Century Art, Centre Georges Pompidou, Paris, France
2004 *Subway Series: The New York Yankees and the American Dream*, Bronx Museum of the Arts, Bronx, NY
Whitney Biennial 2004, Whitney Museum of American Art, New York, NY

Disparities & Deformations: Our Grotesque. Fifth International Biennial Exhibition, SITE Santa Fe, Santa Fe, NM [cat.]

2002 *Documenta XI*, Documenta und Museum Fridericianum Veranstaltungs-GmbH, Kassel, Germany [cat.]

Shoot the Singer: Music on Video, Institute of Contemporary Art, Philadelphia, PA

2001 *In fumo*, Galleria d'Arte Moderna e Contemporanea di Bergamo, Bergamo, Italy [cat.]

American Tableaux, Walker Art Center, Minneapolis, MN; traveled to Miami Art Museum, Miami, FL; University of Iowa Museum of Art, Iowa City, IA; Portland Art Museum, Portland OR; The Winnipeg Art Gallery, Winnipeg, Canada; Plains Art Museum, Fargo, ND

2000 *Mirror's Edge*, Bildmuseet, Umeå, Sweden; traveled to Vancouver Art Gallery, Vancouver, Canada; Castello di Rivoli Museo d'Arte Contemporanea, Turin, Italy; Tramway, Glasgow, Scotland; Charlottenborg Udstillingsbygning, Copenhagen, Denmark

1999 *The American Century: Art and Culture, 1950-2000*, Whitney Museum of American Art, New York, NY

Otto Dix / Raymond Pettibon, Kunsthalle zu Kiel, Kiel, Germany [cat.]

1997 *Whitney Biennial 1997*, Whitney Museum of American Art, New York, NY [cat.]

Heaven: Public View, Private View, P.S. 1 Contemporary Art Center, Long Island City, NY

Michael Craig-Martin and Raymond Pettibon, Kunstverein Düsseldorf, Dusseldorf, Germany [cat.]

Sunshine & Noir: Art in Los Angeles 1960-1997, Louisiana Museum for Moderne Kunst, Humlebaek, Denmark; traveled to Kunstmuseum Wolfsburg, Wolfsburg, Germany; Castello di Rivoli Museo d'Arte Contemporanea, Turin, Italy; The Armand Hammer Museum of Art and Culture Center, University of California, Los Angeles, CA [cat.]

1995 *Temporary Translation(s) - Kunst der Gegenwart und Fotografie: Sammlung Schürmann,* Deichtorhallen, Hamburg, Germany

1993 *1993 Whitney Biennial*, Whitney Museum of American Art, New York, NY [cat.]

1992 *Helter Skelter: L.A. Art in the 1990s*, The Museum of Contemporary Art, Los Angeles, CA [cat.]

Selected Bibliography

Coetzee, Mark. *Not Afraid: Rubell Family Collection*. London: Phaidon Press, 2004.

Coetzee, Mark, ed., *Red Eye: L.A. Artists from the Rubell Family Collection*. Miami: Rubell Family Collection, 2007.

Dàvila, Mela. *Raymond Pettibon: plot laid thick*. Barcelona: Museu d'Art Contemporani de Barcelona, 2002.

Duncan, Michael. "Pettibon's talking pictures." Art in America [Vol. 87, No. 3, March 1999]: 106-109.

Hainley, Bruce. "Raymond Pettibon." Artforum [Vol. 39, No. 3, Nov. 2000]: 159.

Lewis, Jim. "A conversation with Raymond Pettibon." Parkett [No. 47, Sept. 1996]: 56-69.

Ohrt, Roberto, and Raymond Pettibon. *Raymond Pettibon: the books 1978-1998*. New York: Distributed Art Publishers, 2000.

Pettibon, Raymond. *Thinking of you*. Chicago: Renaissance Society at the University of Chicago, 1998.

"Raymond Pettibon: a project for Artforum." Artforum [Vol. 41, No. 8, April 2003]: 86.

Storr, Robert. *Raymond Pettibon*. London: Phaidon, 2001.

Volkart, Yvonne. "Raymond Pettibon." Flash Art [Vol. 28, No. 183, Summer 1995]: 122.

Selected Collections

The Art Institute of Chicago, Chicago, IL
Centre Georges Pompidou, Paris, France
Dallas Museum of Art, Dallas, TX
Kunstmuseum St. Gallen, St. Gallen, Switzerland
Los Angeles County Museum of Art, Los Angeles, CA
Museum Ludwig, Cologne, Germany
Museum of Contemporary Art Chicago, Chicago, IL
The Museum of Contemporary Art, Los Angeles, CA
Museum of Contemporary Art San Diego, San Diego, CA
The Museum of Modern Art, New York, NY
Philadelphia Museum of Art, Philadelphia, PA
Rubell Family Collection, Miami, FL
Saint Louis Art Museum, St. Louis, MO
Sammlung Goetz, Munich, Germany
San Francisco Museum of Modern Art, San Francisco, CA
Tate Modern, London, England
Vancouver Art Gallery, Vancouver, Canada
Walker Art Center, Minneapolis, MN
Whitney Museum of American Art, New York, NY

CHARLES RAY

Born in Chicago, IL, 1953
Lives and works in Los Angeles, CA

Education

1977-1979 M.F.A., Mason Gross School of the Arts, Rutgers University, New Brunswick, NJ
1971-1975 B.F.A., University of Iowa, Iowa City, IA

Selected Solo Exhibitions

2007 Matthew Marks Gallery, New York, NY
A New Sculpture, Regen Projects, Los Angeles, CA
2006 *black & white*, Astrup Fearnley Museet for Moderne Kunst, Oslo, Norway
1998 *Charles Ray*, Whitney Museum of American Art, New York, NY; traveled to the Museum of Contemporary Art, Los Angeles, CA; Museum of Contemporary Art, Chicago, IL [cat.]
1997 *Unpainted Sculpture*, Regen Projects, Los Angeles, CA
1996 Studio Guenzani, Milan, Italy
1994 *Charles Ray*, Rooseum Center for Contemporary Art, Malmö, Sweden; traveled to Institute of Contemporary Arts, London, England; Kunsthalle Bern, Bern, Switzerland; Kunsthalle Zürich, Zurich, Switzerland [cat.]
1990 Burnett Miller Gallery, Los Angeles, CA
Interim Art, London, England
Newport Harbor Art Museum, Newport Beach, CA [cat.]
Charles Ray / Matrix 140, Berkeley Art Museum, University of California, Berkeley, CA [cat.]
1989 Burnett Miller Gallery, Los Angeles, CA
Feature Inc., New York, NY
1987 Feature Inc., Chicago, IL
Burnett Miller Gallery, Los Angeles, CA

Selected Group Exhibitions

2007 *Art Since the 1960s: California Experiments*, Orange County Museum of Art, Newport Beach, CA
Depth of Field: Modern Photography at the Metropolitan, Metropolitan Museum of Art, New York, NY
Dead! Dead! Dead! Ydessa Hendeles Art Foundation, Toronto, Canada
Photography and the Self: The Legacy of F. Holland Day, Whitney Museum of American Art, New York, NY
2006 *Red Eye: L.A. Artists from the Rubell Family Collection*, Rubell Family Collection, Miami, FL [cat.]
Where are we going? Selections from the François Pinault Collection, Palazzo Grassi, Venice, Italy [cat]
Recent Drawings: Robert Gober, Roni Horn, Jasper Johns, Ellsworth Kelly, Brice Marden, Ken Price, Charles Ray, Terry Winters, Matthew Marks Gallery, New York, NY
Small Sculpture, Matthew Marks Gallery, New York, NY [cat.]
2005 *Ecstasy: In and About Altered States*, The Museum of Contemporary Art, Los Angeles, CA [cat.]
2004 *Monument to Now*, Deste Foundation Centre for Contemporary Art, Athens, Greece [cat.]
2003 *La Biennale di Venezia, 50th International Art Exhibition. Dreams and Conflicts: The Dictatorship of the Viewer*, Venice, Italy [cat.]
Selections from the Permanent Collection, Walker Art Center, Minneapolis, MN
2001 *Jasper Johns to Jeff Koons: Four Decades of Art from the Broad Collections*, Los Angeles County Museum of Art, Los Angeles, CA; traveled to Corcoran Gallery of Art, Washington, DC; Museum of Fine Arts, Boston, MA
2000 *Let's Entertain*, Walker Art Center, Minneapolis, MN; traveled to the Centre Georges Pompidou, Paris, France; Portland Art Museum, Portland, Oregon; Kunstmuseum Wolfsburg, Wolfsburg, Germany; Miami Art Museum, Miami, FL [cat.]

1999 *Regarding Beauty: A View of the Late Twentieth Century,* Hirshhorn Museum and Sculpture Garden, Smithsonian Institution, Washington DC; traveled to Haus der Kunst, Munich, Germany [cat.]
The American Century: Art and Culture, 1900-2000: Part II, 1950-2000, Whitney Museum of American Art, New York, NY [cat.]
1998 *16mm films: Jennifer Bornstein, Steve Doughton & Charles Ray,* greengrassi, London, England
1997 *4e Biennale de Lyon d'art contemporain,* Lyon, France [cat.]
Skuptur. Projekte in Münster 1997, Westfälisches Landesmuseum für Kunst und Kulturgeschichte Münster, Munster, Germany
Sunshine & Noir, Art in L.A.1960-1997, Louisiana Museum for Moderne Kunst, Humlebaek, Denmark; traveled to Kunstmuseum Wolfsburg, Wolfsburg, Germany; Castello di Rivoli Museo d'Arte Contemporanea, Turin, Italy; *The Armand Hammer Museum of Art and Culture Center*, University of California, Los Angeles, CA [cat.]
Whitney Biennial 1997, Whitney Museum of American Art, New York, NY [cat.]
1995 *Whitney Biennial 1995,* Whitney Museum of American Art, New York, NY [cat.]
1993 *Whitney Biennial 1993,* Whitney Museum of American Art, New York, NY [cat.]
1992 *documenta IX,* Kassel, Germany [cat.]
*Helter Skelter: L.A. Art in the 1990's,*The Museum of Contemporary Art, Los Angeles, CA [cat.]
1989 *Whitney Biennial 1989,* Whitney Museum of American Art, New York, NY [cat.]

Selected Bibliography

Coetzee, Mark. *Not Afraid: Rubell Family Collection*. London: Phaidon Press, 2004.
Coetzee, Mark, ed., *Red Eye: L.A. Artists from the Rubell Family Collection*. Miami: Rubell Family Collection, 2007.
Fried, Michael, and John Kelsey. *Charles Ray*. New York: Matthew Marks Gallery, 2007.
Fried, Michael. "Early One Morning..." Tate Etc. [No. 3, Spring 2005]: 50-53.
Gaines, Malik. "Charles Ray." Contemporary [No. 64, 2004]: 86-89.
Hainley, Bruce. "Charles Ray." Artforum [Vol. 36, No. 5, Jan. 1998]: 91.
Holte, Michael Ned. "Charles Ray: slow dissolve." ArtReview [No. 8, Feb. 2007]: 62-67.
Kertess, Klaus. "Some Bodies." Parkett [No. 37, 1993]: 36-39.
Knight, Christopher. "Charles Ray's Still Lifes." Parkett [No. 37, 1993]: 46-48
Nittve, Lars, and Ulrika Levén. *Charles Ray*. Malmö: Rooseum Center for Contemporary Art, 1994.
Ray, Charles. *A four dimensional being writes poetry on a field with sculptures*, New York: Matthew Marks Gallery; Göttingen: Steidl Publishers, 2006.
Ray, Charles, Paul Schimmel, and Lisa Phillips. *Charles Ray*. Los Angeles: Museum of Contemporary Art, 1998.
Ray, Charles. "Thinking of Sculpture as Shaped by Space." The New York Times [Oct. 7, 2001]: 34.
Relyea, Lane. "Charles Ray: In the No." Artforum [Vol. 31, No. 1, Sept. 1992]: 62-66.
Schimmel, Paul, and Lisa Gabrielle Mark. *Ecstasy: In and About Altered States*, Cambridge: MIT Press, 2005.
Schimmel, Paul, and Lisa Phillips. *Charles Ray*, Los Angeles: Museum of Contemporary Art, 1998.
Storr, Robert. "Anxious Spaces." Art in America [Vol. 86, No. 11, Nov. 1996]: 101-105, 143-144.
Wagner, Anne M. "Charles Ray." Artforum [Vol. 37, No. 9, May 1999]: 171-172.

Selected Collections

The Art Institute of Chicago, Chicago, IL
Astrup Fearnley Museet for Moderne Kunst, Oslo, Norway
Dallas Museum of Art, Dallas, TX
Kunstmuseum Basel Museum für Gegenwartskunst, Basel, Switzerland
Metropolitan Museum of Art, New York, NY
The Museum of Contemporary Art, Los Angeles, CA
Museum of Fine Arts, Boston, MA
The Museum of Modern Art, New York, NY
Orange County Museum of Art, Newport Beach, CA
Rubell Family Collection, Miami, FL
Tate Collection, London, England
Walker Art Center, Minneapolis, MN
Whitney Museum of American Art, New York, NY

JASON RHOADES

Born in Newcastle, CA, 1965
Died in Los Angeles, CA, 2006

©Courtesy Estate of Jason Rhoades; Galerie Hauser & Wirth, London and Zurich; David Zwirner, New York

Education

1991-1993 M.F.A. University of California, Los Angeles, Los Angeles, CA
1988 Skowhegan School of Painting and Sculpture, Skowhegan, ME
1986-1988 B.F.A, San Francisco Art Institute, San Francisco, CA
1985-1986 One year of study, California College of Arts and Crafts, Oakland, CA

Selected Solo Exhibitions

2007 *Black Pussy*, David Zwirner, New York, NY [cat.]
Multiples (sculptures, 1993-1998), El Sourdog Hex, Berlin, Germany
2006 *Tijuantanjierchandelier*, Centro de Arte Contemporáneo de Málaga, Malaga, Spain
2005 *The Black Pussy...and the Pagan Idol Workshop*, Hauser & Wirth, London, England
My Madinah: Pupp Tent/Puss Tent, Galería Helga de Alvear, Madrid, Spain
2003 *Meccatuna*, David Zwirner, New York, NY
2002 *PeaRoeFoam. The Impetuous Process & From the Costner Complex*, David Zwirner, New York, NY
My Special Purpose, Museum Moderner Kunst Stiftung Ludwig Wien, Vienna, Austria [cat.]
2001 *Jason Rhoades: Costner Complex (Perfect Process),* Portikus, Frankfurt am Main, Germany [cat.]
2000 *of perfect world,* David Zwirner, New York, NY
New Works: 00.4, Artpace, San Antonio, TX
Hauser & Wirth, Zurich, Switzerland
1998 *After the Seven Stomachs of Nurnberg as Part of the Creation Myth,* Van Abbemuseum, Eindhoven, Netherlands [cat.]
1997 *Deviations in Space, VARIOUSVIRGINS,* David Zwirner, New York, NY
1993 *CHERRY Makita - Honest Engine Work*, David Zwirner, New York, NY

Selected Group Exhibitions

2007 *Sympathy for the Devil: Art and Rock and Roll Since 1967*, Museum of Contemporary Art Chicago, Chicago, IL [cat.]
Think with Senses-Feel with the Mind, 52nd Biennale di Venezia, Venice, Italy [cat.]
There is never a stop and never a finish: In memoriam Jason Rhoades, Friedrich Christian Flick Collection, Hamburger Bahnhof - Museum für Gegenwart, Berlin, Germany [cat.]
Eden's Edge: Fifteen LA Artists, Armand Hammer Museum, University of California, Los Angeles, CA, Los Angeles, CA [cat.]
2006 *Red Eye: L.A. Artists from the Rubell Family Collection*, Rubell Family Collection, Miami, FL [cat.]
Wrestle, Hessel Museum of Art, Center for Curatorial Studies, Bard College, Annandale-on-Hudson, NY [cat.]
FASTER! BIGGER! BETTER!, Zentrum für Kunst, und Medientechnologie, Karlsruhe, Germany [cat.]
2005 *Lichtkunst aus Kunstlicht: Licht als Medium der Kunst im 20 Jahrhundert*, Zentrum für Kunst und Medientechnologie, Karlsruhe, Germany [cat.]
Dionysiac, Centre Georges Pompidou, Paris, France [cat.]
2004 *Moving Parts – Forms of the Kinetic,* Kunsthaus Graz, Landesmuseum Joanneum, Graz, Austria [cat.]
Friedrick Christian Flick Collection im Hamburger Bahnhof, Hamburger Bahnhof Museum, Berlin, Germany [cat.]
Das Große Fressen: Von Pop bis heute, Kunsthalle Bielefeld, Bielefeld, Germany [cat.]
Everything is Connected, he, he, he, Astrup Fearnley Museet for Moderne Kunst, Oslo, Norway
2003 *OVER WIJ / ABOUT WE,* Van Abbemuseum, Eindhoven, Netherlands
2002 *L.A. on My Mind: Recent Acquisitions from MOCA's Permanent Collection,* Museum of Contemporary Art at the Pacific Design Center, Los Angeles, CA
Paul McCarthy & Jason Rhoades: Shit Plug, Hauser & Wirth, Zurich, Switzerland [cat.]

2001 *Public Offerings*, The Museum of Contemporary Art, Los Angeles, CA [cat.]
Yokohama 2001: International Triennale of Contemporary Art, Yokohama, Japan [cat.]
1999 *dAPERTutto, 48th Biennale di Venezia*, Venice, Italy [cat.]
Get Together, Kunsthalle Wien, Vienna, Austria [cat.]
Propposition (collaboration with Paul McCarthy),*48th Biennale di Venezia*, Venice Italy [cat.]
Danish Pavilion (collaboration with Peter Bonde), *48th Biennale di Venezia*, Venice, Italy
1998 *Hundert Jahre Secession: (A Century of Artistic Freedom)*, Secession, Vienna, Austria
1997 *47th Biennale di Venezia*, Venice, Italy [cat.]
Whitney Biennial 1997, Whitney Museum of American Art, New York, NY [cat.]
Sunshine & Noir: Art in L.A.1960-1997, Louisiana Museum for Moderne Kunst, Humlebaek, Denmark; traveled to Kunstmuseum Wolfsburg, Wolfsburg, Germany; Castello di Rivoli Museo d'Arte Contemporanea, Turin, Italy; The Armand Hammer Museum of Art and Culture Center, University of California, Los Angeles, CA [cat.]
Biennale de Lyon d'art contemporain, Lyon, France [cat.]
1996 *Nach Weimar*, Neues Landesmuseum, Weimar, Germany [cat.]
Defining the Nineties: Consensus-Making in New York, Miami, and Los Angeles, Museum of Contemporary Art, Miami, FL [cat.]
1995 *Whitney Biennial 1995,* Whitney Museum of American Art, New York, NY [cat.]
Selections of the Permanent Collection, Museum van Hedendaagse Kunst, Ghent, Belgium

Selected Bibliography

Coetzee, Mark, ed., *Red Eye: L.A. Artists from the Rubell Family Collection*. Miami: Rubell Family Collection, 2007.
Felix, Zdenek, and Jason Rhoades. *Jason Rhoades: Perfect World*. Cologne: Oktagon, 2000.
Furness, Rosalind. "Jason Rhoades: Black Pussy... and the Pagan Idol Workshop." Modern Painters [Dec. 2005 / Jan. 2006]: 125.
Hochdorfer, Achim, and Jan Avgikos. *PeaRoeFoam: the impetuous process, my special purpose and the liver pool - Jason Rhoades*. Vienna: Museum Moderner Kunst Stiftung Ludwig Wien, 2002.
Lunn, Felicity. "Jason Rhoades." Artforum [Vol. 43, No. 3, Nov. 2004]: 235.
Princenthal, Nancy. "Jason Rhoades." artUS [Issue 1, Jan. – Feb. 2004]: 41.
Princenthal, Nancy. "Jason Rhoades: pipe dreams." Art in America [Vol. 89, No.1, Jan. 2001]: 98-101, 141.
Rhoades, Jason. *Jason Rhoades: the Costner complext (perfect process)*. Frankfurt: Portikus, 1996.
Rhoades, Jason, and Eva Meyer-Hermann. *Jason Rhoades: volume, and Rhoades referenz*. Cologne: Oktagon, 1998.
Robecchi, Michele. "Jason Rhoades." Contemporary [Issue 81, 2006]: 42-45.
The snowball: A collaborative project by Peter Bonde & Jason Rhoades. Ostfildern: Hatje Cantz, 1999.
Vincent, Steven. "Jason Rhoades." Art Review [Vol. 54, Nov. 2003]: 103.
Wei, Lilly. "Rhoades Abroad." Art in America [Vol. 91, No. 12, Dec. 2003]: 98-99.
West, Kevin. *Black Pussy* (2007). Germany: Steidl; New York: David Zwirner, New York.
Wilson, Michael. "Jason Rhoades." Artforum [Vol. 42, No.4, Dec. 2003]: 145-146.

Selected Collections

Centre Georges Pompidou, Paris, France
Hamburger Bahnhof - Museum für Gegenwart, Berlin, Germany
Los Angeles County Museum, Los Angeles, CA
The Museum of Contemporary Art, Los Angeles, CA
The Museum of Modern Art, New York, NY
Neue Nationalgalerie, Staatliche Museen zu Berlin, Berlin, Germany
Rubell Family Collection, Miami, FL
San Francisco Museum of Modern Art, San Francisco, CA
Solomon R. Guggenheim Museum, New York, NY
Stedelijk Museum, Amsterdam, Netherlands
Stedelijk Museum voor Actuele Kunst, Ghent, Belgium
Tate Modern, London, England
Van Abbemuseum, Eindhoven, Netherlands
Villa Arson, Nice, France
Whitney Museum of American Art, New York, NY

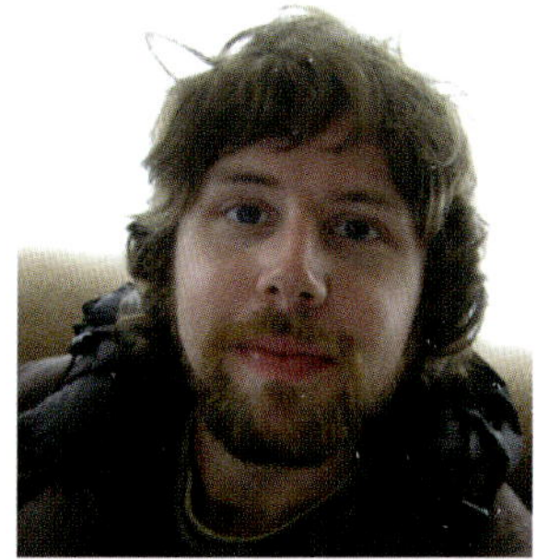
©Carolyn Pennypacker Riggs

RY ROCKLEN

Born in Los Angeles, CA, 1978
Live and works in Los Angeles, CA

Education

2004-2006 M.F.A., University of Southern California, Los Angeles, CA
2001 B.F.A., University of California, Los Angeles, Los Angeles, CA
1996-1998 Two years of study, California Institute of the Arts, Valencia, CA

Selected Solo Exhibitions

2007 *Half Craft*, Me-di-um, St. Barthélemy, French West Indies
Land of Super Neutral, Bangkok University Gallery, Bangkok, Thailand
2006 *Soft Ice*, Zach Feuer Gallery, New York, NY
2004 *Lost / Found*, Dangerous Curve, Los Angeles, CA
2003 *Ry Rocklen: Ground 4 Life*, Black Dragon Society, Los Angeles, CA

Selected Group Exhibitions

2007 *Warhol and...*, Kantor / Feuer Gallery, Los Angeles, CA
Oliver Twist, RENTAL, New York, NY
2006 *Red Eye: L.A. Artists from the Rubell Family Collection*, Rubell Family Collection, Miami, FL [cat.]
L.A. Trash and Treasure, Milliken Gallery, Stockholm, Sweden
Fall, Black Dragon Society, Los Angeles, CA
From L.A. Steve Canaday, Gerald Davis and Ry Rockland, Baronian_Francey, Brussels, Belgium
11:59, Compact Space, Los Angeles, CA
2005 *Drive by and re-LAX*, UPspace, Los Angeles, CA
Bart Exposito & Ry Rockland: In Between Bandwidths, The Nada Art Fair, Miami, FL
2004 *Black Dragon Society*, Apex Art, New York, NY
2003 *3D 7DEEP*, Black Dragon Society, Los Angeles, CA
Golden, Michael Janssen Galerie, Cologne, Germany
Clusterfuck, Latch Gallery, Los Angeles, CA
Something Else, Latch Gallery, Los Angeles, CA
Win, Lose, or Draw / Smoking Pencils, Rolling Papers, Black Dragon Society, Los Angeles, CA
2002 *I'm From Orange County and I Drink Johnny Walker Red*, Galerie Julius Hummel, Vienna, Austria
The Daily Circus, Latch Gallery, Los Angeles, CA
Low Overhead, Todd Hughes Fine Art, Pasadena, CA
A Well Rounded Appetite, Latch Gallery, Los Angeles, CA
2001 *Face Off*, The Smell, Los Angeles, CA
Big Trouble in Little China, Black Dragon Society, Los Angeles, CA
The Backyard Show, The Hatch Gallery, Los Angeles, CA
Battle for the Greatest Drawing in the World Title, Black Dragon Society, Los Angeles, CA
Something of That Nature, Black Dragon Society, Los Angeles, CA
2000 *Chocolate Thunder*, Black Dragon Society, Los Angeles, CA

Selected Bibliography

A Fascinating Arrangement of Particles. Zurich: JPR Ringier, 2008.
ArtReview."Future Greats." ArtReview [No. 9, March 2007]. 77-104.
Coetzee, Mark, ed., *Red Eye: L.A. Artists from the Rubell Family Collection*. Miami: Rubell Family Collection, 2007.
Hargreaves, Kathryn. "Just Us." Artillery [Summer 2007].

Hargreaves, Kathryn. "Real Live Art: Possessed & Transcendent." The Arts District Citizen [February 2006].
Pines, Ethan. "Art Tsunami." The Men's Book [Spring 2006].
Spiegler, Marc. "American Renaissance." The Art Newspaper [July 27, 2006].
Spiegler, Marc and Agnieszka Rokoczy. "Sess, droga e Ground Zero." Giornale dell'Arte [Vol. 24, No. 257, Sept. 2006]: 57-58.
Studer, Margaret. "Shopping Spree: Buying is Strong in Basel." The Wall Street Journal Europe [June 24-26, 2005].

Selected Collections

Rubell Family Collection, Miami, FL
Thomas J. Watson Library, The Metropolitan Museum of Art, New York, NY

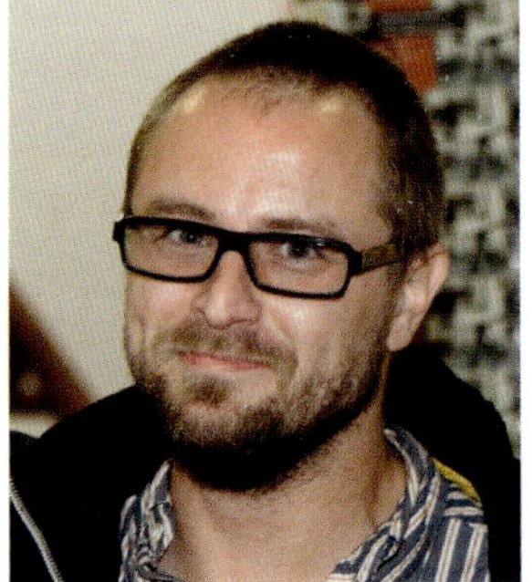
©Simon Hare Photography 2006

STERLING RUBY

Born in Bitburg, Germany, 1972
Lives and works in Los Angeles, CA

Education

2003-2005 M.F.A., Art Center College of Design, Pasadena, CA
2000-2002 B.F.A., The School of the Art Institute of Chicago, Chicago, IL
1992-1996 Fine Arts, Pennsylvania College of Art & Design, Lancaster, PA

Selected Solo Exhibitions

2007 *Paintings and Benches*, Galerie Christian Nagel, Berlin, Germany
Slasher Posters & Pillow Works, Bernier / Eliades Gallery, Athens, Greece
Superoverpass, Foxy Production, New York, NY
Killing the Recondite, Metro Pictures, New York, NY
2006 *Interior Designer*, MARC FOXX, Los Angeles, CA
Recombines, Galleria Emi Fontana, Milan, Italy
Supermax 2006, Galerie Christian Nagel, Cologne, Germany
2005 *This Range*, Guild & Greyshkul, New York, NY
New Work, Foxy Production, New York, NY

Selected Group Exhibitions

2007 *Uneasy Angel / Imagine Los Angeles,* Monika Sprüth Philomene Magers, Munich, Germany
Circumventing the City, D'Amelio Terras Gallery, New York, NY
I Want to Believe, Galerie Eva Presenhuber, Zurich, Switzerland
The Second Moscow Biennale of Contemporary Art, Moscow, Russia [cat.]
2006 *Red Eye: L.A. Artists from the Rubell Family Collection*, Rubell Family Collection, Miami, FL [cat.]
Only The Paranoid Survive, Hudson Valley Center for Contemporary Art, Peekskill, NY
2006 California Biennial, Orange County Museum of Art, Newport Beach, CA [cat.]
Having New Eyes, Aspen Art Museum, Aspen, CO
2005 *Adjoining The Voids*, sister, Los Angeles, CA
T1–Torino Triennale Tremusei, Galleria Civica d'Arte Moderna e Contemporanea, Turin, Italy [cat.]
All the Pretty Corpses, The Renaissance Society at The University of Chicago, Chicago, IL
Sugartown, Elizabeth Dee Gallery, New York, NY
5 X U, Team gallery, inc., New York, NY

Selected Bibliography

Bonami, Francesco, and Carolyn Christov-Bakargiev. *The Pantagruel Syndrome: T1–Torino Triennale Tremusei. 2005.* Milano: Skira, 2005. 404.
Coetzee, Mark, ed., *Red Eye: L.A. Artists from the Rubell Family Collection.* Miami: Rubell Family Collection, 2007.
Hawkins, Richard. "Sterling Ruby: Long Live the Amorphous Law." Flash Art [No. 250, Oct. 2006].
Holte, Michael Ned. "Sterling Ruby." Artforum [Vol. 45, No. 4, Dec. 2006]: 315.
Holte, Michael Ned. "Sterling Ruby." *California Biennial 2006.* Newport Beach: Orange County Museum of Art, 2006:136-139.
Myers, Holly. "Shape Shifter," ArtReview [Issue 6, Dec. 2006].
Taft, Catherine. "Introducing." Modern Painters [Dec. 2006: 75-77].
Taft, Catherine. "Sterling Ruby." Modern Painters [Nov. 2006]: 104-105.

Selected Collections

Armand Hammer Museum, University of California, Los Angeles, Los Angeles, CA
The Dallas Center for Contemporary Art, Dallas, TX
Orange County Museum of Art, Newport Beach, CA
Rubell Family Collection, Miami, FL
Seattle Art Museum, Seattle, WA
The Sender Collection, New York, NY
Solomon R. Guggenheim Museum, New York, NY
Zabludowicz Collection, London, England

LARA SCHNITGER

Born in Harlem, Netherlands, 1969
Lives and works in Los Angeles, CA, and Amsterdam, Netherlands

©Simon Hare Photography 2006

Education

1999-2000 Center for Contemporary Art, Kitakyushu, Japan
1992-1994 de Ateliers, Amsterdam, Netherlands
1991-1992 Degree, Academie Vyvarni Umeni, Prague, Czech Republic
1987-1991 Diploma, Koninklijke Academie van Beeldende Kunsten, The Hague, Netherlands

Selected Solo Exhibitions

2007 Stuart Shave / Modern Art, London, England
2005 *My Other Car is a Broom*, Magasin 3 Stockholm Konsthall, Sweden; traveled to Stroom Den Haag, The Hague, Netherlands [cat.]
Anton Kern Gallery, New York, NY [cat.]
Blacks on Blondes, Triple Candie, New York, NY
2004 *Crazy Horses*, Air 2 Paris / Air de Paris, Paris, France
2003 *Liesje Leerde Lotje lopen langs de lange Lindenlaan*, Revalidatie Centrum Friesland, Beetsterzwaag, Netherlands
2002 Anton Kern Gallery, New York, NY
2001 *Lara Schnitger: Project Room*, Santa Monica Museum of Art, Santa Monica, CA
2000 Kunst-Werke, Berlin, Germany
1999 Anton Kern Gallery, New York, NY
UP & CO, New York, NY
1998 *Lara Schnitger: Space Invader*, De Vleeshal, Middelburg, Netherlands [cat.]
1997 University of Buffalo Art Gallery, Buffalo, NY
1996 Anton Kern Gallery, New York, NY

Selected Group Exhibitions

2007 *Fantastic Politics: Art in Times of Political Crisis*, Nasjonalmuseet for kunst, arkitektur og design, Oslo, Norway [cat.]
Uneasy Angel / Imagine Los Angeles, Monika Sprüth Philomene Magers, Munich, Germany
2006 *Red Eye: L.A. Artists from the Rubell Family Collection*, Rubell Family Collection, Miami, FL [cat.]
USA TODAY: New American Art from The Saatchi Gallery, Royal Academy of Arts, London, England; traveled to The State Hermitage Museum, St Petersburg, Russia [cat.]
2005 *THING: New Sculpture from Los Angeles*, Armand Hammer Museum, University of California, Los Angeles, CA [cat.]
Both Ends Burning, David Kordansky Gallery, Los Angeles, CA [cat.]
My Barbarian, The Power Plant, Toronto, Canada
2004 *Secrets of / de'90s*, Museum voor Moderne Kunst Arnhem, Arnhem, Netherlands
2003 *Nice and Easy*, Sprengel Museum Hannover, Hannover, Germany
Social Fabric, Lothringer13, Munich, Germany
2002 *Civilized Special Zone*, Chinese European Art Center, Xiamen, China
Building Structures, P.S.1 Contemporary Art Center, Long Island City, NY
2002 Shanghai Biennale, Shanghai, China [cat.]
2000 *Trendwände*, Kunstraum Düsseldorf, Dusseldorf, Germany
Raumkorper, Netze und andere Gebilde, Kunsthalle Basel, Basel, Switzerland [cat.]
Gozaimas, Stedelijk Museum Bureau Amsterdam, Stedelijk Museum, Amsterdam, Netherlands
1999 *Provisorium I*, Bonnefantenmuseum, Maastricht, Netherlands

1998 *Een Keuze*, Grote Kerk Den Haag, The Hague, Netherlands
Morning Glory. De Ateliers 1993-1997, de Ateliers, Amsterdam, Netherlands [cat.]
1996 *Sublieme Vormen*, Stedelijk Museum, Amsterdam, Netherlands [cat.]
1995 *Wild Walls*, Stedelijk Museum, Amsterdam, Netherlands [cat.]

Selected Bibliography

Coetzee, Mark, ed., *Red Eye: L.A. Artists from the Rubell Family Collection*. Miami: Rubell Family Collection, 2007.
Elaine, James, and Aimee Chang. *THING: new sculpture from Los Angeles*, Los Angeles: Armand Hammer Museum, 2005.
Eleey, Peter. "Lara Schnitger: Anton Kern Gallery." frieze [No. 70, Oct. 2002]: 97.
My Other Car Is A Broom. Conversation between Richard Julin and Lara Schnitger. Stockholm: Magasin 3 Stockholm Konsthall, 2005.
Saatchi Gallery. *USA TODAY: New American Art from The Saatchi Gallery*. London: Royal Academy of Arts, 2006.
Schnitger, Lara. *Fragile Kingdom*. Amsterdam: Artimo – Gijs Stork, 2004.
Schnitger, Lara. *Lara Schnitger: it ain't gonna lick itself*. New York: Anton Kern Gallery, 2005.
Schnitger, Lara, and Lexter Braak. *Lara Schnitger*. Middelburg: De Vleeshal, 1998.
Smith, Roberta. "Art in Review: Lara Schnitger." The New York Times [July 19, 2002].
Smith, Roberta. "Art in Review: Lara Schnitger." The New York Times [Oct. 7, 2005].
Williams, Gregory. "Lara Schnitger: Anton Kern." Artforum [Nov. 2002]: 186.
Document 8, Middelburg: De Vleeshal, 1998.

Selected Collections

Bonnefantenmuseum, Maastricht, Netherlands
Carnegie Museum of Art, Pittsburgh, PA
Fogg Art Museum, Harvard University, Cambridge, MA
Los Angeles County Museum of Art, Los Angeles, CA
Magasin 3 Stockholm Konsthall, Stockholm, Sweden
The Museum of Modern Art, New York, NY
Nasjonalmuseet for kunst, arkitektur og design, Oslo, Norway
Rubell Family Collection, Miami, FL
Stedelijk Museum, Amsterdam, Netherlands

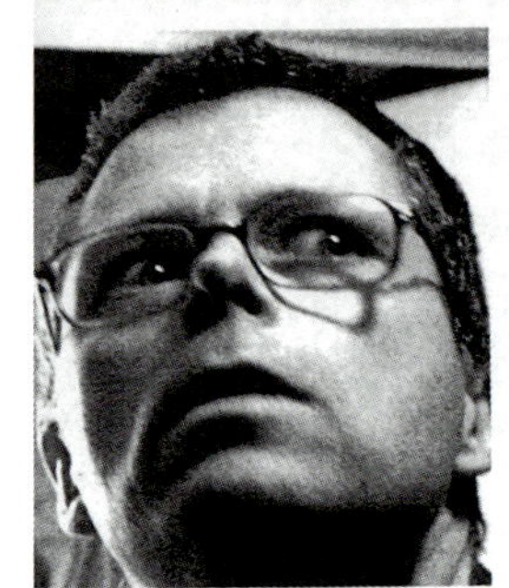

JIM SHAW

Born in Midland, Michigan, 1952
Lives and works in Los Angeles, CA

Education

1976-1978 M.F.A., California Institute of the Arts, Valencia, CA
1971-1974 B.F.A., University of Michigan, Ann Arbor, MI

Selected Solo Exhibitions

2009 CAPC, Musée d'Art Contemporain de Bordeaux, Bordeaux, France
Palais de Tokyo, Paris, France
2007 *Dr. Goldfoot & His Bikini Bombs*, Metro Pictures, New York, NY
2012 - Montezuma's Revenge, Galerie Praz-Delavallade, Berlin, Germany
The Hole, Galerie Praz-Delavallade, Paris, France
Jim Shaw: The Donner Party, P.S.1 Contemporary Art Center, Long Island City, NY
Distorted Faces & Portraits, 1978-2007, Blondeau Fine Art Services, Geneva, Switzerland [cat.]
Jim Shaw, Galleria Massimo De Carlo, Milan, Italy [cat.]
2006 *Left Behind #8, 9, 10*, Patrick Painter Inc., Santa Monica, CA
Dream Object (I was in my Japanese gallery / museum in Japan...), Patrick Painter Inc., Santa Monica, CA
Vise Head, Patrick Painter Inc., Santa Monica, CA
My Mirage 1986-91, Skarstedt Fine Art, New York, NY
Bernier / Eliades Gallery, Athens, Greece
Art & Public, Geneva, Switzerland
Emily Tsingou Gallery, London, England
2005 Galerie Praz-Delavallade, Paris, France
The Inky Depths / The Woman in the Wilderness, Metro Pictures, New York, NY
The Dream That Was No More A Dream, Patrick Painter Inc., Santa Monica, CA
2004 Emily Tsingou Gallery, London, England
2003 *Kill Your Darlings*, Patrick Painter Inc., Santa Monica, CA
Jim Shaw: Drawings, Studies, O-ism, Art & Public, Geneva, Switzerland
Drawings, Metro Pictures, New York, NY
Jim Shaw, Bernier / Eliades, Athens, Greece
O, Magasin, Centre National d'Art Contemporain, Grenoble, France; traveled to Kunsthaus Glarus, Glarus, Switzerland [cat.]
2002 *The Goodman Image File and Study*, Swiss Institute, New York, NY
The Rite of the 360°, Galerie Praz-Delavallade, Paris, France
Jim Shaw, Galleria Massimo de Carlo, Milan, Italy
O-ist Thrift Store Paintings, Metro Pictures, New York, NY
2001 *Dreamt of Drawings*, Emily Tsingou Gallery, London, England
Jim Shaw, Metro Pictures, New York, NY
Galleria Massimo de Carlo, Milan, Italy
Galerie Praz-Delavallade, Paris, France
2000 *Jim Shaw: Thrift Store Paintings*, Institute of Contemporary Arts, London, England [cat.]
Patrick Painter Inc., Santa Monica, CA
1999 Galerie Praz-Delavallade, Paris, France
Metro Pictures, New York, NY
Jim Shaw Everything Must Go 1976 -1999, Casino-Luxembourg – Forum d'Art Contemporain, Luxembourg; traveled to Musée d'Art Moderne et Contemporain, Geneva, Switzerland; The Contemporary Arts Center, Cincinnati, OH [cat.]
1998 Frankfurt Kunstverein, Frankfurt, Germany
Rupertinum, Salzburg, Austria

Selected Group Exhibitions

2008 *In Geneva No One Can Hear You Scream*, Blondeau Fine Art Services, Geneva, Switzerland
2007 *Eden's Edge: Fifteen LA Artists*, Armand Hammer Museum, University of California, Los Angeles, CA [cat.]
If Everybody Had an Ocean - Brian Wilson: An Art Exhibition, Tate St. Ives, St. Ives, England; traveled to CAPC, Musée d'Art Contemporain de Bordeaux, Bordeaux, France [cat.]
2006 *Red Eye: L.A. Artists from the Rubell Family Collection,* Rubell Family Collection, Miami, FL [cat.]
Magritte and Contemporary Art: The Treachery of Images, Los Angeles County Museum of Art, Los Angeles, CA [cat.]
Los Angeles 1955-1985:Tthe Birth of an Art Capital, Centre Georges Pompidou, Paris, France [cat.]
2005 *Masters of American Comics*, The Museum of Contemporary Art, Los Angeles, CA [cat.]
2004 *Disparities & Deformations: Our Grotesque*, SITE Santa Fe, Santa Fe, NM [cat.]
Diaries and Dreams – Contemporary Drawings, Instituzione Galleria d'Arte Moderna di Bologna, Bologna, Italy [cat.]
2002 *Whitney Biennial 2002*, Whitney Museum of American Art, New York, NY [cat.]
2000 Johnen + Schottle, Cologne, Germany
Made in California, Los Angeles County Museum of Art, Los Angeles, CA [cat.]
1998 *From Head to Toe: Concepts of the Body in 20th Century Art*, Los Angeles County Museum of Art, Los Angeles, CA [cat.]
1997 *Sunshine & Noir, Art in L.A.1960-1997,* Louisiana Museum for Moderne Kunst, Humlebaek, Denmark; traveled to Kunstmuseum Wolfsburg, Wolfsburg, Germany; Castello di Rivoli Museo d'Arte Contemporanea, Turin, Italy; The Armand Hammer Museum of Art and Culture Center, University of California, Los Angeles, CA [cat.]
1995 *Art on Paper 1995*, Weatherspoon Art Museum, The University of North Carolina at Greensboro, Greensboro, NC [cat.]
1993 *Der Zerbrochene Spiegel (Thrift Store Painting Collection)*, Staatliche Akademie der Bildenden Kuenste, Vienna, Austria; traveled to Deichtorhallen, Hamburg, Germany [cat.]
1992 *Helter Skelter: L.A. Art in the 1990s*, The Museum of Contemporary Art, Los Angeles, CA [cat.]
American Art of the 80's, Museo di Arte Moderna e Contemporanea di Trento e Rovereto, Rovereto, Italy [cat.]
1991 *Whitney Biennial 1991*, Whitney Museum of American Art, New York, NY [cat.]

Selected Bibliography

Coetzee, Mark, ed., *Red Eye: L.A. Artists from the Rubell Family Collection*. Miami: Rubell Family Collection, 2007.
Dreams, Santa Monica: Smart Art Press, 1995.
Harvey, Doug, and Jim Shaw. *Jim Shaw: Selected Dream Drawings*. Santa Monica: Patrick Painter Inc., 2006.
Jim Shaw: Everything Must Go, 1974-1999. Luxembourg: Casino Luxembourg, 1999.
Jim Shaw: O. Zurich: JRP / Ringier, 2004.
Shaw, Jim, Marc Blondeau, Lionel Bovier, and Philippe Davet. *Jim Shaw: Distorted Faces & Portraits, 1978-2006*. Zurich: JRP/Ringier; New York: D.A.P., 2007.
Shaw, Jim. *Thrift Store Paintings: Paintings Found in Thrift Stores*. Hollywood: Heavy Industry Publications, 1990.

Selected Collections

Albright-Knox Art Gallery, Buffalo, NY
Armand Hammer Museum, University of California, Los Angeles, CA
Centre Georges Pompidou, Paris, France
Des Moines Art Center, Des Moines, IA
Fond national d'art contemporain, Paris, France
Fonds régional d'art contemporain, Normandie, France
Los Angles County Museum of Art, Los Angeles, CA
Musée d'Art Moderne et Contemporain, Geneva, Switzerland
The Museum of Contemporary Art, Los Angeles, CA
The Museum of Modern Art, New York, NY
Rubell Family Collection, Miami, FL
Solomon R. Guggenheim Museum, New York, NY
Walker Art Center, Minneapolis, MN
Whitney Museum of American Art, New York, NY

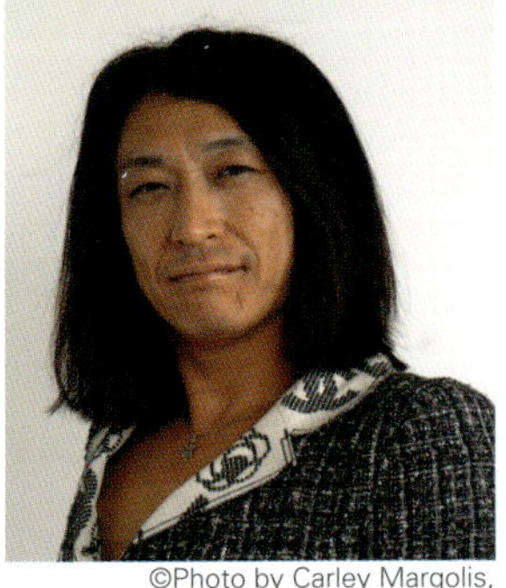
©Photo by Carley Margolis, courtesy of David Zwirner New York

YUTAKA SONE

Born in Shizuoka, Japan, 1965
Lives and works in Los Angeles, CA

Education

1988-1992 M.A. in Architecture, Tokyo National University of Fine Arts and Music, Tokyo, Japan
1983-1988 B.F.A., Tokyo National University of Fine Arts and Music, Tokyo, Japan

Selected Solo Exhibitions

2007 *Yutaka Sone*, Parasol unit foundation for contemporary art, London, England [cat.]
Yutaka Sone, David Zwirner, New York, NY
Yutaka Sone, *Roller coaster Project* (with Damon Mc Carthy) Gallery Side 2, Tokyo, Japan
2006 *Yutaka Sone: It Seems Like Snow Leopard Island,* David Zwirner, New York, NY
Yutaka Sone: Like Looking for Snow Leopard, Kunsthalle Bern, Bern, Switzerland [cat.]
Yutaka Sone: X-Art Show, Aspen Art Museum, Aspen, CO [cat.]
Yutaka Sone. Forecast: Snow, The Renaissance Society at The University of Chicago, Chicago, IL [cat.]
2005 *Snow*, Gallery Side 2, Tokyo, Japan
2004 *Amusement Romana*, David Zwirner, New York, NY
Amusement Romana, Gallery Side 2, Tokyo, Japan
MARS Gallery, Tokyo, Japan
2003 *Yutaka Sone: Jungle Island*, The Geffen Contemporary at MOCA, The Museum of Contemporary Art, Los Angeles, CA
50th Biennale di Venezia, Japanese Pavilion, Venice, Italy [cat]
2002 *Travel to Double River Island*, Toyota Municipal Museum of Art, Toyota City, Japan
2000 *Double Six*, Artpace San Antonio, San Antonio, TX
1999 *Yutaka Sone*, David Zwirner, New York, NY
Alpine Attack, Sogetsu Art Museum, Tokyo, Japan
1997 *Amusement*, Gallery Side 2, Tokyo, Japan
At the End of All the Journeys, Hiroshima City Museum of Contemporary Art, Hiroshima, Japan; traveled to Shiseido Art House, Kakegawa, Japan; Navin Taxi Gallery, Bangkok, Thailand
1996 *Future Perfect*, Bunkamura Gallery, Tokyo, Japan
Scoop, Mitaka City Arts Foundation, Tokyo, Japan [cat.]
1993 *One Hand Clapping*, Yokohama Galleria, Yokohama, Japan
Her 19th Foot, Contemporary Art Gallery, Art Tower Mito, Mito, Japan [cat.]

Selected Group Exhibitions

2007 *CRITICAL MASS- KRITISCHE MASSE: 20 Jahre Stiftung Kunsthalle Bern*, Kunsthalle Bern, Bern, Switzerland
2006 *Red Eye: L.A. Artists from the Rubell Family Collection*, Rubell Family Collection, Miami, FL [cat.]
Tokyo Blossoms: Deutsche Bank Collection Meets Zaha Hadid, Hara Museum of Contemporary Art, Tokyo, Japan
2005 *Chikaku - Time and Memory in Japan*, Kunsthaus Graz am Landesmuseum Joanneum, Graz, Austria [cat.]
IDYL: as to answer that picture, Middelheimmuseum, Antwerp, Belgium [cat.]
25: Twenty-five Years of the Deutsche Bank Collection, Deutsche Guggenheim, Berlin, Germany [cat.]
2004 *Whitney Biennial 2004*, Whitney Museum of American Art, New York, NY [cat.]
100 Artists See God, Contemporary Jewish Museum, San Francisco, CA; traveled to Laguna Art Museum, Laguna Beach, CA; Contemporary Art Center of Virginia, Virginia Beach, VA; Freedman Gallery, Albright College Center for the Arts, Reading, PA; Cheekwood Botanical Garden and Museum of Art, Nashville, Tennessee [cat.]
Brainstorming: Topographie de la morale, Centre international d'art et du paysage de l'île de Vassivière, Ile de Vassivière, France

Climats, Cyclothymie des Paysages, Centre international d'art et du paysage de l'île de Vassivière, Ile de Vassivière, France

2003 *MetaScape*, Cleveland Museum of Art, Cleveland, OH
Sharjah Biennial 6, Sharjah, United Arab Emirates
Happy Trail, Shiseido Gallery, Tokyo, Japan [cat.]

2002 *The Gift: Generous Offering, Insidious Hospitality*, Palazzo delle Papesse, Centro Arte Contemporanea, Siena, Italy; traveled to Bronx Museum of the Arts, Bronx, NY; Scottsdale Museum of Contemporary Art, Scottsdale, AZ; Mary and Leigh Block Museum of Art, Northwestern University, Chicago, IL [cat.]
25th Bienal de São Paulo, São Paulo, Brazil
13th Biennale of Sydney, Sydney, Australia

2001 *Loop*, P.S. 1 Contemporary Art Center, Long Island City, NY
Public Offerings: Works by 25 Young Artists Shaping International Contemporary Art, The Museum of Contemporary Art, Los Angeles, CA
7th International Istanbul Biennial, Istanbul, Turkey

2000 *Acquisizione Recenti / Recent Acquisitions*, Fondazione Sandretto Re Rebaudengo per l'Arte, Palazzo Re Rebaudengo, Guarene d'Alba, Italy
The Greenhouse Effect, Serpentine Gallery, London, England

1999 *Fancy Dance: Contemporary Japanese Art After 1990,* Artsonje Center, Seoul, Korea; traveled to Artsonje Museum, Gyeongju, Korea

1998 *Unfinished History*, Walker Art Center, Minneapolis, MN; traveled to Museum of Contemporary Art, Chicago, IL [cat.]

1997 *Cities on the Move 1*, Wiener Secession, Vienna, Austria; traveled to CAPC Musée d'Art Contemporain de Bordeaux, Bordeaux, France; P.S.1 Contemporary Art Center, Long Island City, NY; Louisiana Museum for Moderne Kunst, Humlebaek, Denmark; The Hayward Gallery, London, England; Kiasma – Museum of Contemporary Art, Helsinki, Finland [cat.]
Skuptur. Projekte in Münster 1997, Westfälisches Landesmuseum für Kunst und Kulturgeschichte Münster, Munster, Germany [cat.]
Promenade in Asia, Shiseido Gallery, Tokyo, Japan [cat.]

1996 *Interzones: a work in progress*, Kunstforeningen, Copenhagen, Denmark [cat.]
Video Art on the Edge, Kita Kanto Museum of Fine Arts, Maebashi, Japan

Selected Bibliography

Coetzee, Mark, ed., *Red Eye: L.A. Artists from the Rubell Family Collection*. Miami: Rubell Family Collection, 2007.

Ghez, Susanne, Philippe Pirotte, Hamza Walker, et al. *Yutaka Sone*, 2006. Chicago: The Renaissance Society at The University of Chicago, 2006

Hasegawa, Yuko. "Yutaka Sone: an architect sculpts a timescape." Flash Art [Vol. 34, No. 218, May-June 2001]: 126-128.

Itoi, Kay. "Land of the rising stars." The Art Newspaper [Vol. 13, No. 140, Oct. 2003]: 39-40.

Matsui, Midori. "Yutaka Sone." Flash Art [Vol. 34, No. 226, Oct. 2002]: 110.

Montreuil, Gregory. "Yutaka Sone." Contemporary [Issue 64, 2004]: 98-101.

Ng, Elaine. "Yutaka Sone: The Blizzard of 2006." ArtAsiaPacific [No. 48, Spring 2006]: 70-75.

Nittve, Lars. *Nutopi*, Malmö: Rooseum Center for Contemporary Art, 1995.

Rousseau, Bryant. "Artist's Walk: Yutaka Sone." ARTINFO.com [Sept. 28, 2006]

Weissman, Benjamin. "High roller." Modern Painters [May 2006]: 84-87,

Wolf, Matt. "Yutaka Sone." Flash Art [Vol. 37, No. 236, May-June 2004]: 83.

Yood, James. "Yutaka Sone." Artforum [Vol. 44, No. 9, May 2006]: 295-296.

Selected Collections

The 21st Century Museum of Contemporary Art, Kanazawa, Kanazawa, Japan
The Art Institute of Chicago, Chicago, IL
Daros Collection, Zurich, Switzerland
High Museum of Art, Atlanta, GA
Kunsthalle Bern, Bern, Switzerland
Mori Art Museum, Tokyo, Japan
The Museum of Contemporary Art, Los Angeles, CA
The Museum of Modern Art, New York, NY
Rubell Family Collection, Miami, FL
Toyota Municipal Museum of Art, Toyota City, Japan

©Simon Hare Photography 2006

CATHERINE SULLIVAN

Born in Los Angeles, CA, 1968
Lives and works in Los Angeles, CA

Education

1997 M.F.A., Art Center College of Design, Pasadena, CA
1992 B.F.A., California Institute of Arts, Valencia, CA

Selected Solo Exhibitions

2007 *Catherine Sullivan: Triangle of Need*, Walker Art Center, Minneapolis; traveling to A Foundation, Liverpool, England, Vizcaya Museum and Gardens, Miami, FL; Metro Pictures, New York, NY; Smart Museum of Art, University of Chicago, Chicago, IL [cat.]
2006 *The Chittendens*, Whitney Museum of American Art, New York, NY; Gió Marconi, Milan, Italy; Galerie Catherine Bastide, Brussels, Belgium
Catherine Sullivan: 'Tis a Pity She's a Fluxus Whore, The Gallery Sketch, London, England
2005 *The Ice Floes of Franz Joseph Land*, Kunsthalle Zürich, Zurich, Switzerland
Richard Telles Fine Art, Los Angeles, CA
The Chittendens, Metro Pictures, New York, NY; traveled to Secession, Vienna, Austria; Tate Modern, London, England [cat.]
2004 *Catherine Sullivan: Getting Out of the 20th Century Alive*, Neuer Aachener Kunstverein, Berlin, Germany
Ice Floes of Franz Joseph Land, Gió Marconi, Milan, Italy
Ice Floes of Franz Joseph Land, house of Alex / house of Peter (and some of those crappy details), Kunstverein Braunschweig e.V., Braunschweig, Germany
2003 *Five Economies (big hunt/ little hunt)*, Metro Pictures, New York, NY; traveled to Centre D'Art Contemporain, Fribourg, Switzerland
Tis Pity She's a Fluxus Whore, Wadsworth Atheneum Museum of Art, Hartford, CT
Catherine Sullivan / MATRIX 201d, Berkeley Art Museum and Pacific Film Archive, University of California at Berkeley, Berkeley, CA [cat.]
Speech Model from 'The Flies,' Collaboration with Lisa Lapinski, Galerie Mezzanin, Vienna, Austria
2002 *Five Economies (big hunt/ little hunt)*, The Renaissance Society at The University of Chicago, Chicago, IL; traveled to Armand Hammer Museum, University of California, Los Angeles, CA; Rubell Family Collection, Miami, FL [cat.]
2001 *Gestus Maximus (Gold Standard)*, Galerie Christian Nagel, Cologne, Germany
Unspoken Evil III – Rites of Ascension and Obscurity, Galerie Catherine Bastide, Brussels, Belgium

Selected Group Exhibitions

2007 *The World as a Stage*, Tate Modern, London, England
To See Dance, Centro Andaluz de Arte Contemporáneo, Seville, Spain
Uneasy Angel / Imagine Los Angeles, Monika Sprüth Philomene Magers, Munich, Germany
Talking Pictures - Theatricality in Contemporary Film and Video Art, K21 Kunstsammlung Nordrhein-Westfalen, Dusseldorf, Germany
Ver Bailar, Centro Andaluz de Arte Contemporáneo, Seville, Spain
Shooting Back, Thyssen-Bornemisza Art Contemporary, Vienna, Austria [cat.]
LEMAITRE: Free electrons, Tabacalera International Contemporary Culture Centre of San Sebastian, Donostia, San Sebastian, Spain
2006 *Red Eye: L.A. Artists from the Rubell Family Collection*, Rubell Family Collection, Miami, FL [cat.]
Figures de l'Acteur: Le Paradoxe du comedien, Collection Lambert en Avignon, Avignon, France
A Short History of Performance – Part IV, Whitechapel Art Gallery, London, England
2005 *Prague Biennale 2*, Prague, Czech Republic
2004 Whitney Biennial 2004, Whitney Museum of American Art, New York, NY
Playlist, Palais de Tokyo, Paris, France

2003 *Brightness*, Thyssen-Bornemisza Foundation in Contemporary Art at the Museum of Modern Art, Dubrovnik, Croatia
In Between / Extra Muros, Centre d'Art Contemporain, Fribourg, Switzerland
Baja to Vancouver, The West Coast and Contemporary Art, Seattle Art Museum, Seattle, WA
Biennale de Lyon d'art contemporain, Lyon, France [cat.]
Silver | dreams, screens, and theories, Art Gallery of Greater Victoria, Victoria, Canada [cat.]
Fast Forward, Media Art Sammlung Goetz, KZM, Karlsruhe, Germany [cat.]
2002 *Crisp*, Marianne Boesky Gallery, New York, NY
2001 *Cosima Von Bonin*, Kunstverein in Hamburg, Hamburg, Germany
2000 *L.A.-ex*, Museum Villa Stuck, Munich, Germany
1999 Galerie Christian Nagel, Cologne, Germany
1998 Lines of Sight, site specific project at the California aqueduct, Lancaster, CA
Still and Otherwise, Margo Leavin Gallery, Los Angeles, CA
1996 *SuperIntellectuals*, Three Day Weekend, Los Angeles, CA
Video Povera, California State University, Los Angeles, CA
1995 Gander Mountain High, Room 10, Pasadena, CA

Selected Bibliography

Amirati, Domenick. "New York Critics' Picks – Catherine Sullivan." artforum.com [March 4, 2003].
Baldissera, Lisa. *Silver: dreams, screens and theories*. Victoria: Art Gallery of Greater Victoria, 2004.
Burton, Johanna. "Catherine Sullivan, 'Five Economies (Big hunt/little hunt).'" Time Out New York, [March 13-20]: 73.
Catherine Sullivan: the Cittendens. Frankfurt am Main: Revolver; Vienna: Secession, 2005.
Chambers, Christopher. "Catherine Sullivan." Flash Art [Vol. 36, No. 230, May – June, 2003]: 149.
Coetzee, Mark. *Not Afraid: Rubell Family Collection*. London: Phaidon Press, 2004.
Coetzee, Mark, ed., *Red Eye: L.A. Artists from the Rubell Family Collection*. Miami: Rubell Family Collection, 2007.
Dunn, Melissa. "Whitney Biennial 2004: A Good-Looking Corpse." Flash Art [Vol. 37, No. 236, May – June, 2004]: 63, 80.
Goldberg, RoseLee. "Catherine Sullivan." Artforum [Vol. 44, No. 5, Jan. 2006]: 208-211.
Heartney, Eleanor. "The Well-Tempered Biennial." Art in America [Vol. 92, No. 6, June – July, 2004]: 70-77.
Jana, Reena. "The Ambiguity of Vision." Tema Celeste [March-April, Issue 102]: 52-57.
Kerr, Merrily. "Recuperating Revolt: Aaron Spangler, Paul Chan, and Catherine Sullivan." Flash Art [Vol. 37, No. 236, May – June 2004]: 106-109.
Ruf, Beatrix et al. *Catherine Sullivan and Co.: Film and theater works, 2002-2004*. Dijon: Presses du reel; Zurich: JRP / Ringier, 2006.
Schjeldahl, Peter. "What's New." The New Yorker [March 22]: 100-101.
Smith, Roberta. "Art in Review: Catherine Sullivan – 'Five Economies (Big Hunt / Little Hunt).'" The New York Times [March 21, 2003].
Sullivan, Catherine, and Tim Griffin. "Catherine Sullivan talks about The Chittendens, 2005." Artforum [Vol. 44, No. 6, Feb. 2006]: 174-177.
Sullivan, Catherine. *Catherine Sullivan: five economies (big hunt / little hunt)*. Los Angeles: Armand Hammer Museum, University of California, 2002.
Sundell, Margaret. "Repeat performances: the art of Catherine Sullivan." Artforum [Vol. 42, No. 2, Oct. 2003]: 136-139.
Yood, James. "Catherine Sullivan." Artforum [Vol. 41, No. 1, Sept. 2002]: 208.

Selected Collections

Armand Hammer Museum, University of California, Los Angeles, CA
Fondazione Sandretto Re Rebaudengo per l'Arte, Turin, Italy
Miami Art Museum, Miami, FL
Musée d'Art Contemporain de Lyon, Lyon, France
Musée d'Art Contemporain, Marseille, France
The Museum of Contemporary Art, Los Angeles, CA
Rubell Family Collection, Miami, FL
Samlung Goetz, Munich, Germany
Tate Modern, London, England
Walker Art Center, Minneapolis, MN
Wadsworth Atheneum Museum of Art, Hartford, CT
Whitney Museum of American Art, New York, NY

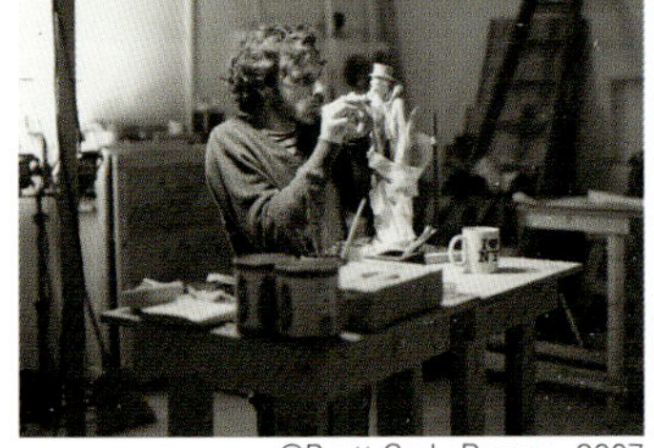

©Brett Cody Rogers, 2007

RICKY SWALLOW

Born in San Remo, Australia, 1974
Lives and works in Los Angeles, CA

Education

1993-1997 B.F.A., Victorian College of the Arts, The University of Melbourne, Melbourne, Australia

Selected Solo Exhibitions

2007 The Douglas Hyde Gallery, Dublin, Ireland [cat.]
Younger Than Yesterday, Kunsthalle Wien, Vienna, Austria
2006 P.S.1 Contemporary Art Center, Long Island City, NY
Long Time Gone, Stuart Shave / Modern Art, London, England
2005 *51st Biennale di Venezia*, Australian Pavilion, Venice, Italy [cat.]
2004 *Killing Time*, Gertrude Contemporary Art Spaces, Melbourne, Australia [cat.]
2003 *Field Recordings*, Tomio Koyama Gallery, Tokyo, Japan
2002 *Tomorrow in Common*, Andrea Rosen Gallery, New York, NY
Karyn Lovegrove Gallery, Los Angeles, CA
2001 Berkeley Art Museum and Pacific Film Archive, University of California at Berkeley, Berkeley, CA
Above Ground Sculpture, Hamish McKay Gallery, Wellington, New Zealand
2000 *Plastruct*, Karyn Lovegrove Gallery, Los Angeles, CA
Darren Knight Gallery, Sydney, Australia
Ricky Swallow: Above Ground Sculpture, Project Room, Dunedin Public Art Gallery, Dunedin, New Zealand [cat.]
1998 *Repo Man*, Darren Knight Gallery, Sydney, Australia

Selected Group Exhibitions

2007 *Goth: Reality of the Departed World*, Yokohama Museum of Art, Yokohama, Japan
Sculptors' Drawings, Aspen Art Museum, Aspen, CO
2006 *Red Eye: L.A. Artists from the Rubell Family Collection*, Rubell Family Collection, Miami, FL [cat.]
2005 *Getting Emotional*, The Institute of Contemporary Art, Boston, MA [cat.]
2004 *Living Together is Easy*, Art Tower Mito, Mito, Japan [cat.]
The Ten Commandments, Deutsches Hygiene-Museum, Dresden, Germany [cat.]
2003 *Art+Film*, Centre for Contemporary Photography, Melbourne, Australia
Still Life, Art Gallery of New South Wales, Sydney, Australia [cat.]
Variations on the theme of illusion, Emily Tsingou Gallery, London, England
Extended play: Art remixing music, Govett-Brewster Art Gallery, New Plymouth, New Zealand [cat.]
The Fourth Sex: Adolescent Extremes, Stazione Leopolda, Florence, Italy [cat.]
2002 *Remix: Contemporary Art & Pop*, Tate Liverpool, Liverpool, England [cat.]
Possible Worlds, ARTSPACE, Auckland, New Zealand
2001 *Bootylicious: A context for new additions to The University of Melbourne Art Collection*, The Ian Potter Museum of Art, The University of Melbourne, Melbourne, Australia
A Person Looks at a Work of Art... The Michael Buxton Contemporary Australian Art Collection, Heide Museum of Modern Art, Bulleen, Australia
Museum of Contemporary Art, Sydney, Australia [cat.]
Terror 2.1 Utopia, Kiasma - Museum of Contemporary Art, Helsinki, Finland
2000 *Keith Edmier, Ricky Swallow, Erick Swenson*, Andrea Rosen Gallery, New York, NY
The Retrieved Object, Linden – St. Kilda Centre for Contemporary Arts, Victoria, Australia
Uncommon World: Aspects of Contemporary Australian Art, National Gallery of Australia, Canberra, Australia [cat.]
Brand New Master Copy, UKS Gallery, Oslo, Norway
1999 *Spellbound*, Karyn Lovegrove Gallery, Los Angeles, CA
Contempora 5, The Ian Potter Museum of Art, The University of Melbourne, Melbourne, Australia [cat.]

Hamish McKay Gallery, Wellington, New Zealand
Signs Of Life, Melbourne International Biennial 1999, Melbourne, Australia [cat.]
Walkmen, Synaesthesia Music, Melbourne, Australia
1998 *Soup*, The Collective Gallery, Edinburgh, Scotland
Metamorphosis, Mornington Peninsula Regional Gallery, Melbourne, Australia
All this and Heaven too: The 1998 Adelaide Biennial of Australian Art, Art Gallery of South Australia, Adelaide, Australia [cat.]

Selected Bibliography

Alexander, George. "Killing Time: Ricky Swallow." ArtAsiaPacific [No. 45, Summer 2005]: 56-62.
"Art & Ideas: Australian Pavilion: Ricky Swallow." Financial Times [June 15, 2005].
Biesenbach, Klaus. "Panem et Circenses: Ricky Swallow in Venice." Art and Australia [Vol. 42, No. 4, Winter 2005]: 572-579.
Brooks, Richard. "A beginner's guide to the Biennale." The Sunday Times [June 19, 2005].
Coetzee, Mark, ed., *Red Eye: L.A. Artists from the Rubell Family Collection*. Miami: Rubell Family Collection, 2007.
Colless, Edward. *Memory made plastic: Ricky Swallow, 1999*. Waterloo: Darren Knight Gallery, 1999.
Collings, Matthew. "Rambling, absurd, magnificent: that's the Venice Biennale." The Daily Telegraph [June 4, 2005].
Conway Morris, Roderick. "Pushing Boundaries at Venice Biennale." International Herald Tribune [June 14, 2005].
Day, Charlotte, and Jennifer Higgie, et al. *Ricky Swallow: this time another year*. Sydney: Australia Council, 2005.
Engberg, Juliana. *Ricky Swallow: no radio*. Artext [No. 62, Aug. – Oct. 1998]: 32-35.
Engborg, Juliana. *Signs of life: Melbourne International Biennial 1999*. Melbourne: City of Melbourne, 1999.
Fenner, Felicity. "Report from Australia: New Life In Melbourne." Art in America [Vol. 88, No. 1, Jan. 2000]: 74-77.
Hainley, Bruce "Spellbound." Artforum [Vol. 38, No. 5, Jan. 2000]: 119-120.
Herbert, Martin. "Bone idol." Modern Painters [May 2005]: 68-73.
Hutak, Michael. "Venice Biennale." The Bulletin [June 29, 2005].
Johnson, Ken. "Art in Review." The New York Times [September 20, 2002].
Johnson, Ken. "Ricky Swallow and Jessica Stockholder: Contrasts in Sculpture, in Theme and in Medium." The New York Times [February 21, 2006].
Nicholson, Tom. "Signs of Life: Melbourne International Biennial 1999." Art & Australia [Vol. 37, No. 2, 1999]: 201-203.
Palmer, Daniel. "Shadowplay." frieze [No. 58, April 2001]: 84-87.
Palmer, Daniel. "Signs of Life: Melbourne International Biennial." frieze [No. 48, Sept. – Oct. 1999].
Palmer, Daniel. Review. "Walkmen." frieze [No. 46, May 1999].
Paton, Justin. *Killing time*, Waterloo: Darren Knight Gallery, 2004.
Paton, Justin. "The Was and May: Ricky Swallow's Wooden problem." Art Monthly Australia [No. 157, March 2003].
Paton, Justin. *Ricky Swallow: field recordings*. Roseville: Craftsman House, 2005.
Ricky Swallow: above ground sculpture. Dunedin: Dunedin Public Art Gallery, 2001.
Ricky Swallow. Dublin: Douglas Hyde Gallery, 2007.
Ricky Swallow: the past sure is tense. Perth: Art Gallery of Western Australia, 2006.
Sooke, Alastair. "Ten hot Biennale artists." The Daily Telegraph [June 4, 2005].
Woodrow, Ross. "Artists as Model Workers." Art Monthly Australia [No. 186, Dec. 2005 – Feb. 2006]: 40-42

Selected Collections

Art Gallery of New South Wales, Sydney, Australia
Art Gallery of Western Australia, Perth, Australia
Berkeley Art Museum and Pacific Film Archive, University of California at Berkeley, Berkeley, CA
Chartwell Collection, Auckland Art Gallery, Aukland, New Zealand
City of Melbourne, Melbourne, Australia
Dunedin Public Art Gallery, Dunedin, New Zealand
Monash University Collection, Monash University Museum of Art, Clayton Australia
Museum of Contemporary Art, Sydney, Australia
The Museum of Modern Art, New York, NY
National Gallery of Australia, Canberra, Australia
National Gallery of Victoria, Melbourne, Australia
Peter Norton Family Collection, Los Angeles, CA
Rubell Family Collection, Miami, FL

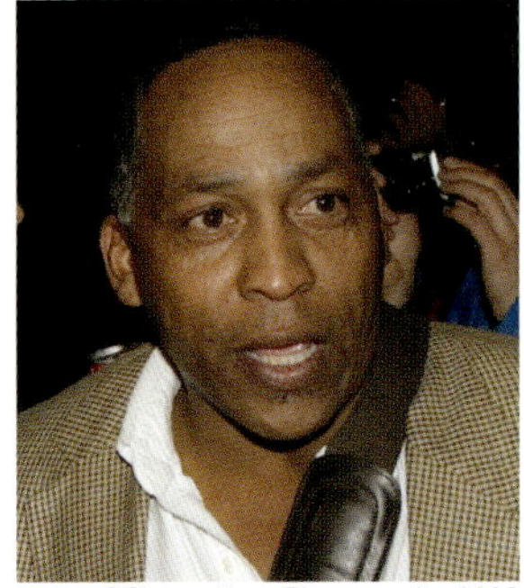
©Simon Hare Photography 2006

HENRY TAYLOR

Born in Oxnard, CA, 1958
Lives and works in Los Angeles, CA

Education

1994-1995 B.F.A., California Institute of the Arts, Valencia, CA

Selected Solo Exhibitions

2007 *Sis and Bra*, The Studio Museum in Harlem, New York, NY
We're all water, but some of us are muddy, Atelier Cardenas Bellanger, Paris, France
2006 *Get Black*, sister, Los Angeles, CA
2005 Daniel Reich Gallery, New York, NY
2004 *Free 99*, sister, Los Angeles, CA

Selected Group Exhibitions

2007 *Paper Bombs*, Jack Hanley Gallery, Los Angeles, CA
Repeat after me: I AM a Revolutionary, RENTAL, New York, NY
2006 *Red Eye: L.A. Artists from the Rubell Family Collection*, Rubell Family Collection, Miami, FL [cat.]
LA Trash and Treasure, Milliken Gallery, Stockholm, Sweden
metro pictures, part two, Museum of Contemporary Art, North Miami, FL [cat.]
Back From the End of the Earth, Galerie Ben Kaufmann, Berlin, Germany
LAXed: Paintings from the Other Side, Peres Projects, Berlin, Germany
2004 *California Earthquakes*, Daniel Reich Gallery, New York, NY
Losing My Head, sister, Los Angeles, CA

Selected Bibliography

Coetzee, Mark, ed., *Red Eye: L.A. Artists from the Rubell Family Collection*. Miami: Rubell Family Collection, 2007.
Gray, Emma. "Oh Brother: Henry Taylor." ArtReview [April 2007]: 40.
Henry, Max. "Exhibition Review." Time Out Magazine [Feb. 17-23, 2005].
Kraus, Chris, Jan Tumlir, and Jane McFadden. *LA Artland: Contemporary Art from Los Angeles*. London: Black Dog Publishing Ltd., 2005.
Smith, Roberta. "Art in Review: Henry Taylor." The New York Times [Feb. 18, 2005].

Selected Collections

Rubell Family Collection, Miami, FL
The Studio Museum in Harlem, New York, NY

Doug Aitken
Diamond Sea, 1997
Installation with sound
Variable dimensions

John Baldessari
Stake: Art is Food for Thought and Food Costs Money, 1985
Black-and-white photographs, color photograph and acrylic paint
144 x 480 in. (365.8 x 1219.2 cm)

John Baldessari
Goya Series: The Same Elsewhere, 1997
Ink jet print and hand lettering on canvas
75 x 60 in. (190.5 x 152.4 cm)

John Baldessari
Blockage (Blue), With Three Persons (One with Tie Orange), 2004
Three dimensional archival digital photographic prints with acrylic paint on Sintra, Dibond and Gatorfoam panels
89 1/4 x 71 7/8 in. (226.7 x 182.6 cm)

John Baldessari
Noses & Ears, Etc. (Part Two): Two (Red) Faces with Noses and Ear and (Blue) Hand and Foodstuffs, 2006
Three dimensional archival digital photographic prints with acrylic paint
71 1/2 x 105 3/4 x 4 in.
(181.6 x 268.6 x 10.2 cm)

Frank Benson
Human Statue, 2005
Forton MG, oil and acrylic paint, fabric and wood
Ed. of 3 + 1 AP
80 x 21 x 20 in. (203.2 x 53.3 x 50.8 cm)

Amy Bessone
Afrikaaniënpietà, 2005
Oil on canvas
96 x 74 in. (243.8 x 188 cm)

Amy Bessone
Sketch for Wrestlers, 2005
Oil on canvas
18 x 20 in. (45.7 x 50.8 cm)

Amy Bessone
Fate, 2006
Oil on canvas
84 x 98 in. (213.4 x 248.9 cm)

Amy Bessone
German God, 2006
Oil on canvas
110 x 64 in. (279.4 x 162.6 cm)

Amy Bessone
Gray Glass, 2006
Oil on canvas
102 x 72 in. (259.1 x 182.9 cm)

Mark Bradford
Whore in the Church House, 2006
Mixed media collage on canvas
103 x 144 in. (261.6 x 365.8 cm)

Chris Burden
21 Foot Truss Bridge, 2003
Stainless steel reproduction Mysto type I Erector parts, Ed. 2/3
45 3/4 x 14 3/4 x 234 1/2 in.
(116.2 x 37.5 x 595.6 cm)

Chris Burden
Gold Bullets, 2003
Ten twenty-two karat gold bullets and two wood and Plexiglas vitrines, Ed. 8/10
Bullets: variable dimensions
Each vitrine: 10 1/4 x 5 3/4 x 6 1/4 in.
(26 x 14.6 x 15.9 cm)

Brian Calvin
When and Where, 2004
Acrylic on canvas
60 x 80 in. (152.4 x 203.2 cm)

Brian Calvin
Heads Believe, 2006
Acrylic on canvas
78 x 60 in. (198.2 x 152.4 cm)

Aaron Curry
New Shack / Old Shack (To Fold and Fuck) [Shack 1, 4-6, 8, 9-15, 17], 2006
Installation; ink, gouache, acrylic paint, paper, paper collage, poster, wood, resin, polyurethane, paint, cardboard, tape and rope
Variable dimensions

Brian Fahlstrom
Light Low, 2006
Oil on canvas
83 1/4 x 67 in. (211.4 x 170.2 cm)

Brian Fahlstrom
Present, 2006
Oil on canvas
74 x 203 1/4 in. (188 x 515.6 cm)

Mark Grotjahn
Untitled (yellow & white butterfly, #543), 2005
Crayon and mixed media on board
23 3/4 x 19 in. (60.3 x 48.2 cm)

Karl Haendel
Big Ricky #1, 2006
Pencil on paper
52 x 38 in. (132.1 x 96.5 cm)

Karl Haendel
Screaming Baby, 2006
Pencil on paper
79 3/4 x 51 3/4 in. (202.5 x 131.6 cm)

Karl Haendel
Times Square, 2006
Pencil and charcoal on nine sheets of paper
67 1/4 x 84 in. (170.8 x 213.3 cm)

Karl Haendel
Untitled (Anita Hill), 2006
Pencil on paper
36 x 52 in. (91.4 x 132.1 cm)

Karl Haendel
Untitled (Boxers), 2006
Pencil on paper
41 x 52 in. (104.2 x 132.1 cm)

Karl Haendel
Untitled (Carter / Mondale), 2006
Pencil on paper
22 x 30 in. (55.9 x 76.2 cm)

Karl Haendel
Untitled (Reagan / Monroe) Part of the Monroe Doctrine Group, 2006
Pencil on paper
41 5/8 x 27 5/8 in. (105.7 x 70.1 cm)

Karl Haendel
Watch #1, 2006
Pencil on paper
26 x 41 in. (66 x 104.2 cm)

Karl Haendel
Watch #2, 2006
Charcoal on nine sheets of paper
66 x 90 3/4 in. (167.6 x 230.5 cm)

Richard Hawkins
Untitled, 2000
Oil on magazine page
10 13/16 x 9 in. (28.8 x 22.9 cm)

Richard Hawkins
Untitled, 2000
Collage and oil on magazine page
10 7/8 x 8 in. (30.2 x 20.3 cm)

Richard Hawkins
Untitled, 2000
Oil on magazine page
11 13/16 x 9 1/8 in. (28.8 x 23 cm)

Richard Hawkins
Untitled, 2000
Oil on magazine page
11 13/16 x 9 1/8 in. (28.8 x 23 cm)

Richard Hawkins
Untitled #30, 2000
Oil on magazine page
11 7/8 x 9 11/16 in. (30.2 x 23.7 cm)

Richard Hawkins
Urbis Paganus III, 3, 2006
Collage
19 11/16 x 15 in. (50.5 x 38 cm)

Richard Hawkins
Urbis Paganus III, 5, 2006
Collage and ink
19 7/8 x 15 in. (50.5 x 38 cm)

Richard Hawkins
Urbis Paganus III, 8, 2006
Collage and ink
19 7/8 x 15 in. (50.5 x 38 cm)

Richard Hawkins
Urbis Paganus III, 12, 2006
Collage
19 7/8 x 15 in. (50.5 x 38 cm)

Evan Holloway
Second Law, 2006
Steel, plaster, batteries and bicycle parts
86 x 86 x 11 in. (218.4 x 218.4 x 27.9 cm)

Evan Holloway
Social Epistemology, 2006
Steel, Celluclay, acrylic medium, spray enamel, lights and lighting controller
149 x 10 x 15 in. (378.5 x 25.4 x 38.1 cm)

Violet Hopkins
I'll be your..., 2006
Colored pencil and acrylic ink on archival paper
80 x 146 in. (203.2 x 370.8 cm)

Thomas Houseago
Untitled, 2005
Plaster, hemp and steel,
32 1/4 x 76 x 25 1/2 in. (81.9 x 193 x 64.8 cm)

Thomas Houseago
Box Figure, 2006
Tuf-Cal, hemp, iron, clay and graphite
40 3/4 x 77 x 42 in. (108.1 x 195.5 x 106.7 cm)

Thomas Houseago
First Light, 2006
Tuf-Cal, hemp, iron, clay and graphite
60 x 53 x 40 in. (152.3 x 134.7 x 101.6 cm)

Thomas Houseago
Sitting Nude, 2006
Tuf-Cal, hemp and iron
36 1/2 x 51 x 33 in. (92.7 x 129.5 x 83.8 cm)

Thomas Houseago
Squatting Man (Toad), 2006
Tuf-Cal, plaster, hemp, iron and graphite
48 x 48 x 30 in. (122 x 122 x 76.2 cm)

Thomas Houseago
Standing Boy, 2006
Tuf-Cal, hemp, iron, clay and graphite
96 x 30 x 37 in. (243.8 x 76.2 x 94 cm)

Thomas Houseago
Striding Man, 2006
Tuf-Cal, hemp, iron, clay and graphite
70 x 37 x 58 in. (177.8 x 94 x 147.3 cm)

Thomas Houseago
Sunrise, 2006
Tuf-Cal, hemp, iron, clay and graphite
72 1/2 x 68 x 30 in. (184.1 x 172.8 x 76.2 cm)

Mike Kelley
Screamin' Smoke, 1985
Acrylic on paper
42 x 107 1/2 in. (106.7 x 273.1 cm)

Mike Kelley
Untitled, 1990
Afghans and stuffed animals
6 x 48 x 287 1/2 in. (15.2 x 121.9 x 730.3 cm)

Mike Kelley
Extracurricular Activity Projective Reconstruction #9 (Farm Girl), 2004-2005
Piezo black-and-white print on rag paper and Chromogenic print, Ed. 5/5
40 1/8 x 53 1/2 in. (101.9 x 135.9 cm)

Mike Kelley
Extracurricular Activity Projective Reconstruction (Singles Mixer) #8, 2005
Piezo black-and-white print on rag paper and Chromogenic print, Ed. 5/5
73.5 x 35.3 in. (186.8 x 88.9 cm)

Mike Kelley
Fresno, 2005
Mixed media with video projection, sound, and photograph
98 x 221 x 185 in. (248.9 x 561.3 x 469.9 cm)

Barbara Kruger
Untitled (Worth Every Penny), 1987
Silkscreen on vinyl
182 x 110 in. (462.3 x 279.4 cm)

Barbara Kruger
Untitled (Money Makes Money), 2001
Silkscreen on vinyl
164 3/8 x 102 6/8 in. (417 x 260 cm)

Nathan Mabry
Gentlemen and Scholars (Smoking L's), 2004
Wood, oil paint, eagle and turkey feathers, beads, alligator clip and leather
33 x 33 x 33 in. (83.8 x 83.8 x 83.8 cm)

Nathan Mabry
A Very Touching Moment (Cunning Linguist), 2005
Bronze, Ed. 2/2
62 x 30 x 30 in. (157.5 x 76.2 x 76.2 cm)

Nathan Mabry
Timeless, 2005
Bronze, Ed.1/3
40 x 29 x 30 in. (101.6 x 73.7 x 76.2 cm)

Nathan Mabry
?, 2006
Cast bronze and welded sheet bronze, Ed. 1/3
66 x 53 x 27 3/4 in. (167.6 x 134.6 x 70.5 cm)

Nathan Mabry
Drifting, Drifted, Drifter, 2006
Stoneware, Ed. of 2 + 1 AP
17 x 144 x 3 in. (43.2 x 365.8 x 7.6 cm)

Nathan Mabry
In Your Face (Number 4), 2006
C-print on Sintra, Ed. 1/3
14 x 11 in. (35.6 x 28 cm)

Nathan Mabry
In Your Face (Number 5), 2006
C-print on Sintra, Ed. 1/3
14 x 11 in. (35.6 x 28 cm)

Nathan Mabry
In Your Face (Number 6), 2006
C-print on Sintra, Ed. 1/3
14 x 11 in. (35.6 x 28 cm)

Nathan Mabry
In Your Face (Number 7), 2006
C-print on Sintra, Ed. 1/3
14 x 11 in. (35.6 x 28 cm)

Nathan Mabry
In Your Face (Number 8), 2006
C-print on Sintra, Ed. 1/3
11 x 14 in. (28 x 35.6 cm)

Nathan Mabry
In Your Face (Number 9), 2006
C-print on Sintra, Ed. 1/3
11 x 14 in. (28 x 35.6 cm)

Nathan Mabry
It Is What It Is (On the Chair, On the Table, On the Bed), 2006
Steel, wood, terracotta
60 x 79 x 48 in. (152.4 x 200.6 x 121.9 cm)

Paul McCarthy
Cultural Gothic, 1992
Metal, wood, pneumatic cylinder, compressor, programmed controller, burlap with foam, acrylic, dirt, fiberglass, clothing, wigs and stuffed goat
96 x 94 x 94 in. (241 x 235 x 235 cm)

Paul McCarthy
MoCA Man, 1992
Latex rubber, urethane foam, clothing, wig, wood, motor, artificial turf and saw horses
36 x 72 x 36 in. (92.4 x 182.9 x 91.4 cm)

Paul McCarthy
Masks, 1999
Seven C-prints, Ed. of 9 + 1/4 AP
Each: 18 3/4 x 13 1/4 in. (47.6 x 33.7 cm)

Paul McCarthy
Documents-Flicker Video, 2005
DVD, Ed. 5/10 + 2 AP
Loop

Paul McCarthy
Peter Paul Skin Sample, 2005
Fifteen color photos, Ed. 32/36
Each: 9 7/8 x 6 11/16 in. (25.1 x 17 cm)

Paul McCarthy
Painter Reformed, 1995-2006
Wood paneling, carpet, paint, furniture, canvas, kitchen utensils, over-sized paint tubes and brush, video projector, latex hands and noses, cardboard boxes, wooden crates, folding chairs, ink jet prints mounted on Gatorfoam, chromogenic prints and DVD projection with sound
Variable dimensions

Paul McCarthy
Tripod, 2006
Fiberglass, resin, pigment and steel, Ed. 3/3
105 x 72 x 80 in. (266.7 x 182.9 x 203.2 cm)

Paul McCarthy and Jason Rhoades
Videos with sound and elements from *Propposition*, 1999
Mixed media
Variable dimensions

Paul McCarthy and Mike Kelley
Fresh Acconci, 1995
Fifteen color photographs and video projection with sound, Ed. 5/30
38 x 45 1/2 in. (96.5 x 115.5 cm)

Jason Meadows
Black Panther, 2001
Wood, steel and spray paint
25 3/4 x 91 x 30 in. (65.4 x 231.1 x 76.2 cm)

Jason Meadows
Web of Spiderman, 2001
Basketball hoops, nylon net, wood, anodized aluminum, aluminum, paint and hardware
37 x 101 x 66 in. (94 x 256.6 x 167.7 cm)

Matthew Monahan
Kopffunk, 2006
Mixed media
60 3/4 x 13 x 13 in. (154.3 x 33 x 33 cm)

Matthew Monahan
Liberator's Retreat, 2006
Drywall, wax, foam, pigment and wood
78.7 x 26 x 27.6 in. (200 x 66 x 70 cm)

Matthew Monahan
Scheintod, 2006
Drywall, paper, acrylic, beeswax, plastic, metal and wood
63 x 63 x 13 in. (160 x 160 x 33 cm)

Matthew Monahan
Smug Magic, 2006
Drywall, glass, canvas, paper and wood,
111.8 x 13.4 x 13.4 in. (284 x 34 x 34 cm)

Kristen Morgin
Carousel Horses, 2006
Wood, unfired clay, paint and wire
72 1/2 x 70 x 35 in. (184.2 x 177.8 x 88.9 cm) and 73 x 67 1/2 x 29 1/2 in. (185.4 x 171.4 x 75 cm)

Catherine Opie
Jo, 1993
Chromogenic print, Ed. 6/8 + 2 AP
20 x 16 in. (50.8 x 40.6 cm)

Catherine Opie
John and Scott, 1993
Chromogenic print, Ed. 6/8 + 2 AP
20 x 16 in. (50.8 x 40.6 cm)

Catherine Opie
Justin Bond, 1993
Chromogenic print, Ed. of 8 + 1/2 AP
20 x 16 in. (50.8 x 40.6 cm)

Catherine Opie
Mike and Sky, 1993
Chromogenic print, Ed. of 8 + AP 1/2
20 x 16 in. (50.8 x 40.6 cm)

Catherine Opie
Mitch, 1993
Chromogenic print, Ed. 6/8 + 2 AP
20 x 16 in. (50.8 x 40.6 cm)

Kaz Oshiro
Kitchen Project, 2004-2005
Acrylic on canvas
Left: 85 x 159 x 26 in. (215.9 x 403.9 x 66 cm)
Right: 85 x 101 x 25 in. (215.9 x 256.5 x 63.5 cm)

Kaz Oshiro
Fender Showman Amp Head, 2006
Acrylic and Bondo on canvas
8 3/4 x 24 x 9 1/4 in. (22.2 x 61x 23.5 cm)

Kaz Oshiro
Fender Super Reverb Amp #3, 2006
Acrylic and Bondo on stretched canvas
24 1/2 x 24 1/2 x 10 1/2 in. (62.2 x 62.2 x 26.7 cm)

Laura Owens
Untitled, 2005
Oil and acrylic on linen
108 x 60 in. (274.3 x 152.3 cm)

Raymond Pettibon
No Title (My first kiss as I), 1988
Pen and ink on paper
14 x 11 in. (35.6 x 27.9 cm)

Raymond Pettibon
No Title (The first water), 1989
Pen and ink on paper
14 x 11 in. (35.6 x 27.9 cm)

Raymond Pettibon
No Title (Give me leave), 1989
Pen and ink on paper
15 1/4 x 22 1/4 in. (35.6 x 27.9 cm)

Raymond Pettibon
No Title (I had to buy her), 1989
Pen and ink on paper
17 x 11 in. (43.2 x 27.9 cm)

Raymond Pettibon
No Title (Is it irksome), 1989
Pen and ink on paper
14 x 11 in. (35.6 x 27.9 cm)

Raymond Pettibon
No Title (Before sending it), 1999
Pen and ink on paper
27 3/4 x 19 3/4 (70.5 x 50.2 cm)

Raymond Pettibon
No Title (How does it), 1999
Pen and ink on paper
26 x 20 in. (66 x 50.8 cm)

Raymond Pettibon
No Title (Man is free), 1999
Pen and ink on paper
22 1/4 x 30 in. (56.5 x 27.9 cm)

Raymond Pettibon
No Title (The night of), 1999
Pen, ink and oil on paper
30 x 22 in. (76. 2 x 55.9 cm)

Raymond Pettibon
No Title (To compare great), 1999
Pen and ink on paper
30 x 22 1/4 in. (76.2 x 56.5 cm)

Charles Ray
Male Mannequin, 1990
Mannequin and painted fiberglass, Ed. of 3
73 3/4 x 27 1/4 x 21 1/4 in. (186 x 69.2 x 54 cm)

Charles Ray
Oh! Charley, Charley, Charley..., 1992
Eight painted cast fiberglass mannequins with wigs
72 x 90 x 90 in. (183 x 457 x 457 cm)

Jason Rhoades
Untitled Chandelier, 2004
Glass, wire, neon, Plexiglas, fabric, plastic
Variable dimensions

Jason Rhoades
Untitled Chandelier, 2004
Glass, wire, neon, Plexiglas, fabric, plastic
Variable dimensions

Ry Rocklen
10,000 Year Wait, 2005
Styrofoam, wine glasses and water, Ed. 2/3
36 x 19 x 19 in. (91.4 x 48.3 x 48.3 cm)

Ry Rocklen
Eighty Ape, 2005
Gorilla suit, concrete, rebar, boots and wooden shackles
63 x 82 1/2 x 46 in. (160 x 209.5 x 116.8 cm)

Ry Rocklen
Healing Home, 2006
Birdhouse, dowels, Sculpey, and ceramic shoes
59 1/2 x 23 3/4 x 15 in. (151.1 x 60.3 x 38.1 cm)

Sterling Ruby
Eyes Staring at Etched Glass, 2005
Lamda print with Plexiglas mount
Suite of four photographs, Ed. 2/3 + 2 AP
Each: 56 x 48 in. (142.3 x 122 cm)

Sterling Ruby
Absolute Contempt for Total Serenity (Double), 2006
Urethane, Formica and wood
72 7/8 x 60 x 45 in. (184 x 152.4 x 114.3 cm)

Sterling Ruby
Balanced Stack of Pottery with Knife, 2006
Unique collage on paper
45 x 29 in. (114.3 x 73.7 cm)

Sterling Ruby
Mapping (), 2006
Nail polish on Plexiglas
49 1/4 x 49 1/4 x 2 in. (125.1 x 125.1 x 5.1 cm)

Sterling Ruby
Monument Stalagmite / Slave Pissing, 2006
PVC pipe, foam, plastic urethane, wood and Formica
180 x 38 x 38 in. (457.2 x 96.5 x 96.5 cm)

Lara Schnitger
Madonna with Child, 2006
Fabric and wood
84 x 58 in. (213.2 x 147.3 cm)

Lara Schnitger
The Mothership, 2006
Fabric and wood
108 x 120 x 138 in. (274.3 x 304.8 x 350.5 cm)

Jim Shaw
Dream Drawing (I'm under the freeways looking...), 1992
Pencil on paper
12 x 9 in. (30.5 x 22.9 cm)

Jim Shaw
Dream Drawing (Marnie + I were driving and I saw lawns burning...), 1992
Pencil on paper
12 x 9 in. (30.5 x 22.9 cm)

Jim Shaw
Dream Drawing (A man's describing stabbing a typewriter...), 1993
Pencil on paper
12 x 9 in. (30.5 x 22.9 cm)

Jim Shaw
Dream Drawing (Marnie + I were lying in bed...), 1993
Pencil on paper
12 x 9 in. (30.5 x 22.9 cm)

Jim Shaw
Dream Drawing (In an old hotel stairway...), 1994
Pencil on paper
12 x 9 in. (30.5 x 22.9 cm)

Jim Shaw
Pit of Penance, 2006
Ink on seven sheets of paper
Each: 20 x 15 in. (50.8 x 38.1 cm)

Yutaka Sone
Alpine Attack, 1999
Metal, plastic and rubber
35 3/4 x 47 x 17 in. (90.8 x 119.4 x 43.2 cm)

Catherine Sullivan
Big Hunt, 2002
16 mm film transferred to five DVDs, Ed. 1/3
Variable dimensions

Catherine Sullivan
Big Hunt Infusions, 2002
Thirty-five black-and-white photographs, Ed. of 3
Each: 8 x 10 in. (20.3 x 25.4 cm)

Ricky Swallow
Model for the Taming of the Moon, 1999
Plastruct, Milliput, PVC and spray paint
12 x 7 x 13.5 in. (30.5 x 17.8 x 34.3 cm)

Ricky Swallow
The First One Now, 2000
Pigmented resin
Variable dimensions

Henry Taylor
Watts County, 2004
Acrylic on canvas
76 x 61 3/4 in. (193 x 157 cm)

Henry Taylor
On Henry, 2006
Acrylic on canvas
96 3/4 x 75 in. (245.7 x 190.5 cm)

Henry Taylor
Slave, 2006
Mixed media on linen
66 x 50 in. (167.7 x 122 cm)

The Staff at the Rubell Family Collection: Director, Mark Coetzee; Registrar, Juan Valadez; Archivist and Assistant Registrar, Carolina Wonder; Designer, Chi Lam; Visitor Services and Bookstore Manager, Stephanie Garcia; Curatorial Assistant, Mark Clintberg; Chief Preparator, Richard Kern; Preparators, Juan Gonzalez, Ricky Jimenez, Diego Machado, Paul Pisoni, Susanne Slauenwhite, Matthew Snitzer and Mark Stark; Museum Educator, Linda Mangual; Housekeeping, Sonia Alvarez; Proofreader and Text Editing, Elizabeth Martinez; Accounting, Liliana Zarif; Lodging, Oscar Barrameda; Bookstore Assistants, Kiwi Farah and Cecilia Fernandez; Design Assistant, Sergio Alvarez; Office Assistant, Katherine Garcia; Research Assistants, Meredith Carruthers, Rebecca Duclos, Larissa Holman, Tatiana Mellema, David Ross and Jacqueline Sischy; Conservation Interns, Anne Blazejack and John Witty Visitor Services Interns, Sheila Cordova, Yadian Fonseca and Jacob Guerin; and Archive Intern, Katrina Miller.

Blake Byrne, Lucy Cai, Ethan Ehrlich, Russell Ferguson, Gary Garrels, Brian Meola, Ann Philbin, Michael Rabkin, Laura Roselione, Paul Schimmel, Glenn Scott Wright, Ali Subotnick, Chip Tom and Dean Valentine.

303 Gallery, New York, NY; ACME Gallery, Los Angeles, CA; Albion Hotel, Miami Beach, FL; The Andy Warhol Museum, Pittsburgh, PA; Anna Helwing Gallery, Los Angeles, CA; Anton Kern Gallery, New York, NY; Arte al Dia International; Art Center College of Design, Pasadena, CA; Artists Space, New York, NY; ARTSPACE, Auckland, New Zealand; Bank of America; Black Dragon Society, Los Angeles, CA; Blum and Poe, Los Angeles, CA; Cherry and Martin, Los Angeles, CA; Corvi-Mora, London, England; Dallas Museum of Art, Dallas, TX; Daniel Reich Gallery New York, NY; Darren Knight Gallery, Sydney, Australia; David Kordansky Gallery, Los Angeles, CA; David Zwirner, New York, NY; Dunedin Public Art Gallery, Dunedin, New Zealand; Flash Art; Foxy Production, New York, NY; Gagosian Gallery, New York, NY; Galerie Catherine Bastide, Brussels, Belgium; Galerie Daniel Buchholz, Cologne, Germany; Galerie Ghislaine Hussenot, Paris, France; Galerie Krinzinger, Vienna, Austria; Galerie Metropol, Vienna, Austria; Galerie Nagel, Cologne / Berlin, Germany; Galerie van Gelder, Amsterdam, Netherlands; Gavin Brown's enterprise, New York, NY; Good / Bad Art Collective, Denton, TX; Harris Lieberman, New York, NY; Hauser & Wirth, London, England / Zurich, Switzerland; International Center of Photography, New York, NY; Ivan Anthony, Newton, Auckland, New Zealand; Karyn Lovegrove Gallery, Los Angeles, CA; Kirkland Arts Center, Kirkland, WA; Linden – Centre for Contemporary Arts, St Kilda, Australia; Lisson Gallery, London, England; Louisiana Museum for Modern Kunst, Humlebæk, Denmark; Lowe Art Museum, University of Miami, Miami, FL; Luckman Fine Arts Complex, California State University, Los Angeles, CA; Luhring Augustine, New York, NY; Mai 36 Galerie, Zurich, Switzerland Marc Foxx, Los Angeles, CA; Marc Selwyn Fine Art, Los Angeles, CA; Marian Goodman Gallery, New York, NY; Mary Boone Gallery, New York, NY; Matthew Marks Gallery, New York, NY; Metro Pictures, New York, NY; Miami Art Museum, Miami, FL; Monika Sprüth Philomene Magers, Munich, Germany; Museum of Contemporary Art San Diego, San Diego, CA; De Nederlandsche Bank, Amsterdam, Netherlands; Parkett Publishers, Zurich, Switzerland New York, NY; Pasco Arts Council, Holiday, FL; Patrick Painter Inc., Los Angeles, CA; Phoenix Art Museum, Phoenix, AZ; Regen Projects, Los Angeles, CA; Richard Telles Fine Art, Los Angeles, CA; Rosamund Felsen Gallery, Santa Monica, CA; Royal Academy of Arts, London, England; Sadie Coles HQ, London, England; San Diego Museum of Art, San Diego, CA; Sikkema Jenkins & Co., New York, NY; Sister, Los Angeles, CA; Sommer Contemporary Art, Tel Aviv, Israel; Southern California Art Projects & Exhibitions, Corona del Mar, CA; Stefan Stux Gallery, New York, NY; Stuart Shave / Modern Art, London, England; Studio Guenzani, Milan, Italy; Tanya Bonakdar Gallery, New York, NY; Tate Liverpool, Liverpool, England; Tate St Ives, Cornwall, England; Taxter & Spengemann, New York, NY; UC Berkeley Art Museum, Berkeley, CA; University Art Museum, College of the Arts, California State University, Long Beach, CA; University of Buffalo Art Gallery, Buffalo, NY; Wadsworth Atheneum Museum of Art, Hartford, CT; Whitewall; and William E. Gahlberg Gallery, McAninch Arts Center at College of DuPage, Glen Ellyn, IL.